AF870121

European Union and its Neighbours in a Globalized World

Volume 3

Series Editors

Marc Bungenberg, Saarbrücken, Germany

Mareike Fröhlich, Saarbrücken, Germany

Thomas Giegerich, Saarbrücken, Germany

Neda Zdraveva, Skopje, North Macedonia

Advisory Editors

Başak Baysal, Istanbul, Turkey

Manjiao Chi, Beijing, China

Annette Guckelberger, Saarbrücken, Germany

Ivana Jelić, Strasbourg, France

Irine Kurdadze, Tbilisi, Georgia

Gordana Lažetić, Skopje, North Macedonia

Yossi Mekelberg, London, UK

Zlatan Meškić, Riyadh, Saudi Arabia

Tamara Perišin, Luxembourg, Luxembourg

Roman Petrov, Kyiv, Ukraine

Dušan V. Popović, Belgrad, Serbia

Andreas R. Ziegler, Lausanne, Switzerland

The series "The European Union and its Neighbours in a Globalized World" will publish monographs and edited volumes in the field of European and International Law and Policy. A special focus will be put on the European Neighbourhood Policy, current problems in European and International Law and Policy as well as the role of the European Union as a global actor. The series will support the cross-border publishing and distribution of research results of cross-border research consortia. Besides renowned scientists the series will also be open for publication projects of young academics. The series will emphasize the interplay of the European Union and its neighbouring countries as well as the important role of the European Union as a key player in the international context of law, economics and politics.

Unique Selling Points:

• Deals with a wide range of topics in regard of European and International Law but is also open to topics which are connected to economic or political science

• Brings together authors from the European Union as well as from accession candidate or neighbouring countries who examine current problems from different perspectives

• Draws on a broad network of excellent scholars in Europe promoted by the SEE | EU Cluster of Excellence, the Europa-Institut of Saarland University as well as in the South East European Law School Network

More information about this series at http://www.springer.com/series/16257

Hava Charlotte Lan Yurttagül

Whistleblower Protection by the Council of Europe, the European Court of Human Rights and the European Union

An Emerging Consensus

Springer

Hava Charlotte Lan Yurttagül
Saarland University
Saarbrücken, Germany

ISSN 2524-8928 ISSN 2524-8936 (electronic)
European Union and its Neighbours in a Globalized World
ISBN 978-3-030-78058-6 ISBN 978-3-030-78059-3 (eBook)
https://doi.org/10.1007/978-3-030-78059-3

© The Editor(s) (if applicable) and The Author(s), under exclusive license to Springer Nature Switzerland AG 2021
This work is subject to copyright. All rights are solely and exclusively licensed by the Publisher, whether the whole or part of the material is concerned, specifically the rights of translation, reprinting, reuse of illustrations, recitation, broadcasting, reproduction on microfilms or in any other physical way, and transmission or information storage and retrieval, electronic adaptation, computer software, or by similar or dissimilar methodology now known or hereafter developed.
The use of general descriptive names, registered names, trademarks, service marks, etc. in this publication does not imply, even in the absence of a specific statement, that such names are exempt from the relevant protective laws and regulations and therefore free for general use.
The publisher, the authors, and the editors are safe to assume that the advice and information in this book are believed to be true and accurate at the date of publication. Neither the publisher nor the authors or the editors give a warranty, expressed or implied, with respect to the material contained herein or for any errors or omissions that may have been made. The publisher remains neutral with regard to jurisdictional claims in published maps and institutional affiliations.

This Springer imprint is published by the registered company Springer Nature Switzerland AG.
The registered company address is: Gewerbestrasse 11, 6330 Cham, Switzerland

Acknowledgements

The present book was submitted in the summer of 2020 as a doctoral thesis, a dissertation I defended at the Saarland University in January 2021. The legal field of European whistleblower protection sparked my interest 4 years ago when I had the chance to participate in the 2018 edition of the moot court Concours Européen des Droits de l'Homme René Cassin. The case study of that year's edition focused on a public official who disclosed evidence of extra-judicial killings ordered by the fictive State of Ricardie and who suffered serious detrimental effects as a result. Our team of the Wirtschaftsuniversität Wien, in the role of defendant, had to argue that those detrimental effects did not amount to a violation of the European Convention on Human Rights. The central issue was whether the applicant could benefit from the whistleblower status and thus fall within the scope of Article 10 of the Convention. Participating in this competition and pleading in front of a jury in the premises of the Council of Europe was an unforgettable experience which inspired me to examine the field of European whistleblower protection in greater length. This book is the result of my research.

I wish to express my deepest gratitude to my supervisor *Prof. Dr. Thomas Giegerich*, whose mentorship, guidance, and support made this book possible. I also feel incredibly privileged to have benefited from his thorough review and evaluation of the submitted thesis. I would like to thank my co-supervisor *Prof. Dr. Torsten Stein* for his insightful remarks, in particular on the Tshwane Principles and the Gesetz über die Rechtsstellung der Soldaten. In the face of the current COVID-19 pandemic, I am especially grateful to have had the chance to present my doctoral research in compliance with the restrictive measures imposed and would like to thank *Prof. Dr. Annette Guckelberger* and *Prof. Dr. Marc Bungenberg* for their stimulating questions and engaging comments during the defense.

I owe special and utmost thanks to *Prof. Dr. Dr. Christoph Grabenwarter* for giving me the honor of representing the Wirtschaftsuniversität Wien during the 2018 edition of the Concours Européen des Droits de l'Homme René Cassin, a unique experience that would shape my academic focus during the years that followed. My gratitude also goes to *Lisa Tabassi and her team* for their supervision and encouragement during my time in the Office of Legal Affairs of the Organization for Security and Co-operation in Europe. Their guidance and constructive feedbacks greatly helped me sharpen my legal mind and build confidence in my abilities. I would also like to thank the *United Nations Office for Disarmament Affairs team* in Vienna and the former Member of the European Parliament *Jo Leinen* for giving me the opportunity to assist them during my internships at the UNODA and the European Parliament.

I am greatly indebted to *Elizabeth Harvey* for the proofreading and editing of this book. It was a real privilege to benefit from her detailed review as a native speaker and legal scholar. I would also like to express my sincere gratitude to *Guy Dehn* and *Thad Guyer* for their valuable insights into the field of whistleblower protection.

The start of this doctoral project coincided with the release of the European Commission Whistleblower Directive proposal. To use this momentum, I took on the challenge of finishing the doctoral thesis by the end of the legislative process. Writing this book became a race against the clock and I will be forever grateful to my friends for their patience, tolerance, and understanding during this time. I would like to thank in particular *Winnie*, *Marion*, *Sarah*, *Bea*, *Loredana*, *Adèle*, *Amelia*, *Nikolina*, *Julia,* and *Virginie* for their loyalty, support, positive reinforcement, and trust in the antisocial hermit I had become.

Last but certainly not least, I would like to thank my family. This undertaking would not have been possible without the unwavering support of my parents, *Laura Vanhué* and *Ali Yurttagül*, and my sister, *Daphné Yurttagül*, to whom I dedicate this book.

Brussels, Belgium Hava Yurttagül
19 April 2021

Contents

Abbreviations

AFCO	Committee on Constitutional Affairs of the European Parliament
APA	Accredited Parliamentary Assistant
CJEU	Court of Justice of the European Union
CM	Committee of Ministers of the Council of Europe
CoE	Council of Europe
CONT	Committee on Budgetary Control of the European Parliament
COVID-19	Coronavirus disease 2019
CPQS	Preparatory Committee for Matters relating to the Staff Regulations
CULT	Committee on Culture and Education of the European Parliament
EASA	European Aviation Safety Agency
ECA	European Court of Auditors
ECB	European Central Bank
ECHR	European Convention on Human Rights
ECON	Committee on Economic and Monetary Affairs of the European Parliament
ECtHR	European Court of Human Rights
EDPS	European Data Protection Supervisor
EEAS	European External Action Service
EESC	European Economic and Social Committee
EIB	European Investment Bank
EMPL	Committee on Employment and Social Affairs of the European Parliament
EMSA	European Maritime Safety Agency
ENVI	Committee on the Environment, Public Health and Food Safety of the European Parliament
EO	European Ombudsman
EP	European Parliament
EPPO	European Public Prosecutor's Office
EU Charter	Charter of Fundamental Rights of the European Union
EU	European Union
EULEX	European Union Rule of Law Mission in Kosovo

FRA	European Union Agency for Fundamental Rights
GDPR	General Data Protection Regulation
GIP	General Implementation Provision
GRECO	Group of States against Corruption
HRC	UN Human Rights Committee
IBA	International Bar Association
ICAO	International Civil Aviation Organization
ICC	International Criminal Court
ICCom	International Chamber of Commerce
IDOC	Investigation and Disciplinary Office
ILO	International Labour Organization
IPW	Implementing Provisions on Whistleblowing
JURI	Committee on Legal Affairs of the European Parliament
LIBE	Committee on Civil Liberties, Justice and Home Affairs of the European Parliament
MARPOL 73/78	International Convention for the Prevention of Pollution from Ships
MEP	Member of the European Parliament
MLC	Maritime Labour Convention
OAS	Organization of American States
OECD	Organization for Economic Co-operation and Development
OLAF	European Anti-Fraud Office
OOPEC	Office for Official Publication of the European Community
OPC	Open Public Consultation
PA	Parliamentary Assembly of the Council of Europe
Paris MoU	Paris Memorandum of Understanding on Port States Control
PIDA	Public Interest Disclosure Act
RSB	Regulatory Scrutiny Board
SARS	Severe acute respiratory syndrome
SOP	Standard operating procedure
TEU	Treaty on European Union
TFEU	Treaty on the Functioning of the European Union
TI	Transparency International
UCITS	Undertakings for Collective Investment in Transferable Securities
UN	United Nations
WBG	World Bank Group

List of Figures

List of Tables

Chapter 1
Introduction

1.1 An Aura of Mystery

Whistleblowers. Individuals cloaked in an aura of mystery. Recent film productions illustrating their stories or the scandals sparked by their disclosures have added a touch of glamour to their persona, the leading roles often played by la crème de la crème of Hollywood.[1] Heroes for some, traitors for others, whistleblowers leave no one indifferent. Criminal or altruistic, the act of blowing the whistle has inflamed passions and sparked fierce controversy over the last few decades, raising the recurrent question: Secrecy at what cost? By revealing unpalatable truths, whistleblowers challenge the status quo, shake up the implicit consensus of what should remain secret, and by doing so, disrupt an existing harmony. "Conflicts over secrecy . . . are conflicts over power: the power that comes through controlling the flow of information".[2] Often member of a small group of individuals with privileged access to information, a whistleblower calls into question the very control of that flow, and aims to recalibrate the established power dynamic. However, dissent against an established order generally meets with strong opposition. Whistleblowing being a form of dissent, opposition against whistleblowers often translates into acts of retaliation for having dared to question the existing status quo. In order words: "snitches get stitches".

[1]Gavin Hood, *Official Secret*, 2019 film, starring Keira Knightley; Scott Z. Burns, *The Report*, 2019 film, starring Adam Driver; Steven Soderbergh, The Laundromat, 2019 film, starring Maryl Streep, Antonio Banderas and Gary Oldman; Steven Spielberg, The Post, 2017 film, starring Maryl Streep and Tom Hanks.

[2]Bok (1989), p. 19.

© The Author(s), under exclusive license to Springer Nature Switzerland AG 2021
H. C. L. Yurttagül, *Whistleblower Protection by the Council of Europe, the European Court of Human Rights and the European Union*, European Union and its Neighbours in a Globalized World 3, https://doi.org/10.1007/978-3-030-78059-3_1

1.1.1 A Legal Perspective

This situation sets the stage for what can be called the whistleblower's dilemma: Remaining silent in the face of misconduct, or blowing the whistle at the risk of suffering retaliation? The dilemma raises a myriad of scholarly issues in a wide variety of academic fields, from psychology to sociology and philosophy, business management to political science and economics, culture to history and law. This book will analyze the different aspects of whistleblowing through a legal lens, and focus on the different considerations in the development of whistleblower laws in Europe.[3] First introduced in the United States (U.S.), whistleblower laws are a decisive stand for whistleblowing as an important contribution to a democratic society. In recent decades, other countries have gradually introduced similar laws, an international trend which reveals the general recognition of whistleblowers as key players in democratic societies.

Notwithstanding this evolution, a number of legal conflicts renders the development of effective whistleblower laws especially arduous. It is particularly evident in the U.S. where, despite a set of leading whistleblower regulations, an increasing number of whistleblowers have been criminally prosecuted in the last decade, thereby emphasizing the blurred lines which define the legal status of whistleblower. Indeed, the complexity of whistleblowing as a legally protected act lies on two main aspects: On the one hand, the qualifying criteria of the status of whistleblower under the law, on the other hand, the formalities and extent of the mechanism established.

1.1.2 Key Questions

Those different elements of a whistleblower law evolve around key questions and related issues: Who can be defined as whistleblower under the law? Could an individual like Julian Assange be considered a whistleblower, for example? What kind of wrongdoing can be the object of a whistleblower report? Does it have to be acts and omissions prohibited by law or can it also include reprehensible conduct which is not per se illegal? What kind of mechanisms should be put in place to receive whistleblower reports? Should the law aim to protect whistleblowers against retaliation or also encourage whistleblowing through different incentives, such as financial incentives? Should individuals be under a legal duty to blow the whistle? Should leaks or anonymous reporting be included in a whistleblower framework? What about disclosures of classified information which posed a potential threat to national security interests? Should individuals who made those disclosures fall

[3] If certain parts of the book touch upon other fields of research, it will do so in general terms without seeking to reflect the complexity of the subject of whistleblowing within those respective disciplines.

within the scope of application of whistleblower laws? To provide context, those questions will be discussed in Part I of this book.

1.1.3 An International Angle

In consideration of the foregoing, the legal ramifications of the balancing exercise around those questions have led to diverging conceptions of the nature of whistleblower laws around the world. However, while heated debates persist, the growing number of countries to adopt whistleblower laws has prompted Non-governmental organizations (NGOs) and intergovernmental organizations to identify best-practices in order to guide countries in the adoption of their national whistleblowing regulations. Notwithstanding those international efforts, the legal protection coverage offered to whistleblowers remains uneven and fragmented worldwide. However, the sensational disclosures made by whistleblowers over the last decade, which revealed international personal data abuses, complex tax-avoidance schemes, and international law violations, brought growing public awareness of the role of whistleblowers for democracies and shifted the debate, from a niche topic to a pop culture issue. This subtle yet unequivocal change of attitude towards whistleblowing is nowhere more evident than in Europe.

1.2 The European Context

Indeed, the European historical background, with the methods used by the Nazi regime, the spying age of the Cold War, as well as the surveillance state in the former Soviet Union, has created a deeply rooted and understandable hostility against so-called 'informers'.[4] Because of this history, we Europeans "have not yet attained even the American level of pro-whistle-blowing rhetoric",[5] and have much to learn from the American experience.[6] Until recently, the act of whistleblowing did not seem to enjoy widespread recognition in Europe.[7] This is particularly well illustrated by the diversity of translations or the lack of equivalence of the term *whistleblowing*,[8] some European countries referring to their laws on witness

[4]Vaughn (2012), pp. 253–254; see also Dehn (1996), p. 10.

[5]Committee on Legal Affairs and Human Rights of the Council of Europe [hereinafter "Committee on Legal Affairs"], *Report on the protection of "whistle-blowers"*, Explanatory memorandum, Doc. 12006, 14 September 2009, para 1.

[6]Ibid., para 97.

[7]Ibid., para 16.

[8]Ibid., para 26.

protection when asked about their whistleblowing regulations,[9] which reveals a general misunderstanding in regard to whistleblower protection.

While certain European countries have kept the terms whistleblower/whistleblowing, others have translated the terms in a variety of ways, evoking different ideas: France uses *lanceur d'alerte* ("the alert launcher"), Germany uses *Hinweisgeber* ("person giving information"), in Latvia, it is *trauksmes cēlējs* ("alarm builder"), in Sweden *visslare* ("whistler"), in Slovenia, *notranji informator* ("internal informant") or in Malta, the term *informatur* ("informant") is used.[10] The act of whistleblowing is also differently defined around Europe, which demonstrates the diversity of understanding of the term. In some European countries, the concept of whistleblowing can be closely related to denunciation or the act of an informant, which can have a particularly negative connotation.[11] This diversity underlines how "the question of whistle-blowing is closely intertwined with the countries' legal cultures in general".[12] While in the U.S., "the term whistleblower was coined as an alternative to these negative epithets",[13] the plurality of European definitions and terms emphasizes how, at least until recently, Europe was lagging behind in regard to the protection of whistleblowers.

1.2.1 An Emerging European Consensus

In the last decade, however, a fundamental shift took place in Europe. Starting in the early 2010s, European initiatives tried to identify common grounds in regard to whistleblowing, which created a positive momentum for change. This book will examine those international and supranational efforts undertaken by the Council of Europe (CoE), the European Court of Human Rights (ECtHR), and the European Union (EU) and analyze their positions in respect to the different issues around whistleblower legislation. This analysis will bring to light an emerging European consensus.

1.2.2 The Position of the Council of Europe and the ECtHR

Since the beginning of the 2010s, the different organs of the CoE started to draw particular attention to the different aspects of whistleblowing, thereby initiating a

[9]Ibid., para 27.

[10]Eurovoc. *Whistleblowing*, EU Vocabularies.

[11]Committee on Legal Affairs, *Report on the protection of "whistle-blowers"*, Explanatory memorandum, para 28.

[12]Ibid., para 28; see also Vaughn (2012), pp. 255–258.

[13]Vaughn (2012), p. 256.

new European dynamic towards stronger whistleblower laws. The Parliamentary Assembly (PA) of the CoE was the first to adopt dedicated recommendations and resolutions on the protection of whistleblowers, laying the groundwork for the development of common European standards (Sect. 3.2). The Committee of Ministers (CM) of the CoE responded with the adoption of its own recommendations, which became leading principles for the establishment of a unified vision of whistleblowing across Europe (Sect. 3.3). On the judicial front, the ECtHR fostered this shared understanding through its case-law on whistleblowing under Article 10 of the European Convention on Human Rights (ECHR).[14] (Chap. 4) The different criteria developed by the ECtHR under Article 10 ECHR, especially in regard to the conflicting relationship between professional loyalty and whistleblowing, underline the determinant role of the judiciary which, with its interpretative authority, can greatly influence the level of protection afforded to whistleblowers (Sect. 4.4). The analysis of the ECtHR's case-law on whistleblowing will also highlight the responsibilities incumbent on the courts in respect to the delicate balancing exercise they must undertake between the competing interests at stake.

While the ECtHR's jurisprudence and the different resolutions and recommendations of the CoE aim to foster a harmonized protection for whistleblowers across Europe through the adoption of national laws established on the basis of common standards, a groundbreaking proposal by the PA called for the adoption of a legally binding Convention, thereby internationalizing the protection coverage for whistleblowers. Such an international legal instrument would truly be revolutionary and seems long overdue (Sect. 3.5.1). Indeed, in an ever more globalized and interconnected world, the cross-border effects of cover-ups have made the need for consistent and coherent whistleblower protection mechanisms increasingly pressing, especially in the security sector (Sects. 2.3.2 and 3.4). The global and deadly consequences of a lack of national whistleblower laws became painfully evident during the Covid-19 pandemic (Sect. 2.3.3).

1.2.3 The European Union Whistleblower Directive

The EU made the first step towards that goal. Indeed, the European patchwork approach hitherto followed (Chap. 7) and lack of "convergence based on uniform standards"[15] between EU Member States encouraged the EU legislator to adopt in 2019 an EU Directive on the protection of persons who report breaches of Union

[14]Convention for the Protection of Human Rights and Fundamental Freedoms (ECHR), 4 November 1950, ETS No. 005.

[15]EU Commission, *Commission Staff Working Document : Impact Assessment Accompanying the document Proposal for a Directive of the European Parliament and of the Council on the protection of persons reporting on breaches of Union law*, SWD(2018) 116 final, 23 Avril 2018, p. 3.

law[16] (hereinafter referred to as "EU Whistleblower Directive"), to remedy the fragmented nature of measures dedicated to whistleblower protection in the EU (Chap. 8). Contrary to the resolutions and recommendations of the CoE, the newly adopted EU Whistleblower Directive is legally binding and imposes an obligation upon EU Member States to transpose the Directive's provisions into national law, a historical step towards a more harmonized legal protection of whistleblowers across Europe. This EU Directive laid down the first stone for the future adoption of an international convention on whistleblowing, which would put an obligation on every country to adopt common rules and establish centralized organs competent to receive reports on wrongdoing. It could also be an opportunity to give international and supranational bodies the ability to intervene and prevent the risk of cover-ups.

1.3 A Long Way Ahead

However, despite a decisive step towards stronger whistleblower laws across Europe, those European initiatives remain to be transposed into national law. The arduous part is therefore still ahead of us. Considering the fragmented scope of application of the EU Whistleblower Directive, it remains to be seen whether EU Member States will go beyond that scope and adopt extensive provisions in regard to their national whistleblower laws. While certain non-EU Balkan countries have already adopted extremely ambitious whistleblower protection frameworks, it is highly uncertain whether other European countries will follow this lead. On an international and supranational level, the European institutions themselves need to address the shortcomings in regard to their own internal rules on whistleblowing to avoid being accused of hypocrisy. Indeed, while they promote stronger whistleblower protection mechanisms within their Member States, the CoE and the EU remain far behind in regard to their own whistleblower protection policies. While the World Bank Group (WBG) and the United Nations (UN) have long established internal whistleblowing regulations, taking into account the particularities in regard to their special legal status as intergovernmental organizations (Sect. 2.6), the Staff regulations within the CoE (Sect. 3.5.3) and the EU (Chap. 5) remain to be reformed in order to comply with the minimum standards those same institutions have imposed on their Member States so as to reflect the new European consensus they helped to define.

[16]Directive (EU) *2019/1937 of the European Parliament and of the Council of 23 October 2019 on the protection of persons who report breaches of Union law*, OJ L 305, 26.11.2019, p. 17.

References

Bok S (1989) Secrets: on the ethics of concealment and revelation. Vintage Books, New York

Dehn G (1996) Whistlebleblowing, fraud & the European Union. Report commissioned by the EU Commission, Public Concern at Work

Eurovoc, Whistleblowing, EU Vocabularies. https://op.europa.eu/en/web/eu-vocabularies/concept/-/resource?uri=http://eurovoc.europa.eu/c_2f00dd5a. Accessed 13 Apr 2021

Vaughn RG (2012) The successes and failures of whistleblower laws. Edward Elgar, Cheltenham/Northampton

Part I
International Perspective

Chapter 2
Introduction to Whistleblower Laws

2.1 The Genesis of "Whistleblowing"

The origin of the concept of "whistleblowing" is unclear. Some credit Ralph Nader, others a British practice.[1] What is certain, however, is that as early as January 1971, the New York Times reported on Mr. Nader's new initiative to promote 'responsible whistleblowing' by scientists, engineers and other professional employees of corporations and government". According to Mr. Nader, "Employed professionals . . . are too often the silent instruments of private and public policies which contravene the public interest, destroy the environment and defraud the taxpayer and consumer.. . . Those professionals who have spoken out, within and beyond their organizations, have too often been demoted, ostracized, discharged or suppressed when in fact they frequently may be heroic figures".[2]

The Conference on Professional Responsibility that followed, "which brought together some of the leading exponent of 'whistle blowing' . . . and some of the individuals who in different circumstances have felt compelled to speak out against the activities of their organizations",[3] resulted in the 1972 published report entitled *Whistle Blowing*, also known as the Nader Report,[4] which illustrates a common narrative of individual responsibility through whistleblowing.[5] From then on, U.S. newspapers started to use the term,[6] revealing the growing public recognition and acceptance for the notion of whistleblowing.

---

[1]Vaughn (2012), p. 256.

[2]Morris (1971, 27 January), p. 32.

[3]Nader et al. (1972), p. vii.

[4]Ibid.

[5]Ibid., p. 38.

[6]e.g. Morris (1971, 27 January); Dudar (1977, 30 October 1977), p. 201; Jensen (1978, 19 May), Section D, p. 1.

© The Author(s), under exclusive license to Springer Nature Switzerland AG 2021
H. C. L. Yurttagül, *Whistleblower Protection by the Council of Europe, the European Court of Human Rights and the European Union*, European Union and its Neighbours in a Globalized World 3, https://doi.org/10.1007/978-3-030-78059-3_2

According to the Nader Report, whistleblowing can be defined as "the act of a man or woman who, believing that the public interest overrides the interest of the organization he serves, publicly 'blows the whistle' if the organization is involved in corrupt, illegal, fraudulent, or harmful activity".[7]

2.1.1 The Pioneering Role of the U.S.

As a pioneer in the field,[8] the U.S. has followed a rather sectorial "piecemeal approach" in regard to whistleblower protection, creating "an inconsistent legislative patchwork".[9] To remedy this situation, the U.S. federal legislator gradually introduced more comprehensive whistleblowers laws.

2.1.1.1 The Sarbanes-Oxley Act

While remaining sector specific, these pieces of legislation introduced some of the most ambitious whistleblowing mechanisms, with a sphere of influence stretching far beyond U.S. borders. The Sarbanes-Oxley Act[10] for example, adopted in response to U.S. corporate scandals, applies to companies listed on U.S. stock exchanges and was praised for being "the most important whistleblower protection law in the world".[11] It establishes both anti-retaliation measures, including criminal charges against individuals who retaliate against whistleblowers,[12] and anonymous reporting channels.[13] Despite its shortcomings,[14] the extraterritorial impact of the Sarbanes-Oxley Act, which may find its legal justification in the voluntary recourse to the U.S. capital market,[15] has greatly enhanced its international relevance as a legal transplant.[16]

---

[7]Nader et al. (1972), p. vii.

[8]Committee on Legal Affairs and Human Rights of the Council of Europe [hereinafter "Committee on Legal Affairs"], *Report on the protection of "whistle-blowers"*, Explanatory memorandum, Doc. 12006, 14 September 2009, para 98.

[9]Boyne (2016), pp. 280–283.

[10]Pub. Law 107-204, 116 Stat. 745 (2002).

[11]Vaughn (2005b), p. 73.

[12]18 U.S.C. § 1513 (e).

[13]15 U.S.C. § 78j-1(m)(4)(A) (Supp. 2004).

[14]See e.g. Moberly (2006), pp. 1107–1180; Moberly (2007), pp. 65–155.

[15]Gerdemann (2018), pp. 366–367.

[16]On U.S. corporate compliance mechanisms as legal transplants, see e.g. Gerdemann (2018), pp. 366 et seq.; Hertel (2019), pp. 56 et seq.

2.1.1.2 The Whistleblower Protection Act

On the public side, the Whistleblower Protection Act[17] represents the ambitious attempt of the U.S. Congress to address the "legal system's schizophrenic perspective on dissent reveal[ing] the inherent consequences of secrecy - sharp contradictions between policies set in the public eye and those implemented outside it".[18] It is the key piece of federal legislation in the field of whistleblower protection[19] and covers public employees who work for federal bodies, with the exception of, inter alia, the Central Intelligence Agency (CIA) and the National Security Agency (NSA).[20] Employees working for these agencies, together with any employee in a position which is "excepted from the competitive [federal] service because of it confidential, policy-determining, policy-making, or policy-advocating character"[21] or "excluded ... by the President based on a determination by the President that is it necessary and warranted by conditions of good administration"[22] thus fall outside the scope of application of the Whistleblower Protection Act. As will be demonstrated below, such exceptions can be particularly detrimental to the effective protection of whistleblowers who disclose classified national security information revealing misconducts committed by the State and its intelligence services.[23]

2.1.1.3 The *Garcetti v. Cebellos* Case

The *Garcetti v. Cebellos* judgment of the U.S. Supreme Court[24] in particular illustrates the vulnerability of public employees when blowing the whistle, some calling it the virus of job duties exclusion.[25] The U.S. Supreme Court indeed held that a public employee does not enjoy constitutional protection for speech "that owes its existence to [his] professional responsibilities"[26] and thus concluded that disciplinary measures adopted because of such speech cannot be considered a violation of the First Amendment. However, with this constitutional background, the wide scope of laws protecting classified national security information[27] and the restrictive application of federal whistleblowers laws thus leave public whistleblowers mostly

---

[17] 5 U.S. Code §§ 1201 et seq. (1989).

[18] Devine (1999), pp. 535–536.

[19] Committee on Legal Affairs, Report on the protection of "whiste-blowers", *Explanatory memorandum*, para 100.

[20] 5 U.S.C. § 2302(a)(2)(C)(ii)(I).

[21] 5 U.S.C. § 2302(a)(2)(B)(i).

[22] 5 U.S.C. § 2302(a)(2)(B)(ii).

[23] On the conflict between whistleblowing and national security see Sect. 2.3.2.

[24] 547 U.S. 410 [2006].

[25] Modesitt (2012), pp. 161–208.

[26] 547 U.S. 410, at 421 (majority opinion).

[27] e.g. 18 U.S.C. § 793(d).

unprotected against retaliation if their disclosure relate to classified national security information.[28]

The existing legal loophole in the U.S. whistleblower protection system gained international attention after the revelations by and prosecution of Edward Snowden, a case presented further below.[29] It will also be particularly interesting to contrast the U.S. Supreme Court's position with that of the ECtHR, which afforded protection to a public official who disclosed classified national security information.[30]

2.1.2 *The Whistleblower's Dilemma*

2.1.2.1 The Challenge of Bureaucracy

The underlying challenge with regard to whistleblowing can be described as follows: "The bureaucracy is a Goliath, and the machinery available to enforce its will is immense".[31] "As the power becomes coagulated, it becomes lazy and entrenched. From there, it is a short step to its becoming corrupt and predatory … In this way, whistle-blowing has moved into a breach left by the failure of the traditional methods of institutional control".[32] However, as a form of bureaucratic opposition, the act of whistleblowing can face strong resistance from the hierarchy[33] and lead to a clash between different bonds of loyalty.[34] In those circumstances, " the possibility of dissent within the hierarchy . . . become[s] so restricted that common candor requires uncommon courage".[35] This is the reason why, despite the diversity of circumstances in which whistleblowers can find themselves, early commentators identified common experiences:[36] Whistleblowers faced great hardship[37] in the form of dismissal, transfers or harassment for having "breached the etiquette of hierarchical management".[38]

[28] Vladeck (2008), p. 313.

[29] See Sect. 2.3.2.2.

[30] On the *Bucur and Toma* ruling of the ECtHR see Sect. 4.4.2.4.

[31] Dudar (1977, 30 October 1977).

[32] Peters and Branch (1972), pp. 293–294.

[33] Weinstein (1979), p. 58.

[34] Elliston (1982b), p. 25.

[35] Nader (1972), p. 3.

[36] Near and Jensen (1983), p. 4.

[37] Ibid., p. 25.

[38] Nader et al. (1972), p. 155.

2.1.2.2 Retaliation

"'Bureaucratic genius for retaliation' . . . is at its most creative in devising reprisals against those who mount oppositions".[39] Retaliation, in relation to whistleblowing, can thus be defined "as undesirable action taken against a whistleblower – in direct response to the whistleblowing – who reported wrongdoing internally or externally, outside the organization".[40] In practice, retaliation in the form of harassment appeared to be particularly common "because it is difficult to prove and quite often the employee has not done anything technically improper to justify formal action".[41] Early studies on retaliation against whistleblowers seem to suggest that acts of retaliation follow different patterns.[42] While retaliatory measures against high-ranking whistleblowers may follow a damage-control reasoning,[43] retaliation against less powerful employees may be motivated by their limited influence in the company and thus increased vulnerability.[44] The likelihood of retaliation was also increased through a situation of power dynamic combined with a lack of support from middle and top management.[45] A 1978 U.S. congressional report on whistleblowing underlined the chilling effect of retaliation, which can deter future potential whistleblowers from reporting wrongdoing.[46] As a consequence, employees, who are amongst the first to become aware of wrongdoing or dangerous dysfunctions within their organization and hierarchy,[47] thus remain silent or suffer serious personal prejudice for having expressed their concerns.[48]

It leads to the crystallization of the whistleblower's dilemma: an employee "motivated by a personal or professional code of ethics, attempts to correct a problem at the risk of his or her career, financial security and reputation".[49]

---

[39]Weinstein (1979), p. 108.

[40]Rehg et al. (2008), p. 222.

[41]Committee on Governmental Affairs of the United States Senate, *The Whistleblowers: A Report on Federal Employees who Disclose Acts of Governmental Waste, Abuse and Corruption* [hereinafter "The Whistleblowers report"]. U.S. Government Printing Office, 1978, p. 27.

[42]Parmerlee et al. (1982), p. 31.

[43]Ibid., p. 30.

[44]Near and Jensen (1983), pp. 23–24.

[45]Near and Jensen (1983), Miceli and Near (1986), Miceli and Near (1989), Near et al. (1993) and Parmerlee et al. (1982).

[46]Committee on Governmental Affairs of the U.S. Senate, *The Whistleblowers report*, p. 2.

[47]Weinstein (1979), p. 62.

[48]Morris (1971, 27 January).

[49]Committee on Governmental Affairs of the United States, *The Whistleblowers report*, p. 6.

2.1.3 *The Essence of Whistleblower Laws*

As the act of whistleblowing gained public recognition, considerations over the need to develop dedicated laws became increasingly relevant.[50] This followed the primary idea that "[b]ureaucracies are not rigid and static but dynamic".[51] Accordingly, organizational culture influences the likelihood of wrongdoing being reported and addressed.[52] In other words, to promote organizational responsibility and accountability, "organizational power must be insecure".[53]

2.1.3.1 Protection vs. Incentives

Different conceptions of whistleblowing emerged during its early development into a fully-fledged legal notion. According to a prevailing view, the main difficulty arising from whistleblowing evolved around the conflict between the duty to society and the duty of loyalty to the employer. In this sense, blowing the whistle brings forward a professional and individual responsibility[54] not to the organization but to society as a whole[55] and represents "the last line of defense ordinary citizens have against the denial of their rights and the destruction of their interests by secretive and powerful institutions".[56] According to this understanding, whistleblowing raises "a tension between an employee's private loyalty to his employer and his public loyalty to the community. . . . The fact that his disclosure would be of "incalculable damage" to his employer can hardly be thought to reduce that duty of disclosure".[57] This conception promotes a utilitarian approach to whistleblowing, putting the emphasis on the public interest of the disclosure. Another view of whistleblowing contradictes this position and places the focus on the balance "between the individual's interest in acting according to his conscience and the employer's interests in his employee's silence",[58] and by extension, loyalty.[59]

Distinguishing those conceptions of whistleblowing helps one understand the different elements at play in the legal reasoning behind whistleblower laws. While the former reasoning offers a broader vision of whistleblowing, underlining the societal contribution of whistleblowers, the latter position emphasizes the difficulties

---

[50]Ibid.

[51]Vaughn (1977), p. 293.

[52]Miceli and Near (1986), p. 137.

[53]Nader (1972), pp. 10–11.

[54]Nader et al. (1972), p. 140.

[55]Nader (1972), p. 7; see also Elliston (1982a), p. 169.

[56]Nader (1972), p. 7.

[57]*Yellow Cab of California*, 65-1 ARB Par. 8256,44 LA 174-445 (164) (Edgar A. Jones, Arbitrator).

[58]Malin (1983), p. 318.

[59]Ibid., p. 278.

around the blurred delimitation between personal convictions and employee loyalty. Different legal consequences follow from those diverging emphases. A legal rationale based on the first position, which highlights the benefits of whistleblowers for society, may expand upon a mere protective framework destined to shield whistleblowers from retaliation and broaden the scope of the law in order to include incentives to encourage whistleblowing. A legal reasoning placing the focus on the balance between personal convictions and duty of loyalty would reject such a conclusion and limit the application of whistleblower laws to a protective aim.[60] The first approach promotes a fundamental vision of whistleblower laws while the second emphasizes its corrective essence.

While being distinct, those different conceptions of whistleblower laws are not mutually exclusive. In fact, they are often complementary. Indeed, the legislator's intention in developing whistleblower laws may often be influenced by those different considerations. Depending on the sector or field of law, the center of gravity of whistleblower regulations may vary and fluctuate between a protective intent and the desire to encourage whistleblowing.

As a consequence, courts may interpret those regulations differently and give more or less importance to the constituent criteria of whistleblower laws, which increases the relevance of the distinction between a law promoting a protective approach and a law which entails an incentive scheme. This divergence of conception can be best illustrated on the international stage. While the Organisation for Economic Co-operation and Development (OECD) promotes a hybrid approach of whistleblower laws, stating that "[o]ne of the main objectives of whistleblower protection systems is to *promote and facilitate the reporting* of 'illegal, unethical or dangerous' activities",[61] the CoE endorsed a protective vision to whistleblower laws, stating that "[t]he normative framework should reflect a comprehensive and coherent approach to *facilitating* public interest reporting and disclosures",[62] in order to "ensure that potential whistleblowers are not discouraged or penalized by conflicting or restrictive legal provisions",[63] rejecting the possibility of financial incentives.[64]

---

[60]Ibid., p. 278.

[61]OECD (2010), p. 9; OECD (2016) p. 44 (emphasis added).

[62]Committee of Ministers of the Council of Europe, Recommendation CM/Rec(2014)7 on the protection of whistleblowers [hereinafter "CoE Recommendation CM/Rec(2014)7"], 30 April 2014, *Appendix*, Point 7.

[63]CoE Recommendation CM/Rec(2014)7, *Explanatory memorandum*, para 50.

[64]Committee on Legal Affairs, *Report on the protection of "whistle-blowers"*, Explanatory memorandum, para 116 (g).

2.1.3.2 A Conflict of Loyalties

Those different definitions of whistleblower highlight another difficulty in the development of whistleblower laws. Indeed, while the OECD defines whistleblowing as the "reporting of "*illegal, unethical or dangerous*"[65] activities", the CoE prefers "*public interest* reporting and disclosures".[66] Both descriptions raise key questions: What are unethical activities? Which information can be defined as being in the public interest? Then come the follow-up questions: Is it enough for an employee to think that the situation she or he became aware of is unethical? Or is there the need for concrete pieces of evidence to demonstrate that those allegations are founded in fact? To what extent should allegations be grounded in evidence for an individual to benefit from the whistleblower status under the law? If an employee becomes aware of wrongdoing, can she or he disclose those wrongdoings publicly or should it first be reported internally? Those questions are central to the development and application of whistleblower laws and evolve, in one way or another, around the primary challenge of whistleblowing: loyalty.

Snitch, denunciator, spy, traitor, anti-patriotic ... These are all different terms to describe the same idea: A breach of loyalty. "Personal loyalties present one of the most genuine, perplexing problems of the whistle-blower".[67] Considering the diversity of circumstances in which wrongdoing is committed and brought to light by individuals, whistleblowers can be confronted with different conflicts of loyalty.[68] Identifying the different layers is key when conducting a balancing exercise and applying whistleblower laws. First and foremost, there is a bond of loyalty to one's personal ethics and beliefs of what is right or wrong. Then follows a bond of loyalty to the supervisor, then to the organization within which the employee is working. As already mentioned above, there is also the bond of loyalty to society as a whole. It can be to the community, to the national interests, or to principles considered universal. Whistleblowing can raise various conflicts in relation to those bonds of loyalty.

To illustrate with some examples: An employee becomes aware of wrongdoing committed by her supervisor, which is contrary to the interests of the company. In this particular setting, there is a conflict between the loyalty to her supervisor and her loyalty to the company. Another example: An employee becomes aware of wrongdoing committed by her company, which have serious detrimental effects to the environment in the region. This time, her loyalty to her company collides with her loyalty to the community. Last but not the least, the third example creates the most sensitive conflict of all in regard to whistleblowing: A public employee becomes aware of wrongdoing committed by her State, which violates constitutional or international law. In this last example, her loyalty to society, to her fellow citizens

[65] OECD (2010), p. 9; OECD (2016), p. 44 (emphasis added).

[66] CoE Recommendation CM/Rec(2014)7, *Appendix*, Point 7 (emphasis added).

[67] Peters and Branch (1972), p. 285.

[68] Elliston (1982b), p. 25.

or to her fellow human beings, can directly clash with the implicit or explicit national interests of her State.

Those standard examples can take the form of more complex variations. Navigating those different bonds of loyalty is the difficult path of whistleblower laws. On the basis of common criteria, those laws have to define in which cases the bond of loyalty "serve[s] the socially useful purpose of preventing deterioration from becoming cumulative", in the "reasoned expectation that improvement or reform can be achieved 'from within'",[69] and in which cases "it must be realized that loyalty-promoting institutions and devices are not only uninterested in stimulating voice at the expense of exit: indeed they are often meant to repress voice alongside exit".[70] In order words, in which cases does the law have to intervene to correct the negative effects of a loyalty-based relationship which can promote silence over accountability, in order to protect an individual who has suffered from the consequences of having broken one bond of loyalty for the benefit of another? Here again, the differentiation between protective and promoting laws has an influence. While protective laws would merely shield individuals who have personally suffered retaliation as a consequence of their "disloyalty", laws promoting whistleblowing through incentives implicitly prioritize one bond of loyalty over another and introduce a hierarchy through a pro-active approach to whistleblowing.

This brings a particular characteristic to light: the constituent criteria of whistleblower laws entail a set of variables which can be the subject to a wide range of interpretations. It thus broadens substantively the margin of appreciation of the judiciary, which plays "the most important roles in determining the meaning of these laws".[71] Depending on the cultural and historical background of the country, the balancing exercise conducted by domestic courts could vary dramatically, expanding or, contrariwise, narrowing the scope of application of whistleblower laws. This observation is particularly relevant for the development of international best-practices. Indeed, while a set of common criteria can be identified as particularly important for the effectiveness of whistleblower legislation, the domestic development, implementation and application of the law greatly depends on the national appreciation of the original challenge surrounding whistleblowing: the conflict of loyalties.

2.1.4 The Justifications for Whistleblower Legislation

In this context, whistleblower law can be a double-edged sword. It can be used to ensure accountability but it can also create a denunciation culture. It can strengthen

[69] Hirschman (1970), p. 79.

[70] Ibid., p. 92

[71] Vaughn (2012), p. 189.

an open government or, contrariwise, promote a surveillance state.[72] Whistleblowing policies could help reveal wrongdoing or be instrumentalized to pursue interests far from general public concerns.[73] This duality to whistleblower legislations makes it all the more important to carefully assess the points of friction and ensure a legislative framework which protects whistleblowers while safeguarding competing interests. The justification for the adoption of whistleblower legislation can be based on different grounds, usually focused on the need for open government, better market regulations, better protection under employment and labor laws, and the effective protection of human rights, especially in the context of the right to freedom of speech.[74]

2.1.4.1 Democratic Accountability and Market Regulation

The most common reason evoked to introduce whistleblower protection provisions is the prevention of corruption and fraud, in the public as well as in the private sector. The open-government and market-regulation perspectives of whistleblower laws aim to further institutional reform and ensure democratic and corporate accountability through the access to information.[75] The former perspective is particularly influenced by a global vision of whistleblowing, in an attempt to promote "open democracies" through the participation of the civil society,[76] while the latter is guided by the awareness that democratic accountability and human rights protection is closely linked to the fight against corruption and financial crimes, a perspective which has regained attention after the 2008 financial crisis.[77]

2.1.4.2 Labor Law and Human Rights Protection

The employment and labor law perspective, based on the Convention No. 158[78] of the International Labour Organization (ILO),[79] justifies the introduction of whistleblowing rules as an effective tool to protect the rights of employees and ensure a safe and fair working environment,[80] some going so far as to promote

72 Ibid., p. 255.

73 Lochak (2016), para 73.

74 Vaughn (2012), p. 286.

75 Ibid., p. 301.

76 Foegle (2015), para 2.

77 Ibid., para 4.

78 Convention Concerning Termination of Employment at the Initiative of the Employer, 22 June 1982, C158.

79 Foegle (2015), para 5.

80 Vaughn (2012), p. 288.

"whistleblowing" as a fundamental employment right.[81] In connection but distinct from the labor law perspective is the protection of the right to freedom of expression as another justification to introduce whistleblower regulations,[82] a position confirmed by the ECtHR which developed its whistleblower protection jurisprudence under Article 10 of the ECHR, the freedom of expression provision.[83] The close relationship between labor law and the right to freedom of expression can be particularly well illustrated by the 2019 United Kingdom (UK) Supreme Court judgment *Gilham v. Ministry of Justice*.[84] While the UK Supreme Court excluded protection under the Public Interest Disclosure Act (PIDA), the UK Whistleblower law, because it denied the status of "worker" to the appellant[85] who is a district judge, it held "that the exclusion of judges from the whistle-blowing protection in Part IVA of the 1996 Act is in breach of their rights under article 14 read with article 10 of the ECHR".[86] This conclusion demonstrates how a human rights approach can strengthen the level of protection for whistleblowers.

2.1.5 Whistleblower Protection in the International Legal Order

2.1.5.1 An Emerging International Consensus

On the international stage, a certain lack of political will to introduce robust whistleblower protection legislations has led to fragmented protection frameworks within domestic jurisdictions.[87] However, there is an increasing international consensus on the need for strong whistleblower laws, a consensus which has materialized with the steady increase in the number of whistleblower protection regulations adopted worldwide.[88] With 48 States having national whistleblower laws today, this number will increase to over 62 by the end of the EU Whistleblower Directive transposition phase at the end of 2021.[89]

[81] Lewis and Fasterling (2014), p. 72.

[82] Vaughn (2012), p. 295.

[83] On the ECtHR case-law on whistleblowing see Chap. 4.

[84] UK Supreme Court Judgment, *Gilham v. Ministry of Justice*, 16 October 2019, [2019] UKSC 44.

[85] Ibid., paras 12–21.

[86] Ibid., para 37.

[87] Wolfe et al. (2014), p. 10.

[88] OECD (2016), pp. 20 and 24; see also GAP, *International Whistleblower Protection Map*, launched in March 2021.

[89] Feinstein et al. (2021), p. 8.

2.1.5.2 The United Nations Convention Against Corruption

In an international legal context, Article 32 of the United Nations Convention against Corruption[90] imposes an obligation upon UN Member States "to provide effective protection from potential retaliation or intimidation for witnesses and experts who give testimony concerning offences",[91] a relevant provision in regard to whistleblowing, but with a particularly narrow personal scope, insufficient to address all aspects of whistleblower protection.[92] On the other hand, even if Article 33 of the UN Convention entitled "Protection of reporting persons", mentions "appropriate measures to provide protection against any unjustified treatment for any person who reports in good faith and on reasonable grounds to the competent authorities any facts concerning offences established in accordance with this Convention", thus offering a particularly forward-thinking approach to whistleblower protection, its relevance is dramatically diminished by the non-binding nature of its formulation; the provision merely encourages UN Member States to *consider incorporating* such measures.

2.1.5.3 The International Covenant on Civil and Political Rights

The particular significance of the UN Convention against Corruption for the protection of whistleblowers was reiterated by Olivier de Frouville in his individual opinion to the Views adopted by the Human Rights Committee (HRC) in the case *Kouider Kerrouche v. Algeria.*[93] Established by the International Covenant on Civil and Political Rights (ICCRP),[94] the HRC is mandated to monitor the implementation of the ICCPR by its State parties,[95] including through the receipt and assessment of individuals complaints.[96] The case *Kouider Kerrouche* concerned a former accountant at the State-owned road-building and engineering corporation ETGR, who had been dismissed after refusing to comply with the ETGR Director's request to falsify a tax statement. He reported the Director's malpractice to the prosecution service but was later criminally charged and convicted for having criticized the judicial authorities of procedural irregularities and abuses of power when they decided to close the

---

[90] UN General Assembly, *United Nations Convention Against Corruption*, 31 October 2003, A/58/422.

[91] Article 32 (1) United Nations Convention against Corruption.

[92] Vaughn (2012), p. 243.

[93] HRC, *Kouider Kerrouche v. Algeria, Views concerning communication No. 2128/2012, Annex, Individual opinion of Olivier de Frouville*, CCPR/C/118/D/2128/2012, 29 December 2016, para 4.

[94] UN General Assembly, *International Covenant on Civil and Political Rights*, 16 December 1966, United Nations, Treaty Series, vol. 999, p. 171.

[95] See Part IV of the ICCPR.

[96] UN General Assembly, *Optional Protocol to the International Covenant on Civil and Political Rights*, 19 December 1966, United Nations, Treaty Series, Vol. 999, p. 171.

preliminary investigations against the ETGR Director.[97] In his communication to the HRC, he claimed, inter alia, that such conviction constituted a violation of his right to freedom of expression under Article 19 ICCPR.[98]

According to Article 19(3) ICCPR, the right to freedom of expression carries with it special duties and responsibilities, the HRC thus recalled that restriction to this right is permitted, provided that it is prescribed by law and necessary for the respect of the rights or reputations of others.[99] In the case at hand however, the HRC held that the State was not able to demonstrate such necessity and thus concluded that the criminal conviction of Mr. Kerrouche was a violation of his right to freedom of expression under Article 19(2) ICCPR. [100] In its individual opinion, HRC member de Frouville expressed his support for the HRC's conclusion,[101] though it regretted "that the Committee has not ... taken the opportunity to develop its own jurisprudence on the legal status of whistle-blowers under article 19 of the Covenant".[102] He indeed considered that the HRC had failed to appreciate the dual aspect of the criminal charges against Mr. Kerrouche, as an act of retaliation and intimidation,[103] stating that "it is broadly accepted today that States have the obligation ... to establish a legislative framework and practices that facilitate and protect the disclosure of information on matters of public interest".[104] According to this reasoning, the HRC member de Frouville considered that Mr. Kerrouche had acted as a whistleblower, the conviction thus constituting a serious violation of Article 19 ICCPR.[105]

2.1.5.4 Whistleblower Protection and International Law

Mr. de Frouville's position illustrates the increasing international acceptance and recognition of the role of whistleblowers in a democratic society and the need to protect their right to freedom of expression under international law. As the former UN Special rapporteur on the promotion and the protection of the right to freedom of expression David Kaye held in his 2015 report, "whistle-blower protections rest upon a core right to freedom of expression".[106] Those views represent a particularly encouraging sign and may be an early indication for the future development of a

[97] HRC, *Kouider Kerrouche v. Algeria,* para 2.9.

[98] Ibid., para 3.5.

[99] Ibid., para 8.8.

[100] Ibid.

[101] HRC, *Kouider Kerrouche v. Algeria, Annex, Individual opinion of Olivier de Frouville*, para 1.

[102] Ibid., para 3 *in fine*.

[103] Ibid., para 1.

[104] Ibid., para 2.

[105] Ibid., para 3.

[106] UN, *Report of the Special Rapporteur on the promotion and protection of the right to freedom of opinion and expression David Kaye* [hereinafter "Special Rapporteur David Kaye whistleblower report"], A/70/361, 8 September 2015, para 5.

whistleblowing jurisprudence under Article 19 ICCPR, thereby aligning with the position of regional human rights courts, such as the ECtHR. Contrary to the UN Convention against Corruption, the right to freedom of expression under Article 19 ICCPR allows for a broad protection coverage for whistleblowers. The HCR has indeed held that "freedoms of information and of expression are cornerstones in any free and democratic society",[107] States have thus the obligation to protect "the right to seek, receive and impart information of all kinds".[108] The HCR also underlined that Article 19 ICCPR includes the right to be protected against attacks aiming to silence individuals,[109] an open door for the future development of a jurisprudence on whistleblower protection under the ICCPR, which may be further encouraged by the emerging international consensus. Such development on the international level, together with the regional initiatives in Europe and elsewhere, may lay the foundation for the adoption of an international whistleblower framework.[110] Indeed, the right to access information, intrinsically linked to the right to the truth, is "one of the central components of the right to freedom of opinion and expression" protected by international law,[111] the adoption of an international legally binding instrument on whistleblower protection would thus make the right to the truth enforceable under international law.

The last decade has also witnessed joined efforts to identify international best-practices for the adoption of specific rules dedicated to the protection of whistleblowers, a particularly encouraging development which can guide national legislators in the process of adopting or reforming national whistleblower laws. On the basis of the principles promoted by the OECD, ILO, UNODC, Transparency International, the International Bar Association and the UN Special Rapporteur David Kaye, this chapter will analyze the international best practices develop over the last decade in regard to whistleblower protection.

2.2 Who Is a Whistleblower Under the Law?

First and foremost, a legislative whistleblower framework should be clearly defined so as to avoid confusion, ensure confidence in the system and promote a "no-loophole" approach through clear delimitations of the scope of application of the

---

[107]HCR, *Adimayo M. Aduayom, Sofianou T. Diasso and Yawo S. Dobou v. Togo*, Views concerning communcations Nos. 422/1990, 423/1990 and 424/1990, 12 July 1996, para 7.4.

[108]HCR, *General comment No. 34 on Article 19 ICCPR: Freedom of opinion and expression*, CCPR/C/GC/34, 12 September 2011, para 11; see also Article 19 of the Universal Declaration of Human Rights, 10 December 1948, 217 A (III).

[109]HCR, *General comment No. 34 on Article 19 ICCPR*, para 23.

[110]On the development of an international convention on the protection of whistleblowers see Sect. 9.5.

[111]UN, *Report of the Special Rapporteur on the promotion and protection of the right to freedom of opinion and expression Frank La Rue*, A/68/362, 4 September 2013, para 2.

law.[112] According to the definition of the OECD, the framework should "protect from discriminatory or disciplinary action employees who disclose in good faith and on reasonable grounds certain suspected acts of wrongdoing or corruption to competent authorities".[113] This definition reveals different key aspects constituent to the personal scope of whistleblower legislations: (1) the employment relationship and (2) the good faith and the reasonable grounds of the reporting individual.

2.2.1 Work-Based Relationship

2.2.1.1 Employees

Most legal definitions of *whistleblower* require a work-based relationship between the individual who reported and the organization she or he reported on. It follows the traditional idea whereby insiders, who are the best placed to become aware of wrongdoing committed within their own organization, reveal information about those wrongdoings and suffer retaliation for having done so. Because of their particular vulnerability linked to their status of employee and thus their professional and financial relationship of dependency, they face interconnected difficulties: on the one hand, their status of employee increases the chance that they remain silent when witnessing wrongdoing because of their dependency towards the organization. On the other hand, if they decide to report on wrongdoing, they are particularly vulnerable to retaliation.

To remedy this situation, whistleblower laws should therefore cover all employees, in the public as well as in the private sector. According to the OECD "no-loophole" approach, the individuals falling within the scope of the law should be clearly defined.[114] The exclusion of certain categories of employees, such as individuals working in the intelligence or defense sector, as is the case in certain countries,[115] shall therefore be considered incompatible with international best practices. As will be described below, it is essential for individuals working in those sectors, which are closely linked to the field of national security, to benefit from strong whistleblower regulations.[116]

---

[112]OECD (2010), p. 9; OECD (2016), p. 43; ILO (2019) p. 14; IBA (2018), p. 18.

[113]OECD (2010), p. 30.

[114]Ibid., p. 9.

[115]Ibid.

[116]On whistleblowing in the security sector see Sect. 2.3.2.

2.2.1.2 Third Parties

The UN as well as advocacy groups have promoted a particularly broad scope of application of whistleblower laws, so as to include individuals "who are outside the traditional employee-employer relationship"[117] or, independently from their employment status, individuals who could be subjected to "unfair treatment as a consequence of whistleblowing".[118] New generations of legislative initiatives have applied these suggestions, expanded upon the primary group of employees and broadened the personal scope of the law to third parties.[119] Accordingly, whistleblower laws may not only protect whistleblowers per se, but also natural or legal persons who are connected to whistleblowers. Under these conditions, it can be envisaged that individuals such as intermediaries, journalists or NGOs could be covered by those new whistleblower regulations if they have suffered detrimental effects as a result of their cooperation with whistleblowers.

2.2.2 *Good Faith and Motives*

One core element of whistleblower laws is the condition of good faith,[120] which aims to prevent abuse of the whistleblower framework while protecting individuals who legitimately believed the accuracy of the information. In this respect, a clarification appears necessary. Domestic courts have indeed interpreted this term differently in respect to whistleblowing and developed a variety of inherent components to accept or deny the good faith of a reporting individual.[121] This diversity of views in regard to the definition of good faith is particularly detrimental to the effectiveness of whistleblower laws as it creates confusion and expands the margin of discretion of authorities at the expense of legal certainty.[122]

2.2.2.1 Reasonable Grounds

The following definition of good faith should be promoted in the context of whistleblower laws: An individual acted in good faith when, in light of the elements

[117] TI (2013), Principle 4, pp. 4–5.

[118] TI (2018), p. 13; Special Rapporteur David Kaye whistleblower report, paras 28-29; Feinstein et al. (2021), pp. 16–17.

[119] e.g. Article 4 in conjunction with Recital 41 Directive (EU) *2019/1937 of the European Parliament and of the Council of 23 October 2019 on the protection of persons who report breaches of Union law* [hereinafter "EU Whistleblower Directive"], OJ L 305, 26.11.2019, p. 17; Article 4(4); Serbian Whistleblower Law, Zakon o zaštiti uzbunjivača, Articles 6 and 7.

[120] OECD (2010), p. 8; OECD (2016), p. 50; ILO (2019), p. 22.

[121] IBA (2018), p. 22.

[122] Ibid., p. 23.

available at the time of the report, she or he had reasonable grounds to believe the information reported to be true, even if it proves to be false or incorrect at a later stage.[123] According to this definition of good faith, the particular circumstances of the case should be analyzed in order to determine whether a reasonable and informed party could have legitimately believed in a wrongdoing. As will be presented below, European organizations have chosen to directly refer to reasonable grounds rather than to the term "good faith", as a way to promote a more harmonized application of whistleblower rules.

The requirements of factual evidence necessary to affirm that an individual had indeed reasonable grounds to believe in the existence of a wrongdoing varies and is closely related to the specific circumstances of the case and the interpretation of the courts. The analysis of the ECtHR and Court of Justice of the European Union (CJEU) case-law will illustrate the different balancing exercises that courts conduct when appreciating the good faith of the reporting individual. The position of the CJEU demonstrates an ambitious yet minority viewpoint in this respect as it puts a particular emphasis on the element of suspicion, a position confirmed by the EU Whistleblower Directive, which describes information on breaches as "information, including reasonable suspicions, about actual or potential breaches".[124] Under this definition, courts would have to determine whether a reasonable and informed party could have legitimately *suspected* the existence of a wrongdoing. With the level of verification and authenticity of the information being at the center of any whistleblower case, only the future will tell whether other national whistleblower laws and the position of domestic courts will move away from the tradition of "reasonable belief" and take the more whistleblower-friendly approach of "reasonable suspicion" in assessing the good faith of the whistleblower.[125]

From a procedural standpoint it is considered best practice to put the burden of proof on the employer, who needs to demonstrate that the reporting person did not act in good faith.[126]

2.2.2.2 The Motivation of the Whistleblower

Another relevant aspect in respect to the good faith criterion is its appreciation in relation to the motive of the whistleblower. While good faith and motives can sometimes be appreciated simultaneously by courts,[127] those two elements should

[123] OECD (2010), p. 8; TI (2013), p. 5; UNODC (2015), pp. 24–25; Special Rapporteur David Kaye whistleblower report, para 62; Feinstein et al. (2021), p. 13.

[124] Article 5(2) *EU Whistleblower Directive*.

[125] Lewis (2010), p. 328.

[126] ILO (2019), p. 22.

[127] e.g. ECtHR, *Guja v. Moldova* [GC], Appl. No. 14277/04, 12 February 2008; Labour Court of South Africa, *Tshishonga v. Minister of Justice and Constitutional Development and Another*, Case No. JS898/04, 26 December 2006, ZALC 104.

be clearly differentiated.[128] Indeed, taking into account the internal motives of an individual to determine whether to afford protection under whistleblower regulations is particularly controversial. While some courts have used the motivations of the reporting individual as a qualifying condition, this element should be rejected as a relevant element to afford the whistleblower status. Aside from the procedural difficulty of establishing the true motives of an individual,[129] determining her or his motivation does not influence the veracity of the information reported.[130] In fact, "logicians have long recognized this strategy as fallacious: whether or not what someone says is true does not depend on his personal motive for saying it".[131] This position has been confirmed in recent years by the UN Special Rapporteur, the CoE and the EU, which exclude the motive as a legitimate criterion of a whistleblower protection framework.[132] Instead of focusing on the personal motivations of the individual, attention should be given to the value of the information reported.

2.2.3 *Gender and Whistleblowing*

2.2.3.1 Gender Differences

The gender differences observed in predicting whistleblowing[133] requires a differentiated approach to whistleblower frameworks so as to increase their effectiveness and address the specificities linked to whistleblowing by women.[134] This is especially important considering that female whistleblowers are more likely to suffer from retaliation.[135] As a form of dissent, whistleblowing by women may be perceived as in greater contradiction with their expected social role and thus lead to more severe retaliation.[136] This difference could also be linked to a more positive attitude towards male whistleblowers, who may be perceived as more prosocial or altruist when blowing the whistle,[137] or portrayed as heroic, a trait traditionally attached to male figures. The increased likelihood of facing retaliation may also explain why women give greater importance to anonymity,[138] confidentiality and

[128] UNODC (2015), p. 25.

[129] Nader et al. (1972), p. 203.

[130] IBA (2018), p. 23.

[131] Elliston (1982a), p. 174.

[132] Special Rapporteur David Kaye whistleblower report, para 31; CoE Recommendation CM/Rec (2014)7, *Explanatory memorandum*, para 85; Article 6(1)(a) *EU Whistleblower Directive*.

[133] Feldman and Lobel (2010), p. 1196.

[134] Tilton (2018), p. 368; Feinstein et al. (2021), p. 67; see also APPG (2020).

[135] Rehg et al. (2008), p. 233.

[136] Ibid., p. 224.

[137] Ibid., p. 236; see also Dozier and Miceli (1985).

[138] Feldman and Lobel (2010), p. 1197.

anti-retaliation measures[139] within whistleblowing frameworks. In this respect, a study has shown that a whistleblower framework encompassing both protective measures and an imposed duty to report increases the likelihood that women will take action and blow the whistle, contrary to men, who appear to be more responsive to high rewards.[140]

2.2.3.2 Sex-Based Discrimination

The appreciation of the whistleblower's good faith can also have a gender component. Indeed, focusing on reasonable grounds rather than on personal motivation to determine the good faith of a whistleblower is all the more important in circumstances where the act of whistleblowing can be closely related to a personal interest. This is particularly relevant in cases of harassment and discrimination, and more specifically in cases of sexual harassment or sex discrimination in the workplace. In this sense, the strength of whistleblowing being the capacity of non-consent,[141] demanding loyalty in a clear situation of power inequality "readily serve[s] to dehumanize and degrade others",[142] and goes against the very purpose of whistleblower protection. Complaints by women against their employers for alleged gender discrimination,[143] like complaints of sexual harassment, should therefore be considered acts of whistleblowing.[144] "While their whistleblowing activities may, in some instances, have more direct personal benefit than would be true for other types of whistleblowers, their activities fall within the accepted definitions of whistleblowing".[145]

2.2.3.3 The #metoo Movement

The particular vulnerability of women to retaliation has attracted international attention in recent years through the *#metoo* movement. This worldwide movement has highlighted the widespread and structural failures of bureaucracies in detecting, addressing and deterring sexual harassment in the workplace. It has further emphasized serious deficiencies in preventing retaliation against women who had rejected the sexual advances of their superiors or men working in their industries. The Harvey

139 Tilton (2018), p. 355.

140 Feldman and Lobel (2010), pp. 1196–1197; For the discussion around an imposed duty to report see Sect. 2.6.3.

141 Vaughn (2012), p. 44.

142 Elliston (1982b), p. 26.

143 Near and Jensen (1983), pp. 4-5.

144 Rehg et al. (2008), p. 222.

145 Near and Jensen (1983), p. 5.

Weinstein revelations[146] brought to light an institutionalized and highly sophisticated silence machinery intended to cover-up sexual harassment and assault cases in the workplace. While the public recognition of the "Silence Breakers"[147] has shifted the focus from the accuser to the accused, the Harvey Weinstein trial has also underlined the particular challenges in relation to sexual harassment and assault cases. To detect and prevent the generalized use of retaliatory measures against women, effective whistleblower regulations can be an effective upstream protection mechanism put in place in order to anticipate potential retaliation and prevent sexual harassment and assault.

2.2.3.4 The Sibyl

In a more general sense, considering whistleblowing in a more gender-balanced manner can also increase the positive public perception of whistleblowers. In this respect, Alison Adam's suggestion to bring the act of whistleblowing closer to the idea of the Sibyl as an alternative to the status of hero, predominantly attached to male traits, could be particularly pertinent to emphasize the collective character of whistleblowing, as opposed to the rather individualistic concept of hero.[148] In more than one way is the shift from hero to sibyl particularly appropriate when portraying whistleblowers. Indeed, "[t]he classic Sibyl delivers an oracle, a divine communication, often a prophecy of some future event. … the element of prophecy is … important as it yields the idea that we should heed the prophetic pronouncements of those who are judged venerable and wise, whether it be the classical Sibyl for her prophecies of war, or the engineers who predicted the loss of Challenger and tried to stop its launch".[149] To change the rhetoric around whistleblowers, from heroes to sibyls, is to emphasize the societal contribution of whistleblowers while promoting a more gender-balanced approach in regard to whistleblowing. Following this systematic, a well-crafted and extensive whistleblower framework can be an effective alternative to the heroism traditionally expected from whistleblowers, thereby becoming an inherent element of the duty of care towards employees.[150]

---

[146] See the first newspaper articles on Harvey Weinstein: Kantor and Twohey (2017, 5 October); Farrow (2017, 23 October); see also Farrow (2019).

[147] Zacharek et al. (2017, 18 December).

[148] Adam (2018).

[149] Ibid., p. 20.

[150] Ibid., p. 18.

2.3 Blowing the Whistle on Wrongdoing

2.3.1 A Broad Material Scope

2.3.1.1 Cross-Sectorial Coverage

A key element of an effective whistleblower law is the clear definition of its material scope, in order words, the description of the kind of information which could be reported under a whistleblower framework. The key is to ensure legal certainty.[151] To follow the "no loophole approach",[152] a horizontal whistleblower regulation promoting a cross-sectorial protection framework can reduce the risk of fragmentation and offer clarity. A broad definition of whistleblowing should thus be recommended,[153] which should include the report of all kinds of wrongdoing,[154] or predicted wrongdoing.[155] "Wrongdoing is defined broadly to cover conduct that is reasonably perceived as actually or potentially unlawful".[156] However, blowing the whistle on acts that are not per se unlawful but can be perceived as unethical or immoral can also be permissible under domestic whistleblower framework.[157] In this context, whistleblower laws should strike a fair balance between a clear description of information susceptible to be reported without over-regulating at the risk of limiting the scope of the law.[158] The main difficulty in this respect is the level of certainty required for blowing the whistle and the authenticity of the information disclosed. As seen above, this should be appreciated in conjunction with the reasonable grounds of the reporting individual.

2.3.1.2 Promoting Legal Certainty

In practice, two main strategies have been pursued:[159] A detailed definition listing the categories covered by the whistleblower framework[160] has the advantage of clarity and legal certainty.[161] However, it can also significantly reduce the scope of application of the law. A more general description using a generic term such as

---

[151] IBA (2018), p. 16; Special Rapporteur David Kaye whistleblower report, para 33.

[152] OECD (2010), p. 9; OECD (2016), p. 44.

[153] UNODC (2015), p. 22; Feinstein et al. (2021), p. 14.

[154] TI (2013), Principle 3, p. 4.

[155] TI (2018), p. 10.

[156] IBA (2018), p. 16.

[157] IBA (2018), p. 16; Special Rapporteur David Kaye whistleblower report, para 32.

[158] OECD (2016), p. 44.

[159] TI (2018), p. 8.

[160] e.g. *EU Whistleblower Directive*.

[161] TI (2018), p. 8.

"disclosure in the public interest"[162] has the advantage of providing a particularly broad coverage, but may be difficult to define and thus lack the legal certainty necessary to establish trust in the whistleblower system.[163] It leaves public authorities and courts a wide margin of discretion which does not guarantee adequate legal foreseeability. The establishment of minimum thresholds has also been developed in some whistleblower systems, requiring "serious" wrongdoing or "gross" mismanagement for example.[164] Limiting the amount of information possible to be disclosed can also be a restricting element imposed by certain domestic systems,[165] especially in regard to disclosure of information related to national security.

2.3.2 *The Conflict Between Whistleblowing and National Security*

The relation between whistleblowing and national security is a conflicting one. While the protection of national security relies heavily on secrecy and confidentiality, whistleblowing is based on the disclosure of information. National security thus challenges the very core of whistleblower laws.[166] No other kind of whistleblowing is therefore more controversial than that of "the person who reveals the wrongdoing of national security forces by leaking classified material".[167]

2.3.2.1 State Secrets and Whistleblower Protection

Classified Information

First and foremost, classified information and information related to national security should be differentiated.[168] This distinction is key in the context of whistleblower laws. The classification of information for national security reasons, even with a rigorous protocol, can be expanded to information which may be linked to national security considerations, but which has been classified for different purposes, in an attempt to withdraw it from public scrutiny. In this context, insiders are the best placed to witness and report abuses in the classification of information. Indeed, protecting whistleblowers is all the more important "in circumstances in which State activities and decisions escape democratic or judicial scrutiny on account of their

[162]e.g. CoE Recommendation CM/Rec(2014)7.

[163]TI (2018), p. 8.

[164]OECD (2016), pp. 44–46.

[165]Ibid., p. 47.

[166]Ibid., p. 212.

[167]Fuller (2014), p. 250.

[168]Vaughn (2012), p. 212.

confidential or secret nature",[169] as "part of the antidote to the poisonous abuse of power",[170] to prevent cover-ups and ensure in this way democratic accountability.[171] However, whistleblower protection regulations in those fields is significantly underdeveloped,[172] which may be the reason why leaks of governmental information often revolve around foreign policy, defense and the intelligence sector.[173] In today's interconnected and digitalized world, the extraterritorial implications of wrongdoing committed by domestic entities working in the field of national security has dramatically increased the international relevance of whistleblower disclosures. The trend of "modern" whistleblowers to "place themselves and their disclosure in a broader global context"[174] seems to confirm this tendency.

State Secrets and National Security

States should have the right to keep information secret. The role of the state to ensure the security of its citizens is one of its core duties. The protection of national security thus entails the need for secrecy in order to best prevent threats and secure the general well-being of the population. However, secrecy hinders scrutiny and creates a fertile ground for undetected abuses and a culture of impunity. This is all the more problematic when those violations or abuses can lead to deadly consequences. In most States, the field of national security and defense represents a significant part of the national budget. The most powerful military powers in the world have close to endless means to follow national security strategies, sometimes at the expense of rights and freedoms protected by national Constitutions or covered by international conventions. The sensitive subject of security versus individual freedoms increases the complexity of whistleblower protection in this field. Indeed, on the one hand, individuals working in the intelligence sector or in the military are the best placed to become aware of abuses or violations of national or international law committed by military forces or intelligence agencies. However, because of the very nature of those activities, the public disclosure could be particularly challenging, if not illegal under national law. Thus follows the question regarding the public interest of the disclosure: Would the benefits in revealing those abuses publicly outweigh the potential damage of the disclosure? This is a particularly difficult question to answer. In this respect, dedicated whistleblower channels could alleviate the burden placed on one individual to determine whether the disclosure of information overrides the need for secrecy.

---

[169]ECtHR, *Stoll v. Switzerland* [GC], Appl. No. 69698/01, 10 December 2007, para 110.

[170]Proxmire (1972), p. 14.

[171]Vaughn (2012), pp. 211–213.

[172]Special Rapporteur David Kaye whistleblower report, para 43.

[173]Vaughn (2012), p. 213.

[174]Fuller (2014), p. 251.

Dedicated Reporting Channels

First and foremost, the existence of whistleblowing mechanisms could ensure the investigation of allegation of wrongdoing without the fear of jeopardizing national security strategies through unnecessary public disclosure.[175] A whistleblower protection framework could balance the different elements at stake and establish strict rules to determine in which circumstances the disclosure of information shall be covered by a whistleblower protection framework and in which instances the need for secrecy outweigh the right to blow the whistle. In this optic, dedicated whistleblower reporting channels tailored to the security sector could be put in place in order to ensure the highest standards of confidentiality and secrecy applicable to security-related whistleblowing.[176]

However, states are generally reluctant to introduce effective whistleblower channels in the field of national security, or if they do, adopt particularly restrictive regulations.[177] The cross-power influence of national security issues, which may link the political interests of the legislative power to the strategies of the executive, adds another layer to the difficulty in establishing effective external reporting channels.[178] Unfortunately, inexistent or inadequate reporting systems could render whistleblowing of wrongdoing close to impossible and incite whistleblowers to report publicly.[179]

The Legitimacy of Public Disclosure

The fundamental question follows: Should a whistleblower be protected when disclosing publicly sensitive information related to national security?

In the last two decades, well-known whistleblowers have publicly disclosed information which has revealed "evidence of significant, and in some cases systematic, international law violations committed by state actors".[180] Those include the disclosures made by Chelsea Manning revealing abuses in Iraq by U.S. and British forces, or the revelations made by Edward Snowden on illegal mass-surveillance

---

[175] Ibid., p. 262.

[176] OECD (2010), p. 32; CoE Recommendation CM/Rec(2014)7, *Appendix*, Point 5; TI (2013), Principle 19, p. 8; UNODC (2015), p. 28.

[177] e.g. New Zealand limits disclosure of national security information to individuals with appropriate security clearance, see OECD (2016), p. 60.

[178] Fuller (2014), p. 262 "it may not be politic for parliamentarians to question the tactics used in a conflict which they themselves have authorized, or those who are willing to question such tactics may lack the clout to take effective action".

[179] Ibid.

[180] Ibid., p. 254.

programs by the NSA.[181] In the same time, the prosecution of whistleblowers has also increased in recent years. Under the Obama Administration for example, there has been more than double the number of prosecutions of whistleblowers under the Espionage Act[182] than under all previous presidents combined.[183] This increasing criminalization of whistleblowers hinders the disclosure of information of outmost importance for the public interest and "threatens meaningful accountability for an increasingly large and sophisticated national security apparatus".[184]

With the lack of effective whistleblower tools, the public disclosure of information increases the control[185] of parts of the executive power traditionally immune to scrutiny.[186] The disclosure of information revealing the extraterritorial impacts of wrongdoing can also prompt other States to adopt protective or corrective measures.[187] The application of the ECHR to Member States' extraterritorial military operations[188] demonstrates how the revelation of violations committed by the military abroad could engage the responsibility of those States under human rights conventions. However, with state support for a system allowing for unconditional disclosure of information related to national security being particularly unlikely,[189] the question remains: When can public disclosure be legitimate and which criteria should States take into account when establishing effective whistleblowing mechanisms in the security sector?

2.3.2.2 Edward Snowden

The Espionage Act and the U.S. Constitution

Edward Snowden is perhaps the most well-known whistleblower of modern times. The U.S. citizen worked for the CIA as a computer technician when he disclosed, in 2013, NSA information regarding numerous U.S. mass-surveillance programs, which sparked an international debate around national security and personal data protection. Having received temporary asylum in Russia, he is prosecuted in the

[181]Ibid., p. 258; see also Vaughn (2012), pp. 314–315, as early as 2001, employees of US intelligence agencies blew the whistle to express their concerns about the legality of new surveillance protocols introduced after 9/11.

[182]Publ.L. 65-24, 40 Stat. 217.

[183]Radack and McClellan (2011), pp. 61–62; Moberly (2012), pp. 75–89; see also Ackerman and Pilkington (2015, 16 March).

[184]Vaughn (2012), pp. 316–317.

[185]Fuller (2014), p. 256.

[186]Proxmire (1972), p. 16.

[187]Fuller (2014), pp. 260–261.

[188]ECtHR, *Al-Jedda v. UK* [GC], Appl. No. 27021/08, 7 July 2011; ECtHR, *Al-Skeini and Others v. UK* [GC], Appl. No. 55721/07, 7 July 2011.

[189]Fuller (2014), p. 261.

U.S. for, inter alia, two counts of violation under the Espionage Act,[190] namely unauthorized communication of national defense information[191] and willful communication of classified intelligence information to an unauthorized person.[192] As mentioned above,[193] the particularly broad scope of Espionage Act provisions, the restrictive application of U.S. whistleblower protection laws and the lack of constitutional protection under the First Amendment have left whistleblowers like Edward Snowden defenseless against criminal prosecution and unable to raise the public interest defense. Contrary to the ECtHR, which systematically conducts a balancing exercise between the public interest of the disclosure and the national interest to keep documents confidential,[194] the U.S. Supreme Court refuses to apply its "Pickering Balancing Test", according to which a balance need to be found "between the interest of the [public employee], as a citizen, in commenting upon matters of public concern and the interest of the State, as an employer, in promoting the efficiency of the public services it performs through its employees".[195] In its *Garcetti* ruling, it indeed held that public officials disclosing information "that owes its existence to [his] professional responsibilities"[196] do not enjoy protection under the First Amendment of the U.S. Constitution.

Protection Under the ECHR

Against this legal background, Edward Snowden consistently declared that he is unwilling to go back to the U.S. unless granted a fair trial,[197] a request backed by the Council of Europe Parliamentary Assembly, which called on the U.S. "to allow Mr. Edward Snowden to return without fear of criminal prosecution under conditions that would not allow him to raise the public interest defence".[198] The public interest defence in cases of unauthorized disclosure of classified information has indeed become a key aspect of international best practices in regard to whistleblower protection.[199] Considering that in late 2020, Mr. Snowden announced that he and his

---

[190]US District Court for the Eastern District of Virginia, *United States of America v. Edward J. Snowden*, Criminal Complaint, Case No. 1:13 CH 265 (CMH), 14 June 2013.

[191]18 U.S.C. 793(d).

[192]18 U.S.C. 798(a)(3).

[193]See Sect. 2.1.1.

[194]See Sect. 4.4.4.

[195]U.S. Supreme Court, *Pickering v. Board of Education*, 391 U.S. 563, at 568 [1968]; see also U.S. Supreme Court, *Arnett v. Kennedy*, 416 U.S. 138 [1983], "Pickering Balancing Test" applicable to federal employees.

[196]U.S. Supreme Court, *Garcetti v. Cebellos*, 547 U.S. 410, at 421 (majority opinion).

[197]see e.g. Daily Show with Trevor Noah (2019, 20 September).

[198]PA Resolution 2060 (2015), *Improving the protection of whistle-blowers*, para 10.2.

[199]UNODC (2015), p. 28; Special Rapporteur David Kaye whistleblower report, para 65.

wife applied for the dual U.S.-Russian citizenship for the sake of their son,[200] the lack of extradition treaty between the U.S. and Russia as well as Russia's refusal to extradite its own citizens for prosecution in other countries renders Mr. Snowden's extradition to the U.S. unlikely. That said, it would be interesting to consider whether Russia and other European countries could be under an obligation to grant protection under the ECHR.

Articles 3 and 6 ECHR

The ECtHR has regularly ruled on whether an extradition to the U.S. is compatible with Article 3 ECHR, which prohibits torture, inhuman or degrading treatment or punishment, and Article 6 ECHR ensuring the right to a fair trial.[201] The ECtHR relies in particular on the proportionality of the sentence, stating that it "is prepared to accept that while, in principle, matters of appropriate sentencing largely fall outside the scope of the Convention ..., a grossly disproportionate sentence could amount to ill-treatment contrary to Article 3".[202] In this respect, the Court held that "a sentence is much more likely to be grossly disproportionate ... if it requires the sentencing court to disregard mitigating factors which are generally understood as indicating a significantly lower level of culpability on the part of the defendant".[203] Thus, "all relevant mitigating and aggravating factors" should be given due consideration for a sentence to be considered proportionate.[204] In regard to the right to a fair trial, the ECtHR has also "not excluded that an issue might exceptionally be raised under Article 6 by an extradition decision in circumstances where the fugitive has suffered or risks suffering a flagrant denial of a fair trial in the requesting country".[205]

Cruel and Inhuman Treatment of Whistleblowers by the U.S.

A number of elements will be relevant to evaluate the prospect of success of a claim before the ECtHR under Articles 3 and/or 6 ECHR. The lack of legal protection for

---

[200]Roth (2020, 2 November).

[201]e.g. ECtHR, *Harkins v. United Kingdom* [GC] (Admissibility), Appl. no. 71537/14, 15 June 2017; ECtHR, *Nivette v. France* (Admissibility), Appl. no. 44190/98, 3 July 2001; ECtHR, *Trabelsi v. Belgium*, Appl. no. 140/10, 4 September 2014; ECtHR, *Findikoglu v. Germany* (Admissibility), Appl. no. 20672/15, 7 June 2016.

[202]ECtHR, *Harkins and Edwards v. United Kingdom*, Appl. nos. 9146/07 and 32650/07, 17 January 2012, para 133.

[203]ECtHR, *Harkins and Edwards v. United Kingdom*, para 138.

[204]ECtHR, *Čalovskis v. Latvia*, Appl. no. 22205/13, 24 July 2014, para 146.

[205]ECtHR, *Soering v. United Kingdom*, Appl. no. 14038/88, 7 July 1989, para 133; see also ECtHR, *Harkins v. United Kingdom*, para 62; ECtHR, *Othman (Abu Qatada) v. United Kingdom*, Appl. no. 8129/09, 17 January 2012, paras 258–287.

whistleblowers disclosing classified information and their treatment in U.S. prison could play a significant role in this respect. Indeed, considering that whistleblowers charged under the provisions of the Espionage Act are unable to raise the public interest defence, it is doubtful whether the ECtHR would consider such exclusion proportionate, as it held in its own case-law on whistleblowing that the assessment of the public interest to disclose classified information has significance and needs to be balance with a State's national security interests. It held in particular that "un système de surveillance secrète destiné à protéger la sécurité nationale comporte le risque de saper, voire de détruire, la démocratie au motif de la défendre",[206] concluding that the public interest to receive such information is so important in a democratic society that it overrides the interest of a State's intelligence service to maintain public trust in the legality of its actions.[207]

The treatment of the whistleblower Chelsea Manning, detained in U.S. prison and accused, inter alia, to have disclosed classified information to unauthorized persons, can also play a role in the ECtHR's assessment. Indeed, in 2012, the UN Special Rapporteur on torture accused the U.S. of cruel, inhuman and degrading treatment towards Chelsea Manning and found that it has violated her right to the presumption of innocence.[208] In a 2019 letter to the U.S. Government, the UN Special Rapporteur reiterated the "open-ended, progressively severe measure of coercion fulfilling all the constitutive elements of torture or other cruel, inhuman or degrading treatment or punishment ... More specifically, the practice of coercive detention appears to be incompatible with the international human rights obligations of the United States under, inter alia, Articles 1, 2, 15 and 16 of the Convention against Torture and other Cruel, Inhuman or Degrading Treatment or Punishment (CAT), as well as under Articles 2, 7 and 9 of the International Covenant on Civil and Political Rights (ICCPR) ".[209]

Being prosecuted on similar charges, it cannot be excluded that Mr. Snowden, if he were to be extradited to the U.S., would not suffer similar treatments, a risk that was identified by the UN Special Rapporteur on torture[210] and the CoE Commissioner for Human Rights[211] in relation to the possible extradition of Mr. Assange to the U.S. Under these circumstances, the ECtHR may well conclude that a potential

---

[206]ECtHR, *Bucur and Toma v. Romania*, Appl. no. 40238/02, 8 January 2013, para 102, *translation* "a system of surveillance designed to protect national security entails the risk of undermining or even destroying democracy on the ground of defending it".

[207]ECtHR, *Bucur and Toma,* para 115.

[208]UN, *Report of the Special Rapporteur on torture and other cruel, inhuman or degrading treatment or punishment, Juan E. Méndez, Addendum*, A/HRC/19/61/Add.4, 29 February 2012, p. 75; see also Pilkington (2012, 12 March) and Peralta (2012, 12 March).

[209]UN, *Special Rapporteur on torture and other cruel, inhuman or degrading treatment or punishment*, *Nils Melzer, Letter to the U.S. Government*, 1 November 2019, AL USA 22/2019, p. 2.

[210]UN, UN Expert says "collective persecution" of Julian Assange must end now, 31 May 2019, *News release*.

[211]CoE Commissioner for Human Rights, *Statement - Julian Assange should not be extradited due to potential impact on press freedom and concerns about ill-treatment*, 20 February 2020.

extradition of Mr. Edward Snowden to the U.S. is incompatible with the ECHR. Such considerations would become particularly relevant if Edward Snowden is allowed to travel in other European countries party to the ECHR.

Asylum for Edward Snowden

Almost a decade ago, Edward Snowden unsuccessfully requested asylum in a number of those countries, including France, Germany and Italy. While the Convention Relating to the Status of Refugees (hereinafter referred to as "Geneva Convention") does not impose an obligation on States to accept asylum seekers who are not on their territory, the preamble of the French Constitution of 1946 provides that "Tout homme persécuté en raison de son action en faveur de la liberté a droit d'asile sur les territoires de la République",[212] opening the door for a possible constitutional asylum procedure in France.[213] While this discussion is ongoing, the French government shows little enthusiasm in considering the question of asylum of Mr. Snowden.[214] However, the increasing popularity of Mr. Snowden[215] and the new European craze for whistleblowers may change the game and announce the beginning of a turning point in European politics, leading maybe in a not too far future to a new chapter for Mr. Snowden in the country who adopted in 1789 the *Déclaration des droits de l'homme et du citoyen*.

2.3.2.3 The Tshwane Principles

In this context, the Global Principles on National Security and the Right to Information, also known as the *Tshwane Principles*,[216] can be particularly useful in identifying the relevant elements to take into consideration when developing whistleblowing regulations in the sector of national security as it aims "to provide guidance to those engaged in drafting, revising, or implementing laws or provisions relating to the state's authority to withhold information on national security grounds or to punish the disclosure of such information".[217] Developed under the leadership of the Open Society Justice Initiative,[218] these guiding principles are the results of a 2-year consultation period with different international experts and regional organizations. While not legally binding, this expert opinion has nonetheless a certain

[212] Preamble of the French Constitution of 1946, IV. Republic, *translation* "Every man persecuted because of his action in favor of freedom has the right of asylum in the territories of the Republic".

[213] Weil (2019).

[214] Bonne and Salvi (2019, 16 September) and Le Monde with AFP (2019, 19 September).

[215] Éditorial Le Monde (2019, 17 September) and Kuper (2018, 24 January).

[216] Open Society Justice Initiative (2013).

[217] Ibid., p. 5.

[218] Part of the Open Society Foundations founded by George Soros.

political significance as it was endorsed by different international bodies, such as the European Parliament,[219] the Council of Europe[220] or the former UN Special Rapporteur on the promotion and protection of the right to freedom of opinion and expression.[221]

Public Interest Disclosure

The Tshwane Principles dedicated to public interest disclosures by public personnel[222] follow the traditional structure of whistleblowers laws: first, they identify the categories of wrongdoing which may be subject to public interest disclosures.[223] Then, they define the personal scope[224] and introduce the necessity to establish internal reporting channels.[225] Then follows the definition of the conditions which have to be fulfilled in order for a public disclosure to be permissible.[226] Last but not least, they introduce an extensive protection mechanism,[227] which includes the provision of a public interest defense.[228] Those guiding principle are particularly ambitious and promote an extensive protection for whistleblowers in the national security sector.

Three Cumulative Conditions

More specifically, under the Tshwane Principles, the following three cumulative criteria have to be met in order for a public interest disclosure to be permissible and thus protected under a whistleblower protection framework applicable to the national security sector: (1) First, the use of internal reporting has proven ineffective or impossible.[229] According to the Tshwane Principles, this is the case: when the competent authority refused or failed to investigate the matter[230] or remained

---

[219]Recital 89 *European Parliament resolution of 12 March 2014 on the US NSA surveillance programme, surveillance bodies in various Member States and their impact on EU citizens' fundamental rights and on transatlantic cooperation in Justice and Home Affairs (2013/2188 (INI))*, P7_TA(2014)0230.

[220]PA Resolution 1954 (2013), *National security and access to information*, paras 7–8.

[221]Special Rapporteur David Kaye whistleblower report, para 44.

[222]Open Society Justice Initiative (2013) *Tshwane Principles*, Part VI, p. 49 et seq.

[223]Ibid., Principle 37, p. 49.

[224]Ibid., Principle 38, p. 50.

[225]Ibid., Principle 39, pp. 50–51.

[226]Ibid., Principle 40, pp. 51–52.

[227]Ibid., Principle 41, pp. 53–55.

[228]Ibid., Principle 43, pp. 55–56.

[229]Ibid., Principle 40 (a), p. 52.

[230]Ibid., Principle 40 (a)(1)(i), p. 52.

inactive for an unreasonable period of time;[231] when the internal disclosure of information could lead to the destruction or concealment of evidence or to retaliation;[232] when there is a lack of a dedicated internal channel[233] or when there is an imminent risk of danger to the life, health, and safety of persons, or to the environment.[234] (2) Secondly, the whistleblower disclosure was limited to the information "reasonably necessary to bring to light the wrongdoing".[235] It is specified, however, that a whistleblower should only be deprived of protection when the harm of having disclosed information deemed unnecessary to demonstrate the wrongdoing outweighs the public interest of disclosure.[236] (3) Lastly, the whistleblower reasonably believed that the public interest in the disclosure of that information outweighed the damage to the public interest following the disclosure.[237]

Guiding Factors for National Authorities

In this context, Principle 43 lays down five guiding elements for domestic authorities when determining whether the public interest in disclosing information had indeed prevailed and thus whether the whistleblower could enjoy protection. Those include the amount of information disclosed,[238] the potential damage caused by the disclosure,[239] the reasonable grounds of the whistleblower,[240] the possibility for internal reporting[241] and the specific circumstances of the case which could have justified the disclosure.[242]

The criteria established by the Tshwane Principles for the legitimacy of public interest disclosures mirror those developed by the ECtHR when determining whether an individual who disclosed information publicly could benefit from the whistleblower status under Article 10 ECHR. However, the road to public disclosure remains uncertain considering the substantial number of variables and the consequently large margin of appreciation of state authorities when determining whether an individual shall indeed be protected. A closer look at the ECtHR case-law will

[231] Ibid., Principle 40 (a)(1)(ii), p. 52.

[232] Ibid., Principle 40 (a)(2), p. 52; see also TI (2013), Principle 19, p. 8.

[233] Ibid., Principle 40 (a)(3), p. 52.

[234] Ibid., Principle 40 (a)(4), p. 52.

[235] Ibid., Principle 40 (b), p. 52.

[236] Ibid., p. 52.

[237] Ibid., Principle 40 (c), p. 52.

[238] Ibid., Principle 43 (b)(i), p. 56.

[239] Ibid., Principle 43 (b)(ii), p. 56.

[240] Ibid., Principle 43 (b)(iii), p. 56.

[241] Ibid., Principle 43 (b)(iv), p. 56.

[242] Ibid., Principle 43 (b)(v), p. 56.

provide an interesting insight into the applicability of those criteria to concrete whistleblower cases.[243]

2.3.2.4 The Future of Whistleblowing in the Security Sector

To ensure democratic accountability, insiders within the security sector should have the opportunity to report wrongdoing. In this context, effective whistleblower protection regulations in the field of security shall not only entail internal reporting channels and external channels, but also protection in case of public disclosures. “Recent cases suggest that states are surprisingly responsive to whistleblowing related to international law infringements and that they often take action to tighten international law compliance. This is particularly evident in the cases of Chelsea Manning and Edward Snowden”.[244] However, those cases have brought to light the limits of whistleblowing as a codified and regulated act and underlined the blurred line of legality between whistleblowing and leaking. In light of the current deficiencies in the protection of whistleblowers working in the security and intelligence sector and the governments’ lack of will in introducing effective whistleblowing channels, those sectors may remain the “dead angle” in the accountability mechanisms established through whistleblower legislations.[245] This is particularly unfortunate considering that “these whistleblowers are an important assurance of an effective national security policy”.[246]

The global extent of the violations committed by national entities working in the security sector underline the urgency for effective domestic whistleblower laws covering the area of national security to ensure not only the respect of constitutional rights in the country itself, but also the protection of human rights world-wide. Rather than considering whistleblowing and national security mutually exclusive, strong whistleblower laws can ensure effective national security policies.[247] This is all the more relevant today in a period of international tension, where the executive branch can often be entrusted with extra-ordinary powers to deal with states of emergency, a breeding ground for abuse and violation of individuals’ freedom.

2.3.3 *The COVID-19 Pandemic*

The global crisis caused by the COVID-19 pandemic has shown how the silencing of professionals in one country can have dramatic consequences around the world. This

[243] On the six whistleblowing criteria developed by the ECtHR see Sect. 4.4.

[244] Fuller (2014), p. 253.

[245] Foegle (2015), para 22.

[246] Vaughn (2012), p. 231.

[247] Ibid., pp. 214, 231.

situation has underlined the increasing necessity for rigorous whistleblower mechanisms on the national level, as well as for cross-border frameworks ensuring whistleblower protection internationally. This is all the more important considering the spill-over effects of cover-ups, which have been brought to light by the COVID-19 pandemic. However, this global crisis has not only showcased the serious consequences of a lack of whistleblower regulations on the national level, it has also highlighted the fragile position of existing national whistleblowing channels and once again illustrated the detrimental effects suffered by whistleblowers who have used those dedicated channels in the hope to raise the alarm.

2.3.3.1 Dr. Li Wenliang

Silencing by Wuhan Public Authorities

Dr. Li Wenliang was one of the first medical professionals to have recognized and warned about the spread of a novel and highly contagious coronavirus disease, which will later be named COVID-19 and become, over the course of 2020, the deadliest pandemic in recent history. As early as December 2019, Dr. Li Wenliang, an ophthalmologist working at Wuhan Central Hospital, China, informed fellow colleagues about the threat of an outbreak of an unknown virus which seemed to provoke severe acute respiratory syndrome (SARS), and encouraged them to take precautionary measures to protect themselves from infections.[248] A few days later, he was summoned by the Public Security Bureau in Wuhan, which pressured him to sign a statement in which he recognized spreading rumors and making false statements disturbing public order.[249] A few days before his death on February 7th, 2020, from COVID-19, when asked about the Wuhan government's action to stop him from warning and informing other medical professionals about the disease, Dr. Wenliang told journalists that "[i]f the officials had disclosed information about the epidemic earlier, I think it would have been a lot better. There should be more openness and transparency".[250]

"Irregular Law Enforcement Procedures"

The silencing attempt by Wuhan's authorities, followed by the death of Dr. Wenliang, caused a public outcry and led the Chinese government to officially apologize to his family,[251] the Communist Party of China going so far as naming him a "martyr", which represents the highest honor for a citizen killed working to

[248] Green (2020), p. 682.

[249] Ibid.

[250] The New York Times (2020, 7 February).

[251] Cheng (2020, 19 March).

serve the country. After the death of Dr. Wenliang, the Chinese National Supervisory Commission had indeed decided to send a team to Wuhan in order to investigate the local authorities' actions against Dr. Wenliang, which concluded that "武汉市公安局武昌分局中南路派出所对李文亮出具训诫书不当，并存在执法程序不规范的问题。调查组已建议湖北省武汉市监察机关对此事进行监督纠正，督促公安机关撤销训诫书并追究有关人员责任，及时向社会公布处理结果。".[252] Following those conclusions, the Wuhan Municipal Public Security Bureau announced disciplinary procedures against the two officials responsible for having reprimanded Dr. Wenliang.[253]

Concealment and Disinformation

While the recognition of Dr. Wenliang's contribution by national authorities should be welcomed, the effectiveness of those measures without structural reforms allowing for individuals like Dr. Wenliang to systematically report on health or safety issues will remain very limited. In particular, considering the global impact of the cover-up by Wuhan's authorities and the national dissimulation of the crisis by China. Indeed, a May 2020 report by the U.S. Department of Homeland Security revealed that Chinese leaders had "intentionally concealed the severity" of the pandemic to the world to stock medical supplies, "denying there were export restrictions and obfuscating and delaying provision of its trade data".[254] That information, if confirmed, is particularly troubling and renders the establishment of cross-border whistleblower channels ever more pressing, which could be made possible through an international whistleblower protection convention establishing international reporting channels. We are living in an ever more interconnected and globalized world. The silencing of whistleblowers in one country can have dramatic effects on the other side of the globe, as the latest events leading to the COVID-19 Pandemic have demonstrated.

[252]Xinhua News Agency (2020, 19 March), *translation* "The Zhongnan Road Police Station of the Wuchang Branch of the Wuhan Municipal Public Security Bureau issued an admonishment to Li Wenliang improperly, and there were problems with irregular law enforcement procedures. The investigation team has recommended that the supervisory authority of Wuhan City, Hubei Province supervise and rectify the matter, urge the public security organ to revoke the admonishment and hold relevant personnel accountable, and promptly announce the results of the treatment to the public".

[253]Junjun (2020, 19 March).

[254]Weissert (2020, 4 May) and Folmer and Margolin (2020, 8 June); See also EU Commission accusing China of disinformation, EU Commission, 'Coronavirus: EU Strengthens action to tackle disinformation', 10 June 2020, *Press release*.

2.3.3.2 The USS Theodore Roosevelt Commander

Leaked Letter

Following a COVID-19 outbreak on board of the USS Theodore Roosevelt, a U.S. military ship docked in Guam, Captain Brett Crozier, commanding officer of the ship, addressed a letter to senior military officials in which he wrote that "the spread of the disease is ongoing and accelerating", asking to evacuate the crew and put them in quarantine.[255] While he acknowledged that "[r]emoving the majority of personnel from a deployed U.S. nuclear aircraft carrier and isolating them for two weeks may seem like an extraordinary measure. ... This is a necessary risk. . . . This will require a political solution but it is the right thing to do. . . . We are not at war. Sailors do not need to die. If we do not act now, we are failing to properly take care of our most trusted asset — our Sailors".[256]

"Too Naïve or Too Stupid"

Following the leak of the letter to the public, the acting Navy Secretary Thomas Modly released the captain from his functions on the ground that he « had allowed the complexity of his challenge with the COVID-19 breakout on his ship to overwhelm his ability to act professionally, when acting professionally was what was needed most at the time".[257] However, in a speech to the USS Theodore Roosevelt crew after Captain Crozier was relieved of his commands on board, the acting Navy Secretary said: "If he didn't think that information was going to get out into the public, in this information age that we live in, then he was ... too naïve or too stupid to be the commanding officer of a ship like this".[258] Although the acting Navy Secretary later apologized for his comments following public backlash,[259] the argument itself and the reasoning behind it are not unfamiliar in relation to whistleblower cases.

In the Maria Bamieh case, which will be analyzed in further details below,[260] letters from the chief prosecutor of the EU Mission in Kosovo (EULEX) addressed to her supervisors leaked to the press, in which she expressed her concerns about suspected wrongdoing committed by different members of the mission. Following those leaks, Ms. Bamieh was suspended to prevent her from leaking other

[255]Extracts of Captain Crozier's letter was first made available see Gafni and Garofoli (2020, 31 March).

[256]Ibid.

[257]Lamothe et al. (2020, 3 April).

[258]Speech of Thomas Modly, acting Navy Secretary to the USS Theodore Roosevelt Crew, 6 April 2020 was first made available see Schogol (2020, 6 April).

[259]O'Brian and Seligman (2020, 6 April 2020).

[260]On the presentation of the Maria Bamieh case see Sect. 5.3.2.3.

confidential information, EU officials in Brussels said.[261] Although the independent legal expert appointed to investigate the situation recognized that Ms. Bamieh should have been considered a whistleblower, he held nonetheless that her suspension was justified "by the fact that, even though she was not responsible for the leaks, the documents used as the basis for the articles had been written by her".[262] Both the comments of the legal expert in the EULEX case and of the U.S. acting Navy Secretary follow the same reasoning: The whistleblower should be held responsible for the leak of reports they made internally, ignoring the fact that such an understanding of whistleblower mechanisms contradict the very spirit of whistleblowing policies and would render internal whistleblower channels obsolete.

Public Support for Captain Crozier

In an unexpected twist regarding the U.S. case, 1 month after Captain Crozier was released from his functions, the U.S. Navy decided to reinstate him,[263] however, conditioned to the outcome of an ongoing investigation into the circumstances around the release of the Captain.[264] In the country with the most advanced whistleblower laws, positive perception towards whistleblowers and the public support for Captain Crozier seem to have played a decisive role in this turnaround, demonstrating once more how public awareness and support for whistleblowers can have a determinant impact on the effective protection of insiders who blew the whistle and suffered detrimental effects for doing so. However, despite public support and the reversal of the U.S. Navy's position towards the Captain, the challenges faced by Captain Crozier will most certainly have a chilling effect on other military officers and deter them from raising concerns,[265] a worrying fallout considering the deadly consequences of silence in those dark times and the desperate need for reactive measures which can only be made possible through a rapid and uninterrupted chain of communication.

2.4 Dedicated Reporting Channels

2.4.1 Horizontal Approach vs. Tiered Model

The establishment of dedicated channels to report wrongdoing is a key aspect of any whistleblowing system. In this context, an effective whistleblower legislation should

---

[261] Rettman (2014, 30 October).

[262] Jacqué (2015, 31 March), pp. 10, 53.

[263] Bowman (2020, 24 April).

[264] Seligman (2020, 29 April); see also Reuters (2020, 25 April).

[265] Cooper et al. (2020, 3 April).

first and foremost "clearly [define] the procedures and prescribed channels for facilitating the reporting of suspected acts of corruption, and [encourage] the use of protective and easily accessible whistleblowing channels".[266] Indeed, according to international best practices, clear information about the reporting channels available to blow the whistle is essential to ensure the effectiveness of whistleblower frameworks.[267]

2.4.1.1 Access to Different Reporting Channels

Three reporting channels could be differentiated in this respect: Internal reporting channels, external reporting channels, and, finally, public disclosure. Internal reporting channels are understood to be communication tools available to individuals within their organizations. It can be a dedicated email address, a special department competent to receive whistleblower reports, an online form, etc. Different kinds of those means of reporting should be made available to employees to report wrongdoing.[268] External channels, as the name suggests, refers to reporting methods to external authorities competent to receive whistleblower reports. Here again, different tools of reporting should be made available. Public disclosure, which some include in the definition of external channels, is the disclosure of information directly to the public with the help of the media, online platforms, etc.

The relationship between those different reporting channels is debated. As early as the 1970s, the development of a tiered model for whistleblower laws was promoted.[269] According to this approach, the duty of loyalty to the organization requires that an employee must first try to solve the issue internally. "Only when his way is blocked there, and only when the matter involves something more than mere trivia, should he put the whistle to his lips and blast away".[270] In the U.S., the discussion about internal and external whistleblower reporting channels of whistleblower laws has been the subject of heated debates and led to different regulations, which either excluded internal reporting from the scope of application of the law, included it, gave priority to internal reporting or applied more favorable conditions to reports made internally.[271] In Europe, the discussion has been focused on two positions: the UK tiered model on the one hand, which strictly prioritizes internal channels over external reporting means, and on the other hand, the horizontal approach, which promotes undifferentiated access to the different reporting channels and gives individuals the freedom to choose the reporting channel they

[266]OECD (2010), p. 32; see also UNODC (2015), p. 29.

[267]OECD (2016), p. 52; IBA (2018), p. 21.

[268]IBA (2018), p. 22.

[269]Miller (1972), p. 30.

[270]Ibid.

[271]Vaughn (2012), pp. 322–323.

consider most appropriate.[272] PIDA establishes a tiered model,[273] "each tier [internal, external, then public disclosure] incrementally requires a higher threshold of conditions to satisfy for the whistleblower to be protection".[274] The strict preference given to internal reporting channels by the UK system, much like the opposition to anonymous whistleblower reports by British whistleblower advocacy groups,[275] illustrates the attempt to reconcile the duty of loyalty incumbent on every employee with the necessity to report wrongdoing.[276] In this sense, the structure of the PIDA aims to achieve "the essential but delicate balance between the public interest and the interests of the employer".[277]

2.4.1.2 Internal Reporting and Corporate Compliance

In the early days of whistleblower legislation, internal reporting channels were considered with some skepticism linked with the expectation that reporting internally would increase the risk of destruction of evidence, cover-ups and acts of retaliation.[278] The 2008 financial collapse revived the lack of trust in the effectiveness of internal reporting channels and increased the distrust in existing corporate compliance mechanisms, some describing those mechanisms as "window dressing" and "existing only on paper".[279] However, the establishment of effective internal whistleblower channels should not be underestimated as it gives organizations the opportunity to self-check and address potential wrongdoing internally while easing the workload of competent authorities receiving external whistleblower reports.[280] In this sense, targeted measures can address the deficiencies which render internal reporting channels ineffective[281] in order for internal whistleblowing policies to become an inherent part of any organizational management strategy.

Indeed, experience has shown that internal reporting by employees can greatly contribute to uncovering criminal misconduct within corporations.[282] As an important early risk identification tool,[283] it is therefore in companies' interest to establish effective whistleblowing systems with experienced staff enjoying a high level of

[272] CoE Recommendation CM/Rec(2014)7, *Appendix*, Point 14.
[273] Lewis et al. (2017), pp. 101 et seq.
[274] OECD (2010), p. 12.
[275] Vaughn (2012), pp. 310–311.
[276] Ibid., p. 323.
[277] Public Interest Disclosure Bill, Hansard HL Deb., 5 June 1998, col. 614, Lord Nolan.
[278] Vaughn (2012), p. 324.
[279] Ibid., p. 326.
[280] Vaughn (2012), p. 323; see also Lobel (2008).
[281] Vaughn (2012), p. 327.
[282] Buchert (2016), para 4; ICCom (2008), p. 2.
[283] Buchert (2016), para 4.

autonomy,[284] independent of the Legal Office or the Human Resource (HR) department, which are competent to receive and follow-up on internal whistleblower reports.[285] In larger companies, the establishment of satellite compliance offices may be particularly useful.[286] In order to ensure the highest standards of confidentiality, the compliance officers could benefit from special employment agreements allowing them to preserve the confidentiality of whistleblowers' identity vis-à-vis their superior or manager.[287] It is also necessary for the compliance office to ensure their permanent availability, with different means at their disposal to receive whistleblower reports.[288] While those measures may be cost-intensive for corporations, it is in their best interest to have an internal contact point competent to address whistleblower reports in order to avoid the unpredicted costs related to the involvement of public authorities or the press.[289] Effective internal whistleblowing policies with adequate internal channels can thus be considered an essential brand communication and image management tool.[290]

2.4.1.3 Middle-Ground Solution

Studies have shown that the majority of employees prefer to report internally and fall back on the use of external reporting means only when the former has proven to be inadequate or unsuccessful.[291] This observation thus raises the question of whether it is truly necessary to impose a legally binding tiered structure between internal and external channels. Indeed, a legally imposed obligation to use internal channels prior to external reporting would put upon the whistleblower the burden to prove that the use of internal channels was inadequate and the recourse to external means therefore legitimate, creating an additional hurdle to overcome in an endeavor already strewn with pitfalls.

On the basis of the considerations developed above, a consensus on a middle-ground solution, in which internal reporting is encouraged but not mandatory, is therefore more promising than a strict tiered model. Whistleblower laws should include the obligation for corporations and public entities to establish internal mechanisms allowing an employee to report on suspected wrongdoing. However, a tiered model between internal and external reporting channels, putting an obligation on employees to first go through internal channels, should not be imposed.

[284] ICCom (2008), Recommendation 3, p. 3.

[285] Buchert (2016), para 4.

[286] Rudkowski and Schreiber (2018), p. 17.

[287] Rudkowski and Schreiber (2018), p. 17; see also Buchert (2016), para 12.

[288] Rudkowski and Schreiber (2018), p. 16.

[289] Ibid.

[290] Lewis and Fasterling (2014), p. 85.

[291] I.a. see Miceli et al. (2008), pp. 9–10; Donkin et al. (2008), pp. 88–89.

2.4.2 *Confidentiality, Anonymity and Leaks*

2.4.2.1 Confidentiality vs. Anonymity

The Confidentiality Criterion

The requirement of confidentiality represents an important element of any effective whistleblower protection framework[292] and is part of most whistleblower laws.[293] Under this criterion, the identity of the whistleblower should remain confidential and can only be revealed if the latter has provided consent. This condition is particularly relevant considering the risk of retaliation for individuals who are identified as being the source of the disclosure. To ensure the highest standards of confidentiality, "identifying information" should also be confidential, so as to prevent an identification based on the context and the circumstances.[294] Clear and precise confidentiality conditions should also be provided in order to inform whistleblowers about the situations in which their identity could be or has to be revealed.[295] In this respect, potential conflicts between this confidentiality requirement and data protection regulations may arise, the balance of which depends on the national data protection laws and the specific conditions laid down by the whistleblower framework itself.[296] As will be illustrated below in the *Stuttgart* case, the condition of confidentiality provided by whistleblower mechanisms, ensuring a specific protection of whistleblowers' personal data, can be challenged by EU data protection rules which provide a right to access one's own personal data.[297] National courts thus have the arduous task to balance the need for a whistleblower's identity to remain confidential with the right of an individual subject of a whistleblower report to have access to her or his personal data.

Some whistleblower laws, such as the U.S. Sarbanes-Oxley Act, have gone further and established an obligation for companies to introduce anonymous whistleblower reports, in the form of hotlines, for example.[298] In this respect, confidentiality and anonymity in relation to whistleblowing should be clearly differentiated. While confidentiality implies the necessity for whistleblowers to reveal their identity when reporting on wrongdoing, anonymous reporting channels remove this requirement and allow individuals to report without having to identify

---

[292]TI (2013), Principle 7, p. 5; TI (2018), p. 18; UNODC (2015), p. 48; Special Rapporteur David Kaye whistleblower report, para 39; Feinstein et al. (2021), p. 18.

[293]OECD (2010), p. 11.

[294]TI (2018), p. 20.

[295]Ibid.

[296]On the relationship between the EU Whistleblower Directive and the EU Data Protection Regulation see Sect. 8.5.3.

[297]On the Stuttgart case see Sect. 7.3.2.

[298]Banisar (2011), p. 35.

themselves. In this regard, the latter means of reporting should also be distinguished from what is commonly known as leaking.

Anonymous Whistleblowing

Anonymous reporting is particularly controversial in the context of whistleblower laws.[299] In the European context, the historical background and privacy considerations often lead to vigorous opposition against the adoption of anonymous whistleblower reporting methods, such as hotlines. For example, when the U.S. Fortune 500 multinationals decided to introduce anonymous hotlines in compliance with the U.S. Sarbanes-Oxley whistleblowing provisions, a French employee sent an e-mail to all France-based employees denouncing the company's "Vichy" tactics.[300] This European opposition as well as EU data protection considerations created some frictions between the European and U.S. conception of whistleblowing and led to a nuanced approach to corporate anonymous reporting in Europe. Indeed, anonymous reporting channels raise specific questions in relation to the proportionality principle established by EU data protection rules, whereby personal data should be collected for specific, explicit and legitimate purposes and be processed fairly and lawfully.[301] In an attempt to find the right balance between the proportionality principle and the need for anonymous whistleblowing channels, European companies were permitted to establish such channels, without being allowed to encourage their use.[302]

Legitimate concerns may be expressed in relation to the introduction of anonymous reporting channels. The most obvious downside of anonymous whistleblower reports is a procedural one. Some jurisdictions have considered anonymous information as insufficient to open criminal investigations.[303] If an investigation into information provided through anonymous reporting channels were to open, the procedure could be slowed by the lack of information about the source of the report.[304] It can also have a detrimental impact on the credibility of the report itself, rejection of anonymous reports being based on moral and ethical objections.[305] Indeed, the alleged wrongdoer might try to focus on the anonymity of the whistleblower and question the motivation of the whistleblower to spread doubts

---

[299] OECD (2016), p. 62.

[300] Dowling Jr. (2008), p. 13.

[301] ARTICLE 29 Data Protection Working Party, *Opinion 1/2006 on the application of EU data protection rules to internal whistleblowing schemes in the fields of accounting, internal accounting controls, auditing matters, fight against bribery, banking and financial crime*, 00189/06/EN, WP 117, 01/02/2006, pp. 9 and 11.

[302] ARTICLE 29 Data Protection Working Party, *Opinion 1/2006*, p. 11; see also Hertel (2019), pp. 349–352; Thüsing (2017), pp. 18–22.

[303] OECD (2010), p. 11.

[304] Vaughn (2012), p. 309; OECD (2010), p. 11; IBA (2018), p. 23; OECD (2016), p. 63.

[305] Elliston (1982a), pp. 175 et seq.; see also OECD (2010), p. 11.

as to the veracity of the information reported.[306] Such a rhetoric can be observed following the whistleblower report which lead to the procedure of Impeachment against President Trump in 2019.[307]

However, even if the decision process of blowing the whistle anonymously is particularly complex[308] and can be linked to different factors,[309] allowing for such a mechanism is essential for encouraging the disclosure of wrongdoing by individuals who otherwise would not have come forward.[310] Indeed, considering that most whistleblowers suffer serious detrimental consequences following their reports, creating a system which would put an obligation to reveal one's identity to report on wrongdoing would imply a level of self-sacrifice for the greater good which cannot reasonably be expected, "moral heroism is not and should not be mandated".[311]

Today, there is an increasing consensus on the need for anonymous whistleblowing mechanisms,[312] some countries going "so far as criminalizing deliberate publication of a whistle-blower's name".[313] Furthermore, an effective framework should be established to protect a whistleblower whose identity has been revealed despite an anonymous procedure.[314] Because anonymous reporting and data protection considerations can collide, those frictions should thus be addressed accordingly, the specific balance varying depending on the jurisdiction and subject to interpretation by domestic courts.[315] However, the whistleblowing mechanism should be sophisticated enough so as to ensure the *de facto* anonymity of the individual who reported[316] to avoid that the identity of the whistleblower can be deducted from the circumstances of the case.[317] In this context, studies have shown that the use of web-based reporting channels significantly increase the protection of anonymity in comparison with traditional reporting channels such as in person, e-mails or phone-call reports.[318]

---

[306] Elliston (1982a), p. 174.

[307] President Trump requested on numerous occasions the disclosure of the identity of the whistleblower who filed a complaint in relation to a phone-call with the President of Ukraine, during which President Trump allegedly pressured the President of Ukraine to investigate his political opponent.

[308] Miceli et al. (1988), p. 295.

[309] Barendt (2016), p. 76.

[310] UNODC (2015), p. 50; Special Rapporteur David Kaye whistleblower report, para 40.

[311] Elliston (1982a), p. 172.

[312] ILO (2019), p. 20; OECD (2016), p. 63; IBA (2018), p. 23.

[313] e.g. Australia, Tunisia and the Republic of Korea, see ILO (2019), p. 20.

[314] TI (2013), Principle 13, p. 6.

[315] IBA (2018), p. 23.

[316] Ibid.

[317] Ibid.

[318] Hauser et al. (2019), p. 59.

This reality has also been recognized by the EU, which introduced anonymous whistleblower tools to receive reports on secret cartels and anti-trust violations.[319] The European Anti-Fraud Office (OLAF) also introduced an anonymous reporting channel to receive reports on suspected fraud or corruption cases affecting the financial interests of the EU. Following the implementation of the EU Whistleblower Directive adopted 2019, whistleblowers who report anonymously may also be protected under certain conditions.[320] This recent development represents a subtle revolution in the field of whistleblower protection in Europe and demonstrates a slow but real conversion towards an European-wide acceptance of anonymous whistleblowing.

While the use of anonymous reporting channels cannot be described as the optimal option to report wrongdoing,[321] it is indicative of the level of confidence in the existing mechanisms to protect whistleblowers and translates the trust, or the lack thereof, in the integrity of the entity concerned.[322] Consequently, stronger whistleblowing frameworks ensuring effective protection for individuals who report could decrease the need for anonymous reporting tools and permit more efficient investigations of allegations of wrongdoing.

2.4.2.2 Leaks and Whistleblowing

Anonymous Whistleblowing vs. Leaks

Anonymous whistleblowing can also be associated with leaking, which can also be defined as the anonymous disclosure of information.[323] Leaking and whistleblowing can thus overlap[324] without being synonymous.[325] In the U.S., a lot of what is called "leaking" appears to evolve in a blurred area where the disclosure of classified information is being tolerated without being fully authorized[326] in an attempt to channel media coverage.[327] However, this permissive attitude towards leaks has been challenged in recent years.[328] Prior to the Internet Age, the media played an essential role as an intermediary[329] in the investigation of leaked information, an influence which has decreased today with the development of online platforms like

[319] On the whistleblower mechanisms introduced in the EU Single Market see Sect. 7.1.2.

[320] On the EU Whistleblower Directive see Sect. 8.4.

[321] IBA (2018), p. 23.

[322] OECD (2016), p. 62.

[323] Walzer (2018), p. 48.

[324] Vaughn (2012), p. 229.

[325] Walzer (2018), p. 48.

[326] Pozen (2013), p. 515.

[327] Ibid., p. 580.

[328] Ibid., p. 599.

[329] Barendt (2016), p. 115.

WikiLeaks,[330] eroding the monopole of traditional news outlets.[331] This new development has shaken the traditional democratic scrutiny procedure and reorganized the power dynamic between public authorities, journalists and leakers.[332] The cards have been reshuffled and the rules of the information game changed, shedding a light on the grey zone between whistleblowing, leaks, and media freedom. Indeed, because the act of whistleblowing can also fall outside of any legal framework, in particular in areas related to national security information, whistleblowing and leaking can intertwine,[333] the latter generally involving information on foreign and national security policies.[334] However, the leak of classified information motivated by personal[335] or partisan political gain has undermined "the credibility of many arguments against unauthorized release of information"[336] and increased the complexity of an already intricate and highly contentious issue. Considering that it has become best practice to exclude the motives of a whistleblower as a condition to afford protection, the release of information for personal or political gain is an invalid criterion to differentiate between unprotected and protected leaks, the latter being a form of whistleblowing. Instead, the overlap and distinction can be found in the nature of the information disclosed, the act of whistleblowing implying a revelation made for the purpose of exposing a threat or harm to the public interest.[337] Leaks reaching that threshold should thus be understood as a form of whistleblowing. But while public interest leaks and whistleblowing should be considered equivalent, not all leaks meet this threshold, which renders the distinction between protected and unprotected leaks pertinent. The case of Julian Assange, the founder of the WikiLeaks platform, best exemplifies the different political and legal ramifications of this distinction.

Julian Assange: A Whistleblower?

Following a 2 year investigation into Russian interference in the 2016 U.S. presidential elections, the 2019 Report[338] from the U.S. Special Counsel Robert S. Mueller, III, revealed that "[i]n order to expand its interference in the 2016 U.S. Presidential election, the GRU units transferred many of the documents they

---

[330]Lewis and Fasterling (2014), p. 74; Pozen (2013), p. 608.

[331]Pozen (2013), p. 581.

[332]Lewis and Fasterling (2014), p. 74.

[333]Walzer (2018), p. 48; Lochak (2016), paras 76–77.

[334]Abel (1987), p. 4.

[335]Lewis and Fasterling (2014), p. 73.

[336]Vaughn (2012), p. 212.

[337]CoE Recommendation CM/Rec(2014)7, *Appendix*, Definitions (a); Special Rapporteur David Kaye whistleblower report, para 28.

[338]Mueller, III Special Counsel (2019) *Report On The Investigation Into Russian Interference In The 2016 Presidential Election* vol I. U.S. Department of Justice, Washington, D.C.

stole from the DNC and the chairman of the Clinton Campaign to WikiLeaks".[339] It also emphasized that the Trump Campaign had expressed interest in the WikiLeaks disclosures[340] and was in direct communication with WikiLeaks during the election campaign.[341] The establishment of this close proximity has led the CIA Director, Mr. Pompeo, to qualify the Wikileaks platform as a "nonstate hostile intelligence service", devoid of any moral.[342]

WikiLeaks disclosures have regularly sparked heated debates on the justifications for leaking and the limits of whistleblower protection regulations. In fact, in the same speech, CIA Director Mr. Pompeo included Edward Snowden, whose status of whistleblower has been recognized worldwide, in the same category as WikiLeaks founder Julian Assange,[343] revealing the ambiguities in relation to leaking and whistleblowing. Indeed, the disclosure of classified information through the WikiLeaks platform, or the revelations made by Mr. Snowden, are in direct contradiction with the U.S. administration's strategic acceptance of "controlled" leaks,[344] and emphasize the specific challenges in regard to whistleblower protection. According to Mr. Pompeo, "[t]rue whistleblowers use the well-established and discreet processes in place to voice grievances".[345] But what if no well-established and discreet processes are available? What role can a platform like WikiLeaks play in this context? And what protection, if any, shall its founder enjoy?

In the prospect of a possible extradition of Mr. Assange to the U.S., those questions have become ever more pressing. U.S. authorities indeed appealed against the *USA v. Julian Assange* judgment of early 2021,[346] which rejected the extradition of Mr. Assange to the U.S.,[347] and declared that they will "continue to seek Mr. Assange's extradition to the United States".[348] In May 2019, Mr. Assange was accused of having conspired with Chelsea Manning in the illegal acquisition and disclosure of classified information related to the U.S. national defense.[349] This new indictment expanding the number of charges against Mr. Assange raises fundamental questions in relation to the application of the First Amendment of the

[339] Ibid., p. 44 (GRU refers to the Russian intelligence service).

[340] Ibid., p. 65.

[341] Ibid., p. 59.

[342] Pompeo, CIA Director (2017, 13 April) *Remarks as Prepared for Delivery by Central Intelligence Agency Director Mike Pompeo at the Center for Strategic and International Studies* [hereinafter "Remarks at CSIS]. Central Intelligence Agency.

[343] Pompeo (2017, 13 April) Remarks at CSIS.

[344] Pozen (2013), pp. 599–600.

[345] Pompeo (2017, 13 April) Remarks at CSIS.

[346] Quinn (2021a, 4 January).

[347] Westminster Magistrates' Court, *The Government of the United States of America v. Julian Assange*, Before District Judge Vanessa Baraitser, 4 January 2021; on an analysis of the judgment see Ambos (2021).

[348] Quinn (2021b, 4 January).

[349] US District Court for the Eastern District of Virginia, *United States of America v. Julian Paul Assange*, Superseding Indictment, Criminal No. 1:18-cr-111 (CMH), 23 May 2019.

U.S. Constitution[350] and sparked an international debate on the general protection of the right to freedom of expression, and in particular, the protection of the press.[351] To put into context, the information leaked by Chelsea Manning (then Bradley Manning) and published by WikiLeaks revealed evidence of international law violations and even war crimes committed by the U.S. military in Iraq.[352] One of those files included the video footage known as "the Collateral Murder video", which shows the killing by fire from a U.S. Apache helicopter of 11 civilians, including journalists, in Baghdad, Iraq.[353]

However, the establishment of the close proximity between WikiLeaks and the Russian interference into the 2016 U.S. Presidential campaign has led some to conclude that "WikiLeaks founder Julian Assange is neither whistleblower nor journalist".[354] But what is he, then? While an extensive analysis of the special status of Julian Assange would go beyond the scope of this book, the following considerations intend to provide some food for thought on the potential application of whistleblower laws in relation to the particular status of Mr. Assange.

The main challenge in considering Julian Assange as a whistleblower is his status of intermediary, between the public and the insiders. Indeed, most whistleblower laws require "work-based" circumstances, during which the whistleblower became aware of wrongdoing. While the exact scope of whistleblower laws can be subject to interpretation, experience suggests that those interpretations tend to promote a rather restrictive approach.[355] Taking the UK Public Disclosure Act as an example, which affords protection to "workers", an extension of its scope of application to Mr. Assange seems to be excluded. But how about Article 10 of the ECHR? The case-law of the ECtHR in regard to the status of whistleblower under Article 10 ECHR promotes a restrictive interpretation of the "work-based" criterion as it requires a "subordinated work-based relationship",[356] which renders the recognition of the status of whistleblower for Julian Assange particularly unlikely under current ECtHR jurisprudence.

More ambitious laws have expanded upon the personal scope to include third parties like "facilitators" as additional beneficiaries of whistleblower laws,[357] leading to a potential extension of the scope of protection to intermediaries, like Mr. Assange, who facilitate public access to information provided by

---

[350]The Editorial Board (2019, 23 May).

[351]Ball (2019, 11 April).

[352]Fuller (2014), p. 280.

[353]The New York Times (2011, 24 January) and Daley (2020, 14 June).

[354]Stanger (2019, 22 April).

[355]Vaughn (2012), p. 189.

[356]ECtHR, *Medžlis Islamske Zajednice Brčko and others v. Bosnia and Herzegovina* [GC], Appl. No. 17224/11, 27 June 2017, para 80.

[357]Article 4(4)(a) *EU Whistleblower Directive*. According to Article 5(8) EU Whistleblower Directive, facilitator is defined as follows: "a natural person who assists a reporting person in the reporting process in a work-related context, and whose assistance should be confidential". The requirement of the work-related context thus remains.

whistleblowers. However, this is the exception. The nature of the charges against Mr. Assange being related to national security issues, a field already highly contentious in respect to whistleblowing,[358] the official recognition of the status of whistleblower would be difficult to imagine under most jurisdictions. A broader approach in the defense of Mr. Assange under the general banner of the protection of freedom of expression and the right to impart information thus seems to be more promising. Considering the difference in the treatment of journalists and whistleblowers today,[359] the former enjoying a higher level of protection when using confidential information related to national security issues, it would not be surprising if the defense team of Mr. Assange elaborates a plea based on his status of journalist rather than on his potential role as whistleblower.

With a view to the future of whistleblower laws, an extension of the personal scope of the new generation of legislations should be promoted, allowing for a more generous protection so as to include individuals, like Mr. Assange, who have suffered negative effects following their involvement in the disclosure of information revealing wrongdoing. Rather than a focus on work-related aspects of whistleblower laws, a more ambitious coverage to all individuals who have been detrimentally impacted by assisting or helping whistleblowers to reveal information of general public importance should be considered.

2.4.2.3 Whistleblowing in the Digital Era

"The great secret about laws against leaking is that they have never been used in a manner designed to stop leaking".[360] This is the reason why the crackdown on platforms like WikiLeaks as well as the prosecution of whistleblowers who have disclosed information using those platforms cannot be considered a sustainable solution.[361] On the contrary, it raises fundamental freedom of expression issues. On the U.S. stage, "selective leaking to favored reporters may violate a principle of the First Amendment that prevents the government, when disclosing information, from preferring some news organizations over others".[362] *A fortiori*, one may wonder whether the selective prosecution of some leakers over others[363] can be considered a permissible governmental interference in the rights protected under the First Amendment or contrariwise, a violation of those rights. In the current context, whistleblower laws could alleviate the favoritism resulting from the lax application of laws against leaking and thus narrow the margin of appreciation of the State towards leaks.

---

[358]On the conflict between whistleblowing and national security see Sect. 2.3.2.

[359]Boot (2019) p. 485.

[360]Pozen (2013), p. 635.

[361]Lewis and Fasterling (2014), p. 90.

[362]Vaughn (2012), p. 214.

[363]Ackerman (2015, 16 March).

As the multiplicity of public interest leaks exposes the lack of effective or adequate whistleblower protection mechanisms,"[b]oth leaking and whistleblowing may be vital to the preservation of life and the promotion of healthy democracies".[364] Considering the particular democratic relevance of the classified information as an object of leaks and anonymous whistleblowing, "disclosure becomes more, not less, important"[365] today. While the need for secrecy and confidentiality cannot be ignored, "even where limited secrecy fulfills an important function, as in protecting certain military secrets, controls are needed in order to reduce the dangers that arise when power and secrecy combine. And whatever the assumed benefits of secrecy, its role in damming up the usual alternatives to whistleblowing is a cost all too often forgotten".[366] Without promoting a transparency at any cost, defending public interest leaks, and by extension WikiLeaks, for lack of a better way to report wrongdoing, is fundamental in democratic societies and can "prompt pre-emptive compliance as states fear the consequences of as-yet-undiscovered violations".[367] In the absence of reliable reporting channels, "it is in the public interest to learn about serious wrongdoing via leaks rather than not to hear about it at all".[368]

The digital Era and the rise of new actors have changed the rules of the modern information game. The disclosures made through platforms like WikiLeaks have offered the public a unique glance at the traditionally hidden cards of State secrets. The existence of those platforms, as a sword of Damocles, can thus encourage States to introduce effective whistleblower reporting channels. Taking into account the empirical studies, which demonstrate that employees generally favor internal reporting and rely on external means as a last resort, the introduction of effective internal reporting channels would render leaking less attractive.[369] To borrow the words of Ralph Nader, "[o]rganizational power must be insecure to some degree if it is to be more responsible", "the creative insecurity ... generates a more suitable climate of responsiveness to the public interest and public rights".[370]

[364] Lewis and Fasterling (2014), pp. 71 et seq.

[365] Vaughn (2012), p. 214.

[366] Bok (1989), pp. 228–229.

[367] Fuller (2014), p. 260.

[368] Lewis and Fasterling (2014), p. 90.

[369] Ibid., p. 90.

[370] Nader (1972), p. 11.

2.5 Protective Measures and Incentives

2.5.1 Protective Shield

2.5.1.1 The Nature of Retaliatory Measures

Because reporting persons can suffer a series of retaliatory measures for having blown the whistle, whistleblower laws should prohibit a broad range of measures susceptible to be considered retaliatory.[371] "[R]recommended, threatened and attempted unfair treatment", as well as retaliation by third parties, should also be covered by whistleblower frameworks.[372]

2.5.1.2 Reversal of the Burden of Proof

It should be considered best practice to reverse the burden of proof.[373] This shift would require the employer to demonstrate that the prejudice suffered by the whistleblower was not retaliatory. In this sense, the lack of a causal link between the prejudice suffered and the report made has to be established by the employer.[374] This reversal of the burden of proof is particularly important considering the power imbalance between employer and employee, the latter having a more restrictive access to elements of proof to demonstrate that those detrimental actions were indeed retaliatory.

2.5.1.3 Protection Measures and Sanction Mechanism

Whistleblowers should also be exempt from disciplinary or criminal proceedings and so-called "gag clauses",[375] those clauses referring to a contractual restriction imposed on employees, limiting their right to disclose information. Interim relief[376] or attenuating circumstances should also be considered as part of an effective whistleblower protection framework. To prevent from possible retaliatory measures, whistleblower legislation should also include a sanction mechanism to penalize the

---

[371] TI (2013), Principle 6, p. 5; see also UNODC (2015), p. 46; Special Rapporteur David Kaye whistleblower report, para 41; Feinstein et al. (2021), pp. 16 and 19.

[372] TI (2018), p. 23; UNODC (2015), pp. 53–54.

[373] OECD (2010), pp. 11, 31; OECD (2016), p. 81; UNODC (2015), p. 64.

[374] TI (2013), Principle 8, p. 5.

[375] TI (2013), Principle 10 and Principle 12, p. 6; see also UNODC (2015), pp. 55-56; Feinstein et al. (2021), p. 21.

[376] OECD (2016), p. 86; UNODC (2015), pp. 63–64; Feinstein et al. (2021), pp. 28–29.

retaliation against whistleblowers,[377] which several countries have already adopted.[378]

2.5.1.4 Obligation to Inform and Follow-up

According to U.S. whistleblower research, one of the key reasons why potential whistleblowers do not come forward is not the fear of retaliation, but the belief that nothing is going to be done following their report.[379] To address this issue, an obligation to evaluate the merits of whistleblower reports and the need to inform the reporting individuals about the ongoing process are essential to build trust and ensure the effectiveness of whistleblowing mechanisms.[380] Authorities competent to receive such reports should thus be qualified and trained in order to ensure that appropriate actions will be duly initiated.[381] Access to information should also be available in order for potential whistleblowers to receive advice and guidance.[382]

2.5.2 Incentives

2.5.2.1 A Duty to Report

An obligation to blow the whistle, introduced in the form of a legal or statutory duty to report, is particularly controversial but rather common.[383] A study has shown that, from 56 large European companies, two-thirds required employees to report wrongdoing.[384] The same trend can be observed in intergovernmental organizations.[385] While some commentators explicitly encourage organizations to introduce an obligation to report wrongdoing,[386] others demonstrate more restraint in regard to such a duty.[387] There are indeed a number of issues arising in relation to the establishment of a duty to report. Such a duty could, for example, promote reports based on

[377]TI (2013), Principle 29, p. 11; Special Rapporteur David Kaye whistleblower report, para 42; Feinstein et al. (2021), p. 31.

[378]OECD (2016), p. 83.

[379]Devine (2004), p. 81.

[380]UNODC (2015), pp. 68 and 73; OECD (2010), p. 32; Feinstein et al. (2021), p. 33.

[381]UNODC (2015), p. 69.

[382]UNODC (2015), p. 75; Feinstein et al. (2021), p. 22.

[383]On Whistleblowing as a moral duty see Ceva and Bocchiola (2019); Santoro and Kumar (2019), pp. 34–35.

[384]Hassink et al. (2007), pp. 25–44.

[385]On the protection of whistleblowers within international organizations see Sect. 2.6.

[386]e.g. IBA (2018), p. 6.

[387]e.g. The Whistleblowing Commission (2013), para 54.

insufficient evidence in a fear to be held responsible if remaining silent,[388] which would be detrimental to an effective compliance management.[389] It also creates new risks for whistleblowers. As the EU General Court held in the landmark cases *Bermejo v. EESC*, a duty to report introduces a risk for employees to be subjected to disciplinary sanctions when remaining silent, restricting thereby their margin of appreciation.[390] If the conclusion of the EU General Court stating that such an obligation can encourage employees to report[391] is theoretically correct, in organizations where there is a lack of trust in the reliability and effectiveness of existing whistleblowing mechanisms, a duty to report can limit disclosure if it is coupled with disciplinary sanctions for nondisclosure, as a tool for bureaucratic surveillance.[392] Instead, the fear of retaliation together with the fear of sanctions for nondisclosure could lead employees to avoid acquiring information that may give rise to such obligation,[393] a counterproductive side-effect of mandatory report system. Lastly, the level of protection for freedom of expression provided by national labor laws can have a determinant impact on the legality of a duty to report imposed by corporations,[394] with a strong protection of the right to freedom of expression for employees restricting the possibility for corporations to introduce such obligation.[395] While private companies are not directly bound by the negative aspect of freedom of expression, which encompasses the right not to be compelled to speak, it is prevailing view that States have a positive obligation to protect human rights and thus ensure that private employers do not impose a disproportionate duty to report on their employees.

Notwithstanding the foregoing, studies have demonstrated that the introduction of an obligation to report may encourage whistleblowing in certain circumstances. Indeed, an imposed duty to report seems to be a particularly effective incentive for women:[396] "Being able to fall back on a legal duty allows for women whistleblowers to play the role of reluctant report, bound by a legal requirement, not driven by pride or greed".[397] This could counterbalance the gender difference linked to the natural predisposition to consider men more prosocial or altruist when blowing the whistle.[398] In view of the foregoing, a differentiated approach to such a duty to report should be promoted, limiting the scope of this obligation to suspected misconduct of

---

388 Lewis (2011).

389 Lewis and Fasterling (2014), p. 88.

390 GC, Case T-530/12 P, *Moises Bermejo Garde v. European Economic and Social Committee (EESC)*, Judgment of 8 October 2014, ECLI:EU:T:2014:860, para 149.

391 Ibid., para 150.

392 Vaughn (2012), pp. 250–151.

393 Ibid.

394 Lewis and Fasterling (2014), p. 87.

395 Ibid., p. 89.

396 Feldman and Lobel (2010), p. 1196; Tilton (2018), p. 355.

397 Tilton (2018), p. 360.

398 Rehg et al., 'Antecedents and Outcomes of Retaliation Against Whistleblowers', p. 236.

a certain seriousness. However, it cannot be ignored that a general statutory duty to blow the whistle has become common practice within public and private entities. Therefore, in those circumstances and to counterbalance the difficulties linked to such a general obligation, a clear description of the scope as well as of the procedure to follow should be provided.[399] It should also be accompanied by the development of whistleblower-friendly administrative practices and jurisprudence, taking into account the restricted margin of appreciation of employees resulting from their statutory duty, which would help consolidate a work environment where blowing the whistle becomes a standard procedure and not a cut-throat endeavor, further accentuated by the duty to report.

2.5.2.2 Financial Incentives…

The question of monetary incentives to encourage whistleblowing is a particularly contentious topic.[400] Even in the U.S., where *quit tam* provisions have a long history[401] and where financial incentives for blowing the whistle have been converted into law, the necessity to introduce such incentives to ensure the effectiveness of whistleblower laws remain controversial. Even if financial incentives to blow the whistle can be interpreted as a democratic mechanism, shifting the power of control from the "big organization" to the "small individual", it can also be seen as the institutionalization of a denunciation culture[402] and thus have a detrimental impact on the efforts to change public perception of whistleblowers, who too often suffer from a negative image.[403]

Notwithstanding the foregoing, in Europe, where financial incentives to encourage whistleblowing have traditionally been regarded with great suspicion, the timid transposition of reward mechanisms into law, as is the case in the 2014 Market Abuse Regulation,[404] hints towards a change in European perception regarding financial incentives and increases the likelihood of such mechanisms becoming more common in the future.[405] Some studies have indeed shown that financial incentives can have an influence on the willingness to report, bearing in mind their varying effect depending on the circumstances, and thus the need to develop a contextualized understanding of such incentives.[406]

---

[399]Lewis et al. (2017), p. 454.

[400]Lewis and Fasterling (2014), p. 84.

[401]Callahan and Dworkin (1992), p. 326.

[402]Vaughn (2012), p. 134

[403]Committee on Legal Affairs, Report on the protection of "whistle-blowers", *Explanatory memorandum*, para 30.

[404]On the EU Market Abuse Regulation see Sect. 7.1.2.3.

[405]Lewis and Fasterling (2014), p. 84.

[406]Feldman and Lobel (2010); Callahan and Dworkin (1992), pp. 301–318; Ferziger and Currell (2000); Langenbucher (2020), pp. 1389 et seq.

The evolution of perception in the development of whistleblower frameworks, putting the focus on the nature of the suspected wrongdoing rather than on the motives of the whistleblower, may well influence the decision-making process when considering financial incentives as part of any future whistleblowing mechanism. Until then, it is expected that the debate around the introduction of financial incentives to blow the whistle will remain particularly controversial, even if those practices have already become common practice in a number of sectors.

2.5.2.3 ... or Adequate Compensation?

If the nature and relevance of financial incentives can be discussed, the payment of adequate compensations for the damage suffered is undeniably necessary.[407] In the U.S., experience has shown that whistleblowers rarely invoke financial incentives as a motivation to act,[408] pursuing a *qui tam* suit as the last resort, when other possibilities to obtain compensation for the retaliatory measures suffered have proven unsuccessful.[409] By a process of *a contrario* reasoning, a culture of silence can therefore be linked back to the fear of retaliation rather than the lack of financial incentives. The American experience and lesson-learned are therefore of particular relevance for other legislators when adopting or reforming whistleblower laws.[410]

2.5.3 Public Awareness and Regular Evaluation

2.5.3.1 Public Recognition

The recognition of the contributions and sacrifices made by whistleblowers can be a particular incentive[411] and foster a change in culture ensuring the effectiveness of whistleblower laws.[412] Whistleblowing challenges bureaucratic authority[413] and introduces a system of democratic accountability by redefining the employer/employee relationship of loyalty[414] through the power of non-consent[415] and the

---

[407]UNODC (2015), p. 55; Feinstein et al. (2021), pp. 27–28.

[408]Bucy (2006), p. 338.

[409]Helmer (2007), p. 9.

[410]Committee on Legal Affairs, Report on the protection of "whistle-blowers", *Explanatory memorandum*, para 97.

[411]Vaughn (2012), p. 139.

[412]Calland and Dehn (2004), p. 20.

[413]Vaughn (2012), p. 116.

[414]Ibid., p. 112.

[415]Ibid., p. 44.

right to disobey.[416] Recognition in the form of awards or honors underlines the integrity and moral courage of whistleblowers and emphasizes their important role in society.[417] "Corporate and government bureaucracies who include these indicia in the physical environment of employees make a statement at least as powerful as those contained in codes of ethics".[418] In light of the above, the almost two decade long fight of Mr. McCoy to be recognized as a *bona fide* whistleblower by the EU Committee of the Regions takes on a special meaning.[419]

2.5.3.2 Awareness Campaigns

Awareness campaigns can also contribute to changing the perception of whistleblowers and promoting a positive image of the act of whistleblowing.[420] In this context, the participation of the civil society in promoting whistleblowing policies can be particularly effective[421] and "represents one of the successes of whistleblower laws".[422]

2.5.3.3 Regular Evaluation

Furthermore, to ensure that existing whistleblower rules adequately address the real-life challenges faced by whistleblowers as well as reflect the reality of ever evolving working conditions, they should also be evaluated on a regular basis. Those periodic assessments would allow for competent authorities to adjust, if necessary, the potential deficiencies revealed.[423] In this respect, the systematic collection of data is key to appreciate the effectiveness of those measures.[424]

[416]Ibid., pp. 112–113.

[417]Ibid., p. 139–140; see also UNODC (2015), pp. 67–68.

[418]Ibid., p. 140.

[419]On the McCoy case see Sect. 6.2.1.

[420]OECD (2016), p. 98; UNODC (2015), p. 78.

[421]OECD (2016), p. 97; UNODC (2015), p. 68.

[422]Vaughn (2012), p. 267.

[423]OECD (2010), p. 33; OECD (2016), p. 99; TI (2013), Principle 30, p. 11; UNODC (2015), p. 80; Feinstein et al. (2021), p. 34.

[424]Feinstein et al. (2021), p. 71.

2.6 Protection of Whistleblowers Within International Organizations

2.6.1 Whistleblowing Policies

Over the last two decades, several intergovernmental organizations have introduced internal whistleblowing policies. While the UN, under the impetus of the U.S. Government,[425] led the way by adopting whistleblowing policies as early as 2005,[426] other intergovernmental organizations adopted internal regulations in the early 2010s, such as the International Criminal Court which adopted whistleblower protection policy in 2014.[427] While the development of whistleblowing policies within intergovernmental organizations can be guided by existing national whistleblower laws,[428] it also has the potential to influence the introduction of similar policies in member States (Fig. 2.1).[429] This mutual influence underlines the important role played by intergovernmental organizations in the advancement of whistleblower protection frameworks worldwide.

However, the very nature of those intergovernmental organizations in the world legal order represents a challenge to the traditional accountability system put in place on the national level through democratic mechanisms.[430] The immunity and legal independence enjoyed by intergovernmental organizations leads to three main challenges with regard to whistleblower protection: external disclosure, external evaluation of allegations of retaliation, and the duty to report.[431] To illustrate those challenges, the case of the UN and the WBG will be taken into focus.[432]

---

[425] Walden and Edwards (2014), p. 430.

[426] UN, *Protection against retaliation for reporting misconduct and for cooperating with duly authorized audits or investigations*, ST/SGB/2005/21, 19 December 2005, updated since by UN, *Protection against retaliation for reporting misconduct and for cooperating with duly authorized audits or investigations*, ST/SGB/2017/2, 20 January 2017, [hereinafter "UN Whistleblower protection policy"].

[427] ICC, ICC Whistleblowing and Whistleblower Protection Policy, Ref. ICC/PRESD/G/2014/003, 8 October 2014.

[428] Vaughn (2012), p. 251.

[429] Ibid., p. 247.

[430] Special Rapporteur David Kaye whistleblower report, para 52.

[431] Vaughn (2012), p. 249.

[432] On recommendations to improve the UN internal justice system see Feinstein et al. (2020, 13 May).

Protection against retaliation policy ratings: best practices indicators for criterion 1

Participating organization	1.1 Requires at least two channels for internal reporting	1.2 Allows for reporting to an oversight body and requires that the reporting line be independent	1.3 Allows a person to report confidentially and anonymously	1.4 Has specific provisions for reporting misconduct/wrongdoing concerning the head of an organization and head of the oversight office	1.5 Allows for reporting in any of the working languages of the organization	1.6 Indicates when and how to report to an external entity (e.g., law enforcement, public interest group or the media)
FAO	✓	✓	✓	O	✓	✗
IAEA	✓	✓	✓	✗	✓	✓
ICAO	✓	✗	O	✗	✗	✗
ILO	O	O	O	O	✓	✗
IMO	✓	✓	O	✗	✓	✓
ITU	✗	O	✗	✗	✓	✗
United Nations Secretariat	✓	✓	✓	O	✓	✓
UNAIDS	✓	✓	✓	✗	✓	✓
UNDP	✓	✓	O	O	✓	O
UNESCO	✓	✓	✓	✗	✓	✓
UNFPA	✓	✓	✓	O	✓	✓
UNHCR	✓	✓	✓	✓	✓	✓
UNICEF	✓	✓	O	O	✓	✓
UNIDO	✓	✓	✓	O	✓	✗
UNOPS	✓	✓	O	✗	✓	✓
UN-Women	✓	✓	✓	O	✓	✓
UNRWA	✓	✓	✓	✓	✓	✓
UNWTO	✓	✗	O	O	✓	✓
UPU	✓	✗	O	✗	✓	✓
WFP	✓	✓	✓	✗	✓	✓
WHO	✓	✓	✓	✗	✓	✓
WIPO	✓	✓	✓	✓	✓	✓
WMO	✓	✓	✓	✗	✓	✓

Key: [✓] = fully addressed; [O] = partially addressed; [✗] = not addressed.

Fig. 2.1 Protection against retaliation in international organizations (Reproduced from UN Joint Inspection, *Review of Whistle-blower Policies and Practices in United Nations System Organizations*, JIU/REP/2018/4, 2018)

2.6.2 *External Reporting and Evaluation*

The establishment of external whistleblower channels by international organizations has been the result of a gradual process, best illustrated by a 2005 Review of the WBG Whistleblower policies, which encouraged the WBG to "consider pathways of disclosure that are analogous to the external disclosures protected by most whistleblower protection laws".[433] Since then, both the UN and WB have included, in some circumstances, external reporting, as an inherent part of their whistleblower

[433]Vaughn (2005a, 30 April) Recommendation 17, p. 27.

policies.[434] In those cases of restrictive access to external reporting channels, strong internal whistleblowing channels are therefore primordial. Considering the inherent democratic deficit of those intergovernmental organizations and the consequential absence of scrutiny necessary to ensure fullest accountability, effective internal whistleblower policies can help to bridge the gap. Unfortunately, the UN Ethics Office, in charge of appreciating the merits of requests for protection under the dedicated UN whistleblower policies,[435] has rejected 96% of applications for protection in the period between 2006 and 2016.[436] The serious deficiencies in the UN Ethics Office's decision-making process and implementation of the UN whistleblowing policies became apparent following a UN precedent[437] allowing for independent legal scrutiny.[438] Contrary to the UN Ethics Office, UN Administrative judges indeed seem to be more favorable towards whistleblowers.[439] Notwithstanding this alternative protection shield, a high number of staff members say they fear to speak out and feel unprotected against reprisals.[440] This is all the more detrimental as most staff members are dependent on the organization for their visa and work permits, increasing thereby their professional vulnerability.[441] In those circumstances, acts of retaliation can have particularly far-reaching consequences for their livelihood.

According to the recommendations of the UN Joint Inspection Unit 2018 review of UN whistle-blower policies, "[i]n United Nations system organizations that do not have an external and independent mechanism for appeals when a prima facie case of retaliation is not determined, the executive head should instruct the relevant office (s) to develop, by 2020, appropriate options to address this deficiency for his or her timely consideration, and to outline any agreed-upon mechanisms and processes in updates to protection against retaliation policies".[442] It remains to be seen whether the alternative options developed by the UN organizations concerned will be adequate to effectively address the absence of external mechanisms. The U.S. Consolidated Appropriations Act, which requires UN bodies to comply with whistleblower best practices to receive a certain percentage of the

434 Section 4 of the UN Whistleblower protection policy; World Bank Group Staff Rule 8.02 – Protections and Procedures for Reporting Misconduct (Whistleblowing), Paragraph 04.

435 Section 7 of the UN Whistleblower protection policy.

436 Hunt-Matthes and Gallo (2017), p. 38.

437 UNDT, *Hunt-Matthes v. Secretary-General of the United Nations*, 2011/UNDT/063, 6 April 2011.

438 Hunt-Matthes and Gallo (2017), p. 38.

439 Martel (2017), pp. 278–284.

440 Walden and Edwards (2014), p. 433: 2011 Survey of 7,000 of the UNHCR found that 70% of responded fear of speaking up.

441 Ibid., p. 432.

442 UN Joint Inspection, *Review of Whistle-blower Policies and Practices in United Nations System Organizations*, Recommendation 2, p. 21.

U.S. contributions,[443] may play an important driver in this respect.[444] For now, the absence of effective internal mechanisms,[445] combined with limited access to external reporting channels and the statutory duty to report wrongdoing, represents a cut-throat work environment for UN Staff who wish to blow the whistle. It is also particularly counterproductive to address the "pervasive culture of secrecy in the decision-making processes of the organizations and little or no accountability".[446]

2.6.3 A Duty to Report

The establishment of a duty to report on wrongdoing is a commonly introduced statutory obligation within intergovernmental organizations. In this respect, both the UN[447] and WBG[448] impose a duty to report. On the European level, the CoE and the EU have also introduced an obligation to report, which will be analyzed further below.[449] As seen above, the introduction of a duty to blow the whistle is particularly controversial.[450] In fact, as early as 2005, the review of the WBG Whistleblowing policies recommended to abandon this requirement,[451] describing such a duty as a "double-edge sword".[452] While this recommendation seems to have encouraged the WBG to adopt a more differentiated approach to this duty, it remains applicable in certain circumstances. In regard to suspected fraud and corruption, WGB Staff remain obliged to report it.[453] In cases of suspected misconduct of a different nature, WGB Staff are merely encouraged to report it, without being required to do so.[454] On the contrary, managers are under a duty to report every kind of suspected misconduct.[455] Far from simplifying the whistleblowing process and facilitating

---

443 Publ. Law No. 114-113 (2015), para 7048.

444 Martel (2017), p. 287.

445 Hunt-Matthes and Gallo (2017), p. 41; Walden and Edwards (2014), pp. 440–448.

446 UN Joint Inspection, *Ethics in the United Nations System*, JUI/REP/2010/3, Geneva, 2010, p. 11.

447 Section 1, paragraph 1.1 of the UN Whistleblower protection policy.

448 WBG Staff Rule 8.02, paragraph 2.02 in conjunction with Staff Rule 8.01, paragraph 2.02 and Staff Rule 3.00, paragraph 7.01.

449 On the Council of Europe internal rules on whistleblowing see Sect. 3.5.3; on the European Union internal rules on whistleblowing see Sect. 5.2.1.

450 On the discussion around a duty to report see Sect. 2.5.2.1.

451 Vaughn (2005a, 30 April) Recommendation 3 and 4, pp. 11-14.

452 Ibid., p. 11.

453 WBG Staff Rule 8.02, paragraph 2.02 in conjunction with Staff Rule 8.01, paragraph 2.02 (a) and Staff Rule 3.00, paragraph 7.01.

454 WGB Staff Rule 8.02, paragraph 2.02 in conjunction with Staff Rule 8.01, paragraph 2.02 (b) and Staff Rule 3.00, paragraph 7.01. The list of misconduct susceptible to be reported can be found under Staff Rule 3.00, paragraph 6.01.

455 WBG Staff Rule 8.02, paragraph 2.02 in conjunction with Staff Rule 8.01, paragraph 2.02 and Staff Rule 3.00, paragraph 7.01.

reports of suspected misconduct within the organization, this differentiated approach may well have a deterring effect on WBG Staff. The line between fraud and corruption, and other kinds of misconduct can be particularly blurred in certain circumstances, which can increase the difficulty for employees to appreciate the extent of their obligation in the specific context. The resulting uncertainty is highly detrimental to the effectiveness of WGB whistleblower policies and curtails the potential benefits of an imposed obligation.

2.7 Intermediate Conclusion

The description of the historical evolution of whistleblowing as a legally regulated act and the analysis of the main challenges arising in the process of adopting whistleblower regulations, on a national level as well as for intergovernmental organizations, set the stage for the purpose of this book: illustrating the positions taken in Europe in regard to those challenges and analyzing the emergence of an European consensus regarding the different legal issues in relation to whistleblower laws.

References

Abel E (1987) Leaking: who does it? Who benefits? At what cost? Unwin Hyman, Crows Nest

Ackerman S (2015, 16 March) Petraeus leaks: Obama's leniency reveals 'profound double standard', lawyer says. *The Guardian*

Ackerman S, Pilkington E (2015, 16 March) Obama's war on whistleblowers leaves administration insiders unscathed. *The Guardian*

Adam A (2018) Heros and Sibyls? Gender and engineering ethics. In: Sakellarious N, Milleron R (eds) Ethics, politics, and whistleblowing in engineering. CPC Press, New York, pp 13–22

Ambos K (2021) Humanitarian victory for assange. EJIL:Talk !

APPG (2020) Making whistleblowing work for society. All Party Parliamentary Group Whistleblowing

Ball J (2019, 11 April) You don't have to like Julian Assange to defend him. *The Atlantic*

Banisar D (2011) Whistleblowing: international standards and developments. In: Sandoval IE (ed) Corruption and transparency: debating the frontiers between states, market and society. World Bank Institute for Social Research. UNAM, Washington, D.C.

Barendt E (2016) Anonymous speech: literature, law and politics. Hard Publishing, Oxford

Bok S (1989) Secrets: on the ethics of concealment and revelation. Vintage Books, New York

Bonne F, Salvi E (2019, 16 September) Snowden demande l'asile, l'Elysée fait la sourde oreille. *Mediapart*

Boot ER (2019) Leaks and the limits of press freedom. Ethical Theory Moral Practice 22:483–500

Bowman T (2020, 24 April) The Navy Has Decided to Restore Capt. Brett Crozier. *National Public Radio*

Boyne SM (2016) Financial incentives and truth-telling: the growth of whistle-blowing legislation in the United States. In: Thüsing G, Forst G (eds) Whistleblowing - a comparative study. Ius Comparatum - global studies in comparative law, vol 16. Springer, Cham, pp 279–310

Buchert R (2016) § 42. Ombudsmann und Hinweisgebersysteme. In: Hauschka CE, Mossmayer K, Lösler T (eds) Corporate compliance: Handbuch der Haftungsvermeidung im Unternehmen, 3rd edn. C.H. Beck, Munich

Bucy PH (2006) Moral messengers: delegating prosecutorial power. SMU Law Rev 59(1):321–344

Callahan ES, Dworkin TM (1992) Do good and get rich: financial incentives for whistleblowing and the false claims act. Villanova Law Rev 37(2):273–336

Calland R, Dehn G (2004) Introduction. Whistleblower around the world: the state of the art - the role of the individual, organizations, the state, the media, the law and civil society. In: Calland R, Dehn G (eds) Whistleblowing around the World: law, culture and practice. ODAC/PCaW, Cape Town/London, pp 2–20

Ceva E, Bocchiola M (2019) Is Whistleblowing a Duty?. Political theory today. Polity Press, Cambridge

Cheng A (2020, 19 March) Chinese authorities admit improper response to coronavirus whistleblower. *National Public Radio*

Cooper H, Gibbons-Neff T, Schmitt E (2020, 3 April) The Navy fired the Captain of the Theodore Roosevelt. See how the crew responded. *The New York Times*

Daily Show with Trevor Noah (2019, 20 September) Edward Snowden – "Permanent Record" & Life as an Exiled NSA Whistleblower | The Daily Show

Daley P (2020, 14 June) Julian Assange indictment fails to mention WikiLeaks video that exposed US 'war crimes' in Iraq. *The Guardian*

Devine TM (1999) Whistleblower Protection Act of 1989: Foundation for the Modern Law of Employment Dissent. Admin Law Rev 51(2):531–579

Devine TM (2004) Whistleblowing in the United States: the gap between vision and lessons learned. In: Calland R, Dehn G (eds) Whistleblowing around the World: law, culture & practice. ODAC/PCaW, Cap Town/London, pp 74–100

Donkin M, Smith R, Brown AJ (2008) How do officials report? Internal and external whistleblowing. In: Brown AJ (ed) Whistleblowing in the Australian Public Sector: enhancing the theory and practice of internal witness management in public sector organisations. ANU E Press, Canberra, pp 83–108

Dowling DC Jr (2008) Sarbanes-Oxley whistleblower hotlines across Europe: directions through the maze. Int Lawyer 42(1):1–57

Dozier JB, Miceli MP (1985) Potential predictors of whistle-blowing: a prosocial behavior perspective. Acad Manag Rev 10(4):832–836

Dudar H (1977, 30 October) The price of blowing the whistle. *The New York Times*

Éditorial Le Monde (2019, 17 September) La France doit donner asile à Edward Snowden. *Le Monde*

Elliston FA (1982a) Anonymity and whistleblowing. J Bus Ethics 1(3):167–177

Elliston FA (1982b) Civil disobedience and whistleblowing: a comparative appraisal of two forms of dissent. J Bus Ethics 1(1):23–28

Farrow R (2017, 23 October) From aggressive overtures to sexual assault: Harvey Weinstein's accusers tell their stories. *The New Yorker*, 2017

Farrow R (2019) Catch and kill: lies, spies, and a conspiracy to protect predators. Little, Brown and Company, Boston

Feinstein S, Devine T, Guyer T (2020, 13 May) Letter to Judge Yvonne Mokgoro, Chairperson of the United Nations Internal Justice Council. Governmental Accountability Project

Feinstein S, Devine T, Pender K, Allen C, Nawa R, Shepard M (2021) Are whistleblowing laws working? A global study of whistleblower protection litigation. International Bar Association/Government Accountability Project

Feldman Y, Lobel O (2010) The incentives matrix: the comparative effectiveness of rewards, liabilities, duties, and protections for reporting illegality. Texas Law Rev 88(6):1151–1211

Ferziger MJ, Currell DG (2000) Snitching for dollars: the economics and public policy of federal civil bounty programs. Univ Illinois Law Rev 1999(4):1141–1208

Foegle JP (2015) Un renforcement en demi-teinte du status du lanceur d'alerte dans l'"Europe des droits de l'homme". La Revue des droits de l'homme:1–26

Folmer K, Margolin J (2020, 8 June) Satellite data suggests coronavirus may have hit China earlier: Researchers, new research also suggest that the virus started spreading earlier than officially reported. *ABC News*

Fuller R (2014) A matter of national security: whistleblowing in the military as a mechanism for international law enforcement. San Diego Int Law J 15(2):249–298

Gafni M, Garofoli J (2020, 31 March) Exclusive: Captain of aircraft carrier with growing coronavirus outbreak pleads for help from Navy. *San Francisco Chronic*

GAP, International Whistleblower Protection Map. https://whistleblower.org/map-2/. Accessed 13 April 2021

Gerdemann S (2018) Transatlanic Whistleblowing: Rechtliche Entwicklung, Funktionsweise und Status quo des Whistleblowings in den USA und seine Bedeutung für Deutschland. Studien zum ausländischen und internationalen Privatrecht 404. Mohr Siebeck, Tübingen

Green A (2020) Li Wenliang. The Lancet 395(10225):682

Hassink H, de Vries M, Bollen L (2007) A content analysis of whistleblowing policies of leading European Companies. J Bus Ethics 75:24–44

Hauser C, Hergovits N, Blumer H (2019) Whistleblowing Report 2019. EQS Group, Munich

Helmer JB (2007) False claims act: whistleblower litigation, 5th edn. Bloomberg, New York

Hertel F (2019) Effective internal control and corporate compliance: a law and economics impact analysis of the mysteries of a German Aktiengesellschaft Listed on the NYSE. Schriften zum europäischen, internationalen und vergleichenden Unternehmensrecht, vol 16. Nomos, Baden-Baden

Hirschman AO (1970) Exit, voice and loyalty: responses to decline in firms, organizations, and states. Harvard University Press, Cambridge

Hunt-Matthes C, Gallo PA (2017) The UN whistleblowing protection gap: implications for governance, human rights and risk management. In: Lewis D, Vandekerckhove W (eds) Selected Papers from the International Whistleblowing Research Network Conference Oslo June 2017. International Whistleblowing Research Network, London

IBA (2018) Whistleblower protections: a guide. https://www.ibanet.org/LPRU/whistleblowing.aspx. Accessed 13 April 2021

ICCom (2008) ICC guidelines on whistleblowing. https://iccwbo.org/publication/icc-guidelines-on-whistleblowing/. Accessed 13 April 2021

ILO (2019) Law and practice on protecting whistle-blowers in the public and financial services sectors. Working Paper, WP328. https://www.ilo.org/sector/Resources/publications/WCMS_718048/lang%2D%2Den/index.htm. Accessed 13 April 2021

Jacqué JP (2015, 31 March) Review of the EULEX Kosovo Mission's implementation of the mandate with a particular focus on the handling of the recent allegations, Report to the attention of Higher Representative/Vice President of the European Commission Ms Federica Mogherini

Jensen MC (1978, 19 May) 'Whistle-Blowing' on Toxics. *The New York Times*

Junjun C (2020, 19 March) Wuhan police deal with the responsible person in the case of Li Wenliang being admonished. *Yicai*

Kantor J, Twohey M (2017, 5 October) Harvey Weinstein paid off sexual harassment accusers for decades. *The New York Times*

Kuper S (2018, 24 January) Opinion: Edward Snowden and the millennial conscience. *The Financial Times*

Lamothe D, Ryan M, Sonne P (2020, 3 April) Navy removes aircraft carrier captain who raised alarm about coronavirus response. *The Washington Post*

Langenbucher K (2020) Financial rewards for whistleblowing and motivation crowding theory - a lesson from psychology for transposing EU Directive 2019/1937. In Liber Amicorum Windbichler, pp 1377–1394

Le Monde with AFP (2019, 19 September) La France exclut toujours d'accorder l'asile à Edward Snowden. *Le Monde with AFP*

Lewis D (2010) Ten Years of Public Interest Disclosure Act 1998 Claims: what can we learn from the statistics and recent research? Indus Law J 39(3):325–328

Lewis D (2011) Whistleblowing and data protection principles: is the road to reconciliation really that rocky? Eur J Law Technol 2(1)

Lewis D, Fasterling B (2014) Leaks, legislation and freedom of speech: how can the law effectively promote public-interest whistleblowing? Int Labour Rev 153(1):71–92

Lewis J, Bowers GCJ, Fodder M, Mitchell J (2017) Whistleblowing: law and practice, 3rd edn. Oxford University Press, Oxford

Lobel O (2008) Citizenship, organizational citizenship, and the laws of overlapping obligations. California Law Review 2008, San Diego Legal Studies Paper No. 08-017: 1–59

Lochak D (2016) Les lanceurs d'alerte et les droits de l'Homme: réflexions conclusives. La Revue des droits de l'homme 10:1–21

Malin MH (1983) Protecting the whistle-blower from retaliatory discharge. Univ Mich J Law Reform 16(2):277–318

Martel B (2017) The protection of United Nations whistleblowers against retaliation. Law Pract Int Courts Tribunals 16(2):264–287

Miceli MP, Near JP (1986) Retaliation against whistle blowers: predictors and effects. J Appl Psychol 71(1):137–145

Miceli MP, Near JP (1989) The incidence of wrongdoing, whistle-blowing, and retaliation: results of a naturally occurring field experiment. Employee Responsibilities Rights J 2(2):91–108

Miceli MP, Roach BL, Near JP (1988) The motivations of anonymous whistle-blowers: the case of federal employees. Public Personnel Manag 17(3):281–296

Miceli MP, Near JP, Dworkin TM (2008) Whistle-blowing in organizations. Routledge, New York/London

Miller AS (1972) Whistle blowing and the law. In: Nader R, Petkas PJ, Blackwell K (eds) Whistle blowing: the report of the conference on professional responsibility. Grossman Publishers, New York, pp 25–33

Moberly RE (2006) Sarbanes-Oxley's structural model to encourage corporate whistleblowers. Brigham Young Univ Law Rev 2006(5):1107–1180

Moberly RE (2007) Unfulfilled expectations: an empirical analysis of why Sarbanes-Oxley Whistleblowers rarely win. William Mary Law Rev 49:65–155

Moberly RE (2012) Whistleblowers and the Obama presidency: the National Security Dilemma. Employee Rights Employment Policy J 16(1):51–141

Modesitt NM (2012) The *Garcetti* Virus. Univ Cincinnati Law Rev 80(1):161–208

Morris JD (1971, 27 January) New Nader Group Seeking Tipsters. *The New York Times*

Nader R (1972) An anatomy of whistle blowing. In: Nader R, Petkas PJ, Blackwell K (eds) Whistle blowing: the report of the conference on professional responsibility. Grossman Publishers, New York, pp 3–11

Nader R, Petkas PJ, Blackwell K (eds) (1972) Whistle blowing: the report of the conference on professional responsibility. Grossman Publishers, New York

Near JP, Jensen TC (1983) The whistleblowing process: retaliation and perceived effectiveness. Work Occupations 10(3):3–28

Near JP, Dworking TM, Miceli MP (1993) Explaining the whistle-blowing process: suggestions from power theory and justice theory. Organ Sci 4(3):393–411

O'Brian C, Seligman L (2020, 6 April) Acting Navy secretary apologizes amid uproar over leaked carrier speech. *Politico*

OECD (2010) G20 anti-corruption action plan: protection of whistleblowers, study on whistleblower protection frameworks, compendium of best practices and guiding principles for legislation. https://www.oecd.org/g20/topics/anti-corruption/48972967.pdf. Accessed 13 Apr 2021

OECD (2016) Committing to effective whistleblower protection. OECD Publishing, Paris

Open Society Justice Initiative (2013) The global principles on National Security and the right to information (*Tshwane Principles*)

Parmerlee MA, Near JP, Jensen TC (1982) Correlates of whistleblowers' perceptions of organizational retaliation. Admin Sci Q 27(1):17–34

Peralta E (2012, 12 March) Treatment of Bradley Manning Was Cruel and Inhuman, Says U.N. Official. *National Public Radio*

Peters C, Branch T (1972) Blowing the Whistle: dissent in the public interest. Praeger Publishers, New York

Pilkington E (2012, 12 March) Bradley Manning's treatment was cruel and inhuman, UN torture chief rules. *The Guardian*

Pompeo (2017, 13 April) Remarks as prepared for delivery by Central Intelligence Agency Director Mike Pompeo at the Center for Strategic and International Studies. Central Intelligence Agency

Pozen DE (2013) The Leaky Leviathan: why the Government condemns and condones unlawful disclosures of information. Harv Law Rev 127(2):512–635

Proxmire W (1972) The whistle blower as civil servant. In: Nader R, Petkas PJ, Blackwell K (eds) Whistle blowing: the report of the conference on professional responsibility. Grossman Publishers, New York, pp 12–19

Quinn B (2021a, 4 January) Julian Assange cannot be extradited to US, British judge rules. *The Guardian*

Quinn B (2021b, 4 January) Julian Assange to seek release from prison after extradition ruling. *The Guardian*

Radack J, McClellan K (2011) The criminalization of whistleblowing. Labor Employment Law Forum 2(1):57–77

Rehg MT, Miceli MP, Near JP, Van Scotter JR (2008) Antecedents and outcomes of retaliation against whistleblowers: gender differences and power relationships. Organ Sci 19(2):221–240

Rettman A (2014, 30 October) EU mission in Kosovo rocked by corruption allegations. *EU Observer*

Reuters (2020, 25 April) Brett Crozier: US navy seeks to reinstate captain fired over covid-19. *The Guardian*

Roth A (2020, 2 November) Edward Snowden applies for Russian citizenship for sake of future son. *The Guardian*

Rudkowski L, Schreiber A (2018) Aufklärung von Compliance-Verstöße: Whistleblowing, Arbeitnehmerüberwachung, Auskunftspflichten, 2nd edn. Springer Gabler, Wiesbaden

Santoro D, Kumar M (2019) Speaking truth to power – a theory of whistleblowing. Philosophy and politics – critical exploration, vol 6. Springer, Cham

Schogol J (2020, 6 April) Acting Navy Secretary blasts USS Theodore Roosevelt captain as 'too naive or too stupid' in leaked speech to ship's crew. *Task & Purpose*

Seligman L (2020, 29 April) Navy delays decision on reinstating fired captain who warned of coronavirus. *Politico*

Stanger A (2019, 22 April) Opinions: The Mueller report confirms it: Assange is not a whistleblower or a journalist. *The Washington Post*

The Editorial Board (2019, 23 May) Opinion: Julian Assange's indictment aims at the heart of the first amendment. *The New York Times*

The New York Times (2011, 24 January) "Collateral Murder" Video. *The New York Times*

The New York Times (2020, 7 February) He warned of coronavirus. Here's What He Told Us Before He Died. *The New York Times*

The Whistleblowing Commission (2013) Report on the effectiveness of existing arrangements for workplace whistleblowing in the UK. Public Concern at Work

Thüsing G (2017) Whistleblowing: Deutsche und europäische Perspektive - insbesondere im Datenschutz. Schriftenreihe des Zentrum für Europäisches Wirtschaftsrecht 219:1–36

TI (2013) International principles for whistleblower legislation: best practices for laws to protect whistleblowers and support whistleblowing in the public interest'. https://www.transparency.org/en/publications/international-principles-for-whistleblower-legislation#. Accessed 13 Apr 2021

TI (2018) A best practice guide for whistleblowing legislation. https://www.transparency.org/en/publications/best-practice-guide-for-whistleblowing-legislation. Accessed 13 Apr 2021

Tilton C (2018) Women and whistleblowing: exploring gender effects in policy design. Colomb J Gender Law 35(2):338–368

UNODC (2015) The United Nations Convention against corruption - resource guide on good practices in the protection of reporting persons. https://www.unodc.org/documents/corruption/Publications/2015/15-04741_Person_Guide_eBook.pdf. Accessed 13 Apr 2021

Vaughn RG (1977) Public employees and the right to disobey. Hastings Law J 29(2):261–295

Vaughn RG (2005a, 30 April) Report on the World Bank's whistleblower procedures

Vaughn RG (2005b) America's first comprehensive statute protecting corporate whistleblowers. Admin Law Rev 57(1):1–105

Vaughn RG (2012) The successes and failures of whistleblower laws. Edward Elgar, Cheltenham/Northampton

Vladeck SI (2008) The Espionage Act and National Security whistleblowing after *Garcetti*. Am Univ Law Rev 57(5):1531–1546

Walden S, Edwards B (2014) Whistleblower protection in international organizations. In: Brown AJ, Lewis D, Moberly R, Vandekerckhove W (eds) International handbook on whistleblowing research. Edward Elgar, Cheltenham/Northampton, pp 430–456

Walzer M (2018) Just or unjust leaks: when to spill secrets. Foreign Aff 97(2):48–58

Weil P (2019) Il faut accorder l'asile constitutionnel à Edward Snowden. Esprit 4:87–93

Weinstein D (1979) Bureaucratic opposition: challenging abuses at the workplace. Pergamon Press, New York

Weissert W (2020, 4 May) DHS report: China hid virus' severity to hoard supplies. *The Associated Press*

Wolfe S, Worth M, Dreyfus S, Brown AJ (2014) Whistleblower Protection Laws in G20 Countries: priorities for action'. Blueprint for free speech

Xinhua News Agency (2020, 19 March) The person in charge of the investigation team of the State Supervision and Administration Commission answered questions from reporters. *The Paper*

Zacharek S, Dockterman E, Sweetland Edwards H (2017, 18 December) TIME Person of the Year 2017: The Silence Breakers. *Time Magazine*

Part II
The Council of Europe

Chapter 3
Whistleblower Protection by the Council of Europe

3.1 Introduction

In the longest period of peace Europe has ever experienced, European bodies have played an important role. The vivid memory of the atrocities committed during the Second World War and the risk that it may happen again encouraged European countries to think about a closer and more unified Europe, based on a common foundation and guided by a set of shared values. "We must build a kind of United States of Europe" Winston Churchill famously said, and to that aim, "the first practical step will be to form a Council of Europe".[1] The Council of Europe in question, created in 1950, with 47 Member States today, was entrusted with the task "to achieve a greater unity between its members for the purpose of safeguarding and realising the ideals and principles which are their common heritage and facilitating their economic and social progress".[2] Throughout its 70 year history, the CoE set and monitored common standards in the area of human rights, democracy and the rule of law.[3] In pursuit of this aim, the CoE adopted a series of instruments intended to establish a common foundation on the basis of which compliance by CoE Member States could be monitored, the most well-known being the ECHR.[4] But it only in the 1990s that the CoE took timid steps towards specific whistleblower protection standards, as part of its "Programme of Action against Corruption".[5] According to this action plan, "corruption of any kind and at any level of society seriously undermines the basic values on which society is founded",[6] a reality which calls

[1]Churchill (1946, 19 September).

[2]Article 1(a) Statute of the Council of Europe, 5 May 1949, ETS No. 001.

[3]Weiß (2017), p. 16.

[4]On the protection of whistleblowers under the ECHR Chap. 4.

[5]CM, Programme of Action against Corruption, GMC (96) 95, November 1996.

[6]Ibid., para 18.

© The Author(s), under exclusive license to Springer Nature Switzerland AG 2021
H. C. L. Yurttagül, *Whistleblower Protection by the Council of Europe, the European Court of Human Rights and the European Union*, European Union and its Neighbours in a Globalized World 3, https://doi.org/10.1007/978-3-030-78059-3_3

for common strategies on the CoE level in order "to defend the fundamental values of the Council of Europe, namely democracy, the Rule of Law and human rights".[7] In pursuance thereof, the CoE adopted in 1999 the Criminal Law Convention on Corruption[8] and the Civil Law Convention on Corruption.[9]

The European Anti-corruption Conventions

Both the Criminal Law Convention on Corruption and the Civil Law Convention on Corruption have introduced provisions relevant to the protection of whistleblowers. Article 22 of the Criminal Law Convention on Corruption stipulates, for example:

> **Article 22 – Protection of collaborators of justice and witnesses**
>
> Each Party shall adopt such measures as may be necessary to provide effective and appropriate protection for:
>
> a. those who report the criminal offences established in accordance with Articles 2 to 14 or otherwise co-operate with the investigating or prosecuting authorities;
> b. witnesses who give testimony concerning these offences.

According to the Explanatory Report to the Criminal Law Convention on Corruption, whistleblowers should also be included within the meaning of the word 'witnesses',[10] "effective and appropriate protection" thus referring to the level of protection necessary to counter the risks faced by, inter alia, whistleblowers.[11]

Article 9 of the Civil Law Convention on Corruption states:

> **Article 9 – Protection of employees**
>
> Each Party shall provide in its internal law for appropriate protection against any unjustified sanction for employees who have reasonable grounds to suspect corruption and who report in good faith their suspicion to responsible persons or authorities.

Contrary to the UN Convention against corruption, the scope of protection of the Civil Law Convention on corruption is broader and includes all employees who report, both in the private and public sector. But while the Group of States against Corruption (GRECO) identified whistleblower protection as an emerging theme in

[7]Ibid., para 27.

[8]ETS No. 173, 1 July 2002.

[9]ETS No. 174, 1 November 2003.

[10]CoE, *Explanatory Report to the Criminal Law Convention on Corruption*, 27 January 1999, para 111.

[11]Ibid., para 113.

its evaluation rounds conducted between 2000 and 2010,[12] it is since the early 2010s that Europe witnessed an exponential increase in the adoption of dedicated legislations to better protect whistleblowers.

The Groundwork of the Parliamentary Assembly
The Parliamentary Assembly, named 'Consultative Assembly' in the Statute of the Council of Europe,[13] is the deliberative organ of the CoE[14] and was the first international parliamentary body established in Europe.[15] It aims to promote "debates on emerging and topical European issues, identify trends and best practices and set benchmarks and standards"[16] and thus has a promoting and initiating role within the CoE.[17] Despite its primary consultative function, the PA's power of initiative plays a pivotal role in the promotion of common democratic standards in Europe.[18] It is composed of members of the CoE Member States national parliaments, who can be either elected by the national parliaments or appointed from among the members of the national parliaments.[19] The PA can discuss and make recommendations on any matter relevant to the mandate of the CoE[20] and present its conclusion in the form of recommendations to the Committee of Ministers,[21] the latter being the second statutory organ of the CoE and the executive branch of the organization. According to the Parliamentary Rules of procedures, the implementation of its recommendations is beyond the competence of the Assembly and in the hands of national governments[22] while its resolutions embody a decision or point of view of the Assembly on a question of substance which it is empowered to put into effect and for which it alone is responsible.[23] In this regard, motions for recommendations or resolutions can forge ahead when it has the support of "at least twenty representatives or substitutes belonging to at least five national delegations or be adopted with the requisite quorum by a committee".[24]

It is following three of those motions that key PA resolutions and recommendations on the protection of whistleblowers were adopted. The Committee on Legal

---

[12]GRECO, *Lessons learnt from the three Evaluation Rounds (2000-2010): Thematic Articles*, 2011, pp. 18–21.

[13]Articles 22 et seq. Statute of the Council of Europe.

[14]Article 22 Statute of the Council of Europe.

[15]Leach (2017), p. 166.

[16]PA, Members Handbook, January 2015, p. 8.

[17]CM, Declaration on the Future Role of the Council of Europe in European Construction, CM (89) PV1, 5 May 1989.

[18]Leach (2017), pp. 168–169.

[19]Article 25 Statute of the Council of Europe.

[20]Article 23 Statute of the Council of Europe.

[21]Article 22 Statute of the Council of Europe.

[22]Rule 25.1.a. Parliamentary Assembly Rules of Procedure.

[23]Rule 25.1.b. Parliamentary Assembly Rules of Procedure.

[24]Rule 25.2. Parliamentary Assembly Rules of Procedure.

Affairs and Human Rights (hereinafter referred to as "Committee on Legal Affairs") played an important role in this respect. As one of the nine permanent committees of the PA in charge of preparing reports in their specific fields, upon which plenary debates are based, the Committee on Legal Affairs is one of the committees with the highest profiles and has a particularly wide mandate,[25] as it is assigned to consider "all legal and human rights matters ... which fall within the competence of the Council of Europe".[26] It is common that permanent committees appoint rapporteurs to address specific subjects in relation to their mandate.[27] In this context, the rapporteur Pieter Omtzigt, in charge of the first and second report on the protection of whistleblowers in Europe, played a crucial role in the identification of guiding principles on whistleblowing (Sect. 3.2), and in particular in relation to national security interests of States (Sect. 3.4), thereby helping to develop the European consensus on the protection of whistleblowers which emerged in the last decade. The general positive feedback from the PA in regard to the EU own legislative initiative on whistleblowing (Sect. 3.5.1) further enforces this consensus.

The Committee of Ministers' Guiding Principles

The Committee of Ministers, the executive organ of the CoE[28] composed of the Ministers for Foreign Affairs of each of the CoE Member States,[29] is, by its very nature, under a dual influence. While its mandate entitles it to act on behalf of the CoE to pursue the altruistic goal of greater unity between CoE Members States through the promotion of fundamental freedoms and human rights, its composition represents a 'forum of multilateral diplomacy' and implies a strong interest in promoting national priorities.[30] To fulfill its mission, *inter alia* by considering "the action required to further the aim of the Council of Europe",[31] the conclusion of which can take the form of recommendations to CoE Member States governments,[32] the CM has to reconcile the aforementioned two objectives.[33] The particular relevance of those recommendations, which can be the result of direct suggestions made by the PA, lies in the ability of the CM to be informed of the actions taken by the CoE Member states in response to those recommendations.[34] The relationship between those two statutory organs is central in the institutional order of the

[25]Leach (2017), pp. 173–174.

[26]PA Resolution 1842 (2011) *The terms of reference of Parliamentary Assembly committees – implementation of Resolution 1822 (2011) on the reform of the Parliamentary Assembly*, Appendix, para 2.1.

[27]Leach (2017), p. 173.

[28]Article 13 Statute of the Council of Europe.

[29]Article 14 Statute of the Council of Europe.

[30]Palmer (2017), p. 138.

[31]Article 15(a) Statute of the Council of Europe.

[32]Article 15(b) Statute of the Council of Europe.

[33]Palmer (2017), p. 138.

[34]Article 15(b) Statute of the Council of Europe.

CoE[35] and helps to ensure the legitimacy of CM initiatives[36] through a certain level of democratic control.[37] The unifying power of the CM, made possible by a constant and harmonizing debate between CoE Member States to reach consensus on common European values, has greatly contributed to the promotion of fundamental democratic principles.[38] Its important contribution to the emergence of an European consensus on whistleblower protection is a perfect illustration of its unifying role in Europe (Sect. 3.3).

The Decentralized Aspects of Whistleblower Protection
In a more decentralized perspective, the Congress of Local and Regional Authorities (hereinafter referred as "Congress"), established in 1994[39] to serve the purpose of increasing the participation of local and regional authorities in the consultative process within the CoE,[40] confirmed this consensus on the local and regional level, emphasizing however the necessity to adjust whistleblowing policies to the specific challenges faced by local and regional entities (Sect. 3.5.2).

Whistleblowing Policies of the Council of Europe
Last but not least, a closer look at the CoE's internal rules on whistleblowing will illustrate the existing gaps in the protection framework offered to whistleblowers within the CoE institution, and pressing need to conduct thorough reforms to raise the standards of protection to those promoted in its own recommendations to CoE Member States (Sect. 3.5.3).

3.2 The Initiating Role of the Parliamentary Assembly

3.2.1 Breaking the Rule of Silence

After the adoption of the PA Resolution "Alleged secret detentions and unlawful inter-state transfers of detainees involving Council of Europe member states" calling on CoE Member States to ensure an effective protection of whistleblowers in their state secrecy laws, as part of a set of measures intended to prohibit the unlawful

---

[35] Palmer (2017), p. 160.

[36] e.g. CM Declaration on the Future Role of the Council of Europe in European Construction, CM (89) PV1, 5 May 1989, para 4: "We are counting on the promotional and initiatory action of the Assembly, which as parliamentary organ of the Council of Europe composed of members of national parliaments is in constant touch with the public's wishes and concerns and provides the essential link with national democratic institutions".

[37] Palmer (2017), p. 161.

[38] Ibid., p. 165.

[39] CM Statutory Resolution (94) 3 relating to the setting up of the Congress of Local and Regional Authorities of Europe, 14 January 1994.

[40] On the Congress of Local and Regional Authorities [hereinafter "Congress"] see Schaffarzik (2017), pp. 269–295.

inter-state transfers of detainees,[41] 26 members of the PA from 16 countries[42] signed a motion for a recommendation entirely dedicated to the protection of whistleblowers.[43] Such a recommendation would introduce "a 'reporting culture' to break the rule of silence"[44] in reference to GRECO's findings[45] acknowledging that such a culture could be an effective way to fight against corruption.[46] Going beyond the anti-corruption considerations of GRECO, the motion also emphasizes "the crucial role of whistle-blowers . . . in the reporting of other illegal activities".[47]

Two years after the motion for a recommendation was signed, the Committee on Legal Affairs released its report on the protection of whistleblowers in Europe and confirmed their essential role "to strengthen accountability, and bolster the fight against corruption and mismanagement, both in the public and private sectors".[48] The rapporteur made clear that the report's primary aim was to change the perception of whistleblowers, from traitors or "informers", to generous and courageous individuals committed to fight abuses and willing to sacrifice their career for the greater good.[49] In countries where whistleblowers are more positively perceived, such as in the US,[50] the rapporteur noted that the two main reasons why individuals still remain silent despite stronger whistleblowing protection laws are, first, the lack of confidence that adequate actions will be taken, and second, the fear of retaliation.[51] On the European side, the rapporteur observed a widespread legal vacuum in regard to whistleblower protection[52] and analyzed the particular challenges facing CoE Member States when considering whistleblowing regulations on the basis of the results from a questionnaire sent to all CoE Member States, to which 26 replied.[53]

---

[41]PA Resolution 1507 (2006) *Alleged secret detentions and unlawful inter-state transfers of detainees involving Council of Europe member states*, para 19.5.

[42]Albania, Andorra, Croatia, Cyprus, Finland, France, Germany, Greece, Latvia, Netherlands, Portugal, Serbia, Spain, Switzerland, Turkey, United Kingdom.

[43]PA Motion for a recommendation, *Protection of "whistle-blowers"*, Doc. 11269, 23 April 2007.

[44]Ibid., para 4.

[45]Ibid., para 2.

[46]GRECO, *Seventh General Activity Report (2006), Including a section on the "Protection of whistleblowers"*, Greco (2007) 1E Final, 21 March 2007, p. 10.

[47]PA Motion for a recommendation, *Protection of "whistle-blowers"*, Doc. 11269, 23 April 2007, para 6.

[48]Committee on Legal Affairs and Human Rights of the Council of Europe [hereinafter "Committee on Legal Affairs"], *Report on the protection of "whistle-blowers"*, Summary, Doc. 12006, 14 September 2009.

[49]Committee on Legal Affairs, *Report on the protection of "whistle-blowers"*, Explanatory memorandum, para 1.

[50]Ibid., paras 97–109.

[51]Ibid., para 8.

[52]Ibid., para 23.

[53]Ibid., paras 14 and 24.

3.2.1.1 Guiding Principles to Protect Whistleblowers

The primary issues identified were linked, on the one hand, to the lack of a common definition,[54] and on the other hand, to the general skepticism towards whistleblowing in certain cultures,[55] which seemed to be related to its negative connotation,[56] the political and administrative norms of a country[57] and concerns in regard to the protection of data and privacy protection.[58] While this reluctance of CoE Member States to adopt strong whistleblower protection regulations leaves individuals defenseless to retaliation and can thus hinder the investigation of alleged wrongdoings or illegal practices,[59] the rapporteur observed a shift of perception in recent years, in part linked to the efforts made by NGOs and international organizations in improving the image of whistleblowers.[60]

3.2.1.2 A Legal Framework

On the basis of the existing whistleblower protection laws applicable in certain States, the Committee on Legal Affairs identified a number of existing best practices to protect whistleblowers effectively: First and foremost, a *specific law* should be dedicated to the protection of whistleblowers, encompassing the report of all kind of wrongdoings,[61] applicable to the public as well as to the private sector,[62] and distinct from witness protection laws, which represents a framework insufficient to address the particular challenges facing whistleblowers, in particular with respect to the retaliatory measures they might suffer from prior to any judicial proceedings.[63] According to the rapporteur, such a *law should not put a duty to blow the whistle* upon employees, except in cases where there is a danger to the life and limb of individuals.[64] In relation to the protection against retaliation, the *confidentiality* of the whistleblower's identity[65] should be preferred to anonymity,[66] while an *effective enforcement mechanism* should be put in place in order to investigate the whistleblower report and allow them to file complaints for compensation if they

[54]Ibid., paras 26–27.
[55]Ibid., para 28.
[56]Ibid., para 30.
[57]Ibid., para 28.
[58]Ibid., para 29.
[59]Ibid., para 31.
[60]Ibid., para 115.
[61]Ibid., para 116 (a).
[62]Ibid., para 116 (b).
[63]Ibid., para 116 (c).
[64]Ibid., para 116 (j).
[65]Ibid., para 116 (e).
[66]Ibid., para 116 (f).

suffer prejudice for having blown the whistle,[67] with a *"whistle-blower-friendly" burden of proof* as an inherent part of such a mechanism.[68] The effectiveness of whistleblower laws should also be *regularly monitored*.[69]

3.2.1.3 The Status of Whistleblower

In regard to the applicability of the law, considerations should be made to *expand its personal scope* so as to include not only workers but also individuals outside of organizations.[70] While the good faith of the whistleblower should not necessarily be defined according to her or his motives, "as a matter of ethics and of the credibility of the information divulged", the rapporteur *excluded pecuniary advantage* for blowing the whistle as an option, and preferred to put the focus on whether the whistleblower had *reasonable grounds* to believe that the information disclosed was true, even if it is later revealed to be incorrect.[71]

3.2.1.4 Awareness Campaign

In order to change the perception of whistleblowing and promote whistleblower mechanisms as an effective tool to combat wrongdoings, whistleblower mechanisms should be promoted among employees within public and private entities[72] and be the subject of *awareness campaigns* in order to inform society as a whole about the positive impacts of whistleblowers and their role to "deter and correct wrongdoing and promote transparency and good governance".[73] The rapporteur encouraged the PA to adopt a resolution promoting the value of whistleblowers, and suggested to establish common standards so as to provide concrete proposals for legislative improvements.[74] Likewise, the PA should also recommend that the CM take further action to promote the protection of whistleblowers within CoE Member States and draw up guidelines to that effect.[75] In order to lead by example, the rapporteur suggested to introduce a strong internal whistleblower protection mechanism "covering all sectors of the Council of Europe".[76]

---

[67] Ibid., para 116 (h).

[68] Ibid., para 116 (i).

[69] Ibid., para 116 (k).

[70] Ibid., para 116 (d).

[71] Ibid., para 116 (g).

[72] Ibid., para 116 (l).

[73] Ibid., para 116 (m).

[74] Ibid., para 117.

[75] Ibid., paras 118–119.

[76] Ibid., paras 116 (n) and 120.

3.2.2 *The First Step Towards Common European Standards for Whistleblower Protection*

On April 29th 2010, the Resolution 1729[77] and the Recommendation 1916[78] on the protection of whistleblowers were unanimously adopted by the PA, in line with the propositions made by the Committee on Legal affairs.

The PA Resolution 1729 was voted in unanimity, sending a strong message of support for the protection of whistleblowers. Using the definition developed by the Committee on Legal Affairs in its 2007 report, Resolution 1729 defines whistleblowers as "individuals who sound an alarm in order to stop wrongdoings that place fellow human beings at risk – as their actions provide an opportunity to strengthen accountability and bolster the fight against corruption and mismanagement, both in the public and private sectors".[79] Acknowledging the specific challenges facing whistleblowers[80] and the courage required to report wrongdoings, the PA recognized the necessity to develop "a safe alternative to silence"[81] and thus promoted four key aspects of an effective whistleblower protection legislation: (1) A comprehensive framework;[82] (2) the establishment of secure reporting channels;[83] (3) in cases where the whistleblower claimed to have suffered from retaliatory measures, the burden of proof should lie on the employer to establish beyond a reasonable doubt that those measures were not linked to the whistleblower report;[84] and finally, (4) the effectiveness of the legislation should be monitored and regularly evaluated by independent bodies[85] in order to recalibrate it if necessary.

3.2.2.1 An Extensive Protection Framework

A Broad Scope of Application and Effective Internal Channels

More specifically, a legislation on the protection of whistleblowers should have the broadest possible scope, extending to a wide variety of wrongdoings[86] and covering the private as well as the public sector, including the military and special units.[87] The

---

[77]PA Resolution 1729 (2010) *Protection of "whistle-blowers"*.

[78]PA Recommendation 1916 (2010) *Protection of "whistle-blowers"*.

[79]PA Resolution 1729 (2010) *Protection of "whistle-blowers"*, para 1.

[80]Ibid., para 2.

[81]Ibid., para 5.

[82]Ibid., para 6.1.

[83]Ibid., para 6.2.

[84]Ibid., para 6.3.

[85]Ibid., para 6.4.

[86]Ibid., para 6.1.1.

[87]Ibid., para 6.1.2.

legislation should encourage private and public entities to set up internal channels of reporting[88] and should ensure that individuals who act in good faith when using those internal channels[89] benefit from protection against retaliation.[90]

Good Faith: Between Reasonable Grounds and Motives

According to the PA Resolution 1729, good faith should be understood as "reasonable grounds to believe that the information disclosed was true, even if it later turns out that this was not the case, and provided he or she did not pursue any unlawful or unethical objectives".[91] Under this definition, both objective and subjective elements are included,[92] promoting a traditional idea of good faith under a whistleblower protection framework, which includes the motive of the whistleblower as a qualifying factor. This position seems to diverge from the viewpoint held by the rapporteur of the Committee on Legal Affairs, who focused on the reasonable grounds of the whistleblower as the leading element of good faith.[93]

In fact, according to the understanding of the European Commission for Democracy through Law (hereinafter referred to as "Venice Commission"), the CoE's advisory body on constitutional matters,[94] while the PA Resolution 1729 places the motives as "the key element in deciding whether the whistleblower should be given protection",[95] it does not provide any information as to who should carry the burden to prove the existence of unlawful or unethical objectives, or lack thereof.[96] In the Venice Commission's opinion however, whistleblowers should not have to prove their good motives, though they can be required to demonstrate that the information disclosed is "at least *prima facie* credible", without having to prove that it is "perfectly accurate".[97] While it agreed that the motive may shed light on the whistleblower's character, the Venice Commission held that the approach promoted by the PA should be reconsidered to align with the more cautious position taken the ECtHR in its *Guja* ruling, protection having to "be primarily based on *the service to society*".[98]

---

[88]Ibid., para 6.2.1.

[89]Ibid., para 6.2.4.

[90]Ibid., para 6.2.2

[91]Ibid., para 6.2.4.

[92]European Commission for Democracy through Law [hereinafter "Venice Commission"], *Opinion on the Law on the protection of privacy and on the Law on the protection of whistleblowers of "the former Yugoslav Republic of Macedonia"*, Op. No. 829/2015, CDL-AD(2016)008, 15 March 2016, para 69 *in fine*.

[93]Committee on Legal Affairs, *Report on the protection of "whistle-blowers"*, Explanatory memorandum, para 116 (g).

[94]On the Venice Commission see Grabenwarter (2017), pp. 732–746.

[95]Venice Commission, *Op. No. 829/2015*, para 72.

[96]Ibid., para 70.

[97]Ibid., para 71.

[98]Ibid., para 73 (on the public interest aspect see also paras 65-66 of the same opinion); on the ECtHR *Guja* ruling see Sect. 4.3.

A Comprehensive Approach to Whistleblowing

Individuals using external reporting channels or reporting to the media shall also be protected under an effective whistleblower protection legislation, if internal channels are inexistent, inefficient or inappropriate to address the report.[99] In parallel to such a legislation, the PA emphasized the necessity to change the culture around whistleblowing[100] and underlined the important role of NGOs in promoting a positive image of whistleblowers.[101]

3.2.2.2 Call for Action

Need for Internal, National and International Reforms

In its Recommendation 1916 on the Protection of whistleblowers,[102] the PA called on the CM to develop guiding principles[103] and envisage the possibility to develop a framework convention on the protection of whistleblowers.[104] It also encouraged the CM to invite all CoE Member and Observer States to review their national legal frameworks in order to determine whether they are in compliance with the whistleblowing guidelines developed by the PA in its Resolution.[105] Last but not least, the PA suggested to strengthen the CoE internal whistleblowing mechanism[106] and organize an European conference on the protection of whistleblowers.[107]

The Response of the Committee of Ministers

In its reply,[108] the CM confirmed the PA's position on whistleblowers, reiterating their key role "in increasing accountability and strengthening the fight against corruption and mismanagement", and the need to establish an effective protection scheme.[109] In this respect, the CM further emphasized that whistleblowing is closely linked to the protection of journalistic sources, which should also be ensured as an effective means to protect whistleblowers.[110] Responding to the call of the PA, the CM confirmed that the possibility to develop common guidelines for the protection

[99] PA Resolution 1729 (2010) *Protection of "whistle-blowers"*, para 6.2.3.

[100] Ibid., para 7.

[101] Ibid., para 8.

[102] PA Recommendation 1916 (2010) *Protection of "whistle-blowers"*.

[103] Ibid., para 2.1.

[104] Ibid., para 2.3.

[105] Ibid., para 2.2.

[106] Ibid., para 3.2; see also PA Resolution 1729 (2010) *Protection of "whistle-blowers"*, para 9.

[107] Ibid., para 3.1.

[108] CM Reply to Recommendation 1916, Doc. 12479, 24 January 2011.

[109] Ibid., para 2.

[110] Ibid., para 4.

of whistleblowers will be carefully examined,[111] and proceeded with the adoption of its own recommendation on the protection of whistleblowers.

3.3 The Committee of Ministers' Recommendation: A Foundation Stone for Whistleblower Protection in Europe

The CM Recommendation on the protection of whistleblowers CM/Rec(2014)/7,[112] adopted in 2014, quickly became the *foundation stone* for a harmonized understanding of whistleblower protection in Europe. Indeed, when reference is made to the CoE Recommendation on whistleblower protection, it generally refers to the Recommendation of the Committee of Ministers rather than that of the PA. The Recommendation CM/Rec(2014)7, in which the Committee of Ministers recalled the principle previously developed by the PA, emphasized that whistleblowers "can contribute to strengthening transparency and democratic accountability", and called on CoE Member States to develop legislation on the protection of whistleblowers using the common principles set by the CM in the appendix to the Recommendation CM/Rec(2014)7. These 29 principles, aiming to guide CoE Member States in the process of strengthening or introducing national legislation on whistleblowing, represented a strong momentum in the establishment of European common rules to protect whistleblowers as it greatly influenced the EU legislator in the development of its own initiative.[113]

3.3.1 A Unifying Approach to Whistleblowing

3.3.1.1 Whistleblower: A Common European Definition

Considering the challenges linked to the lack of a commonly accepted statutory definition of the term "whistleblower" among CoE Member States, the first fundamental achievement of the CM Recommendation was to establish a common definition, which reads as follows: A whistleblower "means any person who reports or discloses information on a threat or harm to the public interest in the context of their work-based relationship, whether it be in the public or private sector".[114] The term *work-based relationship* reveals the aim to base the personal scope not on the

---

[111] Ibid., para 5.

[112] CM, *Recommendation CM/Rec(2014)7 on the Protection of Whistleblowers* [hereinafter "CoE Recommendation CM/Rec(2014)7"], 30 April 2014.

[113] See Sect. 8.1.2.2.

[114] CoE Recommendation CM/Rec(2014)7, *Appendix*, Definitions (a).

specific legal status or nature of the working relationship of the person reporting wrongdoing but rather on the *de facto* relationship between the organization and the reporting individual, allowing for the broadest possible personal scope,[115] the key reason to protect whistleblowers being *their economic vulnerability*.[116] However, according to Principle 3, protection should be afforded, whether the work-based activity is remunerated or not,[117] which implies that the economic vulnerability is not the mere reason to afford protection, the occupational dependency can also justify protection. Principe 4 goes further, extending the personal scope to individuals "whose work-based relationship has ended", and considering the possibility to also include those whose work-based relation has yet to begin.[118] This principle demonstrates that, while an effective whistleblower protection law should be limited to a work-based context and address the specific challenges in that respect, the CM also recognizes the general public interest of whistleblowing and thus the benefit of a framework designed to facilitate reports or disclosures[119] and promote a safe environment for blowing the whistle.[120] Those principles illustrate the balancing exercise conducted by the CM between the interest to receive information of wrongdoing and the necessity to delimit the scope of application in the attempt to establish an European consensus.

3.3.1.2 The Rejection of the Good Faith Criterion

According to Principle 22, protection should be afforded so long as the whistleblower "had reasonable grounds to believe" in the accuracy of the information reported or disclosed.[121] In the explanatory memorandum to the Recommendation CM/Rec(2014)7, the CM emphasizes that "the principle has been drafted in such a way as to preclude either the motive of the whistleblower in making the report or disclosure or of his or her good faith in so doing as being relevant to the question of whether or not the whistleblower is to be protected".[122] With this formulation, the CM seems to want to prevent diverging interpretations linked to the different national definitions of good faith and so promote a more harmonized appreciation of the whistleblower protection framework brought forward by the Recommendation. The EU has also taken this approach, refraining from using the term "good faith" in its EU Whistleblower Directive, preferring to refer to the formulation laid

[115]CoE Recommendation CM/Rec(2014)7, *Explanatory memorandum*, para 31.

[116]CoE Recommendation CM/Rec(2014)7, *Explanatory memorandum*, para 45.

[117]CoE Recommendation CM/Rec(2014)7, *Appendix*, Point 3 (Principle 3).

[118]CoE Recommendation CM/Rec(2014)7, *Appendix*, Point 4 (Principle 4).

[119]CoE Recommendation CM/Rec(2014)7, *Appendix*, Point 1 (Principle 1); on the use of the term 'facilitate', see CoE Recommendation CM/Rec(2014)7, *Explanatory memorandum*, para 36.

[120]CoE Recommendation CM/Rec(2014)7, *Appendix*, Point 12 (Principle 12).

[121]CoE Recommendation CM/Rec(2014)7, *Appendix*, Point 22 (Principle 22).

[122]CoE Recommendation CM/Rec(2014)7, *Explanatory memorandum*, para 85.

down in Principle 22 of the CM Recommendation.[123] It reveals an international trend, away from the use of the term "good faith", towards the "reasonable grounds to believe" requirement, which has the advantage to minimize the national margin of appreciation in regard to the application of international protection standards.

However, while the exclusion of the motive as a qualifying criterion should be welcomed, the CM's categorical rejection of the element of "good faith" may create confusion. Considering that the principle of *bona fides*, good faith, is commonly used in the context of whistleblower protection legislation, a clarification would have been more advisable. Indeed, because some national whistleblower laws include good faith as a qualifying criterion, as does the ECtHR in its case-law on the protection of whistleblowers under Article 10 ECHR, the CM should have taken this reality into account in its explanatory memorandum and specified that if applicable, the element of good faith should be defined as the reasonable grounds to believe in the accuracy of the information, even if it is later revealed as false or incorrect. This formulation would have made clear that the European conception of good faith in a whistleblower protection context is understood to exclude the motive of the whistleblower as relevant criterion, which would have narrowed the interpretative margin of national authorities and unified the level of protection for whistleblowers across Europe. In this respect, the clear stand of the CM on the subject would have provided clarity and promoted a common and consistent analysis of the element of good faith.

3.3.2 A Whistleblowing Framework

3.3.2.1 Dedicated Instruments to Protect Whistleblowers

Because CoE Member States' domestic legal traditions and systems widely differ, the Committee of Ministers used the term *framework* to leave national authorities a margin of discretion in the choice of instruments used to protect whistleblowers.[124] In this context, "framework" should be understood as "an arrangement of various normative, institutional and judicial elements which, together, provide a comprehensive and coherent whole"[125] establishing an effective whistleblowing mechanism[126] empowering competent authorities to conduct prompt investigations,[127]

[123]Article 6(1)(a) Directive (EU) *2019/1937 of the European Parliament and of the Council of 23 October 2019 on the protection of persons who report breaches of Union law* [hereinafter "EU Whistleblower Directive"], OJ L 305, 26.11.2019, p. 17, "they had reasonable grounds to believe that the information on breaches reported was true at the time of reporting".

[124]CoE Recommendation CM/Rec(2014)7, *Explanatory memorandum*, para 29.

[125]CoE Recommendation CM/Rec(2014)7, *Explanatory memorandum*, para 35; see also CoE Recommendation CM/Rec(2014)7, *Appendix*, Point 7 (Principle 7).

[126]CoE Recommendation CM/Rec(2014)7, *Appendix*, Point 9 (Principle 9).

[127]Ibid., *Appendix*, para 19. (Principle).

meaning without delay,[128] and have the resources to be effective.[129] Also, while the CM left it to CoE Member States to determine what constitutes a report or disclosure in the public interests, it emphasized that the scope of the domestic framework should reach a minimum standard and include "violations of law and human rights, as well as risks to public health and safety and to the environment".[130] The balancing exercise conducted by CoE Member States in order to take the different interests into consideration, from the interest of employers to the public interest to receive information on wrongdoing,[131] should be guided by the overall principle that any restrictions or exceptions in regard to the protection of whistleblowers should be "no more than necessary".[132] The nature of the domestic restrictions and exceptions introduced by CoE Member States remain to be seen; their legitimacy will most certainly be the subject of judgments by the ECtHR.

3.3.2.2 The National Security Sector: Exceptions Without Exemption

In this respect, Principle 5 formulates a significant yet common exception, specifying that the whistleblowing of "information relating to national security, defence, intelligence, public order or international relations of the State", may be subjected to different rules.[133] However, in line with the 2006 PA Resolution encouraging CoE Member States to include, in their state secrecy laws, an effective whistleblower framework in order to protect individuals who disclose information on illegal state actions,[134] the CM emphasized that those sectors cannot be fully exempt from whistleblower protection mechanisms.[135] In this respect, it specified that the modified whistleblower protection scheme applicable to those sectors should leave the personal scope untouched and focus on restricting, if necessary, the material scope, namely the information susceptible to be excluded from a whistleblower framework.[136] This principle addresses one of the main points of tension in the development of a legal framework protecting whistleblowers: A legitimate interest of States to keep certain information secret and the extent to which whistleblowers could or should be protected when disclosing such secrets. In this respect, the CM, like the PA in its 2013 Resolution on National security and access to information,[137]

[128] CoE Recommendation CM/Rec(2014)7, *Explanatory memorandum*, para 73.

[129] CoE Recommendation CM/Rec(2014)7, *Explanatory memorandum*, para 55.

[130] CoE Recommendation CM/Rec(2014)7, *Appendix*, Point 2 (Principle 2).

[131] CoE Recommendation CM/Rec(2014)7, *Explanatory memorandum*, para 51.

[132] CoE Recommendation CM/Rec(2014)7, *Appendix*, Point 8 (Principle 8).

[133] CoE Recommendation CM/Rec(2014)7, *Appendix*, Point 5 (Principle 5)

[134] PA Resolution 1507 (2006) *Alleged secret detentions and unlawful inter-state transfers of detainees involving Council of Europe member states*, para 19.5.

[135] CoE Recommendation CM/Rec(2014)7, *Explanatory memorandum*, paras 46–47.

[136] Ibid., para 47.

[137] PA Resolution 1954 (2013) *National security and access to information*, paras 7–8.

endorsed the Tshwane Principles as a guiding text in the development of appropriate whistleblower protection rules within the defense, security and intelligence sector.[138] According to the Committee on Legal Affairs, however, Principle 5 sets an excessively broad derogation for the intelligence sector due to the absence of a specific framework defining "national security" and determining the procedure for national security-related disclosures.[139]

3.3.2.3 Clear Reporting Channels

According to the CM Recommendation, the necessity to establish clear and easily accessible reporting channels,[140] which should include internal, external and public reporting channels,[141] is a key element of an effective whistleblower protection framework. Employers should therefore be encouraged to adopt effective internal reporting procedures,[142] where few to no restrictions should be put in place,[143] and where an effective follow-up, informing the whistleblower on the actions taken in response to her or his report, should be provided.[144] While reports through internal channels or to competent public authorities should be encouraged,[145] the CM further emphasized the democratic relevance of public disclosure of information, as part of the protection of the right to freedom of expression.[146] In this respect, the circumstances of each cases shall determine the most appropriate reporting channel,[147] a position criticized by the Committee on Legal Affairs which suggested to introduce clearer rules under which whistleblowers can use public reporting channels.[148] According to the Committee of Ministers, the coordination between the internal, external and public disclosure procedures should be carefully organized in order to avoid a fragmentation of the protection shield.[149]

---

138 On the Tshwane Principles see Sect. 2.3.2.3.

139 Committee on Legal Affairs and Human Rights, *Report on Improving the protection of whistle-blowers*, Explanatory Memorandum, Doc. 13791, 19 May 2015, para 31.

140 CoE Recommendation CM/Rec(2014)7, *Appendix*, Point 13 (Principle 13).

141 CoE Recommendation CM/Rec(2014)7, *Appendix*, Point 14 (Principle 14).

142 CoE Recommendation CM/Rec(2014)7, *Appendix*, Points 15 and 24 (Principles 15 and 24).

143 CoE Recommendation CM/Rec(2014)7, *Explanatory memorandum*, para 63.

144 CoE Recommendation CM/Rec(2014)7, *Appendix*, Point 20 (Principle 20).

145 CoE Recommendation CM/Rec(2014)7, *Appendix*, Point 17 (Principle 17).

146 CoE Recommendation CM/Rec(2014)7, *Explanatory memorandum*, para 60.

147 CoE Recommendation CM/Rec(2014)7, *Appendix*, Point 14 *in fine* (Principle 14).

148 Committee on Legal Affairs, *Report on Improving the protection of whistle-blowers*, Explanatory memorandum, paras 51–54.

149 CoE Recommendation CM/Rec(2014)7, *Explanatory memorandum*, para 38 *in fine*.

3.3.2.4 Protection Scheme

The CM Recommendation also emphasized that, considering the risk incurred by whistleblowers, confidentiality should be ensured as part of an effective whistleblower protection framework.[150] Protecting their identity eases the reporting process by lowering the restraint to report, thus following the goal to facilitate the report of wrongdoing. In regard to the damage suffered by whistleblowers, the CM underlined that an effective framework should entail protection against any kind of retaliation, which is crucial to ensure a strong confidence in the procedure and its effectiveness[151] and to *avoid the chilling effect* that it can have on future whistleblowers.[152] Retaliation is used intentionally and should be understood as comprising a *close causal link* between the whistleblower report and the sanction imposed on the person reporting,[153] sanctions which can take various forms, such as "dismissal, suspension, loss of promotion opportunities, punitive transfers and reductions in or deduction of wages, harassment or other punitive or discriminatory treatment".[154] The CM leave it to CoE Member States to define the kind of protection which should be afforded, in order to be coherent with their domestic legal principles.[155] However, it specified that the employer should carry the burden of demonstrating that the sanction taken was unrelated to the report made by the whistleblower[156] while *interim relief* should be granted to whistleblowers having suffered damages from reporting.[157]

3.3.3 Information Campaign and Monitoring

On a wider scale, the CM highlighted the necessity to promote the positive image of whistleblowers in CoE Member States[158] and make information and confidential advice on whistleblowing procedures free and easily accessible to the general public.[159] The CM also called on CoE Member States to regularly assess the effectiveness of the national legal framework put in place[160] and undertake

[150] CoE Recommendation CM/Rec(2014)7, *Appendix*, Point 18 (Principle 18).
[151] CoE Recommendation CM/Rec(2014)7, *Appendix*, Point 21 (Principle 21).
[152] CoE Recommendation CM/Rec(2014)7, *Explanatory memorandum*, paras 78 and 80.
[153] CoE Recommendation CM/Rec(2014)7, *Explanatory memorandum*, para 83.
[154] CoE Recommendation CM/Rec(2014)7, *Appendix*, Point 21 (Principle 21).
[155] CoE Recommendation CM/Rec(2014)7, *Explanatory memorandum*, para 82.
[156] CoE Recommendation CM/Rec(2014)7, *Appendix*, Point 25 (Principle 25).
[157] CoE Recommendation CM/Rec(2014)7, *Appendix*, Point 26 (Principle 26).
[158] CoE Recommendation CM/Rec(2014)7, *Appendix*, Point 27 (Principle 27).
[159] CoE Recommendation CM/Rec(2014)7, *Appendix*, Point 28 (Principle 28).
[160] CoE Recommendation CM/Rec(2014)7, *Appendix*, Point 29 (Principle 29).

adjustments if necessary.[161] Those inputs were well received by the rapporteur of the Committee on Legal Affairs.[162]

3.4 Whistleblowers and National Security

3.4.1 The Global Impact of National Security Whistleblowing

3.4.1.1 From an Additional Protocol to the ECHR on the Protection of Whistleblowers…

Shortly after the first media outlets revealed documents leaked by Edward Snowden on the mass-surveillance schemes used by the NSA,[163] members of the PA adopted a motion for a recommendation entitled "Additional protocol to the European Convention on Human Rights on the protection of whistle-blowers who disclose governmental action violating international law and fundamental rights".[164] Referring to the persecution of Chelsea Manning, which resulted from the leak of documents related to allegations of misconduct of the US military in Iraq, the 20 signatories of the motion insisted that "[a]bstract arguments of military and State secrecy as well as national security should not be allowed to hamper the effective implementation of the rule of law" and that thus, an additional protocol to the ECHR should integrate provisions protecting civil servants as whistleblowers who reveal human rights and international law violations.[165] Two years later, the Committee on Legal Affairs published its report on the subject, entitled "Improving the protection of whistle-blowers", moving away from the initial idea of adding a protocol to the ECHR. While recalling the important role of whistleblowers in the fight against corruption and human rights violations,[166] the rapporteur particularly emphasized the significance of the disclosure made by Edward Snowden, which shed light "on abuses by the intelligence sector, which has so far been *de facto* excluded from whistle-blower protection measures",[167] and has thus contributed to the public interest.[168]

---

[161] CoE Recommendation CM/Rec(2014)7, *Explanatory memorandum*, para 94.

[162] Committee on Legal Affairs, *Report on Improving the protection of whistle-blowers*, Explanatory Memorandum, paras 56-57.

[163] MacAskill et al. (2013, 6 June), McCarthy (2013, 9 June) and Greenwald et al. (2013, 11 June).

[164] PA, Motion for a recommendation, *Additional protocol to the European Convention on Human Rights on the protection of whistle-blowers who disclose governmental action violating international law and fundamental rights*, Doc. 13278, 5 July 2013.

[165] Ibid.

[166] Committee on Legal Affairs, *Report on Improving the protection of whistle-blowers*, Explanatory Memorandum, para 1.

[167] Ibid., para 2; see also Committee on Legal Affairs, *Report on Mass surveillance*, Doc. 13734, 18 March 2015.

[168] Ibid., para 60.

3.4.1.2 … to a Legally Binding Framework Convention on Whistleblowing

According to the Committee on Legal Affairs, the change in name from "an additional protocol to the ECHR on the protection of whistleblowers who disclose governmental action violating international and fundamental rights", used in the motion for a recommendation, to "Improving the protection of whistle-blowers",[169] aimed to encourage the adoption of a legally binding framework convention, independent of the ECHR, which would take into consideration the different national legal systems and avoid the necessity of ratification by all CoE Member States as it is the case for additional protocols to the ECHR.[170] Contrary to the Committee on Legal Affairs' claim, protocols to the ECHR which introduce additional human rights guarantees do not have to be ratified by all CoE Member States to enter into force, an additional protocol to the ECHR having the significant advantage of falling within the jurisdiction of the ECtHR,[171] thus opening the door to individual applications.[172] The Committee on Legal Affairs proposal to establish a legally binding framework convention remains nonetheless an ambitious proposal, which would establish a homogenous whistleblower protection framework across Europe and draw upon the Recommendation of the CM adopted in 2014.[173] Its aims to be opened to signature by non-European States[174] would represent the first step towards an internationally binding instrument establishing common rules for the protection of whistleblowers. Such an initiative would promote an internationalization of the status of whistleblower, which would in turn raise the level of protection offered through unified standards.[175]

3.4.2 *"The Sword of Damocles" of Protected Disclosures?*

In its report, the Committee on Legal Affairs emphasized the particular importance of whistleblower protection in the secret service sector given the specific challenges facing whistleblowers working for national intelligence agencies. "The whistleblower's freedom of expression and the people's freedom of information clashes with the intelligence agent's duty to protect secret information; transparency and democratic accountability clash with the need for secrecy for intelligence operations

[169]Ibid., para 3.

[170]Ibid., para 80.

[171]Article 32(1) ECHR.

[172]Article 34 ECHR.

[173]CoE Recommendation CM/Rec(2014)7.

[174]Committee on Legal Affairs, *Report on Improving the protection of whistle-blowers*, Explanatory Memorandum, para 80 *in fine*.

[175]Lochak (2016), para 41.

to be effective".[176] In this respect, the rapporteur observed that the intelligence sector is therefore often excluded from legal whistleblower protection frameworks.[177] Referring to whistleblowers within intelligence agencies as "the 'sword of Damocles' of protected disclosures of abuses", the rapporteur underlined their key role of ensuring that the surveillance activities undertaken by those agencies will not extend beyond the limits of legality[178] and thus the necessity to further the protection of whistleblowers in general and in particular those working in national security-related fields.[179]

3.4.2.1 Freedom of Expression vs. Secrecy

Notwithstanding the need for secrecy and confidentiality in certain state-related affairs, the rapporteur stressed, much like the CM in its Recommendation on the protection of whistleblowers, that the sectors of Intelligence and National Security should not be exempt from scrutiny.[180] The delicate balance between the right to freedom of expression and the duty of confidentiality of an official working in the Intelligence sector or in relation with national security issues should be addressed in a whistleblower protection scheme that prohibits the total exclusion of accountability on be grounds of confidentiality and national security.[181] Keeping in mind the PA Resolution 1838, "Abuse of State secrecy and national security: obstacles to parliamentary and judicial scrutiny of human rights violations", and the Tshwane Principles[182] endorsed by the PA in its Resolution 1854 on "National security and access to information", the rapporteur proposed to reassess and readjust the whistleblower protection schemes in place for individuals working for the intelligence sector in light of the new revelations made, *inter alia*, by Edward Snowden.[183]

3.4.2.2 Democratic Scrutiny of the Intelligence Sector

This position is coherent with previous PA Resolutions which encouraged CoE Member States to include, in their state secret laws, an effective whistleblower

[176]Committee on Legal Affairs, *Report on Improving the protection of whistle-blowers*, Explanatory memorandum, para 4.

[177]Ibid., paras 2, 59–72.

[178]Ibid., para 62; see also PA Resolution 1838 (2011) *Abuse of State secrecy and national security: obstacles to parliamentary and judicial scrutiny of human rights violations*; PA Resolution 1954 (2013) *National security and access to information.*

[179]Ibid., para 104.

[180]Ibid., paras 4, 104.

[181]Ibid., paras 4, 62.

[182]On the Tshwane Principles see Sect. 2.3.2.3.

[183]Committee on Legal Affairs, *Report on Improving the protection of whistle-blowers*, Explanatory memorandum, para 59.

framework, in order to protect individuals who disclose information on illegal state actions,[184] following concerns that some had threatened or attempted to persecute whistleblowers on allegations of breach of state secrecy.[185] It also reflects the position of the European Parliament (EP), which called on EU Member States to guarantee democratic scrutiny of their intelligence agencies through effective internal oversight by parliamentary bodies who shall be authorized to have unrestricted access to information related to the operational work of the agencies,[186] deeming the regulations applicable to the intelligence services of certain EU Member States inadequate to ensure effective control.[187] This scrutiny over the intelligence sector and the limits to state secret laws appeared all the more relevant following whistleblower disclosures revealing serious concerns over human rights violations, especially in regard to US actions in the fight against terrorism. In this context, the EP regretted that the 'war on terror' declared by the US following the 9/11 attacks lead to a "serious and dangerous erosion of human rights and fundamental freedoms".[188] According to an established position of the European Union, "effective counter-terrorism measures and respect for human rights are not contradictory, but are complementary and mutually reinforcing aims",[189] a principle confirmed by the Venice Commission in its opinion on the international legal obligations of CoE Member States in respect of secret detention facilities and inter-state transport of prisoners.[190] The erosion of human rights and fundamental freedoms revealed by whistleblowers and the prize they had to paid following their disclosures was made particularly evident in the Edward Snowden case.

[184]PA Resolution 1507, para 19.5.

[185]PA Resolution 1551 (2007) *Fair trial issues in criminal cases concerning espionage or diverging state secrets*, para 8.

[186]Recital 20 *European Parliament resolution on alleged transportation and illegal detention of prisoners in European countries by the CIA: follow-up of the European Parliament TDIP Committee report (2012/2033(INI))*, P7_TA(2012)0309, 11 September 2012.

[187]Recital 3 *European Parliament resolution on the alleged use of European countries by the CIA for the transportation and illegal detention of prisoners, adopted midway through the work of the Temporary Committee (2006/2027(INI))*, P6_TA(2006)0316, 6 July 2006.

[188]Recital 2 *European Parliament resolution on the alleged use of European countries by the CIA for the transportation and illegal detention of prisoners (2006/2200(INI))*, P6_TA(2007)0032, 14 February 2007.

[189]Recital 2 *European Parliament resolution on alleged transportation and illegal detention of prisoners in European countries by the CIA: follow-up of the European Parliament TDIP Committee report (2012/2033(INI))*.

[190]Venice Commission, *Opinion on the International Legal obligations of Council of Europe Member States in respect of Secret detention facilities and inter-state transport of prisoners*, Op. No. 363/2005, CDL-AD(2006)009, 17 March 2006, para 154.

3.4.2.3 The Position of the Committee on Legal Affairs on the Snowden Case

According to the principles promoted by the Committee on Legal Affairs in its report, the rapporteur stated that a whistleblower like Edward Snowden should be protected from retaliation, any possibility of criminal prosecution for the disclosure of confidential information being prohibited.[191] Indeed, following a thorough analysis of the facts of the case, the Committee on Legal Affairs concluded that the information disclosed by Edward Snowden was authentic and revealed acts of wrongdoings.[192] The Committee on Legal Affairs also considered that Edward Snowden did not have adequate internal channels available to report his concerns and that thus, the public disclosure was legitimate.[193] In regard to the amount of information disclosed and the harm suffered by the State because of the disclosure,[194] the Committee on Legal Affairs was of the opinion that "the extent of the disclosure was reasonably necessary", and that the public interest to receive that information overrode the interest of the State to keep it secret.[195]

3.4.3 *"Improving the Protection of Whistleblowers"*

3.4.3.1 Protection of Whistleblowers in the Security Sector

The report resulted in the adoption of Resolution 2060 entitled "Improving the protection of whistle-blowers",[196] with 88 in favor, 7 against and 10 abstentions[197] and Recommendation 2073 on "Improving the protection of whistle-blowers",[198] adopted 86 in favor, 7 against and 9 abstentions.[199] In Resolution 2060, the PA stressed that whistleblower protection should be afforded to everyone, including those working in the national security and the intelligence sector, "who denounce wrongdoings which place fellow human beings at risk of violations of their rights protected under the European Convention on Human Rights".[200] Considering that individuals disclosing information related to national security are generally excluded

---

[191] Committee on Legal Affairs, *Report on Improving the protection of whistle-blowers*, Explanatory memorandum, para 98.

[192] Ibid., para 84.

[193] Ibid., paras 85–88.

[194] Ibid., para 89.

[195] Ibid., para 98.

[196] PA Resolution 2060 (2015) *Improving the protection of whistle-blowers*.

[197] Voting results for the PA Resolution 2060: 88 in favor, 7 against and 10 abstentions.

[198] PA Recommendation 2073 (2015) *Improving the protection of whistle-blowers*.

[199] Voting results for the PA Recommendation 2073: 86 in favor, 7 against, 9 abstentions.

[200] PA Resolution 2060 (2015) *Improving the protection of whistle-blowers*, para 8.

from whistleblower laws' protection coverage,[201] the PA Recommendation 2073 thus called for the negotiation process of a legally binding framework convention which should also ensure protection for employees working in the intelligence and national security sector.[202]

3.4.3.2 A Legally Binding Instrument?

Such legally binding framework convention having to be draw upon the CM Recommendation CM/Rec(2014)7 on the protection of whistleblowers adopted in 2014,[203] the PA invited the CM to take the initiative in the negotiations.[204] However, the adoption of a convention was viewed with caution by the CM. While it did not exclude such initiative in the long term, the CM recalled that its 2014 Recommendation already included principles related to the disclosure of information on national security and intelligence matters, thus preferring to focus on "the promotion and implementation of Recommendation CM/Rec(2014)7".[205] It also gave the European Committee on Legal Co-operation the task to determine when "a more formal review of the implementation of the recommendation" will be deemed appropriate.[206] The CM reiterated its position in 2020, stating that "the negotiation of a binding instrument, such as a convention, would be time consuming and there would be no certainty as to its outcome".[207]

3.4.3.3 Asylum for Whistleblowers

In its Resolution 2060, the PA animated the CoE Member States to grant asylum to public officials working for intelligence agencies or in the field of national security if they are prosecuted in their home country,[208] provided that the information disclosed falls within one of the categories identified by the PA in its Resolution on national security and access to information,[209] its first Resolution on the protection of whistleblowers[210] or the CM Recommendation CM/Rec(2014)7 on the protection of whistleblowers.[211] Finally, the PA called on the US to allow the return of Edward

[201] Ibid., para 7.
[202] PA Recommendation 2073 (2015) *Improving the protection of whistle-blowers*, para 3.1.
[203] PA Resolution 2060 (2015) *Improving the protection of whistle-blowers*, para 10.1.3.
[204] PA Recommendation 2073 (2015) *Improving the protection of whistle-blowers*, para 3.1.
[205] CM, *Reply to Recommendation 2073*, Doc. 13949, 25 January 2016, para 5.
[206] Ibid., para 6.
[207] CM, *Reply to Recommendation 2162*, Doc. 15099, 29 Avril 2020, para 8.
[208] PA Resolution 2060 (2015) *Improving the protection of whistle-blowers*, paras 9 and 10.1.2.
[209] PA Resolution 1954 (2013) *National security and access to information*.
[210] PA Resolution 1729 (2010) *Protection of "whistle-blowers"*.
[211] CoE Recommendation CM/Rec(2014)7.

Snowden and refrain from prosecuting him without allowing him the public interest defense.[212] While it reiterated the principles established in its recommendation,[213] according to which whistleblowers disclosing information related to national security, defense or intelligence should not be completely without protection,[214] the CM did not address the proposal of the PA to grant asylum to whistleblowers nor did it mention the case Edward Snowden, revealing the particularly sensitive issue around whistleblowers, national security issues and international relations.

3.5 Better Protection for Whistleblowers

3.5.1 On the International Level

3.5.1.1 Preventing a Legal Divide…

Following the April 2019 preliminary agreement on the draft of the EU Whistleblower Directive,[215] the PA adopted Resolution 2300[216] and Recommendation 2162[217] on the protection of whistleblowers, entitled "Improving the protection of whistle-blowers all over Europe", which emphasized the important role of whistleblowers in democratic societies[218] and welcomed the efforts of a number of CoE Member States in the development of national legal frameworks protecting whistleblowers more effectively.[219] Despite the CM's reluctance to adopt such instrument, the PA reiterated its call for a legally binding convention to prevent "a new legal divide" in the area of whistleblower protection between EU Member States and the other CoE Members, a convention which should draw upon the standards set by the EU Whistleblower Directive while including the improvements proposed by the PA.[220] It also called on EU Member States to transpose the EU Whistleblower Directive as soon as possible[221] and include the additional measures

---

[212]PA Resolution 2060 (2015) *Improving the protection of whistle-blowers*, paras 10.2.

[213]CM, *Reply to Recommendation 2073*, para 5.

[214]CoE Recommendation CM/Rec(2014)7, *Appendix*, Point 5 (Principle 5) in conjunction with the explanatory memorandum of the same recommendations, paras 46 et seq.

[215]On the EU Whistleblower Directive see Sect. 8.4.

[216]PA Resolution 2300 (2019) *Improving the protection of whistle-blowers all over Europe*.

[217]PA Recommendation 2162 (2019) *Improving the protection of whistle-blowers all over Europe*.

[218]PA Resolution 2300 (2019) *Improving the protection of whistle-blowers all over Europe*, para 1.

[219]Ibid., para 6.

[220]PA Recommendation 2162 (2019) *Improving the protection of whistle-blowers all over Europe*, para 3.

[221]PA Resolution 2300 (2019) *Improving the protection of whistle-blowers all over Europe*, para 13.1.1.

proposed in its Resolution 2300,[222] such as the establishment of a legal support fund[223] and the creation of a national independent authority responsible for the protection of whistleblowers.[224] To CoE Member States who are not members of the EU, the PA encouraged them to further their whistleblower protection laws by using the model of the EU Whistleblower Directive.[225]

3.5.1.2 ... by Promoting a Legally Binding Convention on Whistleblowing

According to the Committee on Legal Affairs, a legally binding convention would ensure the adoption of a comprehensive legal framework by all CoE Member States and promote a harmonized level of protection for whistleblowers across Europe[226] while preventing the establishment of whistleblower protection rules limited to certain sectors.[227] Such a convention would take into account the particular challenges linked to new data protection regulations and govern the issues related to SLAPP lawsuits.[228] SLAPP stands for "Strategic lawsuits against public participation" and can be defined as "groundless or exaggerated lawsuits and other legal forms of intimidation... against weaker parties... who express criticism or transmit messages uncomfortable to the powerful, on a public matter".[229] According to the PA, a convention on whistleblower protection should include the possibility for legal entities to blow the whistle and be protected as "whistleblowing facilitators"[230] and ensure effective guidance for individuals working within national security-related fields through the provision of specific rules.[231] Under the convention, each signatory State would have to create an independent authority[232] competent to assist

[222]PA Resolution 2300 (2019) *Improving the protection of whistle-blowers all over Europe*, para 13.1.2.

[223]PA Resolution 2300 (2019) *Improving the protection of whistle-blowers all over Europe*, para 12.4.

[224]PA Resolution 2300 (2019) *Improving the protection of whistle-blowers all over Europe*, paras 12.3 and 13.1.2.

[225]Ibid., para 13.2.

[226]Committee on Legal Affairs, *Report on Improving the protection of whistle-blowers all over Europe*, Explanatory memorandum, Doc. 14958, 30 August 2019, para 25.

[227]Ibid., para 23.

[228]Ibid., paras 12 and 23; Paper signed by 119 organizations to end SLAPP lawsuits see N.N. (2020, 9 June).

[229]Bard et al. (2020), p. 4; see also Last Week Tonight (2019, 11 November).

[230]PA Resolution 2300 (2019) *Improving the protection of whistle-blowers all over Europe*, para 12.1.

[231]Ibid., para 12.2.

[232]Ibid., para 12.3.

whistleblowers,[233] ensure that their reports are followed by appropriate measures,[234] and work in cooperation with judicial authorities.[235] Those authorities should be part of an European network in order to create an independent European observatory in charge of sharing best practices and be a reliable focal point for the CoE.[236] The convention should also create a legal support fund to finance high quality legal services for whistleblowers.[237] Last but not least, the PA also proposed to appoint a general rapporteur on whistle-blowers, who would be in charge of promoting whistleblowing cases and ensuring visibility of the subject.[238]

3.5.2 On the Regional and Local level

In the same vein as the PA and the CM, the Congress of Local and Regional Authorities emphasized the importance of disclosures made in the public interest[239] and thus the "vital contribution" of whistleblowers in "promoting greater transparency and accountability in local and regional authorities".[240] According to the Congress, a legal framework which offers effective protection for whistleblowers on the local and regional level increases the chance to bring to light wrongdoings which have a negative impact on the resources available to the local and regional communities, hence increasing the organizational effectiveness and resource efficiency of public institutions.[241] Unfortunately, while progress has been made on a national and international level to better protect whistleblowers, the Congress noted that legal protection on the local and regional level remains the exception.[242] This is particularly unfortunate given the proximity of local and regional authorities with citizens through the provision of public services and the close public-private relationship.[243] Indeed, the conclusion of public service delegation contracts and other forms of contracts between the private and the public sector exposes local and regional authorities in particular to corruptive practices.[244]

---

[233] Ibid., para 12.3.1.

[234] Ibid., para 12.3.2.

[235] Ibid., para 12.3.3.

[236] Ibid., para 12.3.4.

[237] Ibid., para 12.4.

[238] Ibid., para 14.

[239] Congress, *The protection of whistleblowers: Challenges and opportunities for local and regional government*, Explanatory memorandum, Report CG36(2019)14 final, 3 April 2019, para 2.

[240] Congress, *The protection of whistleblowers,* Recommendation 435 (2019), para 2.

[241] Congress, *The protection of whistleblowers*, Explanatory memorandum, paras 2–5.

[242] Congress, *The protection of whistleblowers*, Explanatory memorandum, para 7.

[243] Congress, *The protection of whistleblowers,* Resolution 444 (2019), para 3.

[244] Ibid.

3.5.2.1 The Particular Vulnerability of Local and Regional Authorities

According to the Congress' explanatory memorandum, aside from traditional issues related to the scope of application of whistleblower protection frameworks,[245] from the information on the types of wrongdoings which could be the object of reports[246] to need of follow-ups[247] in order to strengthen the trust in the effectiveness of existing reporting channels,[248] one of the main challenges which could seriously affect the effectiveness of whistleblower protection rules on the local and regional level is the lack of opportunity to blow the whistle anonymously.[249] Based on the conclusion of a report prepared by the Association of Certified Fraud Examiners,[250] the Congress further underlined the lost opportunities of disclosure when stripping individuals of the possibility to report anonymously.[251] This specific complication can be rectified if the regional and local legal framework protecting whistleblowers takes this particularity into account and allows individuals who are working for small entities to have direct access to external channels to report on wrongdoing[252] or have access to hotlines.[253] If the possibility of anonymous reports cannot be offered, providing 'pre-emptive protection' against retaliation should be offered to whistleblowers.[254] The Congress Resolution and Recommendation on the protection of whistleblowers, adopted in 2019, confirmed this position.[255]

3.5.2.2 Whistleblowing Mechanisms Dedicated to the Local and Regional Level

Referring to several CoE documents on the fight against corruption,[256] the Congress called on local and regional authorities to develop whistleblower protection policies in accordance with the guiding principles developed by the CM in its Recommendation CM/Rec(2014)7.[257] The Congress drew upon those guiding principles to

[245]Congress, *The protection of whistleblowers*, Explanatory memorandum, para 88.

[246]Congress, *The protection of whistleblowers*, Explanatory memorandum, para 89.

[247]Congress, *The protection of whistleblowers*, Explanatory memorandum, para 90.

[248]Congress, *The protection of whistleblowers*, Explanatory memorandum, para 85.

[249]Congress, *The protection of whistleblowers*, Explanatory memorandum, para 84.

[250]Association of Certified Fraud Examiners (2016).

[251]Congress, *The protection of whistleblowers*, Explanatory memorandum, para 17.

[252]Congress, *The protection of whistleblowers*, Explanatory memorandum, para 83.

[253]Congress, *The protection of whistleblowers*, Explanatory memorandum, paras 87, 88; see also Congress, *The protection of whistleblowers,* Resolution 444, para 8 f) hotline accessible to employees working for the private sector.

[254]Congress, *The protection of whistleblowers*, Explanatory memorandum, para 84.

[255]Congress Resolution 444, para 8 d); Congress Recommendation 435, para 8 a) ii).

[256]Congress, *The protection of whistleblowers*, Explanatory memorandum, paras 7. a) and b).

[257]Congress, *The protection of whistleblowers*, Explanatory memorandum, para 8 a).

develop its own resolution and called on the local and regional authorities to establish internal and external channels[258] for the public as well as for the private sector.[259] Further, it called on them to ensure that independent authorities have the competence to receive and follow-up on disclosure[260] and provide widely accessible information on the legal protection of whistleblowers as well as on the different reporting methods available.[261] The fact that the Congress acknowledged the confidentiality challenges that whistleblowers might face when reporting on wrongdoing committed by local authorities suggests that the above recommendation to establish internal channels refers to regional rather than local authorities. The Congress also recommended to provide access to confidential advisors within organizations,[262] as well as for the possibility to obtain advice from external entities, which should respect the conditions of confidentiality and gratuitousness set by the Principle 28 of the CM Recommendation.[263] In accordance with Principles 27 and 29 of the CM Recommendation, the Congress called on Regional and Local authorities to raise public awareness to promote a positive image of whistleblowing[264] and introduce periodic assessments in order to evaluate the effectiveness of the whistleblower protection rules put in place.[265]

Finally, it also called on associations to assist local and regional authorities in the development and implementation of policy protection for whistleblowers, create training programs for competent authorities, raise awareness of the instruments in place and ensure coherence between the different regional and local policies through contact with anti-corruption agencies.[266] A harmonized framework across localities and regions appeared also necessary for uncovering wrongdoing more effectively. Indeed, given the fact that the effects of wrongdoings often impact more than one locality or region, cooperation between the different local and regional competent authorities can provide an overall more effective protection of whistleblowers.[267]

---

[258] Congress, *The protection of whistleblowers*, Explanatory memorandum, paras 8 b), c) and d), in reference to CoE Recommendation CM/Rec(2014)7, *Appendix*, Point 14.

[259] Congress, *The protection of whistleblowers*, Explanatory memorandum, para 8 f).

[260] Congress, *The protection of whistleblowers*, Explanatory memorandum, paras 8 c) and g), in reference to CoE Recommendation CM/Rec(2014)7, *Appendix*, Points 19–20.

[261] Congress, *The protection of whistleblowers*, Explanatory memorandum, para 8 e), in reference to CoE Recommendation CM/Rec(2014)7, *Appendix*, Point 28.

[262] Congress, *The protection of whistleblowers*, Explanatory memorandum, para 8 b).

[263] Congress, *The protection of whistleblowers*, Explanatory memorandum, para 8 i).

[264] Congress, *The protection of whistleblowers*, Explanatory memorandum, para 8 h).

[265] Congress, *The protection of whistleblowers*, Explanatory memorandum, para 8 j).

[266] Congress, *The protection of whistleblowers*, Explanatory memorandum, paras 9 a), b) and c).

[267] Congress, *The protection of whistleblowers*, Explanatory memorandum, para 91.

3.5.3 On the Internal Front: Blowing the Whistle Within the Council of Europe

3.5.3.1 A Positive First Step

Following the adoption of the first PA Recommendation on whistleblower protection, which advocated a strong internal whistleblowing mechanism within the CoE itself,[268] the CoE Secretary General adopted, in January 2011, Rule No. 1327 on awareness and prevention of fraud and corruption[269] with the explicit aim of strengthening the protection of individuals reporting, in good faith,[270] on suspicion of fraud or corruption[271] by defining specific reporting procedures to that effect.[272] It introduces an obligation for CoE Secretariat Staff members "to report any reasonable suspicion of misconduct they deem to be fraud or corruption to the Director of Internal Oversight".[273] It also encourages all individuals involved in CoE activities to report any suspicion of misconduct directly to the Secretary General of the CoE.[274] If the particularly broad personal scope and the focus on the element of suspicion demonstrate the willingness of the CoE to establish a wide protection shield for whistleblowers, the introduction of a duty to report is particularly problematic and should be reconsidered by the CoE. In general terms, while the protection mechanism offered to whistleblowers working for or in cooperation with the CoE does entail the key elements of an effective framework, the description of the rules applicable remains rather vague and incomplete.

3.5.3.2 With Room for Improvement

The resulting lack of clarity is unfortunate as it creates uncertainty and can negatively affect the effectiveness of the reporting mechanism introduced. Without fully closing the loopholes left by Rule No. 1327, the section "Investigation" on the CoE website partially compensate for the lack of clarity by providing additional information on what or how to report.[275] In the section "How to report fraud or corruption" for example, different internal reporting means are listed, such as the

[268] PA Recommendation 1916 (2010) *Protection of "whistle-blowers"*, para 3.2.

[269] CoE, Rule No. 1327 of 10 January 2011 on awareness and prevention of fraud and corruption.

[270] Article 7 CoE Rule No. 1327.

[271] Article 3(c) CoE Rule No. 1327.

[272] Article 3(b) CoE Rule No. 1327.

[273] Article 4(1) CoE Rule No. 1327.

[274] Article 4(2) in conjunction with Article 2(2) CoE Rule No. 1327.

[275] CoE, *Investigation* website. https://www.coe.int/en/web/internal-oversight/fraud-reporting-investigation. Accessed 13 April 2021.

report through the online “Fraud reporting form”.[276] That said, the wording of the section “Is fraud reporting anonymous”[277] should be reconsidered to clearly lay out the distinction between confidentiality and anonymity as the current formulation may lead to confusion. Indeed, while Rule No. 1327 specifies that the identity of the reporting individual “shall not be disclosed” unless the latter has explicitly renounced this requirement,[278] it does not provide any specific details regarding anonymous reporting. Particular attention should also be given to the lack of information in regard to reports made outside of the internal channels described under Article 4 of Rule No. 1327.[279] Like other international organizations, the CoE faces the same challenges when introducing external whistleblower channels and should draw on the experience of the WBG and the UN.[280] CoE whistleblower policies should also include a defined period to follow-up and investigate the report of suspicion of fraud or corruption[281] in order to ensure an efficient procedure and build trust in the effectiveness of the investigations conducted.

3.5.3.3 Protection Against Retaliation

In the case of retaliation against an individual who has reported on suspicions of fraud or corruption, the latter has the right to seek advice from the Director General of Administration.[282] The investigation into alleged cases of retaliation follows a two-phase procedure: First, the Director General of Administration shall conduct a preliminary assessment of the situation and, if there are reasonable grounds to believe that those allegations are substantiated, the Secretary General is requested to verify those allegations “in accordance with the relevant internal regulatory instruments of the Council of Europe”.[283] While the individual concerned by those alleged retaliatory measures should remain informed about the progress of the inquiry into the matter,[284] interim protective measures could be taken by the Secretary General pending the outcome of the investigations.[285] Those regulations

---

[276] CoE, *Which means of reporting are available?* link. https://www.coe.int/en/web/internal-oversight/how-to-report-information-on-possible-fraud-or-corruption-. Accessed 13 April 2021.

[277] CoE, *Is fraud reporting anonymous?* link. https://www.coe.int/en/web/internal-oversight/how-to-report-information-on-possible-fraud-or-corruption-. Accessed 13 April 2021.

[278] Article 5(2) CoE Rule No. 1327.

[279] Committee on Legal Affairs, *Report on Improving the protection of whistle-blowers*, Explanatory memorandum, para 75.

[280] On the internal whistleblowing rules of the United Nations and the World Bank Group see Sect. 2.6.

[281] Committee on Legal Affairs, *Report on Improving the protection of whistle-blowers*, Explanatory memorandum, para 76.

[282] Article 6(3) CoE Rule No. 1327.

[283] Article 6(5) CoE Rule No. 1327.

[284] Article 6(8) CoE Rule No. 1327.

[285] Article 6(6) CoE Rule No. 1327.

represent a positive first step towards a stronger internal whistleblowing mechanism applicable to the CoE[286] but it remains insufficient in consideration of the principles promoted by the CM and the PA.[287]

3.6 Intermediate Conclusion

While the CoE needs to reform its own internal rules on whistleblowing, its overall influence in the development of national laws protecting whistleblowers cannot be underestimated. Both the PA, in putting the protection of whistleblowers on the European political agenda at the beginning of the last decade, and the CM, by establishing common European standards, had a significant impact on the general acceptance of the concept of whistleblowing in Europe. This has been all the more evident during the development of the EU Whistleblower Directive adopted in late 2019. As will be illustrated below, the Commission of the European Union (EU Commission) used the model of the CM Recommendation to prepare its own impact assessment for an EU-wide initiative on whistleblowing. The EU Whistleblower Directive is revolutionary in so far as it introduces a legal obligation for EU Member States to establish national whistleblower frameworks within 2 years after the adoption of the Directive. This EU initiative raises the level of protection for whistleblowers not only within EU Member States but also within other CoE Member States, which could be encouraged to introduce similar legislation, as part of the their accession to the EU.[288] The 2019 PA Resolution 2300, which calls on all CoE Member States to use the EU Whistleblower Directive as a model in the development of their own whistleblower protection laws,[289] illustrates the reciprocal influence between the CoE and the EU in the field of whistleblowing, sending an encouraging sign for the future harmonization in regard to whistleblower protection across Europe. This international and supranational legal coverage is particularly welcome considering that in the "flat world"[290] we live in, cases of misconduct and their detrimental consequences have an increasing spill-over effect beyond national borderlines. This observation makes the PA's call for a legally binding convention all the more pertinent. The adoption of an international convention on the protection of whistleblowers, unimaginable only two decades ago, may soon become a reality considering the rising number of national legislations

[286]Committee on Legal Affairs, *Report on Improving the protection of whistle-blowers*, Explanatory memorandum, para 73.

[287]PA Resolution 2060 (2015) *Improving the protection of whistle-blowers*, para 6.

[288]This can be observed in several Balkan countries, which adopted whistleblower laws, such as Albania, Montenegro or Serbia see Zivkovic (2019), p. 4.

[289]PA Resolution 2300 (2019), *Improving the protection of whistle-blowers all over Europe*, para 13.2.

[290]In reference to Friedman (2005).

dedicated to the protection of whistleblowers and the increasing necessity to establish cross-border reporting channels in order to address the growing international effects of national cover-ups, crimes and misconduct. This project is getting tantalizingly concrete following the adoption of the new EU Whistleblower Directive, an important precedent in the internationalization of legal protection for whistleblowers.

References

Association of Certified Fraud Examiners (2016) Report to the Nations On occupational fraud and abuse: 2016 Global Fraud Study

Bard P, Bayer J, Chun Luk N, Vosyliute L (2020) Ad-hoc request: SLAPP in the EU context. EU-CITIZEN: Academic Network on European Citizenship Rights. https://ec.europa.eu/info/sites/info/files/ad-hoc-literature-review-analysis-key-elements-slapp_en.pdf. Accessed 13 Apr 2021

Churchill WS (1946, 19 September) Speech delivered at the University of Zurich

Friedman T (2005) The World is flat: a brief history of the globalized world in the 21st century. Allen Lan, London

Grabenwarter C (2017) Constitutional standard-setting and strengthening of new democracies. In: Schmahl S, Breuer M (eds) The Council of Europe: its law and policies. Oxford University Press, Oxford, pp 732–746

Greenwald G, MacAskill E, Poitras L (2013, 11 June) Edward Snowden: the whistleblower behind the NSA surveillance revelations. *The Guardian*

Last Week Tonight (2019, 11 November) SLAPP Suits: Last Week Tonight with John Oliver (HBO), HBO

Leach P (2017) The parliamentary assembly of the Council of Europe. In: Schmahl S, Breuer M (eds) The Council of Europe: its law and policies. Oxford University Press, Oxford, pp 166–211

Lochak D (2016) Les lanceurs d'alerte et les droits de l'Homme: réflexions conclusives. La Revue des droits de l'homme 10:1–21

MacAskill E, Borger J, Greenwald G (2013, 6 June) The National Security Agency: surveillance giant with eyes on America. *The Guardian*

McCarthy T (2013, 9 June) Edward Snowden identifies himself as source of NSA leaks – as it happened. *The Guardian*

N.N. (2020, 9 June) End gag lawsuits in Europe. https://www.eurocadres.eu/news/ending-gag-lawsuits-in-europe/. Accessed 13 Apr 2021

Palmer S (2017) The Committee of Ministers. In: Schmahl S, Breuer M (eds) The Council of Europe: its law and policies. Oxford University Press, Oxford, pp 137–165

Schaffarzik B (2017) Congress of local and regional authorities. In: Schmahl S, Breuer M (eds) The Council of Europe: its law and policies. Oxford University Press, Oxford, pp 269–295

Weiß N (2017) Origin and further development. In: Schmahl S, Breuer M (eds) The Council of Europe: its law and policies. Oxford University Press, Oxford, pp 3–22

Zivkovic K (2019) Blowing the whistle in the Balkan. International Bar Association, London

Part III
The European Court of Human Rights

Chapter 4
Whistleblower Protection Under the European Convention on Human Rights

4.1 Introduction

4.1.1 The European Convention on Human Rights

In parallel to the PA and CM efforts in promoting the adoption of national laws dedicated to the protection of whistleblowers among CoE Member States, the European human rights aspect of whistleblowing also gained particular attention in the last decade. In this context, the ECHR became a central human rights instrument for the protection of whistleblowers in Europe. Adopted in 1950 by the CoE Member States, the ECHR has become the greatest success story in international human rights protection,[1] taking a close to constitutional status in the European legal order[2] and establishing a pioneering system of human rights protection. As an instrument of international law, the ECHR establishes obligations *erga omnes partes* under international law.[3] However, its real effectiveness can only be appreciated on the basis of its integration in domestic legal systems, which can vary from State to State.[4] In the UK, for instance, the ECHR was incorporated into national law through the 1998 Human Rights Act while Austria has elevated the ECHR to a constitutional rank. To ensure that Contracting parties comply with their obligations under the ECHR, it has also put in place a judicial system: the ECtHR.

[1]Lambert Abdelgawad (2017), p. 505.

[2]Ibid., p. 465.

[3]Ibid., p. 473.

[4]Giegerich (2013).

© The Author(s), under exclusive license to Springer Nature Switzerland AG 2021
H. C. L. Yurttagül, *Whistleblower Protection by the Council of Europe, the European Court of Human Rights and the European Union*, European Union and its Neighbours in a Globalized World 3, https://doi.org/10.1007/978-3-030-78059-3_4

4.1.2 The European Court of Human Rights

Established in 1959, the ECtHR plays an important role in fostering closer unity between the countries of Europe through its interpretation of the ECHR. The European Commission on Human Rights, established in 1954, was one of the three organs constituting the original structure of the institution and created a significant body of work which paved the way for the ECtHR's interpretation of the ECHR.[5] Following the 1994 restructuring of the ECHR judicial system,[6] the European Commission on Human Rights was abolished and the ECtHR became a full-time institution, becoming an established judicial machinery.[7] While the roles of those initial organs were mainly focused on providing opinions,[8] the judgments of the current ECtHR (the effective implementation of which is supervised by the CM according to 46 ECHR) enjoy a high level of compliance[9] despite being primarily declaratory.[10] However, the difference of legal cultures between the 47 State parties to the ECHR raises particular challenges for the ECtHR in the establishment of an European consensus through its interpretation of the text.[11] This plurality of legal influences has lead the ECtHR to promote a dynamic approach to the interpretation of the ECHR,[12] following the teleological principle of *ut res magis valeat quam pereat*,[13] according to which the rights and freedoms protected by the ECHR shall be interpreted so as to ensure their practical and effective safeguard.[14] Likewise, this dynamic interpretation encouraged the ECtHR to establish the ECHR as a "living instrument" which must be interpreted in the light of present-day conditions.[15]

While the ECtHR has a supervisory power through its interpretation of the ECtHR, CoE Member States enjoy a certain margin of appreciation when they limit Convention rights, which can vary depending on the context: "The scope of the margin of appreciation will vary according to the circumstances, the subject-matter and its background; in this respect, one of the relevant factors may be the

---

[5] Ibid., p. 229.

[6] Protocol No 11 to the Convention for the Protection of Human Rights and Fundamental Freedoms, restructuring the control machinery established thereby of 11 May 1994, ETS No 155.

[7] Lambert Abdelgawad (2017), p. 470.

[8] Ibid., p. 231.

[9] Ibid., p. 249.

[10] ECtHR, *Abbaso v. Azerbaijan*, Appl. no. 24271/05, 17 January 2008, para 36.

[11] Lambert Abdelgawad (2017), p. 249.

[12] Ibid., p. 250.

[13] Ibid., p. 472.

[14] ECtHR, *Airey v. Ireland*, Appl. no. 6289/73, 9 October 1979, para 24, "The Convention is intended to guarantee not rights that are theoretical or illusory but rights that are practical and effective".

[15] ECtHR, *Tyrer v. UK*, Appl. no. 5856/72, 25 April 1978, para 31; ECtHR, *Johnston and Others v. Ireland*, Appl. no. 9697/82, 18 December 1986, para 53; ECtHR, *Inze v. Austria*, Appl. no. 8695/79, 28 October 1987, para 41; ECtHR, *Airey v. Ireland*, para 26.

existence or non-existence of common ground between the laws of the Contracting States".[16] For instance, Member States will enjoy a narrow margin of appreciation when an interference in the right to freedom of expression is concerned,[17] as it is one of the essential foundations of a democratic society,[18] while the ECtHR may leave CoE Member States a broader margin of appreciation in regard to their national security interests.[19] The identification of an emerging European consensus by the ECtHR, which requires a constant analysis of development in the different legal systems of the CoE Member States, is a never ending process which can be influenced by international trends or documents adopted by the other organs of the CoE.[20] As will be shown below, the jurisprudence of the ECtHR on the protection of whistleblowers under Article 10 ECHR initiated in 2008 and refined since may follow the same process considering the emerging European consensus on common standards for an effective whistleblower protection framework and the established best practices promoted by international organizations.

4.2 The Protection of Whistleblowers Under Article 10 ECHR

4.2.1 Article 10 ECHR

The ECtHR's case-law on whistleblowing is based on Article 10 ECHR, freedom of expression, which reads as follow:

1. Everyone has the right to freedom of expression. This right shall include freedom to hold opinions and to receive and impart information and ideas without interference by public authority and regardless of frontiers. This Article shall not prevent States from requiring the licensing of broadcasting, television or cinema enterprises.
2. The exercise of these freedoms, since it carries with it duties and responsibilities, may be subject to such formalities, conditions, restrictions or penalties as are prescribed by law and are necessary in a democratic society, in the interests of national security, territorial integrity or public safety, for the prevention of disorder or crime, for the protection of health or morals, for the protection of the reputation or rights of others, for preventing the disclosure of information received in confidence, or for maintaining the authority and impartiality of the judiciary.

[16]ECtHR, *Rasmussen v. Denmark*, Appl. no. 8777/79, 28 November 1984, para 40 ; ECtHR, *Sunday Times v. the United Kingdom (No. 1)*, Appl. no. 6538/74, 26 April 1979, para 59.

[17]ECtHR, *Lingens v. Austria,* Appl. no. 9815/82, 8 July 1986, para 42; ECtHR, *Castells v. Spain,* Appl. no. 11798/85, 23 April 1992, para 43; ECtHR, *Thorgeir Thorgeirson v. Iceland*, Appl. no. 13778/88, 25 June 1992, para 63.

[18]ECtHR, *Handyside v. the United Kingdom*, Appl. no. 5493/72, 7 December 1976, para 49.

[19]ECtHR, *Hadjianastassiou v. Greece*, Appl. no. 12945/87, 16 December 1992, para 47; ECtHR, *Pasko v. Russia*, Appl. no. 69519/01, 22 October 2009, para 87.

[20]Lambert Abdelgawad (2017), pp. 250–252.

4.2.1.1 General Principles

According to the ECtHR, freedom of expression is "one of the essential foundations of [a democratic society], one of the basic conditions for its progress and for the development of every man".[21] The ECtHR derives several freedoms from Article 10 ECHR, including the freedom to impart and receive information and ideas as well as freedom of the press. It also differentiates between fact-based information and judgment-based opinions.[22] In this respect, the ECtHR emphasized that Article 10 ECHR "is applicable not only to 'information' or 'ideas' that are favourably received or regarded as inoffensive or a matter of indifference, but also to those that offend, shock or disturb the State or any sector of the population. Such are the demands of that pluralism, tolerance and broadmindedness without which there is no 'democratic society'".[23] The protection of journalistic sources is also included within the ECtHR interpretative framework of Article 10 ECHR.[24] Particularly relevant in cases of whistleblowing, the ECtHR underlines that Article 10 ECHR also extends to the workplace[25] and covers civil servants[26] as well as individuals practicing liberal professions.[27]

4.2.1.2 The Limits to Freedom of Expression

According to Article 10(2) ECHR, the exercise of the right to freedom of expression carries with it duties and responsibilities and can thus be subjected to some

[21]ECtHR, *Handyside*, para 49.

[22]ECtHR, *Lingens*, para 46; see also ECtHR, *Jerusalem v. Austria*, Appl. no. 26958/95, 27 February 2001, para 42; ECtHR, *Dichand and Others v. Austria*, Appl. 29271/95, 26 February 2002, para 42.

[23]ECtHR, *Handyside*, para 49.

[24]e.g. ECtHR, *Goodwin v. United Kingdom* [GC], Appl. no. 17488/90, 27 March 1996, para 39.

[25]ECtHR, *Guja v. Moldova* [GC], Appl. no. 14277/04, 12 February 2008, para 52 ; ECtHR, *Kudeshkina v. Russia*, Appl. no. 29492/05, 26 February 2009, para 85 ; ECtHR, *Herbai v. Hungary*, Appl. no. 11608/15, 5 November 2019, para 36 ; ECtHR, *Soares v. Portugal*, Appl. no. 79972/12, 21 June 2016, para 39 ; ECtHR, *Balenović v. Croatia (Admissibility),* Appl. no. 28369/07, 30 September 2010 ; ECtHR, *Wojtas-Kaleta v. Poland*, Appl. no. 20436/02, 16 July 2009, para 42; ECtHR, *Gawlik v. Liechtenstein*, Appl. no. 23922/19, 16 February 2021, para 47.

[26]ECtHR, *Glasenapp v. Germany*, Appl. no. 9228/80, 28 Augst 1986, para 50; ECtHR, *Kosiek v. Germany*, Appl. no. 9704/82, 28 Augst 1986, para 36; ECtHR, *Haseldine v. United Kingdom (Admissibility),* Appl. no. 18957/91, 13 May 1992, p. 230 ; ECtHR, *Poyraz v. Turkey*, Appl. no. 15966/06, 7 December 2010, para 56 ; ECtHR, *Vogt v. Germany* [GC], Appl. no. 17851/91, 26 Septembre 1995, para 53 ; ECtHR, *Wille v. Liechtenstein* [GC], Appl. no. 28396/95, para 41 ; ECtHR, *Fuentes Bobo v. Spain*, Appl. no. 39293/98, 29 February 2000, para 38 ; ECtHR, *Guja*, para 52 ; ECtHR, *Kayasu v. Turquie*, Appl. nos, 64119/00 and 76292/01, 13 November 2008, para 77.

[27]ECtHR, *Ana Ioniță v. Romania*, Appl. no. 30655/09, 21 March 2017, para 40.

limitations. However, limitations to this right must be narrowly interpreted[28] and meet a set of specific requirements. Indeed, an interference under Article 10 ECHR is only permissible if it fulfills three cumulative conditions: It is prescribed by law, pursues a legitimate aim, and is necessary in a democratic society. Under the first condition, the ECtHR requires that the law "must be adequately accessible: the citizen must be able to have an indication that is adequate in the circumstances of the legal rules applicable to a given case. Secondly, a norm cannot be regarded as a 'law' unless it is formulated with sufficient precision to enable the citizen to regulate his conduct: he must be able - if need be with appropriate advice - to foresee, to a degree that is reasonable in the circumstances, the consequences which a given action may entail".[29] As regard the second condition, Article 10(2) ECHR enumerates several aims considered legitimate to limit the right to freedom of expression, including the interests of national security, the protection of the reputation or rights of others or preventing the disclosure of information received in confidence. Those aims are particularly relevant in regard to whistleblower cases, which regularly revolve around confidential information or national security issues and can often lead to reputational damage.

However, the main focus of every whistleblower case under the ECHR lies in the appreciation of the third condition: Whether the interference was necessary in a democratic society. According to the ECtHR, "the adjective 'necessary', within the meaning of Article 10 para. 2 of the Convention, is not synonymous with 'indispensable', neither does it have the flexibility of such expressions as 'admissible', 'ordinary', 'useful', 'reasonable' or 'desirable'; rather, it implies a 'pressing social need'".[30] CoE Member States have a certain margin of appreciation in this respect to appreciate the pressing social need of the interference, the extent of which may vary depending on the context.[31] However, according to its subsidiary role[32] and supervisory power, the ECtHR makes "the final determination as to whether the interference in issue corresponds to such a need, whether it is 'proportionate to the legitimate aim pursued' and whether the reasons given by the national authorities to justify it are 'relevant and sufficient'".[33] In this respect, the ECtHR's "task in exercising its supervisory function is not to take the place of the competent domestic

[28] ECtHR, *Thorgeir Thorgeirson*, para 63; ECtHR, *Observer and Guardian v. United Kingdom*, Appl. no 13585/88, 26 November 1991, para 59.

[29] ECtHR, *Sunday Times (No. 1)*, para 49.

[30] ECtHR, *Barthold v. Germany*, Appl. no. 8734/79, 25 March 1985, para 55 ; ECtHR, *Handyside*, para 48; ECtHR, *Sunday Times (No. 1)*, para 59 ; see also ECtHR, *Lingens*, para 39.

[31] ECtHR, *Rasmussen*, para 40.

[32] e.g. ECtHR, *Kudła v. Poland* [GC], Appl. no. 30210/96, 26 October 2000, para 152 ; ECtHR, *Cocchiarella v. Italy* [GC], Appl. no. 64886/01, 29 March 2006, para 38 ; ECtHR, *De Souza Ribeiro v. France* [GC], Appl. no. 22689/07, 13 December 2012, para 77.

[33] ECtHR, *Barthold*, para 55 ; see also ECtHR, *Handyside*, paras 48-49 ; ECtHR, *Sunday Times (No. 1)*, para 59; ECtHR, *Lingens*, para 39.

courts, but rather to review under Article 10 the decisions they have taken pursuant to their power of appreciation".[34]

4.2.2 *Duty of Loyalty vs. Whistleblowing*

4.2.2.1 Duty of Loyalty

In regard to the workplace environment, the ECtHR held that employees have a specific *duty of loyalty, reserve and discretion*,[35] which can legitimately limit the extent to which they can exercise their right to free speech.

For Civil Servants. . .

According to the Court, civil servants have particularly strong duties of loyalty, reserve and discretion[36] due to their mission "to assist the government in discharging its functions",[37] the public having the right "to expect that they will help and not hinder the democratically elected government".[38] By the very nature of their mission they may also be prohibited from disclosing information acquired in the performance of their duties if the State wishes, for legitimate reasons, to keep that information

---

[34] ECtHR, *Aurelian Oprea v. Romania*, Appl. no. 12138/08, 19 January 2016, para 58.

[35] ECtHR, *Guja*, para 70; ECtHR, *Marchenko v. Ukraine*, Appl. no. 4063/04, 19 February 2009, para 45; ECtHR, *Kudeshkina,* para 85; ECtHR, *Wojtas-Kaleta,* para 43 ; ECtHR, *Heinisch v. Germany*, Appl. no. 28274/08, 21 July 2011, para 63 ; ECtHR, *Trade Union of the Police in the Slovak Republic and Others v. Slovakia*, Appl. no. 11828/08, 25 September 2012, para 57 ; ECtHR, *Matúz v. Hungary*, Appl. no. 73571/10, 21 October 2014, para 32; ECtHR, *Rubins v. Latvia*, Appl. no. 79040/12, 13 January 2015, para 78; ECtHR, *Langner v. Germany*, Appl. no. 14464/11, 17 September 2015, para 43; ECtHR, *Kharlamov v. Russia*, Appl. no. 27447/07, 8 October 2015, para 27 ; ECtHR, *Aurelian Oprea*, para 59; ECtHR, *Soares,* para 41; ECtHR, *Marunić v. Croatia*, Appl. no. 51706/11, 28 March 2017, para 52; ECtHR, *Pay v. UK (Admissibility)*, Appl. no. 32792/05, 16 September 2008; ECtHR, *Gawlik*, para 65.

[36] ECtHR, *Guja*, para 70; ECtHR, *Marchenko,* para 45; ECtHR, *Kudeshkina,* para 85; ECtHR, *Trade Union of the Police in the Slovak Republic and Others,* para 57; ECtHR, *Rubins,* para 78; ECtHR, *Langner,* para 43; ECtHR, *Kharlamov*, para 27; ECtHR, *Aurelian Oprea*, para 59; ECtHR, *Soares,* para 41.

[37] ECtHR, *Haseldine (A),* p. 231 ; ECtHR, *Guja*, para 71; ECtHR, *Kosiek*, para 85; ECtHR, *Ahmed and Others v. United Kingdom*, Appl. no. 22954/93, 2 September 1998, para 53.

[38] ECtHR, *Guja*, para 71 ; see also ECtHR, *Ahmed and Others,* para 53.

confidential or secret.[39] Civil servants are thus under a particularly strong duty of discretion,[40] moderation and restrain when speaking publicly.[41]

... and Employees in Private Law Employment Relationships

Although in a lesser extent than in the case of civil servants, the ECtHR held that employees in private law employment relationships also have a duty of loyalty, reserve and discretion towards their employers, which can legitimately limit the exercise of their right to freedom of expression.[42]

4.2.2.2 Reporting of Illegal Conduct or Wrongdoing in the Workplace

While the ECtHR acknowledged that one of the precepts of the rule of law allows citizens "to notify competent State officials about the conduct of civil servants which to them appears irregular or unlawful",[43] in 2008, the ECtHR extended the possibility for employees to make use of their right to freedom of expression and report irregularities within their own institution.

For Civil Servants...

The *Guja v. Moldova* ruling was the first case in which the ECtHR had to decide whether a civil servant who publicly disclosed internal information revealing irregularities should be protected under Article 10 ECHR.[44]

---

[39]ECtHR, *Guja*, para 71.

[40]Ibid.; see also ECtHR, *Vogt,* para 53 ; ECtHR, *Hadjianastassiou*, para 46 ; ECtHR, *Ahmed und Others,* para 56 ; ECtHR, *Rekvényi v. Hungary* [GC], Appl. no. 25390/94, 20 May 1999, para 43 ; ECtHR, *De Diego Nafría v. Spain*, Appl. no. 46833/99, 14 March 2002, para 37 ; ECtHR, *Palomo Sánchez and Others v. Spain* [GC], Appl. nos. 28955/06, 28957/06, 28959/06 and 28964/06, Appl. no. 12 September 2011, para 76 ; ECtHR, *di Giovanni v. Italy*, Appl. no. 51160/06, 9 Juillet 2013, para 69 ; ECtHR, *Catalan v. Romania*, Appl. no. 13003/04, 9 Janvier 2018, para 61 ; ECtHR, *Poyraz*, para 57.

[41]ECtHR, *Catalan*, para 60; ECtHR, *Poyraz*, para 78; see also ECtHR, *Haseldine (A)*, p. 232: "a civil servant in a sensitive post should be subject to at least some restrictions and conditions on his freedom of expression concerning information gained in his official capacity ... or relating directly to his functions, particularly when these concern politically sensitive matters".

[42]ECtHR, *Wojtas-Kaleta,* para 43 ; ECtHR, *Heinisch,* para 64 ; ECtHR, *Matúz*, para 32; ECtHR, *Marunić,* para 52.

[43]ECtHR, *Zakharov v. Russia*, Appl. no. 14881/03, 5 October 2006, para 26 ; ECtHR, *Siryk v. Ukraine*, Appl. no. 6428/07, 31 March 2011, para 42 ; ECtHR, *Bezymyannyy v. Russia*, Appl. no. 10941/03, 8 April 2010, para 40 ; ECtHR, *Kazakov v. Russia*, Appl. no. 1758/02, 18 December 2008, para 28.

[44]ECtHR, *Guja*, para 72.

It recognized that:

> a civil servant, in the course of his work, may become aware of in-house information, including secret information, whose divulgation or publication corresponds to a strong public interest. The Court thus considers that the signalling by a civil servant or an employee in the public sector of illegal conduct or wrongdoing in the workplace should, in certain circumstances, enjoy protection. This may be called for where the employee or civil servant concerned is the only person, or part of a small category of persons, aware of what is happening at work and is thus best placed to act in the public interest by alerting the employer or the public at large.[45]

. . . and Employees Under Private Law Contracts

In its *Heinisch v. Germany* ruling, the ECtHR emphasized that the principles developed in the *Guja* judgment also applied to employees under private law contracts, stating:

> that the principles and criteria established in the Court's case-law with a view to weighing an employee's right to freedom of expression by signalling illegal conduct or wrongdoing on the part of his or her employer against the latter's right to protection of its reputation and commercial interests also apply in the case at hand.[46]

According to established case-law, Article 10 ECHR is indeed binding in private law employment relations, which can thus put, in certain circumstances, an obligation upon CoE Member States to protect employees' right to freedom of expression against interference by private persons.[47] It follows that whistleblowers working in private companies may also, in certain circumstances, enjoy protection under Article 10 ECHR.

---

[45] Ibid.

[46] ECtHR, *Heinisch,* para 64.

[47] ECtHR, *Gawlik*, para 47; ECtHR, *Lichtenstrasser v. Austria (Admissibility)*, Appl. no. 32413/08, 7 October 2014, para 27 ; ECtHR, *Aguilera Jiménez and Others v. Spain*, Appl. nos. 28389/06, 28955/06, 28957/06, 28959/06, 28961/06 and 28964/06, 8 December 2009, para 25; ECtHR, *Heinisch,* para 44 ; ECtHR, *Dink v. Turkey*, Appl. nos. 2668/07, 6102/08, 30079/08, 7072/09 and 7124/09, 14 September 2010, para 106; ECtHR, *Palomo Sánchez and Others*, para 59 ; ECtHR, *Matúz,* para 26; ECtHR, *Skwirut v. Poland (Admissibility)*, Appl. no. 11002, 4 November 2014, para 41; ECtHR, *Kaboğlu and Oran v. Turkey*, Appl. nos. 1759/08, 50766/10 and 50782/10, 30 October 2018, para 71; ECtHR, *Herbai*, para 37; ECtHR, *Fuentes Bobo*, para 38; ECtHR, *Ozgür Gündem v. Turkey*, Appl. no. 23144/93, 16 March 2000, para 43.

4.3 A Precedent-Setting Case: The *Guja* Ruling of the ECtHR

To determine whether an employee can be considered a whistleblower and enjoy protection under Article 10 ECHR, the ECtHR has thus to balance the employees' duty of loyalty, reserve and discretion against their right to freedom of expression. In the case *Guja v. Moldova*, the ECtHR for the first time developed different criteria on the basis of which the protection of whistleblowers should be appreciated under the ECHR, thereby making it a landmark case in European whistleblower protection jurisprudence.

4.3.1 Facts of the Case and Question of Law

4.3.1.1 The Applicant: A Civil Servant

The applicant was Head of the Press Department of the Moldovan Prosecutor General's Office at the time of the occurrence. In February 2002, four police officers arrested ten individuals suspected of infraction in relation to the parliamentary elections, who, after having been released, claimed to have been ill-treated and illegally detained. Following those allegations, the Prosecutor's office opened criminal investigations against the four police officers. In letters addressed to the President, the Prime Minister, and the Deputy Speaker of Parliament, the police officers complained that the criminal investigations were abusive and requested verification of the legality of those criminal charges brought against them. As a result, the Deputy Speaker of Parliament sent a letter to the Prosecutor General's Office which reads as follows: "Dear Mr Rusu, A question arises after reading this letter: is the Deputy Prosecutor General fighting crime or the police? This issue is made even more pressing by the fact that the policemen concerned are from one of the best teams in the Ministry of the Interior, whose activity is now being blocked as a result of the efforts of employees of the Prosecutor General's Office. I ask you personally to intervene in this case and solve it in strict compliance with the law".[48]

4.3.1.2 The Wrongdoing: Parliamentary Pressure on Law-Enforcement Officers

At the beginning of 2003 during a visit at the Centre for Combating Economic Crime and Corruption, the President publicly expressed his discontent about the issues related to the undue pressures put on law-enforcement bodies by public officials through pending criminal proceedings and called on law-enforcement officers to

[48]ECtHR, *Guja*, para 10.

ignore any pressure attempts from public officials.[49] The criminal proceedings were then dropped against the four police officers.[50] Following the President's address, the applicant transmitted to the Jurnal de Chişinău Newspaper copies of the letters sent to the Prosecutor General's Office, the first from the Deputy Speaker of Parliament, the second letter from a deputy minister in the Ministry of the Interior,[51] on the basis of which the newspaper published an article with the title "Vadim Mişin [the Deputy speaker of Parliament] intimidating prosecutors", with the two letters attached as photographs.[52]

4.3.1.3 The Disclosure: Report to the Press

The applicant, in his explanation to the Prosecutor General of why he decided to send the letter to the newspaper, declared that his action was in reaction to the President's address and motivated by the desire to help uncover abuses of power hindering the proper functioning of justice. He also underlined that the documents released were not secrets and that he did not intend to harm but rather promote a positive image of the Prosecutor's Office.[53] Following the dismissal of a prosecutor who was suspected of having disclosed those letters, the applicant wrote a second letter to the General Prosecutor, stating that if a breach of the internal regulation had been made, he should be made responsible for it. He also regretted that the Prosecutor General's Office elevated a letter from a public official to the status of State secret and considered it to be an example of the direct political implication in the administration of justice. He concluded by expressing his concerns as to the effective respect of the rule of law and human rights in the Republic of Moldova.[54]

4.3.1.4 Consequence: Dismissal of the Applicant

A few weeks after he sent that letter, the applicant was dismissed on the ground that the letter he had disclosed was secret and that he did not consult other heads of departments of the Prosecutor General's Office prior to the disclosure, which constituted a violation of the Internal Regulations of the Press Department.[55] The applicant filed a complaint against his dismissal on the following grounds: The letters disclosed were not classified as secret; he was not required to consult the other head of departments prior to the disclosure; he disclosed the letters at the

---

[49] Ibid., para 11.
[50] Ibid., para 12.
[51] Ibid., paras 13–14.
[52] Ibid., para 15–16.
[53] Ibid., para 18.
[54] Ibid., para 18–20.
[55] Ibid., para 21.

Newspaper's request; his dismissal violated his right to freedom of speech.[56] The Chişinău Court of Appeal dismissed the complaint on the grounds that the applicant acted in breach of the Internal Regulations of the Press Department by disclosing a secret document without consulting other heads of departments prior to the disclosure, a position confirmed by the Supreme Court of Justice of Moldova.[57]

4.3.1.5 Question of Law

The applicant alleged a breach of his right to impart information protected by Article 10 ECHR because he was dismissed after having disclosed information which allegedly demonstrated the interference of a high-ranking official in pending criminal proceedings.[58]

4.3.2 The Decision of the ECtHR

In accordance with its constant jurisprudence,[59] the ECtHR recalled that the scope of application of Article 10 ECHR extended to the workplace, and *inter alia* public servants.[60] In regard to the dismissal of the applicant due to the disclosure of the letters, the ECtHR recognized the existence of an interference within the meaning of Article 10(2) ECHR, which can constitute a breach of the right to freedom of expression if the interference did not fulfil the three conditions laid down in that paragraph, namely be prescribed by law, pursue a legitimate aim and be necessary in a democratic society.[61]

4.3.2.1 Prescribed by Law and Pursuing a Legitimate Aim

The ECtHR makes an assumption as to the first condition stating that it will assume that the provisions of the Labour Code and the Internal Regulations of the Press Department on the basis of which the applicant was dismissed fulfilled the first requirement, the action being thus prescribed by law.[62] Regarding the second condition, the ECtHR recognized the legitimacy of the aim pursued, namely to

---

[56]Ibid., para 22.

[57]Ibid., paras 23–25.

[58]Ibid., para 48.

[59]ECtHR, *Vogt,* para 53; ECtHR, *Wille,* para 41; ECtHR, *Ahmed and Others,* para 56 ; ECtHR, *Fuentes Bobo*, para 38.

[60]ECtHR, *Guja*, para 52.

[61]Ibid., paras 55–56.

[62]Ibid., paras 57–58.

prevent the disclosure of information received in confidence. The fact that the applicant refused to disclose the source of the information was deemed significant by the ECtHR, which therefore concluded that this refusal appeared to suggest that the information "was not easily or publicly available".[63]

4.3.2.2 Necessary in a Democratic Society: Free Speech vs. Duty of Loyalty

The ECtHR had therefore to determine whether the dismissal in response to the disclosure of internal information was indeed necessary in a democratic society and thus a legitimate interference of Article 10 ECHR.

While civil servants enjoy the right to freedom of expression, the ECtHR recognized that their "duty of loyalty, reserve and discretion to their employer"[64] is all the more relevant as they could get access, in the performance of their functions, to information that States have a legitimate interest in keeping confidential or secret.[65] The ECtHR notes, however, that some information, including that which is confidential and has come to the knowledge of a civil servant, could legitimately be published or divulged in response to a strong public interest. It therefore considered that civil servants who reported on illegal conduct or wrongdoing could be protected in certain circumstances:

> This may be called for where the employee or civil servant concerned is the only person, or part of a small category of persons, aware of what is happening at work and is thus best placed to act in the public interest by alerting the employer or the public at large.[66]

Consequently, the ECtHR had to respond to the inherent question in regard to whistleblowing: What represents a fair balance between the duty of loyalty and the right to freedom of expression? In its balancing exercise, the ECtHR developed a set of six criteria to determine whether the interest in disclosing internal information outweighs the duty of loyalty, reserve and discretion.

The Priority to Internal Channels

As a starting point, the ECtHR held that the disclosure should first be made to a superior or another competent authority and only as a last resort to the public if the first option is considered "clearly impracticable" and no other effective means to remedy the wrongdoing were available.[67]

---

[63] Ibid., para 59.
[64] Ibid., para 70.
[65] Ibid., para 71.
[66] Ibid., para 72.
[67] Ibid., para 73.

The Public Interest in the Disclosure

The public interest in the disclosure being a key factor in determining whether the interference in the individual's freedom of expression was necessary in a democratic society, the ECtHR recalled that debates on questions of public interest can suffer little restriction under Article 10(2) ECHR.[68] Indeed, in democratic societies, the public interest requires governmental actions or omissions to be closely scrutinized, not only by parliamentary or judicial oversight, but also by the media and the public, which can go as far as to outweigh a legally imposed duty of confidence.[69]

The Authenticity of the Information Disclosed

States can have a legitimate interest in preventing defamatory accusations lacking any basis or the diffusion of information made in bad faith,[70] thus the importance of determining the authenticity of the information disclosed.[71] Because freedom of expression carries with it duties and responsibilities, it is thus all the more important for individuals wishing to disclose information to "carefully verify, to the extent permitted by the circumstances, that it is accurate and reliable".[72]

The Damage Suffered by the Public Authority

After assessing the damage suffered by the public authority following the disclosure, the ECtHR has to determine whether it carries more weight than the public interest to obtain the information.[73] In this respect, the topic of the information disclosed and the nature of the public authority concerned should be taken into consideration.[74]

The Motive Behind the Disclosure

For the ECtHR, the reason which motivates an individual to disclose information has a determinant impact on the level of protection afforded. In reference to the *Haseldine* case, the ECtHR stated that "an act motivated by a personal grievance or a personal antagonism or the expectation of personal advantage, including pecuniary gain, would not justify a particularly strong level of protection".[75]

---

[68]Ibid., para 74.

[69]Ibid.

[70]see ECtHR, *Castells*, para 46 *in fine*.

[71]ECtHR, *Guja*, para 75.

[72]Ibid., para 75.

[73]Ibid., para 76.

[74]Ibid.

[75]Ibid., para 77.

According to the ECtHR, "it is important to establish that, in making the disclosure, the individual acted in good faith and in the belief that the information was true, that it was in the public interest to disclose it and that no other, more discreet, means of remedying the wrongdoing was available to him or her".[76]

The Severity of the Penalties

To determine whether the interference in the individual's right to freedom of expression was proportionate to the legitimate aim pursued, the ECtHR considered it necessary to analyze the penalties and its consequences on the individual having disclosed the information.[77]

4.4 The Six Whistleblowing Criteria

4.4.1 Reporting Channel Used

4.4.1.1 The Tiered Approach of the ECtHR

According to the ECtHR current case-law, an employee has the obligation to report the illegal conduct or wrongdoing internally first. If internal reporting cannot reasonably be expected, "external whistle-blowing should be protected",[78] public disclosure being only permissible as a last resort when the report to the superior or a competent body "is clearly impracticable".[79] This three-tiered model of reporting is coherent with the ECtHR's established jurisprudence connecting the level of protection afforded under Article 10 ECHR to the means used to exercise the right to freedom of expression.[80] In the ECtHR's reasoning, the requirement to report first to the superior would give the latter an opportunity "to investigate the veracity of the allegations".[81] However, the obligation to report internally first does not apply if "redress could not legitimately be expected".[82] An employee could thus be exempt from seeking internal clarification when the employer remained inactive despite being aware of the malpractice,[83] or if the employee "would render him or her liable

[76]Ibid.

[77]Ibid., para 78.

[78]ECtHR, *Heinisch*, para 73.

[79]ECtHR, *Guja*, para 73; ECtHR, *Heinisch,* para 65.

[80]ECtHR, *Haseldine (A)*, pp. 231–232 ; ECtHR, *Balenović (A),* 'wide circulation'.

[81]ECtHR, *Soares,* para 48.

[82]ECtHR, *Heinisch,* para 73.

[83]ECtHR, *Guja*, para 82; ECtHR, *Heinisch,* para 73; ECtHR, *Bucur and Toma v. Romania*, Appl. no. 40238/02, 8 January 2013, para 97; ECtHR, *Matúz*, para 47.

to criminal prosecution" if he or she does not uncover the information.[84] Similarly, the ECtHR considered it unreasonable to expect an employee to notify her or his superior if the latter is directly implicated in the illegal practice or wrongdoing subject of the report.[85] In contrast, if the whistleblower was aware of internal reporting channels and did not make use of it before disclosing the information publicly, the ECtHR denied whistleblower protection under Article 10 ECHR.[86]

4.4.1.2 The Question of Existing External Reporting Procedures

If internal notification to the hierarchical superior cannot be reasonably expected, the ECtHR will have to determine whether the employee had "any other effective means of remedying the wrongdoing which he intended to uncover", other than the public disclosure, which should be used as a last resort.[87] The lack of national "provision concerning the reporting of irregularities by employees",[88] in other words, the absence of a domestic legal whistleblower protection framework, is a key indicator for the ECtHR in determining whether effective means other than the public disclosure are available to the whistleblower. Indeed, in the absence of such legal framework and if the internal reporting to the superior is considered clearly impracticable, the ECtHR has systematically considered the external disclosure as justified.[89]

4.4.1.3 An Incentive to Introduce National Whistleblowing Mechanisms

This position represents a strong incentive for CoE Member States to introduce effective whistleblower protection provisions in their domestic legislation and for corporations to establish internal reporting channels.[90] Following the newly adopted EU Whistleblower Directive, it remains to be seen whether the ECtHR will consider the national transpositions of this Directive as effective means for reporting illegal conducts or wrongdoing. Depending on the ECtHR's position in regard to those national laws, and the implementation of reporting channels by public and private entities, public disclosure made by a whistleblower in those EU countries may be more strictly scrutinized, leading to a more restrictive access to public disclosure. However, given the sectorial character of the EU Whistleblower Directive, the

---

[84]ECtHR, *Heinisch,* para 73.

[85]ECtHR, *Guja*, para 82; ECtHR, *Bucur and Toma*, para 97.

[86]ECtHR, *Soares,* para 48.

[87]ECtHR, *Guja*, para 73; ECtHR, *Heinisch,* para 65.

[88]ECtHR, *Guja*, para 81.

[89]ECtHR, *Guja*, para 81; ECtHR, *Heinisch,* para 75; ECtHR, *Bucur and Toma*, para 96; ECtHR, *Görmüş and Others v. Turkey*, Appl. no. 49085/07, 19 Janvier 2016, para 61.

[90]Schlachter (2012), p. 112; Junod (2009), p. 260.

ECtHR might adopt a more nuanced approach to whistleblowing. In its 2021 *Gawlik* ruling, the Court already hinted at the possibility to depart from its previous case-law and adopt a more undifferentiated approach between reporting channels to align with the Recommendation CM/Rec(2014)7 adopted by the CM.[91] To reflect the consensus which emerged over the last decade in regard to European whistleblower protection, such a revision of the Court's jurisprudence towards a more horizontal approach should be encouraged.

4.4.2 The Public Interest in the Disclosed Information

Because Article 10 ECHR encompasses the right to receive information, the ECtHR held that the public interest to receive information "can sometimes be so strong as to override even a legally imposed duty of confidence".[92] Due to the lack of definition as to what constitutes such public interest, the ECtHR enjoys a certain flexibility in determining whether the information disclosed had indeed a public interest character. Nevertheless, it uses a set of recurrent elements to guide its assessment. If the wrongdoing the employee wishes to uncover has been the subject of a wide media coverage,[93] or was the object of national or international actions to fight against it,[94] the ECtHR will tend to recognize the public interest of the information disclosed. In this context, the ECtHR assesses whether the information disclosed contributed to the public debate.[95]

4.4.2.1 Key Democratic Principles

It will also refer to key democratic principles, such as "the transparent editing of programs of the State television",[96] the "special role in society of the judiciary, which, as the guarantor of justice, [has] a fundamental value in a law-governed State",[97] or "that in a democratic society both the courts and the investigation authorities must remain free from political pressure",[98] to determine the public

---

[91] ECtHR, *Gawlik*, para 82.

[92] ECtHR, *Guja*, para 74.

[93] ECtHR, *Guja*, para 87 ; ECtHR, *Heinisch,* para 91 ; ECtHR, *Bucur and Toma*, para 101 ; ECtHR, *Görmüş and Others*, para 54.

[94] ECtHR, *Guja*, para 87.

[95] ECtHR, *Bladet Tromsø and Stensaas v. Norway* [GC], Appl. no. 21980/93, 20 May 1999, para 63; ECtHR, *Stoll v. Switzerland* [GC], Appl. no. 69698/01, 10 December 2007, paras 117-120 ; ECtHR, *Görmüş and Others*, paras 55-56 ; ECtHR, *Matúz*, para 39.

[96] ECtHR, *Matúz*, para 33.

[97] ECtHR, *Kudeshkina,* para 86.

[98] ECtHR, *Guja*, para 86.

interest of the information disclosed. Similarly, while public institutions or state-owned companies should enjoy public confidence[99] and can impose upon their employees a duty of discretion,[100] the public character of those bodies may subject them to a particularly high level of scrutiny.[101]

4.4.2.2 Function of the Employer in a Democratic Society

The function of the institution or the position of the employee having disclosed the information can also play a role in the balancing exercise between the duty of discretion and the importance for the public to receive internal information about misconduct or illegal practices. As seen above, civil servants have a particularly strong duty of discretion.[102] On the other hand, the ECtHR stated that "the obligation of discretion and confidentiality constraints cannot be said to apply with equal force to journalists, given that it is in the nature of their functions to impart information and ideas".[103] In regard to the function of the institution targeted by the information disclosed, the ECtHR seems to take a particularly wide range of elements into considerations when determining the public interest to receive internal information.

4.4.2.3 The *Heinisch* Ruling

In the case *Heinisch v. Germany*, the applicant, a geriatric nurse working in nursing home run by Vivantes Netzwerk für Gesundheit GmbH, a limited liability company majority-owned by the Land of Berlin, was dismissed[104] after having expressed repeated concerns to the management about the overwork resulting from staff shortage and the consequent insufficiencies in the care provided. She ultimately filed a criminal complaint against Vivantes for aggravated fraud, specifying that this complaint intended to prevent the applicant from holding criminal liability since she regularly pointed out the deficiencies without seeing any willingness from the management team to remedy the situation. In its *Heinisch* ruling, the ECtHR noted that:

[99]ECtHR, *Guja*, para 90 ; see also ECtHR, *Heinisch,* para 89 ; ECtHR, *Kudeshkina,* para 86; ECtHR, *Görmüş and Others*, para 63.

[100]ECtHR, *Hadjianastassiou*, para 46 ; ECtHR, *Ahmed and Others*, para 56 ; ECtHR, *Rekvényi*, para 43 ; ECtHR, *De Diego Nafría*, para 37 ; ECtHR, *Palomo Sánchez and Others*, para 76 ; ECtHR, *di Giovanni*, para 69 ; ECtHR, *Catalan*, paras 60–61; ECtHR, *Vogt,* para 53 ; ECtHR, *Poyraz*, paras 57 and 78.

[101]ECtHR, *Matúz*, para 39 ; ECtHR, *Heinisch,* para 71 ; ECtHR, *Görmüş and Others*, para 63.

[102]ECtHR, *Guja*, para 71.

[103]ECtHR, *Matúz,* para 39.

[104]ECtHR, *Heinisch,* para 6.

> In societies with an ever growing part of their elderly population being subject to institutional care, and taking into account the particular vulnerability of the patients concerned, who often may not be in a position to draw attention to shortcomings in the provision of care on their own initiative, the dissemination of information about the quality or deficiencies of such care is of vital importance with a view to preventing abuse. This is even more evident when institutional care is provided by a State-owned company, where the confidence of the public in an adequate provision of vital care services by the State is at stake.[105]

It remains unclear, however, if the ECtHR would have followed the same reasoning if the company was privately owned[106] or entirely state-owned.[107] Whether the ECtHR's reasoning was based on the necessity to protect the rights of the employee or grounded on the role of the ECHR as a protection mechanism against State action has indeed an influence on the weight of the duty of loyalty in the balancing exercise.[108]

4.4.2.4 The *Bucur and Toma* Ruling

In the case *Bucur and Toma v. Romania*, the first applicant[109] worked within the department of Surveillance-Recording of telephone communications in a military unit of the Romanian Intelligence Service (Serviciul Român de Informații, hereinafter referred as "SRI"). He was assigned to the surveillance and recording of phone calls made by individuals identified by a register maintained for this purpose, during which he had to check the quality of the wiretapping and that the reception conditions (date and time of the wiretapping, the identity of the individuals,. . .) were met.[110]

In the performance of his duties, the applicant noticed multiple irregularities such as the lack of information about the identity of individuals wiretapped or the lack of motives justifying the wiretapping. He also noted the particularly high number of journalists, politicians and business people being wiretapped, especially after cases receiving a lot of media coverage.[111] He decided to disclosed those audio tapes containing several conversations of journalists and politicians[112] and was consequently sentenced to 2 years suspended imprisonment for theft, illegal collection and transfer of secret information and divulgation and use of illegal data affecting the

---

105 Ibid., para 71.

106 Lewis and Fasterling (2014), p. 79.

107 Schubert (2011), p. 758.

108 Ibid., p. 759.

109 The analysis focuses on the first applicant's claim as he raised a violation of his right to freedom of expression under the Convention, while the two other applicants raised violation of their right of privacy under Article 8 of the Convention, an analysis which would go beyond the scope of this book.

110 ECtHR, *Bucur and Toma*, para 7.

111 Ibid., para 8.

112 Ibid., para 10.

private life, the honor and reputation of others, with the decision confirmed by the Military Court of Appeal and the Supreme Court of Justice of Romania.[113]

In determining the public interest of the information disclosed, the ECtHR stated:

> La Cour estime que les informations divulguées par le requérant présentaient indéniablement un intérêt public. L'interception des communications téléphoniques revêtait une importance particulière dans une société qui avait connu pendant le régime communiste une politique d'étroite surveillance par les services secrets. . . . [L]a société civile était directement touchée par les informations divulguées, toute personne pouvant voir intercepter ses communications téléphoniques. . . . Par ailleurs, la Cour elle-même a été soucieuse de se convaincre à maintes reprises de l'existence de garanties adéquates et suffisantes contre les abus en la matière, car un système de surveillance secrète destiné à protéger la sécurité nationale comporte le risque de saper, voire de détruire, la démocratie au motif de la défendre . . . Eu égard à ce qui précède, la Cour estime que les informations divulguées par le requérant avaient un rapport avec des abus commis par des fonctionnaires de haut rang et avec les fondements démocratiques de l'État. Il ne fait désormais aucun doute qu'il s'agit là de questions très importantes relevant du débat politique dans une société démocratique, dont l'opinion publique a un intérêt légitime à être informée.[114]

The *Heinisch* and *Bucur and Toma* rulings demonstrate the variety of elements taken into consideration by the ECtHR when determining the public interest of the information disclosed.

4.4.3 The Authenticity of the Information

4.4.3.1 "Not Entirely Devoid of Any Factual Grounds"

Because the exercise of the right to freedom of expression entails duties and responsibilities, the employee "who chooses to disclose information must *carefully verify*, to the extent permitted by the circumstances, that it is *accurate and*

---

[113] Ibid., paras 41–48.

[114] Ibid., paras 101–103, *translation* "The Court considers that the information disclosed by the applicant was undoubtedly of public interest. The interception of telephone communications is of particular importance in a society which has undergone surveillance by the secret service during the communist regime. . . . civil society was directly affected by the information disclosed as anyone could have had their telephone communication intercepted . . . Furthermore, the Court itself has been repeatedly committed to be satisfied that there exist adequate and effective safeguards against abuse in the area, since a system of surveillance designed to protect national security entails the risk of undermining or even destroying democracy on the ground of defending it. . . In view of the above, the Court considers that the information disclosed by the applicant had to do with abuse by high-ranking officials and with the democratic foundations of the State. There can be no doubt that these are very important issues related to the political debate in a democratic society, of which public opinion has a legitimate interest of being informed". In relation to system of secret surveillance see also ECtHR, *Rotaru v. Romania* [GC], Appl. no. 28341/95, 4 May 2000, paras 59-60; ECtHR, *Klass and Others v. Germany*, Appl. no. 5029/71, 6 September 1978, paras 49–50.

reliable"[115] and must thus have *reasonable grounds* to believe that the information disclosed was true.[116] The extent of this obligation is also determined in accordance with the function and role of the employee, a high-ranking and highly qualified employee having to verify all the information which can substantiate the allegation made.[117] The ECtHR introduced this condition in order to protect the employer from "defamatory accusations devoid of foundation or formulated in bad faith", against which the State has the right "to respond appropriately and without excess".[118]

While the report of incorrect information "knowingly or frivolously"[119] should not enjoy the protection under Article 10 ECHR, the ECtHR accepted that a "certain degree of exaggeration and generalization" is permissible and does not necessarily amount to a gratuitous attack, provided that the statement is "*not entirely devoid* of any *factual grounds*".[120] The ECtHR has thus to verify, on the basis of the circumstances of the case, and taking into account the difference between statement of facts and statement of judgment,[121] the extent to which the employee was able to verify the truthfulness of the information disclosed. In this context, the ECtHR relies on the PA first Resolution on the protection of whistleblowers[122] and states that an employee who disclosed information in the belief that they were true can still enjoy protection under Article 10 ECHR, even if it later turns out to be false.[123]

4.4.3.2 Classified Information

A particular challenge arises in the context of classified information, the truthfulness of which is particularly difficult to verify by the ECtHR. While it recognizes that States may legitimately keep certain information confidential or secret,[124] the ECtHR is mindful that the protection of Article 10 ECHR can have an "even greater importance in circumstances in which State activities and decisions escape democratic or judicial scrutiny on account of their confidential or secret nature",[125]

---

[115] ECtHR, *Guja*, para 75 (emphasis added); ECtHR, *Heinisch,* para 67; ECtHR, *Gawlik*, para 75; see also ECtHR, *Bladet Tromsø and Stensaas,* para 65; *a contrario*, see ECtHR, *Soares,* para 47.

[116] ECtHR, *Bucur and Toma*, para 107.

[117] ECtHR, *Gawlik*, paras 77–78.

[118] ECtHR, *Guja*, para 75; ECtHR, *Heinisch,* para 67; ECtHR, *Marchenko,* para 50; see also ECtHR, *Castells*, para 46.

[119] ECtHR, *Heinisch,* para 79.

[120] ECtHR, *Heinisch*, para 85 (emphasis added); see also ECtHR, *Kudeshkina,* para 95; ECtHR, *Orelian Oprea*, para 71; ECtHR, *Marchenko,* para 50 ; see also in relation to defamation cases : ECtHR, *Palomo Sánchez and Others*, para 73; ECtHR, *Nilsen and Johnsen v. Norway* [GC], Appl. no. 23118/93, 25 November 1999, para 52.

[121] ECtHR, *Kudeshkina,* para 91.

[122] PA Resolution 1729 (2010) *Protection of "whistle-blowers"*.

[123] ECtHR, *Heinisch,* para 80 ; ECtHR, *Bucur and Toma*, para 107; ECtHR, *Gawlik*, para 75.

[124] ECtHR, *Guja*, para 71.

[125] In the context of press freedom see ECtHR, *Stoll,* para 110.

emphasizing that the "publication of documents is the rule and classification the exception".[126]

In this context, the ECtHR places a particular emphasis on the domestic judicial proceeding and review of the State's interference in the applicant's freedom of expression.[127] While the ECtHR cannot substitute its own view for that of the domestic courts[128] or take the place of the States "in defining their national interests, a sphere which traditionally forms part of the inner core of State sovereignty",[129] it can take into consideration the fairness of proceedings in order to assess the proportionality of an interference in the rights protected by Article 10 ECHR.[130]

> Consequently, the Court must determine whether the purely formal notion of secrecy ... is compatible with the requirements of the Convention. In other words it must examine whether, in the instant case, this purely formal notion was binding upon the courts to the extent that they were prevented from taking into consideration the substantive content of the secret document in weighing up the interests at stake, as an inability to take that into consideration would act as a bar to their reviewing whether the interference with the rights protected by Article 10 of the Convention had been justified.[131]

In this context, the ECtHR must determine "whether the 'secret' classification appears justified in the light of the purpose and content of the disclosed documents".[132] The quality of the domestic judicial review in regard to the legitimacy of the confidential classification of the information disclosed may thus determine whether the ECtHR considers the classification as justified and the interference necessary.[133] Indeed, "[i]f the reasoning of the national court demonstrates a lack of sufficient engagement with the general principles of the Court under Article 10 of the Convention, the degree of margin of appreciation afforded to the authorities will necessarily be narrower".[134] Accordingly, the lack of an effective judicial review could lead to a violation of Article 10 ECHR.[135] If the domestic courts failed to examine the interest of the public to receive the classified information for example,

---

[126]In reference to the PA Resolution 1551 (2007) *Fair trial issues in criminal cases concerning espionage or divulging State secrets*; see also ECtHR, *Stoll,* para 111; ECtHR, *Gîrleanu v. Romania*, Appl. no. 50376/09, 26 June 2018, para 88.

[127]ECtHR, *Stoll,* para 112.

[128]ECtHR, *Bucur and Toma*, para 110.

[129]ECtHR, *Stoll,* para 137; ECtHR, *Gîrleanu*, para 94; ECtHR, *Görmüş and Others*, para 64.

[130]ECtHR, *Stoll,* para 137; ECtHR, *Gîrleanu*, para 94; ECtHR, *Bucur and Toma*, para 110; ECtHR, *Kudeshkina,* para 83; ECtHR, *Matúz*, para 35; ECtHR, *Görmüş and Others*, para 64.

[131]ECtHR, *Stoll,* para 137; see also ECtHR, *Bucur and Toma*, para 110; ECtHR, *Görmüş and Others*, para 64.

[132]ECtHR, *Stoll,* para 138; see also ECtHR, *Bucur and Toma*, para 111.

[133]ECtHR, *Görmüş and Others*, para 52; see also ECtHR, *Animal Defenders International v. United Kingdom* [GC], Appl. no. 48876/08, 22 April 2013, para 108.

[134]ECtHR, *Matúz*, para 35.

[135]ECtHR, *Lombardi Vallauri v. Italy*, Appl. no. 39128/05, 20 October 2009, paras 54–56.

the ECtHR tends to conclude that there were no fair proceedings,[136] which in turn can lead to a violation of Article 10 ECHR,[137] the national courts having failed to demonstrate the necessity of the interference in a democratic society.

4.4.4 The Damage Suffered by the Employer

4.4.4.1 "Considerable Damage"

To determine whether a disclosure is legitimate and thus necessary in a democratic society, the ECtHR undertakes a balancing exercise between the extent and seriousness of the detrimental effect suffered by the employer and the importance of the public interest to receive the information disclosed.[138] Depending on the characteristics of the employer, the disclosure of internal irregularities by an employee may indeed have a detrimental effect on the proper function of the tasks undertaken by the public institution or the company concerned. For instance, the disclosure of information about internal wrongdoings or illegal conducts may jeopardize the confidence in the "independence and political neutrality of the prosecuting authorities of a State",[139] in the national intelligence agencies,[140] in the judiciary's authority[141] or in the equal treatment of the press by the State.[142] It can also threaten "the commercial success and viability of companies"[143] or the reputation of individuals.[144] In this respect, the ECtHR has to determine whether the disclosure was susceptible to causing a *considerable damage*[145] capable of outweighing the interest of the public to receive the information disclosed. Determining whether the damage is indeed considerable seems to depend on a series of factors, including the nature of the tasks undertaken by the institution concerned or the interest to maintain confidence in its proper functioning.

---

[136] ECtHR, *Bucur and Toma*, paras 104 and 111-112; ECtHR, *Matúz*, para 49 ; ECtHR, *Görmüş and Others*, paras 64-65.

[137] ECtHR, *Bucur and Toma*, para 120; ECtHR, *Matúz*, para 50; ECtHR, *Görmüş and Others*, paras 76–77.

[138] ECtHR, *Guja*, para 76; see also ECtHR, *Heinisch,* para 68.

[139] ECtHR, *Guja*, para 90.

[140] ECtHR, *Bucur and Toma.*

[141] ECtHR, *Kudeshkina,* para 86.

[142] ECtHR, *Görmüş and Others*, para 63.

[143] ECtHR, *Heinisch,* para 89; see also ECtHR, *Gawlik*, para 79.

[144] ECtHR, *Marchenko,* para 51.

[145] In relation to national security matters see ECtHR, *Hadjianastassiou*, para 45 ; ECtHR, *Stoll,* para 130 ; ECtHR, *Gîrleanu*, para 89; in relation to whistleblowing see ECtHR, *Bucur and Toma*, para 114; ECtHR, *Görmüş and Others*, paras 47 and 62.

4.4.4.2 The Diplomatic Corps, the Military and the Intelligence Sector

For example, the ECtHR stated in its *Hadjianastassiou* ruling that the disclosure of technical information about a weapon used in the national army can give information about its production progress and thus cause a considerable damage to the national security of a country.[146] Similarly, in the case *Stoll v. Switzerland*, the ECtHR considered that the disclosure of an ambassador's internal report during a sensitive period of negotiation undermined the climate of discretion necessary to the proper functioning of diplomatic relations in general and negatively impacted the outcomes of the ongoing negotiations, causing considerable damage.[147] In both cases, the ECtHR thus held that the sanctions imposed on the individuals responsible for the disclosure were not in violation of Article 10 ECHR.

The disclosure of documents related to the military, the diplomatic corps or the intelligence agencies being particularly sensitive due to the traditionally confidential nature of the information, the ECtHR also acknowledged that "secret information concerning military operations in a conflict zone is *a priori* information that must be protected".[148] However, because outdated or declassified military information are unlikely to pose a threat to national security, the ECtHR held that the disclosure of such information is thus not susceptible to cause a considerable damage.[149] In the same spirit, and in reference to the principle whereby the publication of documents should be the rule and the classification the exception,[150] the ECtHR emphasized that the protection of Article 10 ECHR is all the more important when State activities remain beyond the democratic control or the control of the judiciary due to their confidentiality or secrecy, stating that the disclosure of information on those activities can thus play a crucial role in a democratic society and allow the public to control the Government to which it has entrusted the protection of its interests.[151]

In its *Bucur and Toma* ruling, the ECtHR therefore held that even if the intelligence service of a State has a legitimate interest in maintaining public trust, the interest of the public to obtain information about illegal activities within its institution is so important in a democratic society that it overrides the interest of that institution in preserving public confidence.[152] The fact that the State had not invoked the considerable damage of the disclosure during the proceedings before the ECtHR may have also played a role in this conclusion.[153]

---

[146] ECtHR, *Hadjianastassiou*, para 45.

[147] ECtHR, *Stoll,* para 136.

[148] ECtHR, *Gîrleanu*, para 89.

[149] Ibid.

[150] ECtHR, *Görmüş and Others*, para 49; ECtHR, *Stoll*, para 111.

[151] ECtHR, *Görmüş and Others*, para 48.

[152] ECtHR, *Bucur and Toma*, para 115.

[153] Ibid., para 114.

4.4.5 *Motive and Good Faith of the Employee*

4.4.5.1 The Motive

The appreciation of the ECtHR in regard to the motive revives a controversial aspect of whistleblower protection. Indeed, according to the ECtHR, the motive of the reporting individual plays an important role in affording protection under Article 10 ECHR.[154] If the disclosure was "motivated by a personal grievance or a personal antagonism or the expectation of personal advantage, including pecuniary gain", the level of protection under Article 10 ECHR will not be particularly strong.[155] Consequently, while the ECtHR follows a comprehensive approach and takes into account not only the motives but also the factual grounds and the means used to determine the good faith of the reporting individual, it would be more inclined to consider an interference in the right of freedom of expression legitimate and reject a violation of Article 10 ECHR if the disclosure seems to be motivated by professional grievances.[156]

4.4.5.2 The Comprehensive Approach of the ECtHR

It is thus important to determine whether the whistleblower

> acted in good faith and in the belief that the information was true, that it was in the public interest to disclose it and that no other, more discreet, means of remedying the wrongdoing was available to him or her.[157]

If the whistleblower did not have immediate recourse to public disclosure and first reported internally or to competent authorities,[158] the ECtHR seems to be more willing to conclude a lack of alternative means and recognize the good faith of the whistleblower, even if the allegations are subsequently proven to be unfounded, "provided he or she had reasonable grounds to believe that the information disclosed was true".[159] What is more, the good faith of an employer would not necessarily be questioned even if she or he used a certain degree of exaggeration and generalization, as long the allegations "were not entirely devoid of factual grounds".[160]

---

[154]ECtHR, *Guja*, para 77; ECtHR, *Heinisch*, para 69.

[155]ECtHR, *Guja*, para 77; ECtHR, *Kudeshkina*, para 95.

[156]ECtHR, *Haseldine (A)* ; ECtHR, *Balenović (A)*.

[157]ECtHR, *Guja*, para 77; ECtHR, *Heinisch*, para 69.

[158]ECtHR, *Heinisch*, para 84; ECtHR, *Bucur and Toma*, para 117.

[159]ECtHR, *Heinisch*, para 80; *a contrario* see ECtHR, *Soares*, paras 46–49.

[160]ECtHR, *Heinisch*, para 85 ; see also ECtHR, *Kudeshkina* para 95.

4.4.5.3 A Need for Alignment with the New European Consensus

According to a constant jurisprudence and the acknowledgment that the ECHR is a living instrument which must be interpreted in the light of present-day conditions, the ECtHR has given itself the freedom to depart from its earlier decisions "in order to ensure that the interpretation of the Convention reflects societal changes and remains in line with present-day conditions"[161] so as to align the application of the ECHR "to any emerging consensus".[162] In light of the emerging European consensus on whistleblowing, which rejects the motive as a relevant factor to determine the good faith of a reporting individual, the ECtHR may need to reevaluate its fifth criterion. According to international best practices as well as the CoE and the EU position on whistleblower protection, the good faith should be appreciated merely on the basis of the reasonable grounds to believe that the information reported is true.[163] The jurisprudence of the ECtHR should therefore reflect this new European evaluation regarding whistleblower protection. To borrow the words of the Venice Commission, the protection afforded to whistleblowers should be based on her or his contribution to society, "and not on the question whether the person who made this contribution was self-interested or not".[164]

4.4.6 The Severity of the Punishment Imposed on the Employee

The proportionality of the interference in the rights protected by Article 10 ECHR is also determined by the severity of the sanction imposed on the whistleblower.[165] The harsher the sanction, the more fear it will induce, creating a "chilling effect" on potential whistleblowers of the same profession or working in the same sector, dissuading them from disclosing information of wrongdoings or illegal practices in the institution concerned, which would consequently hinder public debate.[166] In

[161] ECtHR, *Cossey v. United Kingdom*, Appl. no. 10843/84, 27 September 1990, para 35.

[162] ECtHR, *Chapman v. United Kingdom* [GC], Appl. no. 27238/95, 18 January 2001, para 70.

[163] See CoE Recommendation CM/Rec(2014)7, *Appendix*, para 22; Article 6(1)(a) Directive (EU) *2019/1937 of the European Parliament and of the Council of 23 October 2019 on the protection of persons who report breaches of Union law* ["EU Whistleblower Directive"], OJ L 305, 26.11.2019, p. 17.

[164] The original phrase by the Venice Commission reads as follow : "the protection the law offers to the whistleblowers should be primarily based on the service to society, and not on the question whether the person who rendered this service was self-interested or not", Venice Commission, *Op. No. 829/2015*, para 73.

[165] ECtHR, *Guja*, para 78 ; see also ECtHR, *Heinisch,* para 70.

[166] ECtHR, *Guja*, para 95; see also ECtHR, *Heinisch,* para 91; ECtHR, *Bucur and Toma*, para 119; ECtHR, *Görmüş and Others*, para 74 ; ECtHR, *Marchenko,* para 51 ; ECtHR, *Kudeshkina,* paras

cases of dismissal for example, which represents the most severe punishment under labor law, the ECtHR tends to consider the interference as disproportionate.[167]

4.5 Additional Limits to the Status of Whistleblower

In addition to the six whistleblowing criteria established by the ECtHR in its *Guja* ruling and presented above, further conditions were developed over the course of the last decade that delimit the status of whistleblower.

4.5.1 Subordination and Intent

The limits to the definition of whistleblowing introduced by the ECtHR in its jurisprudence is particularly indicative: Indeed, it requires a *subordinated work-based relationship*[168] and the *intent to uncover a wrongdoing*,[169] without which the criteria developed by the *Guja* ruling do not find application. Those conditions are particularly restrictive and do not reflect the European consensus which emerged from the Recommendation of the CM in regard to whistleblower protection and the 2019 EU Whistleblower Directive. As a living instrument, the ECHR is anchored to the reality of the CoE Member States in which it applies. Because the ECtHR must *"have regard to the changing conditions in Contracting States and respond, for example, to any emerging consensus as to the standards to be achieved*",[170] special attention should be given to the future development of the ECtHR's case-law in this respect. The latest legislative initiatives in whistleblower protection across Europe demand a revision of the limits imposed by the ECtHR in regard to the whistleblower status in order to be consistent with the new European consensus on whistleblowing.

4.5.2 The *Rubins* and *Aurelian Oprea* Ruling

Furthermore, to ensure the highest level of legal certainty essential for offering potential whistleblowers a realistic perspective of their rights under Article

99-100; in accordance with Art. 46(4) ECHR, the ECtHR can determine whether a State has failed to comply with its ruling, upon request of the CM.

[167]ECtHR, *Guja*, para 95 ; see also ECtHR, *Heinisch,* para 91 ; ECtHR, *Matúz*, para 48.

[168]ECtHR, *Medžlis Islamske Zajednice Brčko and Others v. Bosnia and Herzegovina* [GC], Appl. no. 17224/11, 27 June 2017, para 80.

[169]ECtHR, *Herbai,* para 40; ECtHR, *Langner,* para 47.

[170]ECtHR, *Glor v. Switzerland*, Appl. no. 13444/04, 30 April 2009, para 75.

10 ECHR, the ECtHR may also need to clarify the grey areas left by its *Rubins v. Latvia*[171] and *Aurelian Oprea v. Romania*[172] judgements. While in both decisions, the Court found a violation of Article 10 ECHR, it did so without recognizing the whistleblower status of the applicants.

4.5.2.1 The *Rubins* Ruling

In the former ruling, the applicant, a professor at the Riga Stradina University, a State University, was dismissed following his criticisms of the University's reorganization:[173] The lack of democracy, accountability[174] and transparency,[175] and alleged mismanagement of the University's finances.[176] He claimed that his dismissal was a punishment in violation of Article 10 ECHR.[177] However, even if the ECtHR categorized the national whistleblower protection clause as a relevant domestic law for the case,[178] listed and assessed all the six whistleblowing criteria,[179] noted that "the domestic court explicitly invoked the whistle-blowing protection clause enshrined in the Labour law and touched upon this question",[180] and referred to its two landmark cases on whistleblowing, namely *Guja* and *Heinisch*,[181] it laconically held that it did not consider this case to be "one of the protection of whistle-blowers".[182] By developing the argument under the sub-title "The applicant's motives",[183] stating that the reason of the dispute revolved around the reorganization of the University, "which prompted the applicant to raise complaints and to question the transparency of the procedure",[184] the ECtHR gave a hint as to its possible reasoning. However, the specific rationale explaining its rejection of an exploration of the whistleblowing character of the case, where it had sufficient grounds to do so, remains blurred and leads to a guessing game, which is particularly

[171] ECtHR, *Rubins v. Latvia*, Appl. no. 79040/12, 13 January 2015.

[172] ECtHR, *Aurelian Oprea v. Romania*, Appl. no. 12138/08, 19 January 2016.

[173] ECtHR, *Rubins*, para 8.

[174] Ibid., para 9.

[175] Ibid., para 55.

[176] Ibid., para 9.

[177] Ibid., para 52.

[178] Ibid., para 29.

[179] Ibid. [1) public interest and 3) authenticity of the information, para 85; 2) reporting channels, para 88; 4) motives of the applicant, paras 86–89; 5) damage suffered, paras 90-91; 6) severity of the sanction, para 92].

[180] Ibid., para 87.

[181] Ibid., para 88.

[182] Ibid., para 87.

[183] Ibid., paras 86 et seq.

[184] Ibid., para 88.

detrimental to the objectives of consistency and clarity required to ensure an effective protection for whistleblowers under Article 10 ECHR.

4.5.2.2 The *Aurelian Oprea* Case: Article 10 vs. Article 8 ECHR

In the *Aurelian Oprea* case, the applicant, associate professor at the University of Agronomical Sciences and Veterinary Medicine,[185] a State University, accused the University of corruption involving cases of plagiarism and intellectual theft[186] and was subsequently subjected to different criminal, civil and disciplinary proceedings, including for defamation.[187] According to the applicant, these proceedings were in violation of his rights under Article 10 ECHR,[188] claiming *inter alia* that he had acted as a whistleblower.[189] Here again, the ECtHR stated tersely that it "does not consider the present case as a whistle-blower case", referring to its *Rubins* ruling.[190] However, like in the *Rubins* judgment, the ECtHR addressed all six whistleblowing criteria,[191] reiterating that "the signaling by an employee in the public sector of illegal conduct or wrongdoing in the workplace should, in certain circumstances, enjoy protection", in reference to its *Heinisch* ruling, and that every employee has a duty of loyalty, reserve and discretion to their employer.[192] Contrary to the *Rubins* judgment, in which it briefly mentions the motives of the applicant without settling on a clear position,[193] the ECtHR explicitly affirmed the good faith of the applicant in the case *Aurelian Oprea*,[194] thereby reinforcing confusion in respect to the reasons which prompted the ECtHR to deny, in the two cases, the whistleblowing character.

The *Aurelian Oprea* ruling focused on the balancing exercise between Article 8 and Article 10 ECHR, which might have been the reason why the merits in the applicant's status of whistleblower were neglected. This is particularly unfortunate. Indeed, the act of whistleblowing almost always damages the reputation of a person or institution, which could regularly lead to defamation proceedings.[195] In this sense, the extensive case-law on the protection of individual reputation under Article

---

[185] ECtHR, *Aurelian Oprea*, para 6.

[186] Ibid., paras 9–10.

[187] Ibid., paras 16 et seq.

[188] Ibid., para 41.

[189] Ibid., para 69.

[190] Ibid.

[191] Ibid. [1) public interest, para 65; 3) authenticity of the information; paras 66-67; 4) motives of the applicant, paras 69-71; 2) reporting channel, para 71 *in fine*; 5) damage suffered, para 72; 6) severity of the sanction, para 76].

[192] Ibid., para 59.

[193] ECtHR, *Rubins*, paras 88–89.

[194] ECtHR, *Aurelian Oprea*, para 69.

[195] Junod (2009), p. 249.

8 ECHR and the limits posed to this right is particularly insightful to further define the rights of whistleblowers under Article 10 ECHR.[196] It could have been an opportunity for the ECtHR to extend its previous jurisprudence on whistleblowing by addressing the balance between Article 8 and Article 10 ECHR with the prospect of refining the limits to the rights of whistleblowers under Article 10 ECHR according to the jurisprudential principles laid down under Article 8 ECHR.

The protection of whistleblowers under Article 10 ECHR is as effective as the ECtHR's interpretation allows it to be. Defining a clear line in regard to the delimitations of the status of whistleblower within the meaning of Article 10 ECHR is therefore key to providing individuals with a sense of legal certainty.

4.6 Intermediate Conclusion

The ECtHR's limited powers in monitoring the compliance of CoE Member States with its rulings[197] increases the role of the CM which, according to Article 46 (2) ECHR, has the responsibility to supervise the successful execution of ECtHR judgments and determine whether CoE Member States selected appropriate means to meet the outcome of the rulings.[198] That said, the action of a CoE Member State in the execution of an ECtHR ruling can remain in the ECtHR's jurisdiction if it constitutes a new issue left unaddressed in the first ruling,[199] the novelty of which is determined in accordance with the particular facts of the case.[200] As the *Guja v. Moldova (No. 2)* judgment demonstrates, this competence is particularly relevant in relation to whistleblower protection considering the possibility of new retaliatory measures suffered by an applicant after a first ruling of the ECtHR.[201] The applicant had indeed been dismissed a second time following the first judgment. In its *Guja (No. 2)* ruling, the ECtHR held that the second dismissal of the applicant "was not related to an ordinary labour dispute, but had all the characteristics of *another act of retaliation* for his disclosing the letters in 2003" and thus concluded that the second dismissal was another violation of Article 10 ECHR. [202]

[196]Ibid., pp. 249 et seq.

[197]ECtHR, *Guja v. Republic of Moldova (No. 2)*, Appl. no. 1085/10, 27 February 2018, para 33; see also ECtHR, *Bochan v. Ukraine (No.2)* [GC], Appl. no. 22251/08, 5 February 2015, para 33.

[198]ECtHR, *Guja (No. 2)*, para 34; see also ECtHR, *Scozzari and Giunta, v. Italy* [GC], Appl. nos. 39221/98 and 41963/98, 13 July 2000, para 249 ; ECtHR, *Savriddin Dzhurayev v. Russia*, Appl. no. 71386/10, 25 April 2013, paras 247–249.

[199]ECtHR, *Guja (No. 2)*, para 35; see also ECtHR, *Bochan (No. 2)*, para 36; ECtHR, *Mehemi v. France (No. 2)*, Appl. no. 53470/99, 10 April 2003, para 43.

[200]ECtHR, *Guja (No. 2)*, para 36; ECtHR, *Egmez v. Cyprus (Admissibility)*, Appl. no. 12214/07, 18 September 2012, para 54.

[201]ECtHR, *Guja v. Republic of Moldova (No. 2)*, Appl. no. 1085/10, 27 February 2018.

[202]ECtHR, *Guja (No. 2)*, para 57 (emphasis added).

From a more general perspective, the newly adopted EU Whistleblower Directive together with the different CoE resolutions has brought forward an emerging new consensus in the protection of whistleblowers in Europe. As a living instrument, the ECHR should be interpreted in accordance with those findings, especially in regard to the appreciation of the good faith of whistleblowers and the public interest in the disclosure. In the next few decades, the ECtHR will have the opportunity to rule on a diversity of whistleblower cases allowing it to complete its current jurisprudence.[203] One can look forward to this future development and the consolidation of an established case-law on whistleblower protection, thereby providing the indispensable legal certainty necessary to ensure the highest level of effectiveness in regard to existing European whistleblower laws. Lastly, to lead by example, the ECtHR should also consider establishing its own internal whistleblowing rules.[204]

References

Giegerich T (2013) Wirkung und Rang der EMRK in den Rechtsordnungen der Mitgliedsstaaten. In: Dörr O, Grote R, Marauhn T (eds) EMRK/GG Konkordanzkommentar zum europäischen und deutschen Grundrechtsschutz, 2nd edn. Mohr Siebeck, Tübingen

Junod V (2009) La liberté d'expression du Whistleblower - Cour européenne des droits de l'homme (Grande Chambre). Guja c. Moldavie. Revue trimestrielle des droits de l'homme 20 (77):227–260

Kafteranis D, Brockhaus R (2020) Time to reconsider Strasbourg's whistleblower case law. *European Law Blog*

Lambert Abdelgawad E (2017) European Convention on Human Rights. In: Schmahl S, Breuer M (eds) The Council of Europe: its law and policies. Oxford University Press, Oxford, pp 228–268

Lewis D, Fasterling B (2014) Leaks, legislation and freedom of speech: how can the law effectively promote public-interest whistleblowing? Int Labour Rev 153(1):71–92

Schlachter M (2012) Kündigungen wegen "Whistleblowing"? - Der Schutz der Meinungsfreiheit vor dem EGMR, Besprechung des Urteils EGMR v. 21.7.2011 – 28274/08. Recht der Arbeit:108–112

Schubert C (2011) Whistle-blowing after Heinisch v. Germany: much ado about nothing. German Yearb Int Law 54:753–763

[203] Junod (2009), p. 259; Kafteranis and Brockhaus (2020).

[204] see Reply of the ECtHR to a question by the author, dated 11 March 2021, "[t]he Court has no internal whistleblowing rules".

Part IV
Whistleblowers and the European Union

Chapter 5
Whistleblower Protection Regulations Within EU Institutions

5.1 EU Civil Service Law

The relationship between EU officials and EU institutions is governed by EU Administrative Law[1] and regulated by the Regulation No 31 (EEC), 11 (EAEC), laying down the Staff Regulations of Officials and the Conditions of Employment of Other Servants of the European Economic Community and the European Atomic Energy Community (thereinafter referred to as "EU Staff Regulations"), which was first adopted in 1962[2] and last modified in 2021.[3] Under the Lisbon Treaty, the EU Staff Regulations can be amended following the ordinary legislative procedure,[4] the Staff Regulations Committee playing an advisory role as an inter-institutional consultative organ.[5] This Regulation is applicable to all EU bodies, with the exception of the European Central Bank and the European Investment Bank.[6]

[1]Bradley (2018), p. 559.

[2]*EEC/EAEC Council: Regulation No 31/EEC, 11/EAEC, laying down the Staff Regulations of officials and the conditions of employment of other servants of the European Economic Community and the European Atomic Energy Community*, OJ L 45, 14.06.1962, p. 1442.

[3]Consolidated text: *Regulation No 31 (EEC), 11 (EAEC), laying down the Staff Regulations of Officials and the Conditions of Employment of Other Servants of the European Economic Community and the European Atomic Energy Community* [hereinafter "EU Staff Regulations"], 01.01.2021.

[4]Article 336 TFEU.

[5]Article 10 *EU Staff Regulations*.

[6]Bradley (2018), p. 561.

© The Author(s), under exclusive license to Springer Nature Switzerland AG 2021

H. C. L. Yurttagül, *Whistleblower Protection by the Council of Europe, the European Court of Human Rights and the European Union*, European Union and its Neighbours in a Globalized World 3, https://doi.org/10.1007/978-3-030-78059-3_5

5.1.1 EU Civil Service Principles

EU Civil Service Law being Union law,[7] the general rules of EU law apply, such as the right to equal treatment or the right to a fair trial,[8] but it also includes particular principles, which were first developed by the CJEU.[9] It encompasses principles such as "the interest of the service" or the *devoir de sollicitude*,[10] which are of particular relevance in regard to the protection of whistleblowers within EU institutions.

In accordance with Article 7(1) EU Staff Regulations, the interest of the service, which could be considered as "the touchstone of legality in the exercise of the institution's discretion",[11] is the sole principle limiting the power of the administrative authority of each EU Institution (hereinafter referred to as "appointing authority") in its decision to assign or transfer an EU official to a particular position. The principle of *devoir de sollicitude*, a concept created by the CJEU in its jurisprudence[12] and particularly relevant for EU officials who blow the whistle within EU institutions (hereinafter referred to as "EU whistleblowers"), is the duty of the EU administration to take into consideration all factors in its decision concerning the position of an EU official, which should include not only the interest of the service but also the interests of the EU official.[13]

Various EU organs and mechanisms have been established to ensure compliance with EU Civil Service rules and principles, encouraging a harmonious relationship between EU officials and their institutions and promoting a consistent application and interpretation of the EU Staff Regulations.

5.1.2 Key Organs to Ensure a Harmonized Application of EU Civil Service Rules

In addition to the Staff Committee,[14] an important statutory Committee which has a mediatory role between EU Staff and their institution,[15] non-statutory inter-institutional bodies have been established to ensure a coherent application and interpretation of the EU Staff Regulations across EU Institutions. The College of Heads of Administration of the institutions for example, a shadowy body without a statutory

---

[7] Ibid., p. 559.

[8] Ibid., p. 562.

[9] Ibid.

[10] Ibid., pp. 563–565.

[11] Ibid., p. 563.

[12] Ibid., p. 564.

[13] e.g. CST, Case F-156/12, *Robert McCoy v. European Committee of the Regions*, Judgment of 18 November 2014, ECLI:EU:F:2014:247, para 106.

[14] Article 9(1) in conjunction with Article 9(3) *EU Staff Regulations*.

[15] Bradley (2018), p. 567.

basis whose decisions have no legal values but are generally implemented by EU institutions,[16] is composed of "top officials" of the various institutions of the EU and "aims at ensuring a consistent interpretation and implementation of the Staff Regulations and of other administrative matters, taking decisions at the highest administrative level".[17] Like the College of Heads, the Preparatory Committee for Matters relating to the Staff Regulations (CPQS) is a non-statutory organ constituted of representatives from the different EU institutions and is "in charge of discussing and trying to find harmonised solutions in matters relating to the Staff Regulations".[18]

5.1.3 Administrative Supervisory Procedures

A diverse range of administrative procedures ensure compliance with the EU Staff Regulations,[19] with administrative investigations and administrative complaints being the more relevant in regard to whistleblowing.

5.1.3.1 The Disciplinary Procedure

The appointing authority has an extremely broad margin of appreciation as supervisory authorities.[20] If evidence seems to reveal a failure by an EU official to comply with her or his obligations under the EU Staff Regulations, the appointing authority or OLAF can start an administrative investigation to determine whether those allegations are founded.[21] Following the conclusions of the investigations, the appointing authority has the power to undertake disciplinary actions if appropriate.[22]

Internal Investigation by the Appointing Authority

In accordance with their investigative power, appointing authorities have the obligation to adopt internal regulations governing the investigative procedure.[23] In addition but without mandatory character, EU institutions have the possibility to adopt measures implementing further aspects of the disciplinary proceedings

[16]Ibid., p. 568.

[17]European Ombudsman (EO) *Decision closing her own-initiative inquiry OI/1/2014/PMC concerning whistleblowing*, Case OI/1/2014/PMC, 26 February 2015, footnote 5.

[18]Ibid., footnote 9.

[19]Bradley (2018), p. 567.

[20]Ibid., p. 577.

[21]Article 86(2) *EU Staff Regulations*.

[22]Article 86(1) *EU Staff Regulations*.

[23]Article 2(3) Annex IX to the *EU Staff Regulations*.

described in Annex IX to the EU Staff Regulations.[24] In this respect, the EU Commission has introduced the most comprehensive EU internal rules[25] in its General Implementing Provisions (GIPs) on the conduct of administrative enquiries and disciplinary proceedings,[26] which was mirrored by Eurojust in its 2013 Decision on the General implementing provisions on the conduct of administrative inquiries and disciplinary procedures.[27] The EU Commission established an Investigation and Disciplinary Office (IDOC)[28] in charge of conducting administrative inquiries to "determine whether there has been a failure to comply with the obligations incumbent on Commission officials"[29] and "carry out disciplinary procedures for the appointing authority".[30] However, a certain skepticism was expressed as to the impartiality of IDOC during administrative investigations into allegations of harassments,[31] strengthened by the sobering information provided by the EU Commission in a judicial hearing, stating that during a 4 year period, IDOC "had never established the existence of psychological harassment, even though it had initiated between five and ten investigations each year".[32]

The Conclusions of the Investigation

The report on the conclusions of the investigation, which closes the investigative phase of the disciplinary procedure, together with all the evidence of the file, has to be communicated to the EU official concerned.[33] On the basis of the investigation report and following the hearing of the EU official concerned, the appointing authority can decide to proceed in one of four ways: Drop the proceedings if the

---

[24] Article 30 Annex IX to the *EU Staff Regulations*.

[25] Bradley (2018), p. 570.

[26] EU Commission, *Decision laying down general implementing provisions on the conduct of administrative inquiries and disciplinary proceedings* [hereinafter "GIPs on the conduct of administrative inquiries"], C(2019) 4231 final, 12 June 2019, replacing EU Commission, *Decision adopting general implementing provisions on the conduct of administrative enquiries and disciplinary proceedings*, C(2004) 1588 final/4, 28 April 2004.

[27] Eurojust *Decision on the General implementing provisions on the conduct of administrative inquiries and disciplinary procedures*, 23 September 2013.

[28] EU Commission *Decision on the conduct of administrative inquiries and disciplinary procedures*, C(2002)540, 12 February 2002. Later replaced by the EU Commission, *Decision adopting general implementing provisions on the conduct of administrative inquiries and disciplinary proceedings*, C (2004) 1588 final/4, 28 April 2004.

[29] Article 2(1) EU Commission *Decision adopting general implementing provisions on the conduct of administrative enquiries and disciplinary proceedings*, C(2004) 1588 final/4.

[30] Article 2(3) EU Commission *Decision adopting general implementing provisions on the conduct of administrative enquiries and disciplinary proceedings*, C(2004) 1588 final/4.

[31] Bradley (2018), p. 576.

[32] CST, Case F-46/11, *Marie Tzirani v. European Commission*, Judgment of 11 July 2013, ECLI: EU:F:2013:115, para 143.

[33] Article 2(2) and Article 3(1) Annex IX to the *EU Staff Regulations*.

report has not provided conclusive evidence for a failure of statutory obligations,[34] or drop the proceedings despite evidence of a failure.[35] If the investigation report concluded that the EU official has indeed failed to honor her or his obligations under the EU Staff Regulations, the appointing authority can pursue the disciplinary proceedings with[36] or without[37] the participation of the Disciplinary Board.

5.1.3.2 The Administrative Complaint

The administrative complaint is a procedure which allows EU officials to raise a complaint against acts of the appointing authority affecting them adversely.[38] While this administrative procedure is a precondition for a dispute to be raised in a judicial proceeding,[39] the CJEU went further and developed the rule of correspondence between administrative complaints and legal action,[40] all grievances having to be raised in an administrative complaint for the Court to rule on it during judicial proceedings.[41] This principle aims to give EU Institutions an opportunity to resolve administrative disputes internally.[42] Despite the strict interpretation of this principle in most rulings,[43] the Court has acknowledged on some occasions that a more flexible approach might be more adequate and even pressing given the pre-contentious character of administrative complaint procedures and the evolution of administrative practices.[44] In the context of whistleblower protection, this more flexible interpretation is welcome given the particular vulnerability of whistleblowers to retaliatory measures by the administration itself, as will be demonstrated below.[45]

---

[34] Article 3(1)(a) Annex IX to the *EU Staff Regulations*.

[35] Article 3(1)(b) Annex IX to the *EU Staff Regulations*.

[36] Article 3(1)(c)(ii) in conjunction with Articles 12-22 Annex IX to the *EU Staff Regulations*.

[37] Article 3(1)(c)(i) in conjunction with Article 11 Annex IX to the EU *Staff Regulations*.

[38] Article 90 *EU Staff Regulations*.

[39] Article 91(2) *EU Staff Regulations*.

[40] The Court derived this rule from Article 90(2) *EU Staff Regulations*; see also Bradley (2018), p. 565.

[41] CJ, Case C-58/75, *Jacques Henri Sergy v. Commission of the European Communities*, Judgment of 1 July 1976, ECLI:EU:C:1976:102, paras 31-33; CJ, Joined Cases 75/82 and 117/82, C. *Razzouk and A. Beydoun v. Commission*, Judgment of 20 March 1984, ECLI:EU:C:1984:116, para 9.

[42] The Court uses the term 'amicable settlement' in most judgments.

[43] On the strict application of that rule see CJ, Case C-446/00 P, *Cubero Vermurie v. Commission,* Judgment of 13 December 2001, ECLI:EU:C:2001:703, paras 12, 13 and 16; GC, Joined Cases T-78/96 and T-170/96, *W v. Commission of the European Communities*, Judgment of 25 May 1998, ECLI:EU:T:1998:112, paras 62 to 64; CST, F-60/07, *Martin Bermejo v. Commission of the European Communities,* Order of 11 December 2007, ECLI:EU:F:2007:216, paras 36-39.

[44] CST, Case F-45/07, *Wolfgang Mandt v. European Parliament*, Judgment of 1 July 2010, ECLI:EU:F:2010:72, paras 112, 115 and 118.

[45] See Chap. 6.

5.1.4 *The Supervisory Powers of the European Ombudsman*

5.1.4.1 Guardian of Transparency and Democratic Accountability

In the EU context, the function of ombudsman, as a guardian of transparency and democratic accountability,[46] is key to strengthening the democratic legitimacy of the EU as a supranational organization.[47] Established by the Treaty of Maastricht, the European Ombudsman (EO) is an independent body[48] elected by the EP[49] and mandated to ensure "the sound administration and transparency of EU institutions",[50] through the investigation of maladministration in the EU bodies, either on its own initiative or on the basis of complaints.[51] Those broad horizontal investigative powers[52] entitle the EO to launch inquiries into cases where individuals might not be in the position to file complaints or where a particular situation points to a more general pattern of maladministration.[53] In order to conduct a comprehensive investigation, the EO has "'hard'" investigative powers;[54] requests for information, including files, held by the EU institutions, are thus enforceable, with the exception of confidential or sensitive information which are conditioned to specific requirements.[55] Since 2004, the EO can also initiate investigations on whistleblower reports[56] in an effort to gain and increase confidence in the EU and its institutions,[57] a role embraced by the current EO, Emily O'Reilly.[58]

Following its inquiry and if a case of maladministration has been established, the EO informs the EU institution concerned, and when appropriate, provides draft recommendations, to which the EU institution should answer with a detailed opinion

[46]EO *Speech on Making the EU more accountable to its citizens*, Madrid, 13 November 2008.

[47]Haas (2012), p. 348; see also Guckelberger (2004), pp. 14 et seq.

[48]Article 228(3) TFEU. On the independence of the European Ombudsman see Vogiatzis (2018), pp. 77–82; Haas (2012), pp. 248–250.

[49]Article 228(1) TFEU.

[50]EU, *Ombudsman*, Glossary of summaries.

[51]Article 228(1) TFEU. On the mandate of the European Ombudsman see Hofmann (2017), pp. 1–27; Mastroianni (2017), pp. 178–197; Vogiatzis (2018), pp.185–284. On the definition of maladministration in particular see Haas (2012), pp. 260–269.

[52]Vogiatzis (2018), p. 26.

[53]Hofmann (2017), p. 9.

[54]Haas (2012), p. 726.

[55]Article 3(2) Consolidated text: *Decision of the European Parliament on the regulations and general conditions governing the performance of the Ombudsman's duties* [hereinafter "EO Statute"], 9 March 1994, OJ L 113, 04.05.1994, p. 15.

[56]Hofmann (2017), pp. 9–10.

[57]Harden (2017), p. 213.

[58]Vogiatzis (2018), p. 159.

within 3 months.[59] Even if the EO should, to the extent possible, promote an amicable resolution,[60] the measures undertaken are not legally binding for EU institutions and do not create enforceable rights for complainants, the EO being vested with purely recommendatory powers.[61] Despite this non-binding character, the vast majority of EO inquiries are well received by EU institutions, with a compliance rate of over 80%,[62] which reinforces the position of the EO as a legitimate supervisory body.[63]

5.1.4.2 Quis Custodiet Custodes Ipsos?

Quis custodiet custodes ipsos? While the general performance of the EO's duties is overseen by the EP, the principle of independence precludes it from monitoring the individual decisions of the EO.[64] The determining factor for legal actions against an EO decision is its legally binding nature.[65] Given the particularly wide discretionary power in handling complaints[66] and the non-legally binding nature of EO acts, they are generally not subject to legal actions before the Court.[67] However, in the landmark case *Lamberts*, the EU General Court considered that, although limited, judicial control over non-legally binding EO decisions is possible to the extent permitted considering the specific nature of the EO,[68] thus opening the door to

[59]Article 228(1) TFEU in conjunction with Article 3(6) *EO Statute* and Article 6.3 *Decision of the European Ombudsman adopting Implementing Provisions* [hereinafter "EO Implementing Provisions"], 1 September 2016.

[60]Article 3(5) in conjunction with Article 6.1 *EO Implementing Provisions*.

[61]Hofmann (2017), p. 17.

[62]Seventy-seven percent compliance rate in cases closed in 2018, see EO, *Putting it Rights? – How the EU institutions responded to the Ombudsman in 2018,* Annual Report, 18 December 2019; 81% compliance rate in cases closed in 2017, see EO, *Putting it Rights? – How the EU institutions responded to the Ombudsman in 2017*, Annual Report, 20 December 2018; 85% compliance rate in cases closed in 2016, 83% compliance rate in cases closed in 2015, with the highest compliance rate achieved in 2014 with 90%, see EO, *Putting it Right? – How the EU institutions responded to the Ombudsman in 2014*, Annual Report, 11 December 2015.

[63]Hofmann (2017), p. 26.

[64]Haas (2012), p. 306.

[65]Ibid., pp. 307 et seq.; see also Tsadiras (2007), pp. 607–626.

[66]Vogiatzis (2018), p. 42.

[67]GC, Case T-103/99, *Associazione delle Cantine Sociali Venete v. European Ombudsman and European Parliament*, Order of 22 May 2000, EU:T:2000:135, paras 43–46.

[68]GC, Case T-209/00, *Frank Lamberts v. European Ombudsman*, Judgment of 10 April 2002, ECLI:EU:T:2002:94, para 57; see also CJ, Case C-234/02 P, *European Ombudsman v. Frank Lamberts*, Judgment of 23 March 2004, ECLI:EU:C:2004:174, paras 49–50.

non-contractual claims against the EO[69] and the payment of damages.[70] Indeed, in the EU General Court's view, the measure which caused the damage does not need to be legally binding in order for it to be the subject of an action for damages.[71] It therefore concluded that "in very exceptional circumstances a citizen may be able to demonstrate that the Ombudsman has made a manifest error in the performance of his duties likely to cause damage to the citizen concerned".[72] While Mr. Lamberts lost the case against the EO, the Court judgment remains groundbreaking as it extends the judicial review of the EU courts to almost all EO activities,[73] which could be particularly advantageous for EU whistleblowers wishing to challenge EO acts they consider inappropriate in regard to the complaint they made.

5.2 Whistleblower Protection Under EU Civil Service Law

The 2004 and 2014 Regulations amending the EU Staff Regulations were the most significant amendments in recent years.[74] The 2004 Council regulation amending the EU Staff Regulations[75] strengthened the protection afforded to EU officials, with new statutory prohibitions in regard to psychological and sexual harassment,[76] introducing reporting channels to raise concerns of serious irregularities committed within EU institutions.[77] It also introduced a reporting procedure allowing EU officials to raise concerns about orders they consider tainted with irregularity,[78] which was consolidated in 2013 with the additional phrase: "An official who informs his superiors of orders which he considered to be irregular or likely to give rise to serious difficulties shall not suffer any prejudice on that account".[79] Contrary to the

[69]GC, Case T-209/00, *Lamberts v. European Ombudsman*, paras 45-60; see also CJ, Case C-234/02 P, *European Ombudsman v. Lamberts*, paras 31–71.

[70]GC, Case T-412/05, *M. v. European Ombudsman*, Judgment of 24 September 2008, EU:T:2008:397.

[71]GC, Case T-209/00, *Lamberts v. European Ombudsman*, para 58.

[72]Ibid., para 57.

[73]Haas (2012), p. 313; see also Guckelberger (2004), p. 146; Tsadiras (2007), p. 624.

[74]Bradley (2018), p. 560.

[75]*Council Regulation (EC, Euratom) No 723/2004 of 22 March 2004 amending the Staff Regulations of officials of the European Communities and the Conditions of Employment of other servants of the European Communities*, OJ L 124, 27.04.2004, p. 1.

[76]*Council Regulation (EC, Euratom) No 723/2004*, Amendment No. 14, new Article 12a *EU Staff Regulations*.

[77]*Council Regulation (EC, Euratom) No 723/2004*, Amendment No. 25, new Article 22a and 22b *EU Staff Regulations*.

[78]*Council Regulation (EC, Euratom) No 723/2004*, Amendment No. 24, new Article 21a *EU Staff Regulations*.

[79]*Regulation (EU, Euratom) No 1023/2013 of the European Parliament and of the Council of 22 October 2013 amending the Staff Regulations of Officials of the European Union and the*

administrative complaint described in the previous chapter, the new mechanism introduced in Articles 22a and 22b EU Staff Regulations does not require EU officials to be directly affected by the action they wish to report. As will be demonstrated below, the Article 22a EU Staff Regulations introduced in 2004 draws upon the EU Commission's first internal rules on whistleblowing introduced in 1999.[80]

5.2.1 *General Provisions*

As a general principle, the EU Staff Regulations prohibits EU officials from disclosing information acquired during the performance of their professional duties, unless permitted by the appointing authority or if it is used as evidence before the EU Courts or before the Disciplinary Board of an EU body.[81] However, pursuant to Article 22a(1) EU Staff Regulations, introduced in 2004:

> Any official who, in the course of or in connection with the performance of his duties, becomes aware of facts which give rise to a presumption of the existence of possible illegal activity, including fraud or corruption, detrimental to the interests of the Union, or of conduct relating to the discharge of professional duties which may constitute a serious failure to comply with the obligations of officials of the Union, shall without delay inform either his immediate superior or his Director-General or, if he considers it useful, the Secretary-General, or the persons in equivalent positions, or the European Anti-Fraud Office (OLAF) direct.[82]

5.2.1.1 Blowing the Whistle: A Right or an Obligation Under Article 22a EU Staff Regulations?

In the landmark cases *Bermejo Garde*, which will be further analyzed below,[83] the EU General Court had the opportunity to clarify that, rather than a mere right to report on irregularities,[84] Article 22a(1) EU Staff Regulations imposes an obligation on EU officials to do so.[85] As seen above, a number of issues arises in regard to a

---

Conditions of Employment of Other Servants of the European Union, OJ L 287, 29.10.2013, p. 15, Amendment No. 11, new Article 21a(3) *EU Staff Regulations.*

[80] See Sect. 5.3.1.1.

[81] Article 19 *EU Staff Regulations.*

[82] Article 22a(1) *EU Staff Regulations.*

[83] See Sect. 6.1.

[84] CST, Case F-41/10, *Moises Bermejo Garde v. European Economic and Social Committee (EESC)* [hereinafter "Bermejo Garde v. EESC (2012)"], Judgment of 25 September 2012, ECLI:EU:F:2012:135, paras 54-56, 134 and 136.

[85] GC, Case T-530/12 P, *Moises Bermejo Garde v. European Economic and Social Committee (EESC)* [hereinafter "Bermejo Garde v. EESC (2014)"], Judgment of 8 October 2014, ECLI:EU:T:2014:860, paras 103–106, and 149.

duty to report.[86] The EU Commission defended the legitimacy of this duty by arguing that the mere right to report would imply a right not to report serious irregularities which would be "detrimental to the fight against fraud and therefore to the interests of the Communities".[87] However, such an interpretation would be inconsistent with the general duty of loyalty incumbent on every EU official. Indeed, rather than an alleged incompatibility between a right to blow the whistle and the duty of loyalty under Article 11 EU Staff Regulations claimed by the EU Commission, the right to report should be interpreted in the light of and in conjunction with the duty of loyalty of EU officials. The very nature of a whistleblowing mechanism is the intent to protect workers from retaliatory measures. A duty to report, on the other hand, establishes an additional sanction mechanism and creates an inescapable trap for EU officials: Reporting on irregularities runs the risk of being subjected to retaliation while remaining in silence for fear of retaliation may lead to disciplinary action. Indeed, the EU General Court has held that EU officials may be found liable under Article 86 EU Staff Regulations and be subject to disciplinary sanctions if they fail to report on suspected irregularities.[88] However, it added that as a consequence, the existence of an obligation on the part of EU officials is of particular importance when determining whether they acted reasonably and honestly when reporting on irregularities,[89] such an obligation narrowing their margin of appreciation.[90]

5.2.1.2 Protection Against Retaliation

If an EU official blows the whistle in accordance with Article 22a EU Staff Regulations, she or he "shall not suffer any prejudicial effects on the part of the institution as a result".[91] According to established case-law, "only an act or measure producing binding legal effects that directly and immediately affects the applicant's interest by significantly altering his legal position is an act adversely affecting him".[92] But while the EU whistleblower has to be adversely affected by an act or measure to fall in the scope of application of Article 22a EU Staff Regulations, this provision does not offer a general protection and requires that the adverse act or measure was adopted because of the whistleblower report made.[93] This is the reason

[86]On the issue around a duty to blow the whistle see Sect. 2.4.2.1.

[87]Answer given by Mr. Kallas on behalf of the Commission to a parliamentary question by Paul van Buitenen (Verts/ALE), *OLAF investigations on internal fraud in relation to whistleblower cases*, E-0320/06, 27 March 2006.

[88]GC, Case T-530/12 P, *Bermejo Garde v. EESC (2014)*, para 149.

[89]Ibid., paras 101, 149.

[90]Ibid., para 149.

[91]Article 22a(3) *EU Staff Regulations*.

[92]CST, Case F-41/10, *Bermejo Garde v. EESC (2012)*, para 49.

[93]CST, Case F-2/09, *Riccardo Achille Menghi v. European Union Agency for Cybersecurity (ENISA)* [hereinafter "Menghi v. ENISA"], Judgment of 24 February 2010, ECLI:EU:F:2010:12, para 139; GC, Case T-512/13 P, *AN v. European Commission*, Judgment of 12 December 2014,

why the court must be particularly vigilant as to the circumstances of a case in which a report made by an EU whistleblower, on the basis of Article 22a EU Staff Regulations, is followed by an adverse decision against her or him.[94] However, the court consistently held that it is for the EU whistleblower to prove, "possibly in the form of a set of precise and consistent evidence",[95] that there is indeed a close link[96] between the adverse decision and the report made.[97] This position is unfortunate as it goes against the CoE Recommendations CM/Rec(2014)7[98] and offers a lower level of protection for EU whistleblowers than under the EU Whistleblower Directive.[99] As seen above, letting a whistleblower bear the burden of proof is particularly detrimental to the effectiveness of a whistleblower protection mechanism. It is highly advisable that this case-law is overturned to, on the one hand, comply with international standards, and, on the other hand, offer EU whistleblowers the same level of protection as EU citizens who fall within the scope of the EU Whistleblower Directive, allowing for a consistent level of protection for whistleblowers across the EU and within EU institutions and bodies.

5.2.1.3 The Good Faith of the Whistleblower or the Duty to Act Reasonably and Honestly

According to Article 22a (3) EU Staff Regulations, an EU official shall be protected against acts of retaliation, "provided that he acted reasonably and honestly".[100] While the term "reasonably and honestly" is used in the English, Spanish, Portuguese or Dutch version of the EU Staff Regulations,[101] the French version uses

ECLI:EU:T:2014:1073, para 90; GC, Case T-602/16, *CJ v. European Center for Disease Prevention and Control (ECDC)*, Judgment of 13 December 2017, ECLI:EU:T:2017:893, para 112.

[94] CST, Case F-2/09, *Menghi v. ENISA*, para 138.

[95] GC, Case T-602/16, *CJ v. ECDC*, para 112.

[96] CJ, Case C-170/18 P, *CJ v. European Center for Disease Prevention and Control (ECDC)*, Judgment of 15 May 2019, ECLI:EU:C:2019:410, para 66; see also GC, Case T-602/16, *CJ v. ECDC*, paras 112-113.

[97] GC, Case T-512/13 P, *AN v. Commission*, paras 93-94.

[98] CM, *Recommendation CM/Rec(2014)7 on the Protection of Whistleblowers* [hereinafter "CoE Recommendation CM/Rec(2014)7"], 30 April 2014, *Appendix*, Point 25; see also CoE Recommendation CM/Rec(2014)7, Explanatory memorandum, para 88.

[99] Article 21(5) Directive (EU) *2019/1937 of the European Parliament and of the Council of 23 October 2019 on the protection of persons who report breaches of Union law* [hereinafter "EU Whistleblower Directive"], OJ L 305, 26.11.2019, p. 17. See also Recital 93 *EU Whistleblower Directive*.

[100] Article 22a(3) *EU Staff Regulations*.

[101] CST, Case F-77/09, *Nijs v. European Court of Auditors (ECA)*, Judgment of 13 janvier 2011, ECLI:EU:F:2011:2, para 65.

"bonne foi",[102] and the German version "Treu und Glaube",[103] both expressions usually translated in English by the term "good faith". From Article 22a(3) EU Staff Regulations and the interpretation provided by the CJEU, there seems to be an overlap in meaning and purpose between the concept of good faith traditionally used in the context of whistleblower protection and the expression used in the English version of the EU Staff Regulations, namely "reasonably and honestly". For the sake of consistency, "good faith" and "act reasonably and honestly" will be used as equivalent. The key criteria developed by the EU Civil Service Tribunal to determine whether an EU official acted in good faith, or reasonably and honestly, will be analyzed below.[104]

5.2.1.4 Investigations Against the EU Whistleblower

According to the EU General Court, while Article 22a EU Staff Regulations protects EU whistleblowers against unwarranted investigations against them,[105] it does not prevent the administration from conducting investigations to determine their responsibility in the irregularities they reported.[106] Nonetheless, if disciplinary sanctions are imposed due to the implication of the EU whistleblower into the irregularities she or he reported, having blown the whistle may be considered attenuating circumstances.[107] Article 22a EU Staff Regulations also protects EU whistleblowers against prejudice suffered in the course of an investigation, even if the investigation was warranted.[108] This interpretation promotes a particularly ambitious protection scheme for EU whistleblowers under the EU Staff Regulations and should therefore be welcomed.

---

[102]The French version of Article 22a(3) *EU Staff Regulations* reads as follow: "Le fonctionnaire qui a communiqué l'information visée aux paragraphes 1 et 2 ne subit aucun préjudice de la part de l'institution, pour autant qu'il ait agit de **bonne foi**" (emphasis added).

[103]The German version of Article 22a(3) *EU Staff Regulations* reads as follow : "Dem Beamten dürfen seitens des Organs keine nachteiligen Auswirkungen aufgrund der Tatsache erwachsen, dass er Informationen gemäß den Absätzen 1 und 2 weitergegeben hat, sofern er dabei in **Treu und Glauben** gehandelt hat" (emphasis added).

[104]See Sect. 6.1.3.

[105]GC, Case T-512/13 P, *AN v. Commission*, para 34; GC, Case T-689/16, *Nikolaos Pipiliagkas v. European Commission*, Judgment of 13 December 2018, ECLI:EU:T:2018:925, para 58.

[106]GC, Case T-61/18, *Amador Rodriguez Pieto v. European Commission*, Judgment of 4 April 2019, ECLI:EU:T:2019:217, para 72.

[107]Ibid., para 72.

[108]GC, Case T-512/13 P, *AN v. Commission*, para 34; GC, Case T-689/16, *Pipiliagkas v. Commission*, para 58.

5.2.1.5 A General Protection Across EU Institutions and Bodies

The fact that an EU official shall report the suspected wrongdoing he became aware of "in the course of or in connection with the performance of his duties" emphasizes that the status of whistleblower is not tied to a direct working relation with the EU institution, agency or body. Indeed, according to the EU Commission Legal Service's interpretation of Article 22a and 22b EU Staff Regulations, the status of whistleblower shall be granted independently of whether the EU official reported on alleged irregularities committed within her or his own institution or witnessed in another EU institution or body.[109] This interpretation of Articles 22a and 22b EU Staff Regulations allows for the broadest protection coverage for whistleblowers across the EU bureaucratic apparatus and ensures a horizontal application of those provisions, irrespective of the contractual arrangements with a specific EU institution, agency or body. Indeed, deciding otherwise would "reduce the scope and seriously undermine the effectiveness (*effet utile*) of Articles 22a and 22b SR".[110]

5.2.2 Reporting Channels

5.2.2.1 "If He Considers It Useful"

According to Article 22a(1) EU Staff Regulations *in fine*, an EU official has different reporting channels available to blow the whistle. He should inform "either his immediate superior or his Director-General or, *if he considers it useful*, the Secretary-General, or the persons in equivalent positions, or OLAF direct".[111] The term "useful"[112] represents an unusual qualification to determine whether an external organ such as OLAF could be alerted. That said, one should welcome the fact that it is for EU officials to appreciate the usefulness of the reporting means, leaving them a particularly broad margin of appreciation when determining to whom they wish to report to. Indeed, according to the EU General Court case-law, an EU official could inform OLAF directly without prior notification to a superior[113] and should not be considered as having acted less reasonably and honestly than an EU official who reported first to her or his superiors.[114] The French formulation of the 2002 *Décision de la Commission concernant la conduit à tenir en cas de suspicion d'actes répréhensibles graves* confirms this interpretation of Article 22a(1) EU Staff

[109]EU Commission Legal Service, *Scope of application of Articles 22a and 22b of the Staff Regulations*, Opinion Ares(2011)439054, 19 April 2011, p. 1.

[110]Ibid., p. 2 (SR refers to EU Staff Regulations).

[111]Emphasis added.

[112]Article 22a(1) *EU Staff Regulations.*

[113]GC, Case T-530/12 P, *Bermejo Garde v. EESC (2014)*, para 67.

[114]Ibid., para 65.

Regulations: "en informe sans délai son chef de service ou son directeur général ou, s'il l'estime utile, le secrétaire général, ou les personnes de rangs équivalents, à moins qu'il n'informe directement l'Office européen de lutte antifraud".[115] According to this wording, OLAF can indeed be the direct recipient of whistleblower reports without prior notification to superiors. This interpretation is in compliance with the EU Commission Legal Service's interpretation of this provision as it states that the EU official has indeed "a free choice about whom to inform (among those indicated)".[116] Lastly, the fact that the usefulness, or lack thereof, should not be demonstrated by the EU official[117] further enhances this horizontal approach, an interpretation of Article 22a(1) EU Staff Regulations particularly favorable to EU whistleblowers as it offers them the freedom to choose the reporting channel they consider most appropriate.

5.2.2.2 The Tiered Model Imposed by Article 22b EU Staff Regulations

Article 22b EU Staff Regulations introduces additional reporting channels. Indeed, if an EU official discloses information to the President of either the EU Commission, the European Court of Auditors (ECA), the Council of the European Union (Council), the EP, or to the EO in compliance with Article 22b EU Staff Regulations, she or he should not suffer any detrimental effects on the part of the institution, provided that "the official honestly and reasonably believes that the information disclosed, and any allegation contained in it, are substantially true"[118] and that she or he "has previously disclosed the same information to OLAF or to [her or] his own institution and has allowed OLAF or that institution the period of time set by the Office or the institution, given the complexity of the case, to take appropriate action. The official shall be duly informed of that period of time within 60 days".[119] However, this period can be ignored if the EU whistleblower "can demonstrate that it is unreasonable having regard to all the circumstances of the case".[120]

The tiered model and the burden of proof, which lies on the EU whistleblower, are particularly problematic for a number of reasons: First, the EU Staff Regulations develop an intermediary system of reporting, between the UK inspired tiered model and a more flexible approach promoted by the newly adopted EU Whistleblower

---

[115]Article 1 of the *EU Commission Decision on raising concerns about serious wrongdoing,* C (2002)845, 26 February 2002, "if he or she considers it useful, the Secretary-General, or the persons in equivalent positions, or the European Anti-Fraud Office direct". The French version of the text emphasizes the 'suspicion' aspect of those concerns.

[116]EU Commission Legal Service, *Scope of application of Articles 22a and 22b of the Staff Regulations*, p. 2 "It is therefore clear that the official concerned has a free choice about whom to inform (among those indicated), including the possibility of informing OLAF direct".

[117]GC, Case T-530/12 P, *Bermejo Garde v. EESC (2014)*, para 161.

[118]Article 22b(1)(a) *EU Staff Regulations.*

[119]Article 22b(1)(b) *EU Staff Regulations.*

[120]Article 22b(2) *EU Staff Regulations.*

Directive. This conditional access to alternative reporting channels within the EU institutional framework is particularly unfortunate as it restricts the freedom of EU whistleblowers to determine for themselves which reporting channel is the more appropriate in consideration of the circumstances of the case. This reporting structure is also inconsistent with international standards on whistleblowing and the CoE Recommendation CM/Rec(2014)7.[121]

Likewise, the two cumulative conditions limiting the EU Whistleblower to disclosing wrongdoing only to the presidents of the EU Institutions or to the EO, applied unless the EU whistleblower can demonstrate that the waiting period provided in Article 22b(1)(b) EU Staff Regulations is unreasonable, raises the issue of burden of proof and the potential challenges facing EU whistleblowers having access to limited evidence to legitimate their action. Indeed, leaving the burden of proof on the whistleblower to demonstrate the adequacy of her or his decision to by-pass the waiting period is a responsibility susceptible to hinder reporting given the often limited access to evidence available to the official blowing the whistle and the consequently limited ability to justify the recourse to this means of reporting. On the one hand, this exception merely liberates the EU whistleblower from the obligation to wait a certain period of time until appropriate actions have been taken but does not lift the primary obligation to first report to OLAF or the institution concerned.

5.2.2.3 Report to a Third Party?

Lastly, like other intergovernmental organizations,[122] the EU faces particular challenges when considering the establishment of external reporting channels. While the possibility of reporting to a third party was taken into consideration in the original proposal for the 2004 amendment of the EU Staff Regulations,[123] this option was abandoned for the pretended sake of clarity.[124] Also, while the EU Commission recognized that "public disclosure and debate have great value", it was excluded as an additional reporting channel as it "can have the effect of compromising legal or disciplinary proceedings that may arise from the apprehension of wrongdoing".[125] The detrimental consequences of this categorical exclusion of public disclosure as an integral part of the EU Staff Regulations whistleblower protection framework far

[121]CoE Recommendation CM/Rec(2014)7, Point 14 (Principle 14).

[122]On the internal rules on whistleblowing of the United Nations and the World Bank Group see Sect. 2.6.

[123]Parliamentary question by Erik Meijer (GUE/NGL) to the Commission, *Whistle-blowers (3): encouraging whistle-blowers to use OLAF voluntary by giving practical proof that it is effective and rapid*, E-0113/01, 1 February 2001.

[124]Answer given by Mr. Kinnock on behalf of the Commission to a parliamentary question by Erik Meijer (GUE/NGL), *Whistle-blowers (3): encouraging whistle-blowers to use OLAF voluntary by giving practical proof that it is effective and rapid*, E-0113/01, 11 April 2001.

[125]Ibid.

exceed the risks of introducing such a reporting option. Indeed, the legitimate concerns expressed by the EU Commission can be countered through a conditional access to this reporting channel, as is the case under the newly adopted EU Whistleblower Directive.[126] As will be presented below, the possibility of, under certain conditions, having recourse to public disclosure as a legitimate means of reporting under Article 22a EU Staff Regulations might not be completely excluded as the CJEU's case-law seems to suggest.[127]

5.2.2.4 Obligation to Follow-up

According to Article 24 EU Staff Regulations, an EU official has the possibility to request the assistance of the EU. This provision has the purpose to protect EU officials against harassment or degrading treatment from colleagues, superiors or third parties[128] and is therefore particularly important in relation to Articles 22a and 22b EU Staff Regulations. This is the reason why the administration which received a request for assistance from an EU official who reported under Articles 22a or Article 22b EU Staff Regulations and suffered prejudice in the form of harassment for example, shall process this request within a reasonable timeframe.[129] The administration does not have a broad margin of interpretation in determining what constitutes a reasonable timeframe, especially considering its obligation to act particularly swiftly when cases of harassment are concerned.[130]

5.2.3 *The Road Ahead*

Paradoxically, under the conditions laid down by Article 22a EU Staff Regulations, EU whistleblowers will enjoy less protection under the EU Civil Service law than whistleblowers falling within the scope of the EU Whistleblower Directive. Indeed, under the Directive adopted in 2019, whistleblowers can report through internal reporting channels, or directly through external reporting channels,[131] or by public disclosure under certain conditions.[132]

---

[126] Article 15 *EU Whistleblower Directive*.

[127] See Chap. 6.

[128] CST, F-61/10, *AF v. European Commission*, Judgment of 16 May 2012, ECLI:EU:F:2012:65, para 70.

[129] GC, Case T-730/18, *DQ v. European Parliament*, Judgment of 3 October 2019, ECLI:EU:T:2019:725, para 103.

[130] Ibid., para 107.

[131] Article 10 *EU Whistleblower Directive*.

[132] Article 15 *EU Whistleblower Directive*.

Notwithstanding those weaknesses, Article 22a and Article 22b EU Staff Regulations lay the first milestone towards a stronger protection for EU Officials blowing the whistle on illegal activities committed within EU institutions. A reform of those provisions should consider a wider material scope, including the report of not only illegal activities or serious failure but more generally, all acts or omissions "which do not appear to be unlawful in formal terms but defeat the object or the purpose of the law",[133] in alignment with the newly adopted EU Whistleblower Directive which will be analyzed hereunder.[134] A broader material scope could allow the CJEU to adopt an extensive interpretation of the nature of actions susceptible to be reported.

5.3 EU Institutions and Their Implementation Procedures on Whistleblowing

The Regulation (EU, Euratom) No 1023/2013 amending the EU Staff Regulations, which entered into force in 2014, introduced an obligation for every EU institution to establish internal rules on the procedures designed to receive confidential reports from EU Whistleblowers in accordance with Article 22a or 22b EU Staff Regulations, on the protection of EU whistleblowers against detrimental effects and on the complaint procedure for EU whistleblowers who reported and suffered detrimental effects following their report.[135]

Following the 2014 amendment to the EU Staff Regulations, the EO conducted an inquiry to determine whether the EU institutions complied with their obligations. In letters addressed to nine EU bodies,[136] the EO requested to obtain information about the adoption procedure for internal rules protecting whistleblowers within their respective regulatory frameworks.[137] Despite the sobering results,[138] only two EU Institutions having adopted internal rules in compliance with Article 22c EU Staff Regulations by the end of the inquiry in 2015, namely the EU Commission and the ECA,[139] the EO noted a greater involvement of EU Institutions in discussions for

[133]Recital 42 *EU Whistleblower Directive*. See also Article 5(1) *EU Whistleblower Directive*.

[134]See Sect. 8.4.

[135]*Regulation (EU, Euratom) No 1023/2013*, Amendment No. 13; new Article 22c *EU Staff Regulations*.

[136]The European Parliament, the European Commission, the Council of the European Union, the Court of Justice of the European Union, the European Court of Auditors, the European External Action Service, the European Economic and Social Committee, the Committee of the Regions, and the European Data Protection Supervisor.

[137]EO, *Letter to the European Commission requesting an opinion in the European Ombudsman's own-initiative inquiry OI/1/2014/PMC concerning whistleblowing*, Case OI/1/2014/PMC, 24 July 2014.

[138]EO, *Decision of the European Ombudsman closing her own-initiative inquiry OI/1/2014/PMC concerning whistleblowing*, Case OI/1/2014/PMC, 26 February 2015.

[139]Ibid., para 9.

stronger internal rules on whistleblowing.[140] Confidentiality being "the most effective incentive to encourage staff to report wrongdoing"[141] and to ensure that the EU institutions and bodies comply with their Data protection obligations[142] when implementing internal whistleblower protection frameworks, the European Data Protection Supervisor (EDPS) also released guidelines and a list of recommendations with key elements to take into consideration when processing personal information in the course of a whistleblowing procedure.[143]

5.3.1 *The EU Commission: Forerunner in the Protection of EU Whistleblowers*

The EU Commission did not wait for the introduction of Article 22c EU Staff Regulations to adopt internal rules on whistleblowing. Indeed, as will be illustrated below, the EU Commission had already established an internal whistleblowing protection scheme in the late 1990s and continued to build upon it, with its 2012 Guidelines on whistleblowing representing the latest version of its internal rules on the protection of whistleblowers.

5.3.1.1 The Early Initiatives to Protect EU Whistleblowers

EU Commission Decision of 1999

Following a 1996 report calling on the EU Commission to develop its own internal rules in order to allow "its staff to raise concerns about serious financial malpractice",[144] the EU Commission introduced, as early as 1999, new rules stipulating that staff members who became aware of wrongdoing "shall inform without delay his Head of Service or Director-General or, if he considers it useful, the Secretary-General of the Commission", or OLAF directly and "shall in no way suffer inequitable or discriminatory treatment as a result".[145] According to the EU Commission,

[140] Ibid., para 11.

[141] European Data Protection Supervisor (EDPS), Data Protection and Whistleblowing in the EU Institutions, *Press release*, EDPS/2016/12, 18 July 2016.

[142] *Regulation (EU) 2018/1725 of the European Parliament and of the Council of 23 October 2018 on the protection of natural persons with regard to the processing of personal data by the Union institutions, bodies, offices and agencies and on the free movement of such data*, OJ L 295, 21.11.2018, p. 39.

[143] EDPS, *Guidelines on processing personal information within a whistleblowing procedure*, July 2016.

[144] Dehn (1996), p. 13.

[145] Article 2 of the *EU Commission Decision concerning the terms and conditions for internal investigations in relation to the prevention of fraud, corruption and any illegal activity detrimental*

"an effective balance between the public interests of confidentiality and loyalty of public servants and those of transparency and accountability must be achieved. Indeed, the principal aim of "whistleblowing" provisions is to provide an incentive for staff to report concerns internally, and for their employer to investigate those concerns effectively".[146]

2002 Reforms

In accordance with its opinion that "the most effective way to encourage staff to report concerns within the organization is to provide clearly defined and secure internal reporting channels",[147] the EU Commission introduced an additional reporting channel in 2002,[148] allowing EU Commission officials to inform the EO or the President of the Council, of the EP or of the ECA,[149] if the EU Commission or OLAF did not take appropriate measures within a reasonable period,[150] provided that the EU Commission official honestly and reasonably believed that information was substantially true.[151] According to the EU Commission, this condition has the objective of ensuring that OLAF, as the most competent body to act on wrongdoings within EU bodies, is informed and has the opportunity to act, and thus hinder unfounded accusations.[152] However, while reporting to bodies outside of the EU institutional framework was considered in the EU Commission's consultative document as an option of last resort,[153] this possibility was not retained in the final draft. The position of the EU Commission regarding the external reporting channels

---

to the Communities' interests (notified under document number SEC(1999) 802), 1999/396/EC, ECSC, Euratom, 2 June 1999.

[146] Answer given by Mr. Kinnock on behalf of the Commission to a parliamentary question by MEP Erik Meijer (GUE/NGL): *Whistle-blowers (1): their socially useful function in solving problems in large and small organisations*, E-0111/01, 11 April 2001; see also EU Commission, *Raising Concerns about Serious Wrongdoing,* Communication from Mr. Kinnock to the Commission, Consultative document, 24 Nov. 2000, pp. 2–3.

[147] Ibid.; see also EU Commission, *Raising Concerns about Serious Wrongdoing,* Communication from Mr. Kinnock to the Commission, p. 5.

[148] Article 2(1) of the *EU Commission Decision C(2002)845 on raising concerns about serious wrongdoing*.

[149] Article 2(1)(c) of the *EU Commission Decision C(2002)845 on raising concerns about serious wrongdoing.*

[150] Article 2(1)(b) in conjunction with Article 2(2) and (3) of the *EU Commission Decision C(2002) 845 on raising concerns about serious wrongdoing.*

[151] Article 2(1)(a) of the *EU Commission Decision C(2002)845 on raising concerns about serious wrongdoing*.

[152] Answer given by Mr. Kinnock on behalf of the Commission to a parliamentary question by MEP Erik Meijer (GUE/NGL): *Whistle-blowers (2): how shortcomings in the rules discourage and prevent their activities*, E-0112/01, 11 April 2001.

[153] EU Commission, *Raising Concerns about Serious Wrongdoing,* Communication from Mr. Kinnock to the Commission.

provided seems to suggest that the access to such channels should be strictly interpreted, the report to the President of another EU institution or to the EO having been developed "in order to cover eventualities in the unlikely event that the independent European Anti-fraud Office has not taken appropriate action".[154]

The Shortcomings

The shortcomings of this whistleblower system, in particular in regard to the tiered model imposed between internal and external reporting channels as well as the burden of proof, were identified very early on without being addressed by the EU Commission.[155] Unsurprisingly, in a 2004 Communication to the EU Commission on "'How to enhance effective application of the Whistleblowing rules and protection of Whistleblowers'", the then Vice-President of the EU Commission Mr. Kinnock acknowledged that despite those rules being introduced, "they are rarely followed in practice".[156] He suggested two strategies to improve the effectiveness of the existing whistleblowing protection rules: Promote awareness of those rules among EU Commission officials and ensure the highest level of protection for whistleblowers.[157] To ensure stronger protection, the EU Commission should facilitate the transfer process if a whistleblower "**wishes to be moved** to another Commission department in order to safeguard him or her against potential hostile reactions from his or her immediate work environment".[158] Particular attention should also be paid "during **staff evaluation and promotion procedure** to ensure that the whistleblower suffers no adverse consequences in this context".[159] While those measures were certainly beneficial to ensure greater protection for whistleblowers, and might even be considered forward-thinking considering the

---

[154] Answer given by Mr. Kinnock on behalf of the Commission to a parliamentary question by MEP Erik Meijer (GUE/NGL): *Whistle-blowers (2): how shortcomings in the rules discourage and prevent their activities*.

[155] Parliamentary question by MEP Erik Meijer (GUE/NGL) to the Commission: *Whistle-blowers (2): how shortcomings in the rules discourage and prevent their activities*, E-0112/01, 1. February 2001, (while the MEP referred to the consultative document of the EU Commission, *Raising concerns about serious wrongdoing*, the additional rules adopted in 2002 by the Commission did not address the shortcomings identified by the MEP and thus remain very much relevant).

[156] EU Commission, *How to enhance effective application of the Whistleblowing rules and protection of Whistleblowers*, Communication from Vice-President Kinnock to the Commission, SEC (2004)151/2, 6 February 2004, p. 1.

[157] Ibid., pp. 1–2.

[158] Ibid., p. 2.

[159] Ibid., p. 3.

period in which they were introduced, the shortcomings identified by the Member of the European Parliament (MEP) a few years back[160] were left unaddressed.[161]

Despite this first attempt to encourage whistleblowing and further whistleblower protection within the EU Commission, little results could be observed in the decade that followed.

5.3.1.2 The 2012 Guidelines on Whistleblowing

At the beginning of the last decade, the EU Commission took a more proactive approach to whistleblowing. Referring to Articles 22a and 22b EU Staff Regulations and its *devoir de sollicitude*, the EU Commission acknowledged the necessity "to ensure that members of staff who report serious wrongdoings or concerns in good faith are afforded the utmost confidentiality and greatest degree of protection against any retaliation as a result of their whistleblowing", and thus decided to adopt Guidelines on whistleblowing in order to allow EU Commission Staff members to raise concerns without the fear of negative repercussions.[162] In 2018, it also gave its *ex ante* agreement to EU agencies who adopted guidelines on whistleblowing identical to its own.[163] First and foremost, while this form of "guidelines" was supposedly chosen for its accessibility and binding character,[164] considering the soft law nature of "guidelines", it is questionable whether the EU Commission's 2012 "Guidelines on whistleblowing" convey the necessary element of reliability which could inspire confidence among EU Commission Staff, an essential aspect to ensure the effectiveness and practicality of the protection mechanism described thereunder.

---

160 Parliamentary question by MEP Erik Meijer (GUE/NGL), *Whistle-blowers (2): how shortcomings in the rules discourage and prevent their activities*, (while the MEP refers to the consultative document of the EU Commission, *Raising concerns about serious wrongdoing*, the current EU Staff Regulations has the same system).

161 According to the Commission, from 2002 to 2005, 10 cases of whistleblowing were registered by OLAF: See Answer given by Mr. Kallas on behalf of the Commission to a parliamentary question by MEP Paul van Buitenen (Verts/ALE), *EU whistle-blowers*, E-2863/05, 16 September 2005.

162 EU Commission, *Communication from Vice-President Šefčovič to the Commission on Guidelines on Whistleblowing* [hereinafter "Guidelines on Whistleblowing"], SEC(2012)679/1, 6 December 2012, p. 2.

163 Article 1(1) of the *EU Commission decision on giving the Commission's ex ante agreement to the adoption by agencies of implementing rules laying down guidelines on whistleblowing*, C(2018) 1362 final, 27 February 2018.

164 EO, *Decision of the European Ombudsman closing her own-initiative inquiry OI/1/2014/PMC concerning whistleblowing*, para 4.

The Guidelines *Ratione Personae*

The guidelines impose an obligation on Staff members to report serious irregularities,[165] a strong stand which demonstrates the willingness of the EU Commission to promote a zero tolerance approach against those kind of misconduct within its institution. It defines whistleblower as "a member of staff, acting in good faith, who reports facts discovered in the course of or in connection with his or her duties which point to the existence of serious irregularities",[166] stressing, however, that seconded national experts, trainees, interim staff and local agents are not, "'strictly speaking'", falling under the scope of the whistleblowing rules.[167] This provision falls below the minimum level of protection recommended by the CoE which states that an effective whistleblower protection framework should not be linked to the nature of the working relationship and whether it is remunerated or not.[168] Despite the assurance of the EU Commission that those categories of Staff will be protected against retaliation if they report in good faith, well noted in the footnote, the ambiguity that hangs over this vague affirmation will greatly increase the general uncertainty as to the effective personal scope of the guideline and increase the likeliness that trainees or interim staff will refrain from reporting on serious irregularities they may witness.

The Guidelines *Ratione Materiae*

The EU Commission defines serious irregularities as "illegal activities, including fraud and corruption, and serious professional wrongdoings",[169] which restrict considerably the material scope of the guidelines. In comparison, under the EU Whistleblower Directive adopted in 2019, which will be analyzed below,[170] breaches susceptible to be reported are not restricted to unlawful acts and omissions but also include those which defeat the object or purpose of EU rules.[171] The requirement of seriousness greatly limits the effectiveness of the guidelines as it imposes a high threshold for acts or omissions susceptible to be reported below which EU Commission staff members will not be protected under the guidelines, thus staying vulnerable against retaliatory measures if the incidents they reported are not considered serious enough within the meaning of the Guidelines. When in doubt as to the serious nature of misconduct, EU Commission staff members will therefore most certainly remain silent rather than risk to fall outside of the protective shield of

[165]EU Commission Guidelines on Whistleblowing, p. 3.

[166]Ibid.

[167]Ibid., Footnote 2 of the EU Commission Guidelines on Whistleblowing.

[168]CoE Recommendation CM/Rec(2014)7, *Appendix*, Point 3.

[169]EU Commission Guidelines on Whistleblowing, p. 3.

[170]See Sect. 8.4.

[171]Article 5(1) *EU Whistleblower Directive*.

the guidelines and suffer detrimental effects due to the reporting. Further limitations are included in different parts of the Guidelines,[172] increasing its restrictive character and consequently giving the strong impression that reporting should be exceptional and used as a last resort rather than as a mechanism ensuring accountability.

Dedicated Reporting Channels

Prior to using reporting channels, EU Commission staff members can seek advice from trained ethics correspondents in each Directorate General on the applicability of the Guidelines and the reporting procedures.[173] In regard to the reporting channels themselves, the EU Commission's Guidelines mirror the provisions of the EU Staff Regulations by offering a flexible choice between the report to superiors or to OLAF, and laying down the same requirements as in Article 22b EU Staff Regulations in regard to external reports to presidents of other EU institutions or the EO.[174] On the one hand and due to the confidential nature of information governed by the EU Commission during the performance of its institutional functions, the Guidelines emphasize the duty of discretion and loyalty incumbent upon every EU Commission staff member and thus the exceptional nature of external reporting channels.[175] On the other hand, the Guidelines stress the "effective balance between the public interests of confidentiality and loyalty and those of transparency and accountability"[176] when reporting through the external channel provided in Article 22b EU Staff Regulations and thus concludes that "[i]t is up to the staff member to choose the most appropriate channel for reporting the serious irregularities that they must disclose".[177] Those statements seem to be inconsistent with the prior rationale promoted and this raises some concerns over the lack of clarity and consequent uncertainty resulting from the Guidelines' somewhat incoherent formulation.

Burden of Proof

The EU Commission takes a more favorable stand on the effective protection mechanisms when Commission Staff members suffer retaliation from having reported in compliance with the conditions presented above, putting the burden of proof on the perpetrator of the detrimental action to demonstrate the lack of causality between the prejudicial effects suffered and the report made.[178]

[172] EU Commission Guidelines on Whistleblowing, pp. 4 and 8.

[173] EU Commission Guidelines on Whistleblowing, p. 9.

[174] EU Commission Guidelines on Whistleblowing, pp. 5-6.

[175] Ibid., p. 6

[176] Ibid.

[177] Ibid.

[178] Ibid.

5.3.1.3 The Assessment of the 2012 Guidelines on Whistleblowing

The 2016 Review

As part of the EU Commission's review of its own Guidelines on whistleblowing conducted in 2015 and finalized in 2016, one EU whistleblower testified that while the whistleblower report made was taken seriously by OLAF, the length of the procedure itself lead to a relatively long period of uncertainty.[179] In addition, even if the rules of confidentiality were strictly followed by OLAF and IDOC, some concerns were expressed as to the *de facto* protection of confidentiality considering the often restrictive group of EU officials having access to the information reported by the EU whistleblower.[180] In this respect, the burden of proving the retaliatory nature of actions against the whistleblower was another issue identified.[181] Despite those remarks, the EU Commission concluded that the guidelines complied with international best practices[182] and did not need changes to its content,[183] a conclusion confirmed by its 2019 review of the Guidelines on whistleblowing.[184] Following its 2016 review, it concluded, however, that an EU Commission-wide awareness campaign should be launched[185] and considered extending the Guidelines' personal scope of application to non-EU officials.[186] Following those conclusions, IDOC and the EU Commission's unit responsible for ethics launched a campaign to raise the awareness of EU Commission managers about "their rights and obligations regarding whistleblowing".[187] Those efforts are beginning to come to fruition, as revealed by an ECA survey showing that more than 50% of managers from the EU Commission, the EP and the Council combined reported having good knowledge of whistleblowing rules, compared to 32,2% of administrators.[188] In regard to EU

[179]EU Commission, *Report on the Review of the Guidelines on whistleblowing* [hereinafter "2016 Review of the Guidelines on whistleblowing"], 2016, p. 2.

[180]Ibid.

[181]Ibid., p. 3.

[182]Ibid., p. 8.

[183]EU Commission, *Annexes on the EU Whistleblower Directive proposal*, Annex 5, p. 93.

[184]EU Commission, *Report on the 2019 Review of the Guidelines on whistleblowing* [hereinafter "2019 Review of the Guidelines on whistleblowing"], 2019, p. 8.

[185]EU Commission, *2016 Review of the Guidelines on whistleblowing*, p. 9

[186]Ibid., pp. 5–6.

[187]Answer given by Mr. Oettinger on behalf of the European Commission to a parliamentary question by Ingeborg Gräßle (PPE): *Guidance for whistleblowers at the Commission*, E-002035/2019(ASW), 28 June 2019.

[188]European Court of Auditors (ECA), *Special Report: The ethical frameworks of the audited EU institutions: scope for improvement* [hereinafter "Special Report on ethical frameworks"], Annex II—Results of the Survey, No. 13/2019, 19 July 2019, p. 50. Under the definition of the ECA Survey, Managers include Secretaries-General, Directors-General, Directors, Heads of Cabinet, Heads of Unit and Principal Advisers while administrators are staff holding "AD" posts without managerial duties such as general administrators, translators, lawyers, contract agents of function group IV and seconded national experts.

Commission Staff specifically, there is still room for improvement as only 5.5% seem to have in-depth knowledge of rules on whistleblowing while 32,5% have good knowledge of those requirements.[189]

The 2019 Review

According to the EU Commission's 2019 Report reviewing its Guidelines on whistleblowing, IDOC started to give presentations on whistleblowing to the Directorates-General of the EU Commission as well as to EU agencies.[190] To ensure a harmonized implementation and application of the Guidelines on whistleblowing, the Unit HR.E3 "'Ethics and Ombudsman" became the main body tasked with addressing ethics processes and ensuring a centralized information service for EU staff members.[191] According to the 2019 report, the EU Commission intranet portal is regularly updated in order to reflect the latest developments in the area of whistleblowing.[192] In this regard, the EU Commission expressed its willingness to adjust its own Guidelines on the basis of the lessons learned by EU Member States when transposing and implementing the EU Whistleblower Directive.[193]

A Call for Reform

Despite those positive measures, the EU Commission's answers to parliamentary questions concerning its guidelines on whistleblowing[194] accentuate the doubts as to their real effectiveness. Indeed, the EU Commission stated that "[i]n the last five years, there were three cases in which staff members mentioned a status of whistleblower when filing a request for assistance under Article 24 of the Staff Regulations, or a complaint under its Article 90",[195] while OLAF registered five cases of internal whistleblowing concerning EU Commission staff members since

[189] Ibid.

[190] EU Commission, *2019 Review of the Guidelines on whistleblowing*, p. 2.

[191] Ibid.

[192] Ibid., p. 3.

[193] Ibid., p. 4.

[194] Parliamentary question by Ingeborg Gräßle (PPE) to the Commission, *Whistleblowers at the European Commission*, E-002034-19, 18 April 2019; Parliamentary question by Ingeborg Gräßle (PPE) to the Commission, *Guidance for whistleblowers at the Commission*, E-002035-19, 18 April 2019.

[195] Answer given by Mr. Oettinger on behalf of the European Commission to a parliamentary question by Ingeborg Gräßle (PPE): *Guidance for whistleblowers at the Commission*, E-002035/19 (ASW), 28 June 2019.

2015,[196] but opened and investigated only one of the cases registered.[197] Those numbers are strikingly low considering the period of time and the more than 30,000 employees working in the EU Commission. Furthermore, the fact that a single investigation was initiated following a whistleblower report underlines the sentiment of inaction and increases the risk of EU Commission staff members considering this procedure ineffective for remedying irregularities, which seems to be confirmed by the particularly low number of cases in which Staff members refer to the Guidelines. In consideration of the above, the restrictive nature of the Guidelines, the general lack of awareness and the lack of trust in the effectiveness of the procedure appear to be the main reasons leading to an underutilization of the whistleblowing mechanism developed by the EU Commission in 2012.

In Summer 2019, the EU Commission decision laying down general implementation provisions on the conduct of administrative inquiries and disciplinary proceedings, which replaced its 2004 GIPs,[198] introduced a new article entitled "Protection of Whistleblowers", which refers to the 2012 Guidelines on whistleblowing and states that "[i]f the information triggering the proceedings laid down in this Decision has been submitted on the basis of the procedure set out in Article 22(a) of the Staff Regulations, the provisions of the Commission's Guidelines on whistleblowing shall be taken into account in the context of the proceedings referred to in this Decision".[199] However, while this new provision underlines the significance of the Guidelines and the protection of whistleblowers within the EU Commission's internal administrative rules, it does not compensate the shortcomings of the Guidelines itself, which could only be addressed through a comprehensive reform, a prospect made particularly likely following the transposition and implementation of the EU Whistleblower Directive.[200] One can hope that the next review of the EU Commission's Guidelines on whistleblowing, planned in 2025, will trigger a structural and thorough reform.

---

[196]Answer given by Mr. Oettinger on behalf of the European Commission to a parliamentary question by Ingeborg Gräßle (PPE): *Whistleblowers at the European Commission*, E-002034/2019 (ASW), 10 July 2019; see also EU Commission, *2019 Review of the Guidelines on whistleblowing*, p. 5.

[197]Ibid.; see also EU Commission, *2019 Review of the Guidelines on whistleblowing*, p. 5.

[198]Recital 1 *EU Commission GIPs on the conduct of administrative inquiries.*

[199]Article 8 *EU Commission GIPs on the conduct of administrative inquiries.*

[200]EU Commission, *2019 Review of the Guidelines on whistleblowing*, p. 9.

5.3.2 *Other EU Institutions and Their Implementing Provisions on Whistleblowing*

5.3.2.1 Varying Levels of Protection

"To lead by example", the EO adopted internal rules on whistleblowing following her 2014 own-initiative inquiry,[201] encompassing all the key elements of a strong whistleblower framework.[202] Since then, all nine EU institutions which were the object of the 2014 EO inquiry adopted Implementing Provisions on Whistleblowing (IPW).[203] The EP[204] and the Council[205] chose to introduce internal rules while the CJEU,[206] like the EU Commission, adopted guidelines on whistleblowing. In its 2019 Special report on the ethical frameworks applicable in the EP, the EU Commission and the Council, the ECA confirmed the assessment of the EO and stated that all the EU institutions examined had established "adequate whistleblowing policies".[207] However, as will be demonstrated below, despite the introduction of internal rules on whistleblowing, there is still a long way to go to encourage and protect EU whistleblowers effectively and create a reliable mechanism allowing for the systematic report and investigation of irregularities within EU institutions. A broader personal scope of those internal rules could ensure that individuals working directly or indirectly with or within EU institutions, agencies and bodies feel

---

[201]EO, *Decision of the European Ombudsman on internal rules concerning disclosure in the public interest ('whistleblowing')* [hereinafter "Internal rules on whistleblowing"], Case OI /1/2014/PMC, 20 February 2015; see also EDPS, *Opinion on a notification for Prior Checking regarding the European Ombudsman's Whistleblowing Procedure*, Case 2014-0828, 4 December 2014.

[202]EO, *Decision of the European Ombudsman closing her own-inquiry OI/1/2014/PMC concerning whistleblowing*, para 12.

[203]EO, *Speech at the Council of Europe Group of States against Corruption (GRECO), Plenary Meeting, Council of Europe*, Strasbourg, 20 October 2016.

[204]EP, *Internal Rules Implementing Article 22c of the Staff Regulations* [hereinafter "Internal rules on whistleblowing"], 4 December 2015; see also EDPS, *Prior-checking Opinion on the European Parliaments Whistleblowing procedure*, Case 2017-0379, 11 July 2017.

[205]Council of the European Union (Council), *Decision No 3/2016 of the Secretary-General of the Council adopting internal rules for reporting serious irregularities – Procedure for the implementation of Article 22a, 22b and 22c of the Staff Regulations and 66.8 of the Financial Regulation* [hereinafter "Internal rules on whistleblowing"], DE 3/16, 29 February 2016; Following a question by the author, the Council held "that since the entry into force of the Decision n°3/2016..., the General Secretariat of the Council (GSC) has not received any report on serious irregularities within the meaning of that Decision", *Ref. 20/0513-em/jg*, 27/03/2020; See also EDPS, *Prior checking Opinion on the whistleblowing procedure from the General Secretariat of the Council of the European Union*, Case 2015-0349, 15 September 2015.

[206]CJEU, *Décision du Comité Administratif de la Cour de Justice de l'Union européenne adoptant des lignes directrices relatives à l'information et à la protection des lanceurs d'alerte* [hereinafter "Guidelines on Whistleblowing"], 22 February 2016; see also EDPS, *Prior Checking Opinion on Initial Processing in the event of whistleblowing*, Case 2017-0304, 7 July 2017.

[207]ECA, *Special Report on ethical frameworks*, p. 15.

comforted by the fact that they will enjoy strong whistleblower protection, irrespective of their work-based relationship with the EU.

Broader Scope

Indeed, while seconded staff members are excluded from the application of the EU Commission's Guidelines, the Council explicitly extended the scope of application of its IPW to seconded national experts, "irrespective of their administrative position", but excluded trainees and interim or external staff.[208] On the other hand, the CJEU's Guidelines on whistleblowing are applicable to special advisers, temporary officials and contract agents.[209] In the same spirit as the EU Commission's Guidelines[210] and the EP IPW,[211] the Council also discourages anonymous reports[212] but considers the possibility for staff members to anonymously enter into dialogue with OLAF investigators to seek advice and determine whether the information they wish to report is relevant under the IPW.[213]

Improved Follow-ups

There is also room for improvement in regard to the follow-up and feedback to individuals having raised concerns about potential irregularities within EU bodies. Indeed, the reactions of OLAF in cases of whistleblower reports, such as transferring a case to the EU agency which has been the very subject of the whistleblower report, without having sufficiently explained to the EU whistleblower the reason for its decision,[214] or stating that it is under no obligation "to inform whistleblowers of the reasons for closing an investigation without recommendations",[215] seem to demonstrate a general reluctance to follow-up and provide feedback to EU whistleblowers.

---

[208] Council Internal rules on whistleblowing, Annex, p. 4.

[209] Recital 1 of the CJEU Guidelines on whistleblowing.

[210] EU Commission Guidelines on whistleblowing, pp. 7-8.

[211] Article 4(1) of the EP Internal rules on whistleblowing.

[212] Council Internal rules on whistleblowing, Annex, p. 8.

[213] Ibid., p. 11.

[214] EO, *Decision in case* 45/2015/PMC *concerning the European Anti-Fraud Office's (OLAF) actions following the receipt of a whistleblowing report*, Case 45/2015/PMC, 11 August 2015, para 17. As further remark, the EO recommended that OLAF should "consider informing whistleblowers in a more explicit way that its decision not to take immediate action, but to transmit a case first to another EU institution or body for their assessment, does not imply that OLAF has dismissed the matter altogether, but should rather be considered as constituting an appropriate first step in assessing the grievance reported by the whistleblower".

[215] EO, *Decision of the European Ombudsman closing the inquiry into complaint 1183/2012/MMN against OLAF*, Case 1183/2012/MMN, 23 June 2014, para 17. In this cases, the EO "invited OLAF

5.3.2.2 The Vulnerability of Accredited Parliamentary Assistants

The Shortcomings of the European Parliament Internal Rules on Whistleblowing

In this context and despite a wider application of the EP internal rules on whistleblowing, which extend *mutatis mutandis* to trainees and national experts,[216] the ECA identified some weaknesses in regard to the protection of Accredited Parliamentary Assistants (APAs)[217] and recommended adjusting the EP internal rules on whistleblowing to the particular nature of those specific positions.[218] This recommendation was rejected by the EP on the grounds that Article 24 EU Staff Regulations already offers sufficient protection for APAs if they decide to blow the whistle on serious irregularities.[219] This conclusion is devoid of any basis and is particularly unfortunate given the privileged position of APAs in becoming aware of irregularities within the EP and their vulnerability to retaliation. This particular vulnerability is illustrated by the EO case 1517/2017/JF on the early termination of an accredited parliamentary assistant's contract by the EP.[220] In his complaint, "the complainant claimed that his contract had been terminated early as a retaliatory measure for "whistleblowing" steps he had taken, notably in his decision to contact the Parliament's Secretary-General, on 4 October 2016, to highlight certain concerns. As a result of this, he claimed that he was eligible for protection, according to the provisions of the Staff Regulations on whistleblowing. He also claimed he had suffered moral and material damages, and should be duly compensated".[221]

"Broken Trust"

In its response to the complainant, the EP asserted that the early termination complied with internal rules[222] and was legitimate due to the deteriorating working relationship between the complainant and the MEP and the resulting broken

---

to provide additional clarifications as regards its reasons to close the investigation" (para 22 of its decision), which OLAF did.

[216] Article 1(2) EP Internal rules on whistleblowing.

[217] Definition of APAs, see Article 5a *EU Staff Regulations*.

[218] ECA, *Special Report on ethical frameworks*, Recommendation 1(5), p. 37. According to Article 127 *EU Staff Regulations*, Article 11 to Article 22a *EU Staff Regulations* apply by analogy to APAs.

[219] ECA, *Special Report on ethical frameworks*, Attachment, Replies of the European Parliament adopted by the Bureau to the Observations by the European Court of Auditors, on the Special Report "The ethical frameworks of the audited EU Institutions: Scope for Improvement", Reply to Observation 84, On Recommendation 1, Point 5.

[220] EO, *Decision of the European Ombudsman in case 1517/2017/JF on the early termination of the complainant's contract as an accredited parliamentary assistant by the European Parliament*, Case 1517/2017/JF, 8 February 2018.

[221] Ibid., para 6.

[222] Ibid., para 9.

"trust".[223] According to the EP, the complainant was also not able to establish that the MEP bears sole responsibility for the deterioration of the working relation[224] and took the view that "the provisions of the Staff Regulations on whistleblowing do not prevent the adoption of administrative measures that are both objectively justified and unrelated to any possible illegal activity raised by a whistleblower. According to the Parliament, the complainant has not brought forward any evidence to demonstrate that the request for the termination of his contract was a measure taken in retaliation for his attempt to contact the Secretary-General of the Parliament in October 2016 to report potential wrongdoing".[225]

The EO was satisfied by this reasoning, stating that the EP replied appropriately to the concerns raised by the complainant[226] and thus concluded that no further inquiries were justified.[227] This conclusion is regrettable because the interpretation of the EU Staff Regulations promoted by the EP is fundamentally inconsistent with the key principles of an effective whistleblower protection framework. First and foremost, putting the burden of proof on the whistleblower to demonstrate the causal link between the detriment suffered and the report made is contrary to the emerging European consensus[228] and demonstrates the flaws in the EP internal rules implementing Article 22(c) EU Staff Regulations.[229] In addition, the EP did not seem to have considered whether the whistleblower acted in good faith, independently of the accuracy of the allegations, in accordance with Article 2 in conjunction with Article 4(5) EP internal rules implementing Article 22(c) EU Staff Regulations. Finally, the condition of a relationship of trust between the APA and the MEP,[230] the lack of which can legitimately lead to the early termination of an APA's contract,[231] can be particularly challenging in regard to the effective protection of APA whistleblowers. Indeed, while whistleblowing should be balanced with the duty of loyalty to the employer, the mere act of blowing the whistle is per se a break of trust and could thus systematically lead to the early termination of a APA's contract. A thorough reform of the EP's internal rules implementing Article 22(c) EU Staff Regulations introducing all key principles of an effective whistleblower protection framework and the strict respect of confidentiality rules can alleviate the issues arising from the particular status of APAs when blowing the whistle.

---

[223] Ibid., para 10.

[224] Ibid.

[225] Ibid., para 11.

[226] Ibid., para 13.

[227] Ibid., Conclusion.

[228] Article 21(5) *EU Whistleblower Directive*; CoE, Recommendation CM/Rec(2014)7, *Appendix*, Point 25.

[229] Article 6(1) EP Internal rules on whistleblowing does not specify who carries the burden to prove that the detriment suffered by the whistleblower was indeed a retaliatory measure.

[230] Article 127 *EU Staff Regulations*.

[231] Article 139(1)(d) *EU Staff Regulations*.

5.3.2.3 EU External Actions

Offering the widest possible scope of application for internal rules on whistleblowing is all the more important for EU institutions with external relations or regular working relations with contractors or suppliers, such as the European External Action Service (EEAS). In this respect, the case of Maria Bamieh, former chief prosecutor at the European Union Rule of Law Mission in Kosovo (EULEX), perfectly illustrate the challenges facing EU officials when reporting on alleged misconduct within EU bodies working outside of the Union.

The Maria Bamieh Case

In October 2014, the Kosovo daily newspaper Koha Ditore published a series of articles revealing leaked documents which suggested, *inter alia*, that EULEX officials colluded with criminal suspects and accepted payment in exchange for closing ongoing cases.[232] The EULEX internal files leaked to the press included letters from Maria Bamieh, then EULEX chief persecutor, addressed to her supervisor in which she expressed concerns of wrongdoing by members of the mission.[233] After Koha Ditore contacted the EULEX Mission to obtain their side on the leaked documents, Ms. Bamieh was quickly suspended "as a precaution to stop her from leaking more confidential information" EU officials in Brussels said.[234] However, according to Koha Ditore, she was not the source and started speaking only after she got suspended.[235] Her testimony reveals the attacks and death threats she had to endure following the revelations and demonstrates the particularly challenging situation EU whistleblowers can face for raising concerns over allegations of corruptions.

Following the public backlash, Federica Mogherini, the EU High Representative at the time, appointed an independent legal expert to review the EULEX mission's mandate, and more specifically, the adequacy of its actions in regard to allegations of corruption within the mission.[236] While the name of Maria Bamieh does not appear in the report, it can be assumed following a correlation analysis. In his report, the expert considered that the allegation of retaliation in the form of disciplinary procedures against Ms. Bamieh did not seem to be founded[237] and that the signature of confidentiality agreements by EULEX staff members should not be considered as an

[232] Rettman (2014b, 31 October).

[233] Rettman (2014a, 30 October).

[234] Ibid.

[235] Ibid.

[236] European External Action Service (EEAS), *Statement by EU High Representative/Vice President Federica Mogherini on the appointment of legal expert to review EURLEX Kosovo mandate*, 10. November 2014.

[237] Jacqué (2015, 31 March), pp. 9 and 42–43.

attempt to prohibit whistleblowing.[238] Furthermore, while the source of the leaks could not be confirmed, the expert was of the opinion that Ms. Bamieh should have demonstrated more restraint when communicating with the media on the allegation of corruption,[239] in compliance with the presumption of innocence.[240] He also considered her suspension justified "by the fact that, even though she was not responsible for the leaks, the documents used as the basis for the articles had been written by her".[241] This reasoning seems to be difficult to reconcile with the presumption of innocence and appear to reveal a presumption of guilt, especially considering the lack of evidence proving her responsibility or involvement in the leak. In fact, contrary to the reasoning followed by the independent legal expert, such a suspension could, in addition to a potential violation of the EU administration's *devoir de sollicitude*, be also interpreted as an indirect retaliatory act for having blown the whistle internally, within the meaning of Article 22a EU Staff Regulations, the causal link between the letters sent to her superiors and the detrimental measure suffered being clearly established both by EU officials and the independent legal expert.

While the expert's reasoning can be understandable considering the sensitive nature of the documents disclosed and the legitimate interest of the mission to contain the leak of further internal documents, the particularly severe consequence for an individual having reported internally can have a dissuasive effect for future EU whistleblowers. Indeed, with the risk of leaks being omnipresent, potential EU whistleblowers could be deterred from reporting concerns of wrongdoing internally for fear of being suspended if their internal reports are leaked to the public. Considerations should be given to alternative measures aiming to temporarily limit an individual's access to confidential information during ongoing investigations into the leaks while maintaining the presumption of innocence of the EU whistleblower who reported internally, a suspension having the potential to violate this presumption and irrevocably damage the reputation of the EU whistleblower. Those investigations and control over disciplinary measures may be conducted by an independent external body as recommended by the EO,[242] a recommendation confirmed by the legal expert.[243]

Notwithstanding the foregoing, the expert dedicated a short but separate part of its report to the status of whistleblower.[244] First and foremost, the legal expert

[238]Ibid., p. 34.

[239]Ibid., p. 52.

[240]Ibid., p. 51.

[241]Ibid., pp. 10 and 53.

[242]EO, *Decision of the European Ombudsman closing the own-initiative inquiry OI/15/2014/PMC into the way in which the European External Action Service (EEAS) handles allegations of serious irregularities involving the EU rule of Law Mission (EURLEX) in Kosovo*, Case OI/15/2014/PMC, 4 December 2014, para 31.

[243]Jacqué (2015, 31 March), pp. 20–21.

[244]Ibid., pp. 56–57.

underlined that Ms. Bamieh should have been considered an internal whistleblower[245] and should therefore not have suffered prejudice for her action.[246] The expert also acknowledged that she could have reasonably felt sidelined due to the general lack of efforts to make her feel comfortable in her job.[247] He also noted that Article 22a EU Staff Regulations does not provide for external whistleblowing, for example to the press.[248] Despite this observation and in reference to the ECtHR's case-law in regard to external whistleblowing, the expert concluded that "the conditions for applying the status of external whistleblower under the European Convention on Human Rights have not been met in this case".[249] While this interpretation of the ECtHR's case-law seems to be particularly narrow,[250] the expert erred in discussing whether Ms. Bamieh fulfilled the criteria of external whistleblowing under Article 10 ECHR. Indeed, assuming that Ms. Bamieh was not the source of the leak, which seems to be confirmed in the report, she cannot be considered as having used external channels merely because the leaked files included documents of which she is the author. On the contrary, she should be considered a victim of those leaks, even if she confirmed her concerns to the media after the articles were published. While Ms. Bamieh, as the chief prosecutor of the mission, should have demonstrated a certain restraint and moderation when speaking publicly,[251] she cannot be treated as if she intentionally disclosed those documents. External whistleblowing in the form of public disclosure implies the active choice to reveal information publicly, a choice she did not make.[252]

The EEAS Standard Operating Procedure on Whistleblowing

The Bamieh case was not the first instance in which serious shortcomings in the protection of whistleblowers working in EU missions were identified.[253] In a 2015 decision, the EO indeed called on the EEAS to establish adequate rules to protect whistleblowers.[254] One year later, the EEAS provided the EO a copy of newly adopted Standard Operating Procedure (SOP) on whistleblowing, a measure deemed

[245] Ibid., p. 7.

[246] Ibid., p. 9.

[247] Ibid.

[248] Ibid., p. 56.

[249] Ibid., p. 57.

[250] Kusari (2015, 16 April).

[251] On the duty of discretion of civil servants under the ECHR see Sect. 4.2.2.1.

[252] On the application of the ECHR and the extraterritorial application of national employment laws see the decision of the UK domestic court in the Bamieh case, *Bamieh v. Kosovo & Others*, UKEAT/0268/16/RN, Judgment of 19 January 2018, see in particular paras 123 et seq.

[253] EO, *Decision of the European Ombudsman closing the inquiries into complaints 26/2011/DK and 1307/2012/DK against the European External Action Service*, Cases 26/2011/DK and 1307/2012/DK, 4 June 2015, para 23.

[254] Ibid., 'Further remark'.

satisfactory by the EO[255] to address the procedural and systemic issues identified in its own-initiative inquiry.[256] According to the EO, the EEAS SOP on whistleblowing has a generous personal scope as it encompasses all Mission members.[257] Furthermore, the EU stated that the SOP on whistleblowing includes the possibility to report externally to the EEAS' Civilian Operations Commander, the Chair of the Political Committee of the Council, the High Representative, OLAF and the EO.[258] The EEAS specified that the SOP on whistleblowing should be read in conjunction with the EU Commission's Guidelines on whistleblowing.[259] For the EO, the adoption of the SOP on whistleblowing represents "a great improvement",[260] but it nonetheless encouraged the EEAS to consider similar measures for EU delegations and suggested to provide easily accessible online information about the general Guideline on whistleblowing and alternative procedures of reporting.[261]

However, when asked about the SOP on whistleblowing, the EEAS replied that "such a single document does not exist".[262] In its statement, the EEAS emphasized that "[t]he EEAS staff is bound by the Staff Regulations which include rules on whistleblowing, setting out procedures for reporting any fraud, corruption or serious irregularities, and providing protection to whistleblowers from adverse consequences of this reporting. The EEAS applies also the EU Commission Guidelines on Whistleblowing which complement the rules on whistleblowing set out in the Staff Regulations".[263] In addition to the statement, the EEAS provided five documents in an annex which included the EU Commission Guidelines on Whistleblowing, a Q&A on the EU Commission Guidelines on Whistleblowing, two parliamentary questions and their respective answers from EU High

---

[255]EO, *Follow-up on to my own-initiative inquiry OI/15/2014/PMC concerning alleged irregularities affecting EURLEX Kosovo*, Correspondence of the European Ombudsman to the EU High Representative for Foreign Affairs and Security Policy, Case OI/15/2014/PMC, 27 April 2016.

[256]EO, *Decision of the European Ombudsman closing the own-initiative inquiry OI/15/2014/PMC*, para 31.

[257]EO, *Follow-up on to my own-initiative inquiry OI/15/2014/PMC concerning alleged irregularities affecting EURLEX Kosovo,* Annex (iii)(a).

[258]Ibid., Annex (iii)(b).

[259]In its 2019 reply to an EO inquiry, the EEAS reiterated that it applies the Commission's Guidelines on whistleblowing, which implies that those documents, the Commission's Guidelines on whistleblowing and the SOP on whistleblowing, should be considered complementary, see EO, *Decision in case 1234/2018/TM on how an EU delegation to a non-EU country dealt with an individual who raised concerned about an EU-funded project*, Case 1234/2018/TM, 27 June 2019, para 7.

[260]EO, *Follow-up on to my own-initiative inquiry OI/15/2014/PMC concerning alleged irregularities affecting EURLEX Kosovo*, Annex (iii)(b).

[261]OE, *Decision in case 1234/2018/TM on how an EU delegation to a non-EU country dealt with an individual who raised concerned about an EU-funded project*, paras 11-12.

[262]EEAS, Reply to a request by the author for the document SOP on whistleblowing, *Ref. 2020/039*, p. 1.

[263]Ibid., p. 2.

Representative Federica Mogherini and finally, a note from the Director-General for Budget and Administration at the attention of EEAS staff members in Headquarters and in Delegations.[264]

The statement of the EEAS thus seems to suggest that the protection of whistleblowers within the EEAS headquarters and in EU delegations around the world shall be interpreted on the basis of those five documents. Accordingly, the SOP on whistleblowing appears to be an assembly of existing procedures rather than a new single standardized procedure. In the note from the Director-General for Budget and Administration, it is emphasized that the obligation to report on irregularities "fall on all staff, whether official, other agent or staff member not submitted to Staff Regulations",[265] which confirms the broad personal scope of application underlined by the EO in the follow-up to its own-inquiry. However, contrary to the EO's observation, nothing in the provided documents states that Mission members have additional external reporting channels to those provided by the EU Staff Regulations and the EU Commission Guidelines.

The particular emphasis on the EU Commission Guidelines on Whistleblowing demonstrates that the EEAS rely heavily on those provisions to define its own internal rules on whistleblowing. The deficiencies of the EU Commission Guidelines observed above thus apply in the case of the EEAS. Furthermore, the particular role of the EEAS and the status of the EU delegations and its Staff members around the world call for more targeted rules designed to address those specificities, considerations left unaddressed by the EEAS current whistleblowing policies.

5.3.2.4 EU Banks and the EULeaks Initiative

The ECB and EIB Whistleblowing Policies

Because Staff members of the European Central Bank (ECB) and of the European Investment Bank (EIB) are employed under contract,[266] different Staff rules

---

[264]References of the documents provided by the EEAS in its reply: Parliamentary question by MEP Derek Vaughan (S&D) to the Commission (Vice-President/High Representative), *VP/HR – Whistle-blower protections*, E-002610-18, 18 May 2018; Answer given by Vice-President Mogherini on behalf of the Commission, E-002610-18(ASW), 26 June 2018; Parliamentary question by MEP Luke Ming Flanagan (GUE/NGL) to the Commission: *Whistleblower protection at the UN in Switzerland*, E-004636/2017, 10 June 2017; Answer given by Vice-President Mogherini on behalf of the Commission, E-004636/2017(ASW), 11 October 2017; EEAS, *Note for the attention of EEAS Staff Members in Headquarters and in Delegations: Ethical and organizational values (Internal Control Standard 2)*, Director-General, Directorate-General of Budget and Administration, 01.06.2016.

[265]EEAS, *Note for the attention of EEAS Staff Members in Headquarters and in Delegations*, p. 1.

[266]Bradley (2018), p. 560.

apply.[267] Nonetheless, while the EIB adopted a whistleblowing policy in 2009,[268] the ECB introduced whistleblower protection rules as early as 2006 in its internal Administrative Circular.[269] To encourage the report of breaches,[270] the ECB also established a confidential whistleblowing platform[271] to receive information about violations of EU law concerning the prudential supervision of banks.[272] Mirroring the EU Staff Regulations provision on whistleblowing, the ECB further introduced an internal duty to report information about illegal activities following a tiered model and the possibility to report directly to OLAF if certain requirements are fulfilled,[273] thereby strengthening the cooperation between the ECB and OLAF in investigative matters.[274] In accordance with the ECB's intent to review its whistleblowing policy,[275] the then President of the ECB, Mr. Draghi, informed the EP in a letter dated September 2015 that "the Executive Board has identified the enhancement of its whistleblowing framework as one of its strategic priorities for the years 2018 to 2020", and that it "is fully committed to implementing a modern and comprehensive whistleblowing policy and has a genuine interest in instilling a positive culture of speaking up".[276]

EULeaks

In parallel to the internal rules implementing whistleblower protection mechanisms within EU institutions, some MEPs from The Greens/EFA Group in the EP decided to launch a whistleblower platform, EULeaks,[277] in 2016 with an email address and a PGP key, through which individuals could "blow the whistle in defence of the

---

[267]European Central Bank (ECB) Staff Rules, 1 August 2019; European Investment Bank (EIB) Staff Regulations, 16 January 2018.

[268]EIB' Whistleblowing policy; See also EDPS, *Prior-check Opinion on the Whistleblowing Policy of the European Investment Bank,* Case 2016-0381, 29 November 2017.

[269]ECB, *Administrative Circular 01/2006 on internal administrative inquiries*, 21 March 2006.

[270]ECB, *Supervision explained: Whistleblowers act in the greater good*, 8 September 2015. Link.

[271]ECB, *ECB Breach reporting mechanism (whistleblowing)*. Link.

[272]ECB, *Supervisory practices: Important legal information before using the whistleblowing platform*. Link.

[273]Article 3 of the *Decision (EU) 2016/456 of the European Central Bank concerning the terms and conditions for European Anti-Fraud investigations of the European Central Bank, in relation to the prevention of fraud, corruption and any other illegal activities affecting the financial interests of the Union (ECB/2016/3)*, 4 March 2016.

[274]ECB, *Administrative Arrangements between the European Central Bank and the European Anti-Fraud Office*, 16 June 2016.

[275]ECB, *Letter from Danièle Nouy, Chair of the Supervisory Board of the ECB, to Sven Giegold, Member of the European Parliament*, 29 June 2017.

[276]ECB, *Letter from Mario Draghi, President of the ECB, to Sven Giegold, Member of the European Parliament*, L/MD/19/331, 26 September 2019.

[277]EP, Pana Committee: Greens/EFA MEPS Launch EULeaks whistleblower platform. *Press release*, The Greens/EFA Group of the EP, 27 September 2016.

public interest, whilst remaining anonymous".[278] As of April 2019, no statistics on the number of reports made through the platform EULeaks or on the nature of those reports were made available, making the effectiveness of this platform difficult to appreciate.[279]

5.4 The Future of Whistleblower Protection Within EU Institutions

Having strong whistleblower protection rules for employees working in EU institutions is key to ensure the highest level of transparency and help address the growing distrust in EU bureaucracy. Encouraging reports of fraud, corruption, mismanagement, abuse of power and other misconduct within EU institutions would strengthen the integrity of the EU institutions and help improve the image of the EU as a whole. While all EU institutions are moving in the right direction, consistent data collection on internal whistleblower reports within each institution will allow for effective and relevant adjustment of internal rules in order to be in compliance with international best practices and ensure the highest whistleblower protection standards so as to gain the trust of EU officials and encourage them to report breaches.

There is indeed a pressing need to reform the EU Staff Regulations and the implementing procedures on whistleblowing of each EU Institution, agency and body in order to align the whistleblower protection framework applicable within EU institutions to the new minimum standards imposed by the 2019 EU Whistleblower Directive.[280] Paradoxically, if the EU Staff Regulations are not amended to raise the level of protection afforded to individuals raising concerns of irregularities within EU institutions, agencies and bodies, EU Member States domestic public institutions would be held to a higher standard in regard to whistleblower protection than EU institutions themselves, which can only further a sense of hypocrisy.

References

Aiossa N (2020) Make 2020 the year of the EU Staff whistleblower. Transparency International EU. https://transparency.eu/euwhistleblower/. Accessed 13 Apr 2021

---

[278]EP, *EULeaks platform*. https://www.greens-efa.eu/en/article/news/eu-leaks/. Accessed 13 April 2021.

[279]Reply from the Office of the MEP Sven Giegold to a question by the author, " [es wird] keine entsprechende Statistik darüber geführt..., da es sich ja jeweils um vertrauliche Inhalte handelt, welche nicht zentral von einer Stelle bearbeitet werden und je nach Fall die Personen mit fachlicher Zuständigkeit hinzugezogen werden", Email reply from 18 April 2020.

[280]Aiossa (2020, 22 January).

Bradley K (2018) European Union civil service law. In: Hofmann HCH, Rowe GC, Türk AH (eds) Specialized administrative law of the European Union: a sectorial review. Oxford University Press, Oxford, pp 559–578

Dehn G (1996) Whistlebleblowing, Fraud & the European Union. Report commissioned by the EU Commission

EU, *Ombudsman*, Glossary of summaries, available at https://eur-lex.europa.eu/summary/glossary/ombudsman.html. Accessed 13 April 2021

Guckelberger A (2004) Der Europäische Bürgerbeauftragte und die Petitionen zum Europäischen Parlament. Eine Bestandsaufnahme zu Beginn des 21. Jahrhunderts. Schriftenreihe der Deutschen Universität für Verwaltungswissenschaften Speyer 162. Duncker & Humblot, Berlin

Haas J (2012) Der Ombudsmann als Institution des Europäischen Verwaltungsrechts. Zur Neubestimmung der Rolle des Ombudsmanns als Organ der Verwaltungskontrolle auf der Grundlage europäischer Ombudsmann-Einrichtung. Mohr Siebeck, Tübingen

Harden I (2017) The European Ombudsman's role in promoting good governance. Accountability in the EU – the role of the European Ombudsman: the role of the European Ombudsman. Edward Elgar Publishing, Cheltenham, pp 198–216

Hofmann HCH (2017) The developing role of the European Ombudsman. In: Hofmann HCH, Ziller J (eds) Accountability in the EU – the role of the European Ombudsman: the role of the European Ombudsman. Edward Elgar Publishing, Cheltenham/Northampton, pp 1–27

Jacqué JP (2015, 31 March) Review of the EULEX Kosovo Mission's implementation of the mandate with a particular focus on the handling of the recent allegations, Report to the attention of Higher Representative/Vice President of the European Commission Ms Federica Mogherini

Kusari F (2015, 16 April) EU Review wrongly and superficially applies ECtHR precedent on Whistleblowing. Strasbourg Observers

Mastroianni R (2017) New perspective for the European Ombudsman opened by the Lisbon Treaty. In: Hofmann HCH, Ziller J (eds) Accountability in the EU – the role of the European Ombudsman: the role of the European Ombudsman. Edward Elgar Publishing, Cheltenham, pp 178–197

Rettman A (2014a, 30 October) EU Mission in Kosovo rocked by corruption allegations. *EU Observer*

Rettman A (2014b, 31 October) Whistleblower urges external probe into EU mission in Kosovo. *EU Observer*

Tsadiras A (2007) The position of the European Ombudsman in the community system of judicial remedies. Eur Law Rev 32(5):607–626

Vogiatzis N (2018) The European Ombudsman and good administration in the European Union. Palgrave Macmillan, London

Chapter 6
When EU Whistleblowers Go to Court

The road to reporting wrongdoing when working for EU institutions is, as it is often the case for whistleblowers, filled with challenges. The introduction of Articles 22a and 22b EU Staff Regulations was a first step in establishing a whistleblowing mechanism and developing a culture of transparence within EU institutions and bodies. However, the interpretation of those provisions by the judicial branch of the EU plays a key role in determining the real effectiveness of the protection mechanism put in place. The analysis of selected cases will illustrate the CJEU's interpretation of these provisions and provide an insight into their practicality and the extent to which this protection mechanism can effectively shield EU officials wishing to report on suspected wrongdoing in their workplace.

6.1 The Landmark Cases on EU Whistleblowing: *Bermejo Garde v. EESC*

The *Bermejo Garde v. European Economic and Social Committee (EESC)* judgments are particularly interesting as they illustrate the textbook example of a whistleblower case: An official with a particular expertise and several years of work experience in the same institution suspects irregularities in his workplace and reports it to his superiors. Following his report, the official suffers drastic changes in his professional career. In the different decisions, the CJEU not only established the key criteria relevant to determine the scope of application of Article 22a EU Staff Regulations, it also defined the interaction between Article 22a EU and Article 12a EU Staff Regulations, the latter provision prohibiting harassment in the workplace.

© The Author(s), under exclusive license to Springer Nature Switzerland AG 2021

H. C. L. Yurttagül, *Whistleblower Protection by the Council of Europe, the European Court of Human Rights and the European Union*, European Union and its Neighbours in a Globalized World 3, https://doi.org/10.1007/978-3-030-78059-3_6

6.1.1 The Facts of the *Bermejo Garde* Case

The applicant, Mr. Moises Bermejo Garde, started working as Legal Adviser in the Directorat for Administration, Personnel and Finances of the EESC in 1991 and became Head of the Legal Service Unit of the Department in 1997.[1] In October 2008, Mr. W became new Secretary-General of the EESC. From then on, the relation between the applicant and Mr. W gradually deteriorated, in part because, according to the applicant's statement, Mr. W put "illegitimate" pressure on the Legal Service.[2]

At the beginning of December 2009, the applicant, expressly referring to Article 22a(1) EU Staff Regulations, sent a note to the Office of the President of the EESC, informing the latter about numerous and serious irregularities committed by the Secretary-General in the performance of his duties, and in a lesser extent, by the Chief of the Recruitment, Career and Formation Unit of the EESC. The applicant lodged three complaints: The pressure put on the Legal Service, the refusal to impose disciplinary sanctions on a Staff Member who was allegedly guilty of criminal offenses and neglecting to refer the matter to OLAF, and lastly, the irregular filling of director positions within the EESC.[3]

To address those complaints, the applicant called for an investigation into those irregularities to determine the respective personal responsibilities after the intervention of OLAF. He also asked for actions to restore the proper functioning of the secretariat general and ensure the independence of the Legal Service in accordance with the conditions imposed by the CJEU.[4] Lastly, he asked for the assistance of the Office, in compliance with Article 24 EU Staff Regulations, to take measures to end the psychological harassment against him committed by the Secretary-General.[5]

A few days after the receipt of the applicant's note, the president instructed his chief of Staff to start a preliminary examination of the information communicated by the applicant.[6] At the end of January 2010, the Chief of Staff issued a report in which he rejected the applicant's allegations as unfounded but noted that there is indeed a "tense climate" between the Legal Service and the Secretariat General, which seemed to be the result of a difference of views as to the role of the Legal Service. In the words of the Chief of Staff, the applicant's sense of harassment originated in those diverging opinions, the different legal culture and tradition as well as the different personal characters of the individuals involved.[7]

---

[1] CST, Case F-41/10 RENV, *Moises Bermejo Garde v. European Economic and Social Committee (EESC)* [hereinafter "Bermejo Garde v. EESC (2016)"], Judgment of 2 June 2016, ECLI:EU: F:2016:123, paras 12–13.

[2] Ibid., paras 15–17.

[3] Ibid., para 18.

[4] Ibid., para 19.

[5] Ibid., para 20.

[6] Ibid., para 22.

[7] Ibid., para 24.

Following this report, the President of the EESC invited the applicant to withdraw his requests.[8] The latter declined, stating that withdrawing his request would amount to contradicting his obligations under the EU Staff Regulations.[9] In a decision released at the beginning of March 2010, the President rejected the applicant's requests on the grounds that the little evidence on the alleged psychological harassment contradicted the applicant's arguments and that the accusations of abuse of power and authority from the Secretary-General were not justified. In the same decision, the president designated the Secretary-General to assign the applicant to another position in a different unit from the Legal Service.[10] By decision of the 24 March 2010 and with the agreement of the Secretary-General, the president terminated the appointment of the applicant as Head of the Legal Service with immediate effect and reassigned him in the Directorate for Logistics as Head of Unit.[11]

The applicant lodged a complaint against, *inter alia*, the decisions of the President of the EESC to reject his request to transfer the matter to OLAF, to terminate his appointment as Head of the Legal Service and reassign him to another Unit.[12] Following a brief overview of the court proceedings, an analysis of the different Courts' reasoning and conclusions will illustrate the principles they developed regarding the interpretation of Article 22a EU Staff Regulations.

The EU Civil Service Tribunal rejected the applicant's claims in 2012 (hereinafter referred to as "the initial judgment"),[13] a decision appealed by the applicant.[14] The EU General Court set aside the judgment of the Civil Service Tribunal (hereinafter referred to as "the judgment on appeal")[15] and referred the case back to the EU Civil Service Tribunal. In his written observations after referral, the applicant requested, *inter alia*, the annulment of both the decision of termination of his previous functions and the decision of reassignment to another unit, as well as the payment by the EESC of €25,000 as damages and interest.[16] The EESC on the other hand, requested the dismissal of the action and the order for the applicant to bear all the costs of

[8]Ibid., para 25.

[9]Ibid., para 26.

[10]Ibid., para 27–29.

[11]Ibid., para 33–34.

[12]CST, Case F-41/10, *Bermejo Garde v. EESC*, Action brought on 7 June 2010, OJ C 209, 31.07.2010, p. 55.

[13]CST, Case F-41/10, *Moises Bermejo Garde v. European Economic and Social Committee (EESC)* [hereinafter "Bermejo Garde v. EESC (2012)"], Judgment of 25 September 2012, ECLI:EU:F:2012:135.

[14]GC, Case T-530/12 P, *Bermejo Garde v. EESC*, Appeal brought on 5 Dec. 2012 by Moises Bermejo Garde against the judgment of the Civil Service Tribunal of 25 September 2012 in Case F-41/10, Bermejo Garde v. EESC, OJ C 55, 23.02.2013, p. 15.

[15]GC, Case T-530/12 P, *Moises Bermejo Garde v. European Economic and Social Committee (EESC)* [hereinafter "Bermejo Garde v. EESC (2014)"], Judgment of 8 October 2014, ECLI:EU:T:2014:860.

[16]CST, Case F-41/10 RENV, *Bermejo Garde v. EESC (2016)*, para 48.

proceedings.[17] The EU Civil Service Tribunal, after referral, annulled the decisions of the President of the EESC and ordered the latter to pay €25,000 to the applicant, as compensation for the prejudice suffered (hereinafter referred to as "the judgment after referral").[18]

6.1.2 *An Act Adversely Affecting the Whistleblower*

First and foremost, the EU Civil Service Tribunal and the EU General Court had to delimit the scope of protection granted by Article 22a EU Staff Regulations and determine against which kind of acts or measures this provision is supposed to protect EU whistleblowers. Article 22a(3) EU Staff Regulations stipulates that "[a]n official shall not suffer any prejudicial effects on the part of the institution as a result" of having reported on irregularities, "provided that he acted reasonably and honestly". As a reminder, "only an act or measure producing binding legal effects that directly and immediately affects the applicant's interest by significantly altering his legal position is an act adversely affecting him".[19]

6.1.2.1 Termination and Reassignment

According to the applicant, the decision to terminate his appointment as Head of the Legal Service and reassign him to another Unit was a "disguised disciplinary measure" for having blown the whistle on serious irregularities committed by the EESC Secretary-General.[20] While the EU Civil Service Tribunal, in its initial judgment, recognized that these decisions taken following the applicant's report[21] constituted acts adversely affecting him,[22] it recalled that these measures are only in violation of Article 22a EU Staff Regulations if the applicant acted honestly in providing evidence giving rise to a presumption of an illegal activity or of serious failure to comply with the obligations of officials.[23] In the case at hand, the EU Civil Service Tribunal considered that the applicant not only failed to provide evidence of irregularities "so serious as to give rise to the presumption" of such misconduct,[24] he

[17] Ibid., para 50.

[18] CST, Case F-41/10 RENV, *Bermejo Garde v. EESC (2016)*, para 104.

[19] CST, Case F-41/10, *Bermejo Garde v. EESC (2012)*, para 49.

[20] CST, Case F-41/10, *Bermejo Garde v. EESC (2012)*, para 129.

[21] CST, Case F-41/10, *Bermejo Garde v. EESC (2012)*, para 132.

[22] CST, Case F-41/10, *Bermejo Garde v. EESC (2012)*, para 103.

[23] CST, Case F-41/10, *Bermejo Garde v. EESC (2012)*, para 133.

[24] CST, Case F-41/10, *Bermejo Garde v. EESC (2012)*, para 149.

also failed to comply with his obligation "to show the greatest prudence and the greatest discretion" in reporting those allegations.[25]

In its judgment on appeal, the EU General Court rejected the EU Civil Service Tribunal's reasoning[26] and held that in order to appreciate whether the applicant acted reasonably and honestly in accordance with Article 22a EU Staff Regulations, the EU Civil Service Tribunal should have appreciated the report made by the applicant in its proper context.[27] It thus referred the case back to the EU Civil Service Tribunal, which concluded, in its judgment after referral, that the applicant had in fact acted in accordance with Article 22a EU Staff Regulations and that the decisions to terminate his appointment as Head of the Legal Service and reassign him to another Unit were thus a violation of Article 22a (3) EU Staff Regulations.[28]

6.1.2.2 The Refusal to Transfer Information to OLAF

In the case *Bermejo Garde*, after the applicant had transmitted his note with information on alleged irregularities, the President of the EESC refused to transfer the information to OLAF, a decision criticized by the applicant. In the initial judgment, the EU Civil Service Tribunal had thus to decide whether this refusal to transfer the matter to OLAF could be considered an act adversely affecting the applicant,[29] which could thus entitle him to request its annulment, on the basis of Article 22a EU Staff Regulations. In the initial judgment, the EU Civil Service Tribunal considered that this refusal was not an act adversely affecting the applicant because the information disclosed did not directly affect him.[30] On this ground, the request of the applicant to annul the decision of the President of the EESC should therefore be considered as inadmissible.[31]

While it came to the same result, the EU General Court rejected the above reasoning in its judgment on appeal[32] and based its conclusions on different considerations.[33] Indeed, according to the EU General Court, due to the fact that the applicant could inform OLAF directly at any time without any intervention of his superiors, the refusal of the President of the EESC to transfer the information to OLAF could not be considered as an act adversely affecting the applicant, independently of whether the irregularities reported affected him directly or not.[34] It is

[25]CST, Case F-41/10, *Bermejo Garde v. EESC (2012)*, para 150.

[26]GC, Case T-530/12 P, *Bermejo Garde v. EESC (2014)*, para 165.

[27]GC, Case T-530/12 P, *Bermejo Garde v. EESC (2014)*, para 153.

[28]CST, Case F-41/10 RENV, *Bermejo Garde v. EESC (2016)*, para 94.

[29]CST, Case F-41/10, *Bermejo Garde v. EESC (2012)*, para 59.

[30]Ibid., para 60.

[31]Ibid., para 64.

[32]GC, Case T-530/12 P, *Bermejo Garde v. EESC (2014)*, para 68.

[33]Ibid., paras 65–70.

[34]Ibid., para 67.

questionable whether this interpretation is compatible with Article 22a (2) EU Staff Regulations, which expressly stipulates that "[a]ny official receiving the information ... shall without delay transmit to OLAF any evidence of which he is aware from which the existence of the irregularities ... may be presumed". According to this wording, the EU whistleblower's superiors would be under an obligation to inform OLAF, an interpretation confirmed by the EU Civil Service Tribunal in the 2012 initial judgment and in the 2016 judgment after referral.[35] It follows therefrom that the refusal of a superior to transfer information to OLAF could indeed be considered a violation of Article 22a EU Staff Regulations in certain circumstances and thus may constitute an act adversely affecting the EU whistleblower. Indeed, according to the General Court, "un tel refus ne saurait *en principe* affecter sa situation juridique et statutaire"[36] considering that under Article 22a EU Staff Regulations, the EU whistleblower has the possibility to report directly to OLAF. In this context, the term "in principle" used by the General Court suggests that a refusal should not in general be understood as constituting an act adversely affecting the EU whistleblower, but it could be the case in certain exceptional circumstances.

6.1.3 Good Faith Under Article 22(a) EU Staff Regulations

6.1.3.1 The *Bermejo Garde* Criteria

According to Article 22a(3) EU Staff Regulations, an EU official shall act reasonably and honestly, in other words, in good faith, when reporting suspicions of irregularities. As a general principle, the good faith of the EU official is to be established on the basis of concrete facts and all the elements of the context.[37] To this end and drawing on the ECtHR case-law, the EU Civil Service Tribunal developed, in the initial judgment, a set of criteria to determine whether the EU whistleblower acted reasonably and honestly in accordance with Article 22a(3) EU Staff Regulations.[38]

Seriousness of the Irregularity Reported

First and foremost, the report made by an EU whistleblower under Article 22a EU Staff Regulations should concern information on irregularities of a serious nature,[39]

[35]CST, Case F-41/10, *Bermejo Garde v. EESC (2012)*, para 56; CST, Case F-41/10 RENV, *Bermejo Garde v. EESC (2016)*, para 83.

[36]GC, Case T-530/12 P, *Bermejo Garde v. EESC (2014)*, para 67 (emphasis added). Translation "Consequently, such a refusal cannot in principle affect his legal situation".

[37]GC, Case T-530/12 P, *Bermejo Garde v. EESC (2014)*, para 148.

[38]CST, Case F-41/10, *Bermejo Garde v. EESC (2012)*, para 134.

[39]Ibid., para 135.

implied by the examples provided in Article 22a (1) EU Staff Regulations, namely "fraud or corruption".[40] If several irregularities are being reported, the Court has to determine whether the accumulation of those irregularities could form a unified set of events which together could be of a serious nature.[41]

The latter finding is particularly relevant when the report made includes allegations of harassment in violation of Article 12a EU Staff Regulations. Indeed, according to the EU Civil Service Tribunal, who referred to the Charter of Fundamental Rights of the European Union (hereinafter referred to as "EU Charter"), and more specifically to Articles 1 and 31 thereof, as well as to Article 12 and 12a of the EU Staff Regulations which aim to ensure the protection of EU officials in the workplace, harassment constitutes in itself a serious failure to comply with statutory obligations within the meaning of Article 22a(1) EU Staff Regulations.[42] According to the EU General Court however, the duty to report established by Article 22a (1) EU Staff Regulations may be incompatible with the special protection conferred by Article 12a EU Staff Regulations.[43] Based on this observation, it concluded that a distinction should be drawn between harassment and other forms of serious failure to comply with statutory obligations. Accordingly, while EU officials who consider themselves victim of harassment shall not be obliged to report under Article 22a EU Staff Regulations, they could still do so if they wish.[44]

Authenticity of the Information Reported

The seriousness of the irregularity reported should be appreciated in the light of the second criterion, namely whether the information reported could be considered authentic, or at the very least, likely.[45] As a reminder, Article 22a(1) EU Staff Regulations stipulates that:

> Any official who, in the course of or in connection with the performance of his duties, becomes aware of **facts which give rise to a presumption of the existence of possible** illegal activity, including fraud or corruption, detrimental to the interests of the Union, or of conduct relating to the discharge of professional duties which may constitute a serious failure to comply with the obligations of officials of the Union[46]

[40] GC, Case T-530/12 P, *Bermejo Garde v. EESC (2014)*, para 123.

[41] GC, Case T-530/12 P, *Bermejo Garde v. EESC (2014)*, para 155; see also CST, Case F-41/10 RENV, *Bermejo Garde v. EESC (2016)*, para 79.

[42] CST, Case F-41/10 RENV, *Bermejo Garde v. EESC (2016)*, para 80.

[43] GC, Case T-530/12 P, *Bermejo Garde v. EESC (2014)*, para 106.

[44] GC, Case T-530/12 P, *Bermejo Garde v. EESC (2014)*, para 106.

[45] CST, Case F-41/10, *Bermejo Garde v. EESC (2012)*, para 136; GC, Case T-530/12 P, *Bermejo Garde v. EESC (2014)*, para 158; CST, Case F-41/10 RENV, *Bermejo Garde v. EESC (2016)*, para 81.

[46] Emphasis added.

As a general principle, Article 22a EU Staff Regulations does not release EU officials from their statutory obligations under the EU Staff Regulations.[47] In this sense and paraphrasing the ECtHR case-law on Article 10 ECHR, the EU Civil Service Tribunal held that freedom of expression upon which EU officials shall report information on irregularities according to Article 22a EU Staff Regulations carries with it duties and responsibilities.[48] It includes the obligation to act in accordance with the dignity of their functions, as it is required by Article 12 EU Staff Regulations, as well as with their duty of objectivity, impartiality and loyalty enshrined in Articles 11 and 21 EU Staff Regulations.[49] It also implies respect for the presumption of innocence and the dignity of others.[50] While a personal assessment of the facts is permissible,[51] those duties and responsibilities require EU officials to exercise the greatest prudence and the greatest discretion,[52] as well as discernment[53] and reserve[54] when reporting information on irregularities according to Article 22a EU Staff Regulations. This necessity is consistent with an established case-law which imposes "the obligation to show the greatest prudence and the greatest discretion in the publicity given to allegations coming within the competence of OLAF".[55]

In view of the above, EU officials shall verify, to the extent permitted by the circumstances, whether the information they wish to report "are supported by accurate facts or, at least, that they are founded on a 'sufficient factual basis'", in reference to the ECtHR case-law on whistleblowing.[56] In practical terms, the disclosure must be preceded by a minimal assessment of concrete facts leading the EU official to form a reasonable presumption of the existence of serious irregularities.[57] That is not to say, however, that EU officials must establish a presumption of serious irregularities to fall within the scope of Article 22a EU Staff Regulations, which would represent, according to the EU Civil Service Tribunal, a particularly

[47] GC, Case T-91/17, *L v. European Parliament*, Judgment of 14 February 2019, ECLI:EU:T:2019:93, para 46.

[48] CST, Case F-41/10, *Bermejo Garde v. EESC (2012)*, para 136.

[49] CST, Case F-77/09, *Nijs v. ECA*, para 67; CST, Case F-41/10, *Bermejo Garde v. EESC (2012)*, para 136; GC, Case T-530/12 P, *Bermejo Garde v. EESC (2014)*, para 128; CST, Case F-41/10 RENV, *Bermejo Garde v. EESC (2016),* para 73.

[50] CST, Case F-77/09, *Nijs v. ECA*, para 68; CST, Case F-41/10, *Bermejo Garde v. EESC (2012)*, para 136; GC, Case T-530/12 P, *Bermejo Garde v. EESC (2014)*, para 128.

[51] CST, Case F-77/09, *Nijs v. ECA*, para 73.

[52] CST, Case F-77/09, *Nijs v. ECA*, para 80.

[53] GC, Case T-530/12 P, *Bermejo Garde v. EESC (2014)*, para 129.

[54] CST, Case F-77/09, *Nijs v. ECA*, para 70.

[55] Ibid., para 80.

[56] CST, Case F-41/10, *Bermejo Garde v. EESC (2012)*, para 136; more specifically, the court refers to the *Heinisch* case of the ECtHR, which uses the term "no devoid of factual ground" to determine whether the information reported can be considered authentic.

[57] CST, Case F-77/09, *Nijs v. ECA*, paras 65-66; GC, Case T-530/12 P, *Bermejo Garde v. EESC (2014)*, paras 130 and 156.

complex endeavour.[58] Instead, the concrete facts on the basis of which an EU official presumed the existence of possible serious irregularities should be examined in relation with her or his function.[59] The determination of whether an EU official could have reasonably and honestly presumed the existence of possible irregularities within the meaning of Article 22a EU Staff Regulations should be established in particular on the basis of the level of responsibility[60] and the nature of the duties performed by the EU official.[61]

As seen above, Article 22a EU Staff Regulations imposes upon EU officials an obligation to report. The good faith of the EU official shall thus be determined in relation with this obligation, which narrows the margin of appreciation of the EU official when determining whether the suspected wrongdoing falls within the scope of Article 22a EU Staff Regulations and should be reported.[62] Indeed, because an EU official who did not report suspected wrongdoing could be subjected to disciplinary sanctions under Article 86 EU Staff Regulations,[63] EU officials who are under such an obligation may be more inclined to report than if they had a mere right to do so.[64]

The Reporting Means

Article 22a EU Staff Regulations

The third relevant criterion used by the Court for determining whether the EU official acted reasonably and honestly within the meaning of Article 22a(3) EU Staff Regulations is the reporting channel used to make the disclosure.[65] In order to protect the professional reputation of the EU official who is the subject of the report,[66] it is important to establish whether the official or body to which the EU official communicated the information is one of the authorities enumerated in Article 22a(1) EU Staff Regulations entitled to receive such reports,[67] or is part of a group which can be interpreted as of equivalent rank.[68] In this context, the EU Civil Service

58CST, Case F-41/10 RENV, *Bermejo Garde v. EESC (2016)*, para 83.

59Ibid., para 84.

60GC, Case T-530/12 P, *Bermejo Garde v. EESC (2014)*, para 152.

61CST, Case F-41/10 RENV, *Bermejo Garde v. EESC (2016)*, para 84.

62GC, Case T-530/12 P, *Bermejo Garde v. EESC (2014)*, para 149.

63Ibid.

64Ibid., para 150.

65CST, Case F-41/10, *Bermejo Garde v. EESC (2012)*, para 137; GC, Case T-530/12 P, *Bermejo Garde v. EESC (2014)*, para 136.

66CST, Case F-126/11, *José António de Brito Sequeira Carvalho v. European Commission*, Judgment of 11 September 2013, ECLI:EU:F:2013:126, para 77.

67GC, Case T-530/12 P, *Bermejo Garde v. EESC (2014)*, para 135.

68GC, Case T-530/12 P, *Bermejo Garde v. EESC (2014)*, para 161; CST, Case F-126/11, *de Brito Sequeira Carvalho v. Commission*, para 78.

Tribunal held that the protection afforded by Article 22a EU Staff Regulations cannot be granted to EU officials who disregarded this reporting requirement.[69]

Article 22b EU Staff Regulations

As a reminder, Article 22b EU Staff Regulations provides for further reporting channels available to EU officials if two cumulative conditions are met: First, the EU official had reasonably and honestly believed that the information reported are true;[70] secondly, she or he had previously reported to one of the authorities competent under Article 22a EU Staff Regulations and waited a certain period of time.[71] According to this reference system, the conditions of application and criterion of good faith developed by the jurisprudence in regard to Article 22a EU Staff Regulations shall therefore also apply to Article 22b EU Staff Regulations.[72] Notwithstanding those observations, Article 22b (2) EU Staff Regulations exempts EU officials from the obligations laid down in Article 22b(1) EU Staff Regulations if they can "demonstrate that it is unreasonable having regard to all the circumstances of the case". To date,[73] the Court did not have the opportunity to rule on the conditions applicable to determine whether an EU official had indeed acted reasonably within the meaning of Article 22b(2) EU Staff Regulations when reporting directly to the institutions listed in Article 22b(1) EU Staff Regulations.

The Possibility of Public Disclosure

Neither Article 22a nor Article 22b EU Staff Regulations provide for the possibility to report publicly. On the contrary, Article 17(1) EU Staff Regulations provides that EU officials "shall refrain from any unauthorized disclosure of information received in the line of duty, unless that information has already been made public or is accessible to the public". However, an exception from this rule in respect to public disclosure of information giving rise to the presumption of the existence of possible irregularities could potentially be drawn from Article 17a(1) EU Staff Regulations, which institutes the right to freedom of expression for EU officials. Although Articles 17 and 17a EU Staff Regulations are formulated in particularly restrictive terms so as to send the signal that public disclosure of any kind is strongly discouraged, and if permitted, shall be subjected to very strict conditions, the

[69]CST, F-126/11, *de Brito Sequeira Carvalho v. Commission*, para 78 *in fine*.

[70]Article 22b (1)(a) *EU Staff Regulations*.

[71]Article 22b (1)(b) *EU Staff Regulations*; see also CST, F-126/11, *de Brito Sequeira Carvalho v. Commission*, para 79; CST, Joint cases F-88/09 and F-48/10, *Z v. Court of Justice of the European Union (CJEU),* Judgment of 5 December 2012, ECLI:EU:F:2012:171, para 250; CST, Case F-119/07, *Guido Strack v. European Commission*, Judgment of 17 February 2011, ECLI:EU: F:2011:16, para 16.

[72]CST, Case F-77/09, *Nijs v. ECA*, paras 65-70; CST, Joint cases F-88/09 and F-48/10, *Z v. CJEU,* para 184.

[73]1 July 2020.

possibility to disclose information publicly on suspected irregularities shall not be entirely excluded. Drawing from the ECtHR case-law, upon which the EU Civil Service Tribunal modelled its own criteria, and the EU Whistleblower Directive adopted in 2019, it is essential to authorize the use of public channels if no other option can be considered adequate to address the irregularities subject of the report, all while requiring the utmost respect of the duties and responsibilities incumbent on every EU official. To date, the CJEU did not have the opportunity to explicitly address this particular issue, even if the EU Civil Service Tribunal had hinted at the fact that this possibility should not entirely be ruled out.[74] If future reform of the EU Staff Regulations includes the possibility, in certain circumstances, to use public reporting channels while enjoying protection against prejudice, and in doing so, equalizes the protection of whistleblowers within EU institutions and bodies to the same level as individuals falling within the scope of the EU Whistleblower Directive, it would be for the CJEU to ensure that EU officials who had legitimate reason to report publicly remain protected under the EU Staff Regulations and can enjoy their full right to freedom of expression. The accession of the EU to the ECHR would make such a reform indispensable.

The Motive of the Reporting Official, a Fourth Criterion?

The motive of the EU official who disclosed information is the fourth and last criterion mentioned by the EU Civil Service Tribunal in the initial judgment.[75] According to the latter, the EU official motivated by a personal grievance or animosity, or by the prospect of a personal gain shall not be considered as having acted honestly within the meaning of Article 22a(3) EU Staff Regulations. Surprisingly, the Court did not examine whether the applicant was in fact prompted by improper motives.[76] Likewise, even if in the judgment on appeal, the EU General Court referred to an excerpt from the initial judgment in which the four criteria are listed,[77] acknowledging that the EU Civil Service Tribunal had indeed outlined four criteria in its initial judgment,[78] it concluded that because the initial judgment evaluated only the three first criteria, only those three criteria should be taken into consideration to determine the good faith of the EU official.[79] This conclusion was confirmed by the judgment after referral.[80] Therefore, it appears from the foregoing that the fourth criterion mentioned by the EU Civil Service Tribunal in 2012 shall not be considered as an integral part of the evaluation process to determine the good faith

[74] CST, Case F-77/09, *Nijs v. ECA*, paras 76 and 80.

[75] CST, Case F-41/10, *Bermejo Garde v. EESC (2012)*, para 138.

[76] Ibid., paras 150-151. The CST does not examine the motivation of the applicant.

[77] GC, Case T-530/12 P, *Bermejo Garde v. EESC (2014)* para 25.

[78] Ibid., para 117.

[79] Ibid.

[80] CST, Case F-41/10 RENV, *Bermejo Garde v. EESC (2016)*, para 78.

of an EU official under Article 22a EU Staff Regulations, which represents a surprising yet welcome deviation from the ECtHR case-law.

6.1.3.2 The Application of the *Bermejo Garde* Criteria to the Case

In their judgments, the different Courts had to determine whether the applicant had acted in good faith when sending his note alleging irregularities and psychological harassment in accordance with Article 12a (2) and Article 22a (3) EU Staff Regulations and whether those allegations could be considered authentic, or at the very least, credible.[81] As a reminder, the EU General Court laid down three criteria to determine the good faith of the EU official: The seriousness of the reported acts, the authenticity or credibility of the information transmitted and lastly, the methods of communication used.

The Seriousness of the Allegations

As to the first criterion, the EU Civil Service Tribunal considered in its initial judgment that the note sent by the applicant did not reveal the existence of irregularities "so serious as to give rise to the presumption of the existence of psychological harassment ... or ... illegal activity ... or of a serious failure to comply with the obligations of officials".[82] In its judgment on appeal, the EU General Court held however that the EU Civil Service Tribunal examined the different occurrences in isolation where it should have assessed them jointly in order to determine whether the accumulation ("cumul") of those actions could have constituted a serious infringement as a whole.[83] Following this reasoning, the EU Civil Service Tribunal did in fact conclude, in its judgment after referral, that the accumulation ("cumul") of the occurrences which did not directly impact the applicant and those which directly concerned him, especially the incident reflecting potential cases of psychological harassment, leads to the presumption of a wrongful act of an undeniably serious nature.[84]

The Authenticity of the Reported Information

As seen above, this observation should be appreciated in the light of the second criterion, namely the authentic character of the facts reported by the applicant's note and whether it provided grounds to presume that the Secretary-General did usurp his

[81] CST, Case F-41/10 RENV, *Bermejo Garde v. EESC (2016)*, paras 54 et seq.
[82] CST, Case F-41/10, *Bermejo Garde v. EESC (2012)*, para 149.
[83] GC, Case T-530/12 P, *Bermejo Garde v. EESC (2014)*, para 155.
[84] CST, Case F-41/10 RENV, *Bermejo Garde v. EESC (2016)*, paras 79–80.

power.[85] In the initial judgment, the EU Civil Service Tribunal failed to determine *in concreto* whether the information reported was in fact authentic, or at the very least, credible which could give rise to the presumption of the existence of serious irregularities within the meaning of Article 22a EU Staff Regulations, a shortcoming identified by the EU General Court in its judgment on appeal.[86]

The Function of the Applicant As Head of the Legal Service Unit

In the proceedings after referral, the EESC admitted that the Secretary-General did indeed commit some irregularities, but argued that the big picture given by the evidence presented in the applicant's note were not sufficient to raise the presumption that the Secretary-General acted illegally or seriously failed to comply with his obligations under Article 22a(1) EU Staff Regulations, claiming that the non-compliance with the rules of conduct or procedure cannot be used as a presumption for the existence of serious illegality or serious breach.[87] In the judgment after referral, the EU Civil Service Tribunal rejected this argument[88] and, considering the functions of the applicant as Head of the Legal Service which made him more sensitive to his statutory obligations,[89] concluded that he could legitimately have presumed the existence of serious and continuous breaches committed by the Secretary-General.[90]

The Harassment Claims of the Applicant

Concerning the harassment claims made by the applicant, the EU Civil Service Tribunal noted that the relation between the applicant, as Head of the Legal Service, and the Secretary-General greatly deteriorated, which lead to dysfunctions, such as the exclusion of the applicant from a case which would have normally fallen under his competence, due to the lack of action from the administration in regard to the difficulties experienced by the applicant. In this context, the applicant recalled without being contradicted by the EESC, that he had tried on numerous occasions to find a solution to the deteriorating work situation before he sent his note in December 2009.[91] In light of those observations, the EU Civil Service Tribunal thus concluded that those alleged facts should be considered authentic, or at the very least, likely, giving rise to a presumption of the existence of psychological harassment against the applicant within the meaning of Article 12a EU Staff Regulations.[92]

[85] CST, Case F-41/10 RENV, *Bermejo Garde v. EESC (2016)*, para 81.

[86] GC, Case T-530/12 P, *Bermejo Garde v. EESC (2014)*, paras 156–158.

[87] CST, Case F-41/10 RENV, *Bermejo Garde v. EESC (2016)*, para 82.

[88] Ibid., para 83.

[89] Ibid., para 84.

[90] Ibid., para 86.

[91] Ibid., para 58.

[92] Ibid., para 59.

Whistleblowing and the Breach of the Bond of Trust

While the EECS recognized in its written observations that the applicant did suffer pressure from the Secretary-General, it justified those actions as the consequence of pressure put on the Secretary-General himself by another member of the office.[93] The EECS also argued that the accusations made against the Secretary-General had destabilized the level of trust that the Head of the administration had to have in the Head of the Legal Service.[94] The EU Civil Service Tribunal rejected those justifications, stating that this line of argument would lead to disregard of the very concept of harassment and exempt the highest administrative authority of his statutory obligations.[95] Indeed, it emphasized that any harassment complaint against a supervisor usually leads to a breach of the bond of trust, which is the very reason why Article 12a EU Staff Regulations offers a special protection to shield victims against those kind of prejudices, especially when the relationship of trust between the victim of harassment and her or his superior as alleged harasser was breached.[96]

The Role of the Legal Service in EU Institutions

In its written observations and in reference to the different legal culture allegedly at the source of the tense climate between the Secretary-General and the Legal Service, the EESC claimed that the former was entitled to expect from the latter that he adapts to his expectation in regard to the form of legal advice provided by the Legal Service. Being Anglophone, the Secretary-General expected more practical advice rather than a lengthy analysis of the different options available.[97]

The EU Civil Service Tribunal stated that this line of argument ignored the fact that the Legal Service should provide all the necessary information to the institution it serves to enable it to fully exercise its power in compliance with Union law. In that respect, the Legal Service and its Head should not be obliged to adjust automatically to the expectations of the Secretary-General, especially when the latter is perceived by the Legal Service to act in potential conflict with statutory provisions. While it is in the interest of every institution of the Union to ask and receive from its Legal Service "frank, objective and comprehensive" legal advice,[98] it should keep a proper professional relationship appropriate in a good administration of services if it chooses to disregard the advice provided by its Legal Service.[99] The EU Civil Service Tribunal also noted that the Chief of Staff's report did not attribute the tense climate to any acts committed by the applicant and representing a violation of

---

[93]Ibid., para 62.

[94]Ibid., para 75.

[95]Ibid., paras 69–71.

[96]Ibid., para 76.

[97]Ibid., para 66.

[98]e.g. CJ, Joint cases C-39/05 P and C-52/05 P, *Kingdom of Sweden and Maurizio Turco v. Council of the European Union*, Judgment of 1. July 2008, ECLI:EU:F:2011:16, para 42.

[99]CST, Case F-41/10 RENV, *Bermejo Garde v. EESC (2016)*, para 67.

his obligations from article 11 and 12 EU Staff Regulations.[100] On the other hand, it held that the same report provided sufficient ground to presume that the Secretary-General had an attitude toward the applicant which was inconsistent with the statutory provisions governing the rights and obligations of EU officials in the performance of their duties.

The Reporting Channel Used

Finally, in regard to the third criterion, namely the reporting channel used by the applicant, the EU Civil Service Tribunal held in its initial judgment that the applicant had given his allegations a particularly wide publicity by sending his note not only to the President of the EESC but also to the other members of the President's Office, thereby violating his obligation to demonstrate the greatest prudence and the greatest discretion in reporting allegations falling within the competence of OLAF.[101] The EU General Court rejected this conclusion by emphasizing that the members of the President's Office can be considered "persons in equivalent positions" within the meaning of Article 22a(1) EU Staff Regulations and that the EU Civil Service Tribunal failed to provide any reasons why the applicant should not have sent his note to those members.[102] In its judgment after referral, the EU Civil Service Tribunal confirmed the legitimate interest of an EU whistleblower to inform all members of an internal decision-making body and thus concluded that the applicant, in sending his note to all the members of the President's Office, the EESC's collegial decision-making body, acted in accordance with Article 22a(1) EU Staff Regulations.[103]

6.1.4 Conclusions in the *Bermejo Garde* Case

6.1.4.1 The Position of the EU Civil Service Tribunal

In accordance with those observations, the EU Civil Service Tribunal concluded in its judgment after referral that the note sent by the applicant to the Office of the President of the EESC in accordance with Article 22a EU Staff Regulations was in compliance with his duties of objectivity, impartiality and loyalty enshrined in Article 11 EU Staff Regulations and consistent with the dignity of the function set out in Article 12 EU Staff Regulations. It therefore held that the decision to terminate the applicant's appointment as Head of the Legal Service and reassign him to another

[100]CST, Case F-41/10 RENV, *Bermejo Garde v. EESC (2016)*, para 61.

[101]CST, Case F-41/10, *Bermejo Garde v. EESC (2012)*, para 150.

[102]GC, Case T-530/12 P, *Bermejo Garde v. EESC (2014)*, para 161.

[103]CST, Case F-41/10 RENV, *Bermejo Garde v. EESC (2016)*, para 91.

Unit was in violation of Article 12a(2) EU Staff Regulations[104] and should thus be overturned.[105]

The EU Civil Service Tribunal also noted that the three conditions for the applicant's right to compensation were fulfilled, namely the illegality of the EU institution action, the reality of the damage suffered by the applicant and the causal link between the illegal action and the damage suffered.[106] While the annulment of administrative acts at the source of the damage suffered could represent a sufficient and adequate compensation for the damage suffered,[107] in this case the annulment of the decision to terminate his appointment as Head of the Legal Service and transfer him to another unit, the EU Civil Service Tribunal was of the opinion that such annulment could not compensate the appropriate extent of the non-pecuniary damage suffered by the applicant due to the breach of Article 12a and 22a EU Staff Regulations.[108] Following those conclusions, the Tribunal ordered the EESC to pay the sum of €25,000 in damages for the moral prejudice suffered by the applicant.[109]

6.1.4.2 Final Remarks on the *Bermejo Garde* Rulings

A parallel can be drawn between the criteria used by the EU Civil Service Tribunal and the ECtHR in respect to whistleblowing. According to the latter, six criteria should be considered to determine whether an individual can be considered a whistleblower under the ECHR, namely the public interest of the reported information, the reporting channel used, the authenticity of the information, the good faith of the individual, the damage suffered by the employer and the severity of the sanction imposed upon the individual who reported. In the case at hand, the EU Civil Service Tribunal assessed the information reported by the applicant, namely the alleged irregularities and the harassment claims, in the light of 22a EU Staff Regulations. In doing so, it laid down several criteria defining the scope of application of Article 22a EU Staff Regulations. First and foremost, the definition of good faith used by the EU Civil Service Tribunal is a welcome distinction from the ECtHR case-law on whistleblowing. While the latter links the good faith of the reporting individual to his or her motivation, the former focusses on the seriousness of the reported information, the authenticity of the information and the channel used.[110]

Furthermore, the fact that the EU whistleblower is not under an obligation to establish a presumption of serious illegality on the basis of Article 22a EU Staff

[104]Ibid., para 77.
[105]Ibid., para 94.
[106]Ibid., para 101.
[107]Ibid., para 102.
[108]Ibid., para 103.
[109]Ibid., para 104.
[110]Ibid., para 78.

Regulations, since the EU institution concerned has to bear the burden of proof and transmit all necessary information to OLAF,[111] reveals a particularly whistleblower-friendly position of the EU General Court. In addition, because allegation of harassment could be interpreted as a serious failure under Article 22a EU Staff Regulations and thus be the subject of a whistleblower report,[112] any EU whistleblower who reported on suspicions of irregularities which did not meet the standards laid down under Article 22a EU Staff Regulations could still benefit from the status of whistleblower if she or he could demonstrate the authenticity or credibility which could give rise to a presumption of the existence of harassment. That said, the CJEU should take into account the emerging European consensus on whistleblower protection and shift the burden to prove the retaliatory nature of measures imposed on an EU official following her or his report, requiring the perpetrator to demonstrate the lack of a close link between the adverse decision taken against the EU whistleblower and the report made.

6.2 Similar Circumstances, Different Conclusions

6.2.1 The *McCoy* Case

By revealing evidence of systematic fraud and embezzlement within the Committee of the Regions of the European Union (hereinafter referred to as "Committee of the Regions"), Mr. McCoy became one of the most well-known EU whistleblowers. The description of the McCoy case illustrates the particularly grim consequences of blowing the whistle within EU institutions and the two decades long struggle of an EU official, fighting for the recognition of his status as whistleblower.

6.2.1.1 The Facts of the Case *McCoy v. Committee of the Regions*

The applicant, Mr. McCoy, was an EU official who worked first as a financial controller from 2000 to 2002 and became internal auditor from 2002 onwards. In the performance of his duties as financial controller, the applicant identified some irregularities, primarily in the budgetary management of the Committee of the Regions. He first informed the administration and the Secretary-General of the Committee of the Regions, which rejected the concerns expressed by the applicant as being vague and not consistent with the actual audit. In a note addressed to the applicant, dated January 2003, the Secretary-General stated that the applicant did not understand the precise nature of the functions and tasks assigned to him as internal auditor under the new financial regulation and that his notes did not correspond to

[111] Ibid., para 83.

[112] Ibid., para 54.

the services expected from him, which lead to increased work load for others in the services without bringing any positive contribution to improve the budgetary management. The Secretary-General further declared that the applicant's claims were incorrect and that he would not hesitate to open an investigation against him on his activities as internal auditor if he continued to neglect his true obligations and continue to produce inappropriate, damaging and unfounded notes.[113] Thereupon, the applicant informed the Committee on Budgetary Control of the EP of those irregularities, before which he testified in 2003 as part of the investigation of the general budget of the EU.[114] OLAF, upon alerts from MEPs and members of the Committee on Budgetary Control, started an investigation on the irregularities reported by the applicant and interviewed him for the purpose of this investigation.[115] In the context of its report, OLAF underlined "an endemic culture of unprofessionalism . . . where intransparency is preferred above openness".[116]

In a meeting of the Commission for Financial and Administrative Affairs of the Committee of the Regions attended by the applicant, the Secretary-General declared that the latter should not have alerted the Committee on Budgetary Control and instead should have reported those irregularities to the Commission for Financial and Administrative Affairs. Another member of the Committee declared that a lack of loyalty cannot be tolerated in the Committee of the Regions. The applicant's collaborator responded that the Committee had been alerted. Following this meeting, the applicant contested in writing the words used by the Secretary-General and the other member of the Committee.[117] In a letter to the applicant, the Secretary-General declared that the only reason why the applicant believed he had the duty to cry out scandal and appeal for help to the Committee on Budgetary Control was because his work was put into question on the form and on the substance. The fact that the Secretary-General did not agree with the way the financial controller performed his duties did not represent a case of defamation.[118]

While the ECA stated, upon request from the President of the Committee of the Regions for an enquiry, that it did not find any major breach of the budgetary and

[113]CST, Case F-156/12, *Robert McCoy v. European Committee of the Regions* [hereinafter "McCoy v. CoR (2014)"], Judgment of 18 November 2014, ECLI:EU:F:2014:247, paras 8–10.

[114]Ibid., para 11.

[115]Ibid., para 14.

[116]OLAF, *Final report dated 8 October 2003*, not accessible to the public. OLAF's reply to a request made by the author for access to that document: "The requested document is covered by the exceptions under Article 4(2), third indent of Regulation 1049/2001 which stipulates that the institution shall refuse access to a document where disclosure would undermine the protection of the purpose of inspections, investigations and audits", Ref. no. *olaf.c.4(2020)14250*. The fact that OLAF bases its refusal on the ground that it would undermine the purpose of inspections, investigations and audits, despite the fact that the investigation was conducted almost two decades ago, demonstrates the particularly sensitive nature of its findings and suggests that the issues and shortcomings identified may remain pertinent and relevant today; see Mangan (2004, 26 February).

[117]CST, Case F-156/12, *McCoy v. CoR (2014)*, para 13.

[118]Ibid., para 17.

financial rules,[119] OLAF released its investigation report which contradicted these conclusions a few months later, finding that a number of different irregularities had been committed in the budgetary management of the Committee of the Regions and commending the opening of a disciplinary inquiry on different members of the Committee, especially the former Secretary-General. In its conclusions, OLAF underlined that the Committee of the Regions attempted to discourage and destabilize the applicant in the performance of his duty as financial controller and internal auditor. The Committee of the Regions therefore seemed to have ignored its own decision dated 1999 concerning the conditions and modalities of internal investigations on fraud, corruption and other illegal activities detrimental to the interests of the European Community whereby "les fonctionnaires et agents du secrétariat général ne doivent en aucun cas subir un traitement inéquitable ou discriminatoire du fait d'une communication visée aux premier et deuxième alinéas".[120]

In November 2003, the applicant sent a letter entitled "Request for assistance under Article 22 of the Statute for psychological harassment in the work place and request for compensation for the loss suffered", referring directly to the OLAF investigation report and specifying that the performance of his function of control subjected him to psychological harassment, pressure, accusations, intimidation attempts and threats of disciplinary proceedings coming from his direct supervisors. He considered that those serious violations affected his function as internal auditor and constituted not only a discriminatory treatment and a harm to his dignity and reputation but also a psychological destabilization and psychological harassment. He specified that these attacks had medical consequences and undermined his physical integrity. This is the reason why he requested the payment of €5000 and the bearing of his costs and expenditures.[121] Following the investigative report of OLAF, the President sent a letter to the applicant, ensuring him of his commitment in relation to the importance of his role as internal controller in the Committee of the Regions and as key player in the internal reform, informing that the new Secretary-General has ensured his availability in order to enable him to perform his duties as internal auditor with all the assistance, support and cooperation from the members of the Committee of Regions. The President also informed the applicant that the transmission of information to OLAF should not legitimate inequitable or discriminatory treatment and that the internal provision of whistleblower protection would be applied to him.[122]

At the end of the year 2003, the Committee on Budgetary Control presented its report on the discharge relative to the general budget implementation of the EU and, naming expressly the Committee of the Regions and referring to the OLAF report,

---

[119] Ibid., para 18.

[120] Ibid., para 21. *Translation* "officials and agents of the secretariat general shall in no way suffer inadequate or discriminatory treatment as a result of having communicated an information referred to in the first and second paragraphs".

[121] Ibid., para 23.

[122] Ibid., para 25.

criticized the official obstructions of the Committee of the Regions which targeted the applicant and his staff and expressed its expectation that the reforms considered by the Committee of the Regions in order to report irregularities or fraud would prevent any risk of individual or institutional harassment which was the case in the past.[123] The EP reaffirmed those critics in a resolution adopted in January 2004 containing observations on the decision of discharge relating to the budget implementation of the EU and requested that the Committee of the Regions officially apologize to the internal auditor for the harassment and obstructions he suffered.[124]

The following month, the Committee of the Regions rejected unanimously the request for assistance on the ground that the applicant did not demonstrate the reality of the alleged acts of harassment, attacks and intimidations. The Committee of the Regions also informed the Committee on Budgetary Control that its Secretary-General did not find any proof of psychological harassment or intimidation targeting the applicant and stated that the OLAF report merely reproduced the applicant's claims without bringing any evidence, consequently, it decided to reject the request for assistance.[125] The applicant responded through letters to the Committee on Budgetary Control, describing the Committee of Regions' position as erroneous and scurrilous, underlining that this declaration was another manifestation of the negative attitude towards him and the degrading treatment by the Committee's administration. He expressed his primary desire to be recognized by the Committee of the Regions as a person deserving trust and respected in his prerogatives as internal auditor.[126]

In April 2004, the applicant was informed that the Committee of the Regions wrote a report on the possible opening of a disciplinary procedure against him in which it stated that the applicant failed to fulfill his official obligations by not providing sufficient information to his supervisors and OLAF, but that this failure was not serious enough to open a disciplinary procedure against him.[127] Meanwhile, the applicant, who suffered from anxiety and depression and presented symptoms of post-traumatic stress disorder, was placed on medical leave, with an interruption of 6 weeks, until June 2007 when he was put in compulsory retirement for invalidity.[128] During this period, the applicant experienced degrading treatments such as the locking down of his office without prior notice and without having been handed out the new keys.[129] Another instance concerned the boxes containing the applicant's personal belongings and the request of the Secretary-General to verify its content in presence of members of the Committee of the Regions in attendance of the

[123]Ibid., para 28.

[124]Ibid., para 31.

[125]Ibid., paras 34–35.

[126]Ibid., paras 36–37.

[127]Ibid., para 40.

[128]Ibid., para 41.

[129]Ibid., paras 46–47.

applicant himself.[130] During the verification of the content in which three boxes were put under seal and three others put at the disposal of the new internal auditor, the applicant was victim of an attack and brought to the infirmary.[131] The applicant introduced a request on the basis of the Insurance Regulations to recognize the occupational origin of his disease. The Commission examining his invalidity did indeed confirm his invalidity but did not find sufficient elements to make a statement on the link between the invalidity and the occupation of the applicant, and requested the administration to provide authentic elements for that sake.[132]

However, the Office for the administration and payment of individual entitlements (hereinafter referred to as "the Office") contradicted this conclusion and stated that the documents of the file were sufficient for the Office's medical doctor to do an analysis. The latter observed the gradual appearance of symptoms linked to the reprehensible professional conducts of certain members of the Committee of the Regions. He also noted that the applicant was not able to carry out any occupational activity in the European institutions any longer, especially given the fact that his clinical situation was linked to the psychological harassment he experienced in the work-place and to the burn-out that resulted from it. On the basis of this medical analysis, as well as a psychological expertise report, a neuropsychological evaluation and a psychiatric investigation report conducted by different medical professionals, the Office recognized the occupational origin of the applicant's disease and decided to set at 10% of invalidity rate as recommended by the medical doctor, ordering consequently the payment of a lump sum of €128,079.92, in accordance with Article 73 EU Staff Regulations. This decision, dated 2 March 2010, was sent to the Invalidity Committee.[133]

The Invalidity Committee insisted on its original position and concluded that the invalidity of the applicant did not result from an occupational disease, with the decision endorsed by the Committee of the Regions in a decision dated 10 September 2010.[134] In September 2011, the applicant brought an appeal before the EU Civil Service Tribunal for, *inter alia*, the annulment of this decision, stating that the Committee of the Regions' decision was tainted by a violation of the obligation to state reasons and a manifest error of assessment, pleas partially upheld by the EU Civil Service Tribunal.[135] The applicant also sent a request to the Committee of the Regions on the basis of article 90 EU Staff Regulations to compensate the loss he suffered due to its misconduct not entirely repaired by the lump sum attributed in accordance with article 73 EU Staff Regulations. After his request was rejected by

[130] Ibid., para 45.

[131] Ibid., para 48.

[132] Ibid., paras 55–56.

[133] Ibid., paras 58–62.

[134] Ibid., paras 65–66.

[135] CST, Case F-86/11, *Robert McCoy v. European Committee of the Regions* [hereinafter "McCoy v. CoR (2013)"], Judgment of 7 May 2013, ECLI:EU:F:2013:56.

the Committee of the Regions,[136] he brought another appeal to the EU Civil Service Tribunal, with the request to annul the latest decision rejecting his request for compensation on the basis of article 90 EU Staff Regulations,[137] claiming, inter alia, that the Committee of the Regions violated its *devoir de sollicitude*.[138]

6.2.1.2 The Decision of the EU Civil Service Tribunal

Although the EU Civil Service Tribunal acknowledged : "it is common ground that, in its report, OLAF found that the Committee of the Regions had attempted to discourage or destabilise the applicant and that the Parliament, in its discharge resolution, went so far as to require the Committee of the Regions to apologise to the applicant specifically on account of its behaviour towards him",[139] the focus of the *McCoy v. Committee of the Regions* judgments was not whether Mr. McCoy could benefit from the status of whistleblower but whether the invalidity of Mr. McCoy had an occupational origin. In this context, the EU Civil Service Tribunal focused its attention on the report produced by the invalidity committee and held that the report contained inadequate reasoning, which resulted in a discrepancy between the medical findings and the conclusions brought forward in the report,[140] and that the invalidity committee committed a manifest error of assessment.[141] While it annulled the decision of the Committee of the Regions which had refused to recognize the occupational origin of Mr. McCoy's disease,[142] the EU Civil Service Tribunal considered that the latter was not able to demonstrate that the annulment of the decision was insufficient to compensate the damage suffered and thus rejected the claim for damages.[143]

The second judgment went further and ordered the Committee of the Regions to pay Mr. McCoy 20 000 Euro[144] for the non-material damage resulting from the destabilization, the lack of consideration, the waiting period, the frustration endured by Mr. McCoy and the general *manque de sollicitude* on the part of the Committee of the Regions, confirming the causal link between the disease of the former and the conduct of the latter.[145] Mr. McCoy also argued that the Committee of the Regions violated Article 22a EU Staff Regulations by trying, inter alia, to cover up the

[136] CST, Case F-156/12, *McCoy v. CoR (2014)*, paras 68–70.

[137] Ibid., para 71.

[138] Ibid., para 92.

[139] CST, Case F-86/11, *McCoy v. CoR (2013)*, para 113.

[140] Ibid., paras 97–98.

[141] Ibid., para 114.

[142] Ibid., Conclusions of the case, para 153.

[143] Ibid., para 146.

[144] CST, Case F-156/12, *McCoy v. CoR (2014)*, para 129.

[145] Ibid., para 128.

irregularities reported,[146] a claim backed by the EP.[147] However, this plea was rejected by the EU Civil Service Tribunal on the grounds that Mr. McCoy did not provide sufficiently clear and precise arguments and elements of facts for that claim to be considered admissible.[148] This conclusion is particularly surprising as it was generally accepted that Mr. McCoy had indeed been the victim of pressure following his report.[149] Because the causal link between the Committee of the Regions' conduct and Mr. McCoy's health issues was established, confirming the occupational origin of the disease, the EU Civil Service Tribunal could have continued its reasoning and examined the existence of a causal link between the report made and the prejudice suffered, determining in that respect whether, on the basis of the criteria developed in 2012 in its Bermejo judgment, Mr. McCoy could be considered a whistleblower within the meaning of Article 22b in conjunction with Article 22a EU Staff Regulations. The fact that the report was made prior to the 2004 amendment of the EU Staff Regulations is irrelevant as the EU General Court recognized that any EU official having blown the whistle before 2004 had the same right to be protected against retaliation.[150]

6.2.1.3 The Widespread Support for Mr. McCoy

The experience of Mr. McCoy demonstrates how the lack of implementation of whistleblowing regulations can escalate and have a serious impact on the health and well-being of whistleblowers. The failure to address whistleblower reports can also have a detrimental effect on the EU as a whole and promote a general image of lack of transparency and accountability particularly harmful for a supranational body like the EU. Given the nature of the irregularities uncovered by Mr. McCoy and the inquiry conducted by OLAF following his report, the case received particular attention from the general public and enjoyed broad media coverage. The disclosure made by Mr. McCoy, the failure of the Committee of the Regions to apply the whistleblower protection regulation and the detrimental impact suffered by Mr. McCoy as a result prompted the EP to call on the Committee of the Regions

[146] Ibid., para 119.

[147] Recital 23 *Resolution of the European Parliament containing the comments accompanying the decision concerning the discharge in respect of the implementation of the general budget of the European Union for the 2001 financial year — Section VII — Committee of the Regions*, OJ L 57, 25.02.2004, p. 8; see also Recital 21 in fine *Resolution (EU) 2018/1332 of the European Parliament of 18 April 2018 with observations forming an integral part of the decision on discharge in respect of the implementation of the general budget of the European Union for the financial year 2016, Section VII, Committee of the Regions*, OJ L 248, 03.10.2018, p. 138.

[148] CST, Case F-156/12, *McCoy v. CoR (2014)*, paras 120–121.

[149] CST, Case F-86/11, *McCoy v. CoR (2013)*, para 113.

[150] GC, Case T-61/18, *Amador Rodriguez Pieto v. European Commission* [hereinafter "Rodriguez v. Commission"], Judgment of 4 April 2019, ECLI:EU:T:2019:217GC, para 71.

to reform its rules on whistleblowers[151] so as "to ensure that in future bona fide whistle-blowers do not receive the same treatment to which the Financial Controller was subjected",[152] and demanded that the President and the Secretary-General of the Committee of the Regions issue a formal apology to Mr. McCoy.[153]

A decade later and in reference to the same case, the EP reiterated "the considerable cost to Union taxpayers and the harm done to the whistle-blower"[154] and stressed that it "will not tolerate any mistreatment of whistle-blowers in its own ranks or in any other Union Institution and reiterates its total commitment to the spirit and the letter of the legislation on whistle-blower protection",[155] calling on the Committee of the Regions to establish internal rules on whistleblowing[156] and comply with the EU Civil Service Tribunal 2013 judgment in the case *McCoy v. Committee of the Regions*.[157] A year later, while it welcomed the adoption of internal whistleblowing rules by the Committee of the Regions, the EP considered it "unacceptable that the Committee has been dealing with the same whistleblowing case since 2003", and urged "the Committee to take all necessary steps to resolve this situation without further delay and to admit publicly that the whistleblower's findings were correct, as stated by the European Anti-Fraud Office and other Union bodies".[158] In 2017, the EP noted that the Committee of the Regions had still to comply with the two McCoy judgments of the EU Civil Service Court and considered it fundamental to "bring the whistleblower case of the former internal auditor of the Committee to a just,

[151] Recital 8(b) *Resolution containing the comments accompanying the decision concerning the discharge in respect of the implementation of the general budget of the European Union for the 2001 financial year, Section VII, Committee of the Regions.*

[152] Recital 23 *Resolution containing the comments accompanying the decision concerning the discharge in respect of the implementation of the general budget of the European Union for the 2001 financial year, Section VII, Committee of the Regions.*

[153] Recital 24 *Resolution of the European Parliament containing the comments accompanying the decision concerning the discharge in respect of the implementation of the general budget of the European Union for the 2001 financial year, Section VII, Committee of the Regions.*

[154] Recital 28 *Resolution of the European Parliament of 29 April 2015 with observation forming an integral part of the decision on discharge in respect of the implementation of the general budget of the European Union for the financial year 2013, Section VII, Committee of the Regions*, OJ L 255, 30.09.2015, p. 132.

[155] Recital 29 *Resolution of the European Parliament of 29 April 2015 with observation forming an integral part of the decision on discharge in respect of the implementation of the general budget of the European Union for the financial year 2013, Section VII, Committee of the Regions.*

[156] Recital 27 *Resolution of the European Parliament of 29 April 2015 with observation forming an integral part of the decision on discharge in respect of the implementation of the general budget of the European Union for the fincnail year 2013, Section VII, Committee of the Regions.*

[157] Recital 28 *Resolution of the European Parliament of 29 April 2015 with observation forming an integral part of the decision on discharge in respect of the implementation of the general budget of the European Union for the financial year 2013, Section VII, Committee of the Regions.*

[158] Recital 33 *Resolution (EU) 2016/1479 of the European Parliament of 28 April 2016 with observations forming an integral part of the decision on discharge in respect of the implementation of the general budget of the European union for the financial year 2014, Section VII, Committee of the Regions*, OJ L 246, 14.09.2016, p. 152.

honourable and equitable settlement".[159] To describe Mr. McCoy's situation, MEP Tomáš Zdechovský said in November 2020: "When I look at this case, it reminds me of the American film 'Groundhog Day' where the protagonist becomes trapped in a time loop".[160] In the same month, two documents were made public, a draft amicable settlement of € 259 997,21 to compensate for the material and non-material damages of Mr. McCoy,[161] and a draft statement of the Committee of the Regions recognizing the good faith of Mr. McCoy, stating that the latter "acted as a whistleblower in the general sense of the word before a provision on whistleblowing was introduced in the Staff Regulations in the year 2004".[162] In a joint statement by the Committee of the Regions and Mr. McCoy dated December 4, 2020, they announced that an amicable settlement was reached, the Committee of the Regions officially confirming the good faith and whistleblower status of Mr. McCoy. The Committee of the Regions also presented its formal apologies to Mr. McCoy and recognized that "the case should never have been allowed to remain unresolved for more than seventeen years".[163] With this recognition and a financial settlement reached, the time loop has finally come to a close.

6.2.2 *Amador Rodriguez Prieto v. EU Commission*: A Pending Question

While the *Amador Rodriguez Prieto v. EU Commission*[164] judgment remains particularly elusive in regard to whistleblowing, it illustrates some of the remaining uncertainties in the CJEU jurisprudence on Article 22a and Article 22b EU Staff Regulations.

6.2.2.1 The Facts of the Case

The applicant, Mr. Amador Rodriguez Prieto, was an employee of the EU Commission from 1987 to 2003 and worked as Chief of Unit of one of the directorates of Eurostat, the Office of Statistics of the EU. From 1996 onwards, Eurostat ensured the

[159] Recital 21 *Resolution (EU) 2017/1625 of the European Parliament of 27 April 2017 with observations forming an integral part of the decision on discharge in respect of the implementation of the general budget of the European Union for the financial year 2015, Section VII, Committee of the Regions*, OJ L 252, 29.09.2017, p. 134.

[160] Von Der Burchard (2020, 11 November).

[161] CoR, *Draft Amicable settlement*, 10 November 2020, p. 2.

[162] CoR, *Draft public statement of the European Committee of the Regions about an amicable settlement with former staff member Robert McCoy*, 10 November 2020.

[163] CoR & Mr McCoy, *Joint statement on principles governing the resolution of Mr McCoy's bone-fide whistle-blower case*, 4 December 2020.

[164] GC, T-61/18, *Rodriguez Pieto v. Commission.*

distribution of statistical data based on the work of the Office for Official Publication of the European Community (OOPEC) which created a network of points of sale (hereinafter referred to as "data-shops"). The tripartite contracts between Eurostat, the OOPEC and the data-shops provided a complex billing circuit which allowed Eurostat to earn up to 55% of the invoiced price of the data placed on the market. The applicant was in charge of approving the expenditure resulting from those tripartite contracts. With a note, dated 22 October 1998, the applicant requested to conduct an internal audit on the management of those tripartite contracts and asked to be removed from the power to sign the expenditure orders resulting from those contracts. In 1999, the internal audit concluded that there had been some irregularities in the financial management of the tripartite contracts.[165]

In January 2000, the internal audit report was transmitted to the Directorate-General in charge of the financial control of the EU Commission. OLAF was notified and opened several investigations regarding the tripartite contracts, the subsidies granted to certain companies and the billing system put in place. In 2003, OLAF forwarded the case regarding a contract concluded with a French company to the Paris Public Prosecutor, who opened a judicial investigation for concealment. Following new reports of the internal audit in June 2003, the EU Commission mandated its legal service to lodge a complaint against X with the Paris Public Prosecutor on two counts: Concealment and complicity in breach of trust, which was later extended to abuse of trust. The complaint related to possible embezzlement committed by EU officials or agents to the detriment of the financial interests of the EU.[166] In 2008, the applicant informed the EU Commission that he had been summoned by the French police to testify as a witness in the criminal proceeding and requested the appointing authority (hereinafter referred to as "AIPN") to waive his duty of confidentiality in accordance with article 19 EU Staff Regulations and obtain the reimbursement of his travel costs from Luxembourg to Paris. The AIPN waived the applicant's duty of confidentiality but rejected his request for a travel costs reimbursement.[167] Following his hearing with the French police in October 2008, the applicant made a first request for assistance on the basis of article 24 EU Staff Regulations, claiming that by requesting an internal audit, he acted as whistleblower and that the community of interests between him and the EU Institution legitimated the EU's assistance in the procedure, which should include the fee of the attorney present during the police hearing. This request was rejected on the grounds that the two conditions laid down in Article 24 EU Staff Regulations, namely the existence of a threat or contempt against the person and the EU officials' assets and the existence of a causal link between those facts and the statute EU official, were not fulfilled.[168]

[165]Ibid., paras 1–6.

[166]Ibid., paras 7–11.

[167]Ibid., paras 11–13.

[168]Ibid., paras 14–16.

In 2013, the investigative Judge of the Tribunal de grande instance de Paris ordered the dismissal of criminal proceedings against all individuals put under investigation, including the applicant, which was confirmed by the Court of Appeal of Paris and the Cour de Cassation.[169] In 2016, the applicant made a second request for assistance on the basis of Article 24 EU Staff Regulations in order to obtain from the EU Commission the reimbursement of his attorneys' fee arising from his involvement during the French criminal proceeding. He also requested to be granted the status of whistleblower in order to regain his professional integrity. The AIPN declared the request for assistance as inadmissible on the ground that the applicant had not justified this second request with new facts.[170] In a letter, dated 10 April 2017, the EU Commission informed the applicant of the existence of a disciplinary file on him in the context of the Eurostat case.[171]

6.2.2.2 The Position of the EU General Court

This judgment is particularly relevant as it further defines the scope of protection of the whistleblower provisions under the EU Staff Regulations. In the case, the applicant tried "to establish the EU's non-contractual liability for the EU Commission's alleged disregard of his status as a whistle-blower".[172] Indeed, in reference to the *devoir de sollicitude* and principle of equal treatment, the applicant asserted that the EU Commission should have taken his status of whistleblower into account to distinguish his case from other individuals involved in the Eurostat incident. The fact that the EU Commission disregarded his status of whistleblower should therefore be seen as a violation of Article 22a EU Staff Regulations and of its *devoir de sollicitude* and thus engaged the non-contractual liability of the EU.[173] On the basis of those considerations, the applicant requested the annulment of the AIPN's decision[174] and the payment of €68,831 for his material loss and €10,000 for his moral prejudice.[175] For the applicant, the introduction of Article 22a EU Staff Regulations in 2004 did not go against the possibility for the EU Commission to recognize in 2016 the role he played as whistleblower in accordance with his obligations under Article 11 and 12 EU Staff Regulations.[176] The EU General Court indeed confirmed that an EU official who reported on potential irregularities which could adversely affect the interests of the EU prior to 2004 "had already been entitled to the protection of the institution for which he worked against any

[169] Ibid., paras 17–21.

[170] Ibid., para 23.

[171] Ibid., para 24.

[172] Ibid., para 31.

[173] Ibid., para 64.

[174] Ibid., para 31.

[175] Ibid., para 29.

[176] Ibid., para 64.

retaliation resulting from such disclosure and against any prejudicial effects on the part of that institution provided that he acted in good faith".[177]

However, the EU General Court also recognized that, while this principle ensures the protection of an official against detrimental measures from EU institutions, it did not shield him from investigations aiming to establish if and to what extent he was involved in the irregularities he denounced. The EU General Court indicated that at most, the initiative to report those irregularities could be a mitigating factor if the investigation confirmed his involvement in reducing the penalties imposed.[178] The EU General Court therefore concluded that the status of whistleblower claimed by the applicant did not protect him against proceedings aimed at establishing his involvement in the facts reported by him.[179]

On the basis of those considerations, the EU General Court focused its attention on the question of whether, with regard to the particular facts of the case, the EU Commission committed any violations in pursuing a criminal procedure against the applicant after the French courts decided to dismiss proceedings.[180] The EU General Court found that the only explanation for refusing to grant the applicant's request for assistance, after the Cour de Cassation confirmed the dismissal of proceedings, lay in the fact that the EU Commission remained convinced that the applicant did not comply with his statutory obligations, notwithstanding his exoneration by the French court from any criminal charges.[181] This observation in turn revealed a violation by the EU Commission of the fundamental principle of presumption of innocence,[182] which is a fundamental right protected by the ECHR and enshrined in Article 48 (1) EU Charter.[183] On the grounds of those considerations, the EU General Court annulled the decision rejecting his request for assistance, ordered the EU Commission to bear its costs as well as those of the applicant, but rejected the claims for damages.[184] In the EU General Court's view, "the circumstances of the present case do not appear sufficiently exceptional as to support a finding that the appeal lodged against that order and the application for review of that judgment constituted a breach of administrative duty on the part of the Commission".[185] The applicant appealed this decision, claiming that the above judgment erred in law in regard to the EU Commission's conduct towards him considering his whistleblower status[186] but

[177]Ibid., para 71.

[178]Ibid., para 72, referring to the EU Commission Guidelines on whistleblowing.

[179]Ibid., para 73.

[180]Ibid., para 74.

[181]Ibid., para 85.

[182]Ibid., para 93.

[183]Ibid., paras 91–92.

[184]Ibid., para 100.

[185]Ibid., para 76.

[186]CJ, C-457/19 P, *Amador Rodriguez Prieto v. European Commission*, Appeal brought against the judgment of the General Court delivered on 4 April 2019 in Case T-61/18, Rodriguez Prieto v. Commission, 16 June 2019, 2019/c 312/08, OJ C 312, 16.9.2019, p. 6.

an amicable agreement was reach at the end of 2019,[187] leaving open questions in regard to the exact nature of the whistleblower status under the EU Staff Regulations.

6.3 The Judicial Protection Offered to EU Whistleblower: A Tumultuous Affair

Those cases demonstrate the harsh reality for whistleblowers working within EU institutions. Much remains to be done in order for EU whistleblowers to feel safe and supported in their quest to reveal misconduct, mismanagement or corruption committed within EU institutions, agencies and bodies. The chilling effect that those cases can have is particularly detrimental to the effectiveness of the existing protection mechanism established by the EU Staff Regulations. According to Mr. McCoy, "unless you're willing to lose your job and cause irreparable harm to your health, never, ever even think about blowing any whistles".[188] Considering the already tarnished image and the perceived opacity of the EU bureaucracy, the effective protection of EU whistleblowers could play a crucial role in promoting transparency and accountability within EU institutions and be used as an effective tool to improve their image amongst EU citizens. EU whistleblowers, like Mr. McCoy,[189] are convinced Europeans, who moved away from their home countries to contribute to the EU project. In most cases, EU whistleblowers have occupied high level positions within EU institutions. Being the best placed to appreciate the damage caused by cover-ups, dysfunctions or mismanagement within EU institutions and bodies, they can make a valuable contribution to increase the effectiveness of the EU as a supranational body. While a reform of the current EU Staff Regulations can dramatically improve the protection of EU whistleblowers, the interpretation of the CJEU in regard to those statutory provisions is key and should not be underestimated. The increasing attention to the protection of whistleblowers in Europe, and in the EU, following the adoption of the EU Whistleblower Directive, may encourage the CJEU to further develop its jurisprudence on whistleblowing. The position of the CJEU on the subject may in turn have a positive impact on the effective application of the whistleblowing policies within EU institutions and encourage appointing authorities to be proactive so as to offer EU whistleblowers effective support and protection. The negative health impacts of retaliatory measures, which have been illustrated in the different EU whistleblower cases described above, could be prevented, deterring in this way a hostile work environment within EU institutions and bodies.

---

[187] CJ, C-457/19 P, *Order of the President of the Court*, 20 November 2019, ECLI:EU:C:2019:1021.

[188] Panichi (2015, 20 November).

[189] QuantoFilm for Channel 4 News (2020, 9 February).

References

Mangan L (2004, 26 February) Whistleblowers: What happened next?. *The Guardian*

Panichi J (2015, 20 November) MEPs support whistleblower's 15-year saga. *Politico*

QuantoFilm for Channel 4 News (2020) Meet Robert McCoy, the whistleblower who exposed EU fraud

Von Der Burchard H (2020, 11 November) POLITICO Brussels Playbook: Health power grab - Budget deal - Whistleblower saga. *Politico*

Chapter 7
Existing Whistleblowing Rules in Sectorial Secondary Legislation

Prior to the adoption of the EU Whistleblower Directive in 2019, the EU had adopted, over the course of the last decades, a series of legal instruments incorporating certain elements of a whistleblower framework, yet limited to selected sectors. Because the EU Whistleblower Directive built upon those sectorial provisions, a closer look at some of those existing EU instruments will provide a general overview of the EU's whistleblowing approach so far in order to better assess the potential impact of the newly adopted EU Whistleblower Directive for the future protection of whistleblowers in the EU and its integration into the EU legal landscape.

7.1 Whistleblowing in the EU Financial and Trade Sector

7.1.1 Whistleblowers in the EU Financial Sector

7.1.1.1 From LuxLeaks to the Panama Papers

EU whistleblower protection rules are most prolific in the sector of finance and banking, which is linked to the vulnerability of those sectors to fraud, tax evasion, or tax avoidance, causing losses in tax revenues for EU Member States estimated at around €50–70 billion each year.[1] The abuses and violations occurring in those sectors gained European and international attention in the last decade after the economic crisis and more recently through the media resonance of the LuxLeaks,

[1]EU Commission, *Commission Staff Working Document: Impact Assessment Accompanying the document Proposal for a Directive of the European Parliament and of the Council on the protection of persons reporting on breaches of Union law* [hereinafter "Impact Assessment accompanying the EU Whistleblower Directive proposal"], SWD(2018) 116 final, 23 Avril 2018, p. 19.

© The Author(s), under exclusive license to Springer Nature Switzerland AG 2021
H. C. L. Yurttagül, *Whistleblower Protection by the Council of Europe, the European Court of Human Rights and the European Union*, European Union and its Neighbours in a Globalized World 3, https://doi.org/10.1007/978-3-030-78059-3_7

SwissLeaks[2] and the Panama Papers scandals, which revealed, through disclosures made by whistleblowers, widespread and well-coordinated tax-evasion schemes and tax fraud practices. In this context, Algirdas Semeta, former Lithuanian Finance Minister and EU Commissioner for Taxation and Customs Union from 2009 to 2014, acknowledged: "Citizens, people in member states have started paying much more attention to how their countries can collect taxes which are due under national law . . . If you ask me, I personally think Offshore Leaks could be identified as the most significant trigger behind these developments".[3] The 2013 LuxLeaks scandal, for example, revealed how companies could benefit from advantageous schemes to minimize their taxes if their seat was located in the Luxembourg, distorting competition against companies not having access to such variable taxes.[4] The Panama Papers,[5] the greatest leak of confidential information linked to grand scale tax avoidance scheme using offshore companies named after the location of the law firm concerned, Mossack Fonseca, in Panama, was estimated to have cost a revenue loss of around €109-237 billion for the entire 28 EU Member States.[6]

Not only can those offshore scheme have serious detrimental effects on competition and cause significant revenue losses for States, they are also more likely to be linked to criminal activities, including money laundering.[7] Because those tax evasion and avoidance schemes are known to be particularly well masked through complex and multilayered legal arrangements combined with a strong reluctance of financial and bank institutes to share information with States authorities, the contribution made by whistleblowers in those fields are of paramount importance to encourage accountability and deter future abusive tax schemes.[8] Considering the close financial ties between EU Member States and the international character of tax evasion and fraud practices as well as money laundering, individual efforts by EU Member States have rather limited impacts in deterring well-oiled and reactive machinery capable of transferring funds from one jurisdiction to the next with one click. The modern financial system, with its new technologies and transnational interlinks, is particularly impermeable to national actions. This is the reason why EU-wide, harmonized rules are of utmost importance to track down financial abuses. As the Panama Papers case demonstrates, the role of individuals working in those institutions with questionable, if not illegal financial practices, is key to revealing information otherwise inaccessible to public authorities. Access to that information

---

[2]Carvajal and Minder (2013, 8 August), Minder (2012, 18 December) and Kausch (2014).

[3]Rettman (2013, 5 June).

[4]International Consortium of Investigative Journalists. *Luxembourg Leaks*.

[5]Süddeutsche Zeitung. *Dossier Panama Papers*; see also Obermayer and Obermaier (2016), book written by the two journalists from the Süddeutsche Zeitung who were first contacted by the whistleblower who leaked the panama papers.

[6]EU Commission, *Impact Assessment accompanying the EU Whistleblower Directive proposal*, p. 19.

[7]Ibid., p. 20.

[8]Ibid.

is key to effectively enforcing or adjusting national tax-laws, and fight against money laundering. The EU has therefore invested constant efforts to introduce whistleblower protection mechanisms applicable to the EU financial sectors,[9] which included the creation of reporting channels and protection from retaliation.

7.1.1.2 Directive 2013/36/EU

The EU Directive 2013/36/EU[10] on access to the activity of credit institutions and the prudential supervision of credit institutions and investment firms[11] is a reaction to the 2008 financial crisis[12] as it aims to counter the generalized public suspicion towards financial institutions and encourage EU citizens to regain trust in the financial sector.[13] To ensure the enforcement of that objective, the EU Directive underlines the importance of implementing effective mechanisms which should encourage individuals to report on breaches of the national rules transposing the Directive.[14] A particular emphasis is put on employees reporting on breaches committed within their own institutions, as they too should enjoy full protection.[15] As part of those reporting mechanisms, the Directive provides for an obligation to establish effective reporting channels and offer appropriate protection against retaliation.[16] However, leaving the discretion to determine what constitutes "appropriate protection" to EU Member States is highly problematic as it creates a flexibility which can result in widely different levels of protection amongst national transpositions of the Directive and lead to a heterogeneous protection coverage for whistleblowers across the EU.

---

[9]EU Commission, *Annexes on the Proposal for a Directive on the protection of persons reporting on breaches of Union law COM(2018) 218 final – 2018/0106(COD)* [hereinafter "Annexes on the EU Whistleblower Directive proposal"], 23 April 2018, Annex 5, pp. 109–110.

[10]*Directive 2013/36/EU of 26 June 2013 on access to the activity of credit institutions and the prudential supervision of credit institutions and investment firms, amending Directive 2002/87/EC and repealing Directives 2006/48/EC and 2006/49/EC*, OJ L 176, 27.06.2013, p. 338.

[11]*Directive 2013/36/EU; Regulation (EU) No 575/2013 of 26 June 2013 on prudential requirements for credit institutions and investment firms and amending Regulation (EU) No 648/2012*, OJ L 176, 27.06.2013, p. 1.

[12]Recital 51 *Directive 2013/36/EU*; see also EU Commission, *Reinforcing sanction regimes in the financial services sector*, Communication from the Commission to the European Parliament, the Council, the European Economic and Social Committee and the Committee of the Regions, COM (2010) 716 final, 8 December 2010.

[13]Recital 52 *Directive 2013/36/EU.*

[14]Recital 40 *Directive 2013/36/EU.*

[15]Recital 61 *Directive 2013/36/EU.*

[16]Article 71 *Directive 2013/36/EU.*

7.1.1.3 The Supervisory Role of the ECB

The 2008 financial crisis brought to light a number of deficiencies in the macro-prudential supervision mechanisms applicable within the EU area and marked the beginning of a supranationalisation of those responsibilities.[17] In 2013, the competences of the ECB were eventually developed to include specific tasks related to the prudential supervision of credit institutions.[18] As part of the efforts to "ensure the highest standards of supervisions",[19] the ECB had the obligation to establish effective reporting mechanisms, which should include reporting channels and follow-up procedures, in accordance with the principles already developed above: Appropriate protection of the reporting and accused individual.[20] In accordance with those newly acquired competences, the ECB implemented a whistleblowing platform[21] with information on the reporting procedure and the breaches susceptible to be reported.[22]

7.1.1.4 The Risk of Money Laundering and Terrorist Financing

In its 2015 EU Directive on the prevention of the use of the financial system for the purposes of money laundering or terrorist financing,[23] the EU highlights the risk of retaliation against individuals who have expressed their concerns about or reported on cases of money laundering or terrorist financing.[24] The EU Directive therefore stipulates that EU Member States should ensure that protection is afforded to those individuals, especially when hostile actions are taken against them in the work place.[25] The nature of this protection is not left to the complete discretion and authority of the EU Member States. To ensure the enforcement of the Directive and the effective application of its transposition on the national level, the Directive imposes the obligation to create mechanisms which should encourage the reporting

---

[17] Zilioli (2016), p. 126.

[18] *Council Regulation (EU) No 1024/2013 of 15 October 2013 conferring specific tasks on the European Central Bank concerning policies relating to the prudential supervision of credit institutions* [hereinafter "SSM Regulation"], OJ L 287, 29.10,2013, p. 63; see also ECA, *Special Report: European banking supervision taking shape – EBA and its changing context*, No. 5/2014, 25 June 2014.

[19] Article 4(3) *SSM Regulation*.

[20] Article 23 *SSM Regulation*.

[21] ECB Whistleblowing Platform.

[22] ECB, 'Whistleblowing' website, available at https://www.bankingsupervision.europa.eu/banking/breach/html/index.en.html [last accessed on 10/07/2020].

[23] *Directive (EU) 2015/849 of 20 May 2015 on the prevention of the use of the financial system for the purposes of money laundering or terrorist financing, amending Regulation (EU) No 648/2012 of the European Parliament and of the Council, and repealing Directive 2005/60/EC and Directive* 2006/70/EC, OJ L 141, 05.06.2015, p. 73.

[24] Recital 41 *Directive 2015/849*.

[25] Article 38 *Directive 2015/849*.

of breaches to competent authorities.[26] These mechanisms should comprise procedures to receive and follow-up on reports,[27] appropriate protection to individual and employees reporting on breaches,[28] as well as ensure the respect of personal data rules[29] and confidentiality requirements.[30] Those rules reflect some of the key elements of an effective whistleblower protection framework and demonstrate the EU's recognition that the protection of individuals, and in particular employees, who report on breaches of EU laws is fundamental to ensuring its effective implementation and enforcement. However, those rules are far from perfect for encouraging reporting since they do not ensure a robust shield against retaliation in the workplace. The vague qualifier "appropriate protection" raises the same concerns as the EU Directive 2013/36/EU discussed above.

7.1.1.5 Final Remarks on Whistleblowing in the EU Financial Sector

Despite broad discretion being left to EU Member States regarding whistleblower protection, the measures introduced by the EU were a positive step towards harmonizing Member States' diverse provisions applicable to financial institutions. This is in accordance with the EU Commission's 2010 call on EU Member States to consider common mechanisms to detect breaches of Union law, in particular those committed inside the financial sector.[31] However, despite those already existing whistleblower protection provisions on the EU level, sectorial and incoherent whistleblower protection laws on the national level sometimes that mean whistleblowers experience a paradoxical situation, being praised on the European level but prosecuted on the national one.[32] This was the case in the 'LuxLeaks' revelations: As the State of Luxembourg's whistleblower protection provisions only cover cases of corruption, the whistleblowers who revealed the information were not able to enjoy protection under this law.[33] The new EU Whistleblower Directive adopted in October 2019 could play a key role in harmonizing rules on whistleblower protection across the EU and encourage a stronger and more coherent legal framework.

---

[26] Article 61(1) *Directive 2015/849*.

[27] Article 61(2)(a) *Directive 2015/849*.

[28] Article 61(2)(b) *Directive 2015/849*.

[29] Article 61(2)(d) *Directive 2015/849*.

[30] Article 61(2)(e) *Directive 2015/849*.

[31] EU Commission, *Reinforcing sanctioning regimes in the financial services sector*, Communication from the Commission, COM(2010) 716 final, 8 December 2010, p. 15.

[32] Abazi (2016).

[33] EU Commission, *Impact Assessment accompanying the EU Whistleblower Directive proposal*, p. 12.

7.1.2 The Role of Whistleblowers in the EU Internal Market

The internal market is the sector in which the EU demonstrates a particularly strong commitment to providing for ambitious whistleblower protection mechanisms in order to fight against market abuse. Given that market abuse is highly detrimental to competition on a level playing field, several EU instruments and tools have been developed to remedy market distortion, including stronger whistleblowing provisions, with the intention to deter, through the promotion of whistleblower reports, future anti-competition conduct.

7.1.2.1 The Anonymous Whistleblower Tool

In 2017, the EU Commission introduced The Anonymous Whistleblower Tool, a new mechanism allowing individuals to remain anonymous when reporting on secret cartels and antitrust violations.[34] The system implements two distinct procedures, the anonymous and non-anonymous road. For individuals who accept revealing their identity when reporting on breaches of single market rules, the EU Commission provides two contact possibilities, an email address[35] and a phone number,[36] to which information about EU competition violations could be shared. For individuals wanting to remain anonymous, a special online-form is available,[37] which is accompanied by a detailed description of the process. In parallel to the Treaty provisions relevant to EU competition rules, the description gives advice on the best way to proceed in order to preserve anonymity. The procedure also provides for the possibility to obtain a response to the message sent through the online-form, in which case the reporting individual has to create a password prior to sending the message, which can be used, in combination with the ID message, to have a secured access to the EU Commission's reply, which is expected to take approximately 10–15 working days.

The detailed and exhaustive description of the procedure and the reminder to exclude any contact information helps to create a comprehensive image of the procedure and a strong sense of anonymity. This is one of the key elements of a strong whistleblower protection framework as it is shown that the most common reasons why individuals are reluctant to report on breaches are the inaccessibility of reporting procedures, fear of retaliation and the lack of trust in that the report will be followed by actions from the authorities. Through this reactive approach, a

[34]EU Commission, Antitrust: Commission introduces new anonymous whistleblower tool, 16 March 2017, *Press release*.

[35]EU Commission Email-address dedicated to whistleblower reports: comp-whistleblower@ec.europa.eu.

[36]EU Commission Phone number dedicated to whistleblower reports: 0032-2-29 74800 (BE).

[37]EU Commission Website dedicated to anonymous whistleblower reports: https://comp-eu.whistleblowernetwork.net/FrontPages/Default.aspx. Accessed 13 April 2021.

follow-up taking between 10 and 15 days via the anonymous platform on which reports can be made, the EU Commission offers an effective way to counter the traditional burden to reporting breaches. The fact that the message can be written in all the EU languages also helps to open the door to reports from individuals who would otherwise be hindered by the language barrier.

Even if this mechanism is only applicable to one particular sector and for specific violations related to Article 101 and 102 TFEU, this new tool should be welcomed as it demonstrates the willingness of the EU Commission to adopt a forward-thinking approach on whistleblowing. It indicates the EU Commission's general acceptance that whistleblowers can play a key role in detecting breaches of the law and should therefore enjoy the strongest protection, going so far as offering whistleblowers complete anonymity. This tool is revolutionary for two reasons: First, it introduces the concept of anonymous reporting as an official EU whistleblowing mechanism. Second, it also encourages this form of whistleblowing through an official reporting platform.

7.1.2.2 Whistleblowing and Confidential Trade Documents

In this context, the 2004 EU Commission Regulation (EC) No 773/2004 states a limitation to the documents which could be transmitted to the EU Commission, namely any information related to business secrets or confidential information.[38] Under this Regulation, business secrets should be understood as "information of which not only disclosure to the public but also mere transmission to a person other than the one that provided the information may seriously harm the latter's interests".[39] Other confidential information should be understood as information "whose disclosure would significantly harm a person or undertaking",[40] or information on military secrets.[41] This includes letters sent to customers if it could expose the author to retaliatory measures.[42] On the contrary, information which can be known or

[38]Article 16 (1) *Commission Regulation (EC) No 773/2004 of 7 April 2004 relating to the conduct of proceedings by the Commission pursuant to Articles 81 and 82 of the EC Treaty*, OJ L 123, 27.04.2004, p. 18.

[39]GC, Case T-353/94, *Postbank NV v. Commission of the European Communities*, Judgment of 18 September 1996, ECLI:EU:T:1996:119, para. 87.

[40]*Commission Notice on the rules for access to the Commission file in cases pursuant to Articles 81 and 82 of the EC Treaty, Articles 53, 54 and 57 of the EEA Agreement and Council Regulation (EC) No 139/2004*, 2005/C 325/7, OJ C 325, 22.12.2005, p. 7, para. 19.

[41]Ibid., para. 20.

[42]GC, Case T-65/89, *BPB Industries plc and British Gypsum Ltd. v. Commission of the European Communities*, Judgment of 1 April 1993, ECLI:EU:T:1993:31; CJ, Case C-310/93P, *BPB Industries plc. and British Gypsum Ltd. v. Commission of the European Communities*, Judgment of 6 April 1995, ECLI:EU:T:1995:101; GC, Case T-221/95, *Endemol Entertainment Holding BV. v. Commission of the European Communities*, Judgment of 28 April 1999, ECLI:EU:T:1999:85, para 69; GC, Case T-5/02, *Tetra Laval BV. v. Commission of the European Communities*, Judgment of 25 October 2002, ECLI:EU:T:2002:264, paras 98 *et seq.*

deducted by individuals outside of the circle to whom it was initially limited to,[43] or simply the passing of time[44] can be disqualifiers when considering the business secret relevant or the confidential character of the information.

How can those rules be compatible with the necessity for whistleblowers to be protected when disclosing information likely to expose breaches of EU competition laws but revealing business secrets or confidential information? The Directive (EU) 2016/943 on the protection of undisclosed know-how and business information against unlawful acquisition, use and disclosure (hereinafter referred to as "Trade Secrets Directive")[45] adopted in 2016 is a step towards addressing this very thorny issue. For the purpose of this Directive, "trade secrets" is defined as information which is not generally known or readily accessible to individuals usually in charge of receiving that kind of information,[46] information whose secrecy represents commercial significance[47] and information which has been subjected to reasonable steps in order to remain secret.[48]

The Trade Secrets Directive provides a general sanction mechanism for individuals disclosing trade secrets but formulates a protection for whistleblowers as an exception to this general rule, referring to the right to freedom of expression enshrined in Article 11 EU Charter.[49] The Trade Secrets Directive represents an anomaly in the EU whistleblower protection landscape because the protection of whistleblowers laid down in the Directive does not represent a means to reach its objective but rather an exception to that means.[50] Under the title "Exception", Article 5 Trade Secrets Directive explicitly stipulates an obligation for EU Member States to exempt from any sanctions individuals who acquired, used or disclosed information containing trade secrets "for revealing misconduct, wrongdoing or illegal activity, provided that the respondent acted for the purpose of protecting the general public interest".[51]

How the newly adopted EU Whistleblower Directive will interplay with the Trade Secrets Directive within EU Member States' legislative framework remains to be seen. An analysis of the potential options for developing a national

[43]GC, Case T-89/96, *British Steel plc v. Commission of the European Communities*, Order of 29 May 1997, ECLI:EU:T:1997:77, paras 26–27.

[44]GC, Case T-341/12, *Evonik Degussa GmbH v. European Commission*, Judgment of 28 January 2015, ECLI:EU:T:2015:51, paras 84-85 ; CJ, Case C-162/5 P, *Evonik Degussa GmbH v. European Commission*, Judgment of 14 March 2017, ECLI:EU:C:2017:205, paras 64–67.

[45]*Directive (EU) 2016/943 of 8 June 2016 on the protection of undisclosed know-how and business information (trade secrets) against their unlawful acquisition, use and disclosure* [hereinafter "Trade Secrets Directive"], OJ L 157, 15.06.2016, p.1.

[46]Article 2 (1)(a) *Trade Secrets Directive*.

[47]Article 2(1)(b) *Trade Secrets Directive*.

[48]Article 2(1)(c) *Trade Secrets Directive*.

[49]Article 5 (a) *Trade Secrets Directive*.

[50]EU Commission, *Annexes on the EU Whistleblower directive proposal*, Annex 5, p. 90.

[51]Article 5 (b) *Trade Secrets Directive*.

whistleblower framework coherent with the requirements put in place under the Trade Secrets Directive will be discussed below.[52]

7.1.2.3 The Market Abuse Regulation

Financial Incentives to Blow the Whistle

The 2014 Market Abuse Regulation,[53] which aims to regulate and prevent abuses in the single market, explicitly refers to whistleblowers as useful, yet vulnerable actors to detect abuses in the single market.[54] Acknowledging the risk of retaliation, the Regulation states a necessity to develop adequate arrangements to encourage whistleblowing and protect individuals from retaliatory measures following their reporting.[55] Much like the Directives related to the financial sector, the Regulation puts an obligation on EU Member States to establish secure reporting channels for employees who report on breaches of market rules.[56] Internal reporting channels should also be introduced within the institutions regulated by financial services regulations.[57]

The Regulation does not formulate a hierarchy between internal and external channels, which offers a greater freedom to individuals in determining which reporting channel will be the most effective. Moving away from the tiered model inspired by the UK PIDA's system, the EU in this way adopts a more ambitious plan regarding whistleblower protection when reports on breaches and market abuses is at stake. By following an undifferentiated approach between internal and external reporting channels, the EU acknowledges the limits to the tiered model and demonstrates a willingness to alleviate the conditions imposed on whistleblowers when reporting on breaches of market laws by following a horizontal approach to reporting channels.

Furthermore, the Regulation introduces an ambitious novelty as it provides for the possibility to offer financial incentives to individuals reporting on breaches.[58] This possibility, left to the discretion of EU Member States ("may"), is revolutionary in EU law as it opens the door to an "americanized" vision of whistleblowing. The US system offering generous financial incentives for information is heavily disputed among European scholars and far from unanimously accepted by EU Member

---

[52]See Sect. 8.5.2.

[53]*Regulation (EU) No 596/2014 of 16 April 2014 on market abuse (market abuse regulation) and repealing Directive 2003/6/EC and Directives 2003/124/EC, 2003/125/EC and 2004/72/EC* [hereinafter "Market Abuse Regulation"], OJ L 173, 12.06.2014, p. 1.

[54]Recital 74 *Market Abuse Regulation.*

[55]Ibid.

[56]Article 32 (1) and (2) *Market Abuse Regulation.*

[57]Article 32 (3) *Market Abuse Regulation.*

[58]Article 32 (4) *Market Abuse Regulation.*

States.[59] However, independently of whether financial incentives should be welcomed or rejected, this Regulation represents the most far-reaching sectorial framework for the protection of whistleblowers in the EU regulatory landscape.

From Special Training to Anonymous Reports

In accordance with Article 32 (5) of the Market Abuse Regulation, the EU Commission adopted an Implementing Directive to further develop the procedures concerning the reporting channels mechanism introduced in the Regulation.[60] In accordance with the CoE Recommendation CM/Rec(2014)7 and taking its own Anonymous Whistleblower Tool as a model and, the EU Commission requires EU Member States to offer easily identifiable and accessible online information on the reporting options available and the expected timeframe for the follow-up.[61] Explicitly using the term "whistleblower" to define individuals reporting on infringements,[62] the Implementing Directive reiterates the necessity to adopt an undifferentiated approach to internal and external reporting channels.[63] Those channels should be secure and ensure the confidentiality of the reporting individual.[64] It also introduces an anonymous reporting channel,[65] a strong incentive to report.

Another important element of the Implementing Directive is the requirement to train dedicated officials to receive and address reports of breaches,[66] an essential step towards ensuring the efficient and competent handling of whistleblower reports. However, even if the particular threats faced by individuals in a contractual relationship with the institution they reported on[67] are mentioned, the Implementing Directive has a limited impact on the actual protection of whistleblowers as it refers to existing national legislation to effectively fight against retaliatory measures linked to whistleblowing.[68] If there is no existing national procedure or remedy against retaliation, the provision is devoid of substance. Individuals having blown the whistle on infringements of EU market abuse regulations would therefore remain vulnerable to retaliatory measures due to a lack of a specific protection mechanism in the EU Member States' legislation. Considering that until recently, only few EU

[59]On the debate around financial incentives see Sect. 2.5.2.2.

[60]*Commission Implementing Directive (EU) 2015/2392 on Regulation (EU) No 596/2014 of the European Parliament and of the Council as regards reporting to competent authorities of actual or potential infringements of that Regulation*, OJ L 332, 18.12.2015, p. 126.

[61]Article 4 *Commission Implementing Directive (EU) 2015/2392.*

[62]Recital 1 *Commission Implementing Directive (EU) 2015/2392.*

[63]Recital 2 *Commission Implementing Directive (EU) 2015/2392.*

[64]Articles 6 and 9 *Commission Implementing Directive (EU) 2015/2392.*

[65]Article 5(1)(a) *Commission Implementing Directive (EU) 2015/2392.*

[66]Article 3 (1) *Commission Implementing Directive (EU) 2015/2392.*

[67]Article 8(1) *Commission Implementing Directive (EU) 2015/2392.*

[68]Article 8(2)(a) *Commission Implementing Directive (EU) 2015/2392.*

Member States had some sort of whistleblower protection legal framework, this substantive legal vacuum on the national level has significant consequences for the effective implementation of the EU Regulation on market abuse. The newly adopted EU Whistleblower Directive is a first step to address this legal gap.

7.2 Blowing the Whistle on Environmental and Safety Issues

7.2.1 Environmental Protection

The protection of the environment and the concerns about climate change and global warming have attracted a renewed wave of international public mobilization in the past year, such as the Fridays for Future or the movement Extinction Rebellion, thanks to young activists like Greta Thunberg, who was named Person of the Year by Time Magazine in 2019.[69] Those movements for the protection of the climate have urged heads of State and governments to undertake ambitious plans to curb the consequences facing the international community today due to climate change. It has also highlighted the insufficiencies in the regulatory frameworks in place today on the national and international level, and the need to put in place stricter rules to effectively address the issues related to environmental protection and climate change. To fill the gap, civil society actors established different whistleblower mechanisms, with the aim to receive reports on wildlife crimes for example.[70]

On the EU level, the rules aiming to ensure an effective protection of the environment have proven to be insufficient, despite having been the subject of numerous Regulations and Directives.[71] This has led to an estimated cost of 50 billion euro per year.[72] To encourage the implementation of already existing EU rules, the EU Commission released a roadmap in 2018 to provide information to EU Member States and professionals working in the field in order to better enforce environmental protection Regulations.[73] In that respect, encouraging individuals to report on breaches of those Regulations has proven essential.

[69]Alter et al. (2019, 23–30 December).

[70]Earth League International (2020).

[71]EU Commission, *Impact Assessment accompanying the EU Whistleblower Directive proposal*, p. 21; see also EU Commission, *The Environment Implementation Review*. https://ec.europa.eu/environment/eir/index_en.htm. Accessed 13 April 2021.

[72]EU Commission, 'The costs of not implementing the environmental acquis: Final report', *DG Environment*, ENV.G.1/FRA/2006/0073, September 2011, p. 9.

[73]EU Commission, 'Environmental compliance: European Commission launches Action Plan to help Member States improve environmental protection', 19 January 2018, *Press release*.

To ensure compliance with its Regulations, the EU introduced Directive 2013/30/EU on safety of offshore oil and gas operations,[74] which entails an obligation for EU Member States to establish confidential reporting mechanisms in order for individuals to express any safety or environmental concerns related to offshore oil and gas operations[75] while remaining anonymous if further investigations are undertaken.[76] In anticipation of the transposition of the EU Whistleblower Directive, which could expand the scope of those rules to further sectors related to environmental protection, the provisions on reporting mechanisms provided in the Directive 2013/30/EU, solely applicable to offshore oil and gas operation, has a limited impact on the effective protection of the much broader range of environmental issues.

7.2.2 Nuclear Safety

The relationship between whistleblowing and nuclear safety has a long history in the US.[77] In Europe, however, despite having introduced the "most advanced nuclear safety regulatory frameworks in the world",[78] much needs to be done in order to regain the confidence of the public in that sector, which was dramatically affected following a number of European scandals concerning the deterioration of some nuclear power plants. In this context, the Directive 2014/87/EURATOM on the effective nuclear safety culture[79] encourages for example the ability to question and report safety practices.[80]

7.2.3 Transportation Safety

The role of whistleblowers working as engineers in the transportation sector has gained particular international attention in recent years following the crashes of two Boeing 737 Max airplanes in 2018 and 2019. Those tragic incidents brought to light serious deficiencies in the 737 Max production line, and revealed that a number of whistleblowers working in the company had expressed their concerns but were

---

[74] *Directive 2013/30/EU of 12 June 2013 on safety of offshore oil and gas operations and amending Directive 2004/35/EC*, OJ L 178, 28.06.2013, p. 66.

[75] Article 22(1)(a) *Directive 2013/30/EU*; see also Recital 41 of the same Directive.

[76] Article 22(1)(b) *Directive 2013/30/EU*.

[77] See Fitzgerald (2018), pp. 121–123.

[78] EU Commission, *Impact Assessment accompanying the EU Whistleblower Directive proposal*, p. 22.

[79] *Council Directive 2014/87/Euratom of 8 July 2014 amending Directive 2009/71/Euratom establishing a Community framework for the nuclear safety of nuclear installations*, OJ L 219, 25.07.2014, p. 42.

[80] Article 8b(2)(a) *Directive 2014/87/Euratom*.

ignored,[81] underlining the deadly consequences of inexistent or weak whistleblowing policies in private companies.

7.2.3.1 Aviation Safety

In the EU, a range of legislative measures were adopted[82] following the EU Commission's 1999 Recommendation to create a single European sky,[83] advocating for a collective management of airspace[84] in accordance with the Convention on International Civil Aviation (ICAO), which promotes common minimum standards in international civil aviation to prevent "a threat to the general security".[85] The main purpose being safety in air navigation,[86] the European Aviation Safety Agency (EASA) was established in 2002.

In this context, and whilst acknowledging the limits of a reactive approach to further lower the number of casualties in civil aviation, the EU adopted the Regulation (EU) No 376/2014 on the reporting, analysis and follow-up of occurrences in civil aviation.[87] This, indeed, encourages a more reactive mechanism[88] to promote a "safety culture" which should further spontaneous reporting of occurrences in civil aviation.[89] An occurrence, in the sense of this Regulation, is defined as "safety-related events which endangers or which . . . could endanger an aircraft".[90] The lack of effective whistleblower protection framework in the civil aviation sector can lead

---

[81]Marsh and Wallace (2019, 11 December), Gelles (2019, 9 December) and Ma (2019, 10 December).

[82]*Regulation (EC) No 549/2004 of 10 March 2004 laying down the framework for the creation of the single European sky (the framework Regulation)*; OJ L 096, 31.03.2004, p. 1; *Regulation (EC) No 550/2004 of 10 March 2004 on the provision of air navigation services in the single European sky (the service provision Regulation)*, OJ L 96, 31.03.2004, p. 10; *Regulation (EC) No 551/2004 of the Council of 10 March 2004 on the organisation and use of the airspace in the single European sky (the airspace Regulation)*, OJ L 96, 31.03.2004, p. 20; *Regulation (EC) No 552/2004 of 10 March 2004 on the interoperability of the European Air Traffic Management network (the interoperability Regulation)*, OJ L 93, 31.03.2004, p. 26.

[83]EU Commission, *The creation of the single European sky*, Communication from the Commission to the Council and the European Parliament, COM/99/0614 final, 1. December 1999.

[84]Ibid., Recital 13.

[85]Preamble of the *Convention on International Civil Aviation* (Chicago Convention), 7 December 1944; see also Article 37 of the same Convention.

[86]Bieber and Maiani (2015), p. 271.

[87]*Regulation (EU) No 376/2014 of 3 April 2014 on the reporting, analysis and follow-up of occurrences in civil aviation, amending Regulation (EU) No 996/2010 and repealing Directive 2003/42/EC and Commission Regulations (EC) No 1321/2007 and (EC) No 1330/2007*, OJ L 122, 24.04.2014, p. 18.

[88]Recital 5 *Regulation (EU) No 376/2014.*

[89]Recital 36 *Regulation (EU) No 376/2014.*

[90]Article 2(7) *Regulation (EU) No 376/2014.*

to occurrences left unaddressed because of fear to report,[91] so the reporting mechanisms dedicated to receiving reports should be secure, allowing confidentiality of personal data, and independent of other reporting systems.[92]

The EU Member States have a discretionary power to strengthen the protection afforded to individuals reporting on occurrences,[93] thus allowing the development of varying levels of protection among EU Member States, which is particularly problematic given the transnational nature of civil aviation. Furthermore, while the Regulation prohibits the use of information obtained through occurrence reports for other purposes than safety,[94] it does not protect individuals having reported on occurrences from disciplinary or administrative proceedings.[95] The fear of potential self-incrimination[96] thus remains, which in turn decreases the likelihood of making use of the reporting channels developed by the Regulation. Therefore, the absence of strong legal protection for whistleblowers on the national level, which could shield employees from those proceedings when reporting on occurrences, greatly diminishes the relevance and effectiveness of the Regulation.

7.2.3.2 Maritime Safety and Anti-pollution Measures

As part of the EU Common Transport Policy,[97] the EU has a rather reactive approach to maritime safety.[98] One of the most ambitious steps to further maritime safety on the EU level was taken following two oil tanker incidents, "Erika" and "Prestige".[99] This was the creation of the European Maritime Safety Agency (EMSA), an EU body in charge of furthering the EU maritime safety regime through specialized competences, including oil pollution responses, with the purpose to complement the EU Member States responsibilities.[100] The Directive 2005/35/EC[101] built upon those competences[102] with the introduction of "CleanSeaNet", a satellite-based oil spill and vessel detection service.[103] It is complemented by the vessel traffic

[91] Recital 43 *Regulation (EU) No 376/2014.*

[92] Article 6(3) and (4), Article 15 and Article 16 *Regulation (EU) No 376/2014.*

[93] Article 16(7) *Regulation (EU) No 376/2014.*

[94] Article 6(1) and (3) *Regulation (EU) No 376/2014.*

[95] Article 16(7)(a) *Regulation (EU) No 376/2014.*

[96] Recitals 41 and 43 *Regulation (EU) No 376/2014.*

[97] Article 91(1)(i) TFEU.

[98] Bieber and Maiani (2015), p. 227.

[99] Coleman and Jessen (2016), p. 572.

[100] Ibid., pp. 572–573.

[101] *Directive 2005/35/EC of 7 September 2005 on ship pollution and on the introduction of penalties for infringements* OJ L 255, 30.09.2005, p. 11.

[102] Coleman and Jessen (2016), p. 573.

[103] European Maritime Safety Agency (EMSA), *CleanSeaNet Service*. http://www.emsa.europa.eu/csn-menu.html Accessed 13 April 2021.

monitoring and information system established by the Regulation 2002/59/EC,[104] which entails the key aspects of an EU reporting mechanism and surveillance program to alert about large scale discharges of oil and other noxious substances by ships.[105] It aims to enhance the safety of maritime traffic, improve the reaction of EU Member States to incidences and better detect pollution by ships[106] through a computerized data exchange system[107] known as "SafeSeaNet".[108] The mechanism implemented by the Directive 2002/59/EC puts an obligation on the master of ships to report any incident or accident which may affect the safety of the ship or which can lead to pollution of the water.[109]

The general acceptance of leaving the responsibility of ensuring that ships comply with security, safety and employment obligations to flag States was called into question after the 1978 Amoco Cadiz oil spill, as it increased public awareness about the risks related to pollution and safety at sea and encouraged the international community to entrust more responsibilities to port states through the adoption of the Paris Memorandum of Understanding on Port States Control, also known as the 'Paris MoU', and the International Convention on the Prevention of Pollution from Ship (MARPOL 73/78),[110] which in turn animated the EU to strengthen the responsibilities of EU port states.[111] In that spirit, the Directive 2009/16/EC[112] on port state control made the Paris MoU binding to EU Member States[113] and implemented a common inspection regime on ships under close cooperation with the EMSA.[114] This regime also includes a complaint mechanism,[115] through which "information or report [can be] submitted by any person or organisation with a legitimate interest in the safety of the ship, including an interest in safety or health hazards to its crew, on-board living and working conditions and the prevention of pollution".[116]

This mechanism was updated in 2013 to extend the confidentiality clause,[117] which should prohibit the disclosure of the complainant's identity to the master or

---

[104] *Directive 2002/59/EC of 27 June 2002 establishing a Community vessel traffic monitoring and information system and repealing Council Directive 93/75/EEC*, OJ L 208, 05.08.2002, p. 10.

[105] Coleman and Jessen (2016), p. 574.

[106] Article 1 *Regulation 2002/59/EC.*

[107] Article 14 *Regulation 2002/59/EC.*

[108] EMSA, *Vessel traffic monitoring in EU waters (SafeSeaNet).* http://www.emsa.europa.eu/component/flexicontent/113.html?Itemid=58. Accessed 13 April 2021.

[109] Article 17 *Regulation 2002/59/EC.*

[110] Pimm (2016), pp. 858–859.

[111] Bieber and Maiani (2015), p. 227; Pimm (2016), p. 858.

[112] Consolidated text: *Directive 2009/16/EC of 23 April 2009 on port State control*, OJ L 131, 28.05.2009, p. 57.

[113] Pimm (2016), pp. 858–859.

[114] Recital 10 *Directive 2009/16/EC.*

[115] Article 18 *Directive 2009/16/EC.*

[116] Article 2(14) *Directive 2009/16/EC.*

[117] Pimm (2016), p. 880.

the ship owner,[118] and include breaches of the 2006 MLC into the complaint mechanism of the Directive.[119] The latter amendment aims to find a resolution at the lowest level[120] as it encourages the inspector to resolve issues at the ship-board level when appropriate.[121] The Directive also includes the possibility for pilots to report "apparent anomalies" related to the safety or environment at sea, which they became aware of in the performance of their "normal duties".[122] EU Member States then have a duty to follow-up on these reports and record the actions taken in that regard.[123] Other Directives related to maritime safety, such as the Directive 2009/18/EC[124] establishing the fundamental principles governing the investigation of accidents in the maritime transport sector, also provide for confidentiality clauses which protect individuals having provided evidence during the course of investigations.[125]

Due to the large number of international agreements in regard to safety in maritime transportation, the EU legislative competence is often limited to the implementation of international standards.[126] The Directive 2013/54/EU concerning certain flag State responsibilities for compliance with and enforcement of the MLC[127] is one of those examples as it aims to implement compliance and enforcement provisions[128] provided in Title 5 of the 2006 MLC.[129] This Directive puts an obligation on EU Member States to adopt appropriate on-board complaint procedures,[130] which should ensure the confidentiality of the individual lodging the complaint,[131] and offer effective investigation of and remedial measures to potential defects.[132] Although very concise, this provision is a first step towards encouraging whistleblowing with regard to anomalies and deficiencies in the maritime sectors to prevent safety and environmental catastrophes.

---

[118] Article 18 *Directive 2009/16/EC.*

[119] Article 18a *Directive 2009/16/EC.*

[120] Pimm (2016), p. 881.

[121] Article 18a(3) *Directive 2009/16/EC.*

[122] Article 23(1) *Directive 2009/16/EC.*

[123] Article 23(4) *Directive 2009/16/EC.*

[124] *Directive 2009/18/EC of 23 April 2009 establishing the fundamental principles governing the investigation of accidents in the maritime transport sector*, OJ L 131, 28.05.2009, p. 114.

[125] Article 9(b) *Directive 2009/18/EC.*

[126] Bieber and Maiani (2015), p. 227.

[127] *Directive 2013/54/EU of the European Parliament and of the Council of 20 November 2013 concerning certain flag State responsibilities for compliance with and enforcement of the Maritime Labour Convention, 2006*, OJ L 329, 10.12.2013, p. 1.

[128] Recital 8 *Directive 2013/54/EU.*

[129] *Maritime Labour Convention*, 23 February 2006. UNTS Vol. no. 2952.

[130] Article 5(1) *Directive 2013/54/EU.*

[131] Article 5(3) *Directive 2013/54/EU.*

[132] Article 5(2) *Directive 2013/54/EU.*

7.3 Whistleblowers and Data Protection

Public concern over the protection of privacy and data protection in the internet era has increased in recent years following large scale data abuse cases such as in the Cambridge Analytica scandal, the extent of which was revealed following the testimony of insiders.[133] This scandal has increased concern and public awareness about the vulnerability of the democratic process due to the manipulation of personal data and the inadequacy of contemporary legal frameworks for regulating the modern technologies able to gather the personal data of millions of citizen.

7.3.1 The GDPR

While 2018 was a big year for EU Data protection as the General Data Protection Regulation (GDPR)[134] came into force and introduced stronger protection of the right to private life in relation to the processing of personal data, it follows a history of EU initiatives seeking to organize the world online, for example through stronger data privacy regulations such as the 2002 e-privacy Directive,[135] or the NIS Directive,[136] which aim at strengthening the EU against cyber-incidents. The GDPR aims to protect "fundamental rights and freedoms of natural persons and in particular their right to the protection of personal data",[137] which refers to Article 8(1) EU Charter, "Protection of personal data", through the Regulation of the processing of personal data.[138]

Under the GDPR, supervisory authorities in charge of monitoring the implementation of the Regulation[139] have a duty of professional secrecy during and after their term of office, especially when receiving reports from individuals on potential breaches of the Regulation.[140] This condition of secrecy demonstrates the necessity of ensuring confidentiality in order to encourage reporting and thus detect potential infringements of the Regulation more efficiently.

---

[133] Cadwalladr (2018, 18 March), Perrigo (2019, 8 October) and Ottesen (2020, 3 March).

[134] *Regulation (EU) 2016/679 of 27 April 2016 on the protection of natural persons with regard to the processing of personal data and on the free movement of such data, and repealing Directive 95/46/EC (General Data Protection Regulation)* [hereinafter "GDPR"], OJ L 119, 04.05.2016, p. 1.

[135] *Directive 2002/58/EC of 12 July 2002 concerning the processing of personal data and the protection of privacy in the electronic communications sector*, OJ L 201, 31.07.2002, p. 37.

[136] *Directive (EU) 2016/1148 of 6 July 2016 concerning measures for a high common level of security of network and information systems across the Union*, OJ L 194, 19.07.2016, p. 1.

[137] Article 1(2) *GDPR*.

[138] Article 1(1) *GDPR*.

[139] Article 51(1) *GDPR*.

[140] Article 54(2) *GDPR*.

7.3.2 The *Stuttgart* Case

However, the adoption of this new Data protection regulation raises some issues in regard to already existing whistleblowing frameworks and the specific protection of whistleblowers' data when using reporting channels, leaving EU Member States with the laborious task of balancing the different interests at stake. In Germany for example, following the criticism of new data protection rules in regard to whistleblowing hotlines, the German Data Protection authorities updated their guidelines[141] to introduce exceptions to the general information obligation.[142] They also reversed their position regarding anonymous whistleblower reports by starting to promote this reporting channel.[143]

The decision of the *Arbeitsgericht Stuttgart*,[144] which was confirmed by the *Landesarbeitsgericht Baden-Württemberg*,[145] laid a cornerstone in regard to the balancing interests between whistleblowing and the GDPR.[146] In the case at hand, the applicant, who was dismissed following a whistleblower report against him, requested to obtain his personal data information, including those in relation to the whistleblower report. While the German court agreed that the right to access to personal data can be limited in particular cases by the legitimate interest of third parties in maintaining secrecy, it found that the balancing of interests at hand did not justify such a limitation of the applicant's right to full access to his own personal data.[147] The court thus agreed with the applicant and ordered Daimler to give him full access to his personal data in accordance with Article 15 GDPR, inclusive data in relation to internal investigations and a whistleblower report concerning him.[148] To comply with its obligation under its internal whistleblowing framework and ensure the anonymity of the whistleblower, the employer carries the burden of obliterating relevant passages concerning the identity of the whistleblower or which could indirectly reveal the identity of the whistleblower.[149] It remains to be seen if this position is going to be consolidated in the future. The evolution of this issue promises to be particularly interesting and should be followed with great attention.

The GDPR and its delimitation in the context of whistleblower protection thus brings new challenges which remain to be solved, such as the technological means through which data privacy of whistleblowers can be processed, how data

[141] Datenschutzkonferenz (2018, 14 November).

[142] Article 14 *GDPR*.

[143] McKenzie (2019).

[144] ArbG Stuttgart, Judgment of 19.12.2017, 17 Ca 4075/17.

[145] LAG Baden-Württemberg, Judgment of 20.12.2018, 17 Sa 11/18, *Auskunftsanspruch nach der Datenschutzgrundverordnung EUV 2016/679 - berechtigte Interessen Dritter an einer Geheimhaltung*.

[146] Ibid., para 20.

[147] Ibid., paras 184–188.

[148] Ibid., para 209.

[149] Ibid., para 187.

minimization can be achieved, the appropriate time of storage in regard to whistleblower data, or the possible exceptions to the information obligation in regard to whistleblower reports. In this respect, the EDPS Guidelines,[150] though for the attention of EU institutions, agencies and bodies, could also be a helpful tool to define national whistleblower protection rules in compliance with the new GDPR.

7.4 The Shortcomings of the Sectorial Approach to EU Whistleblower Protection

Unfortunately, those EU initiatives did not prompt EU Member States to extend those sectorial whistleblowing schemes to other areas and establish a more comprehensive legal protection framework.[151] However, over the last decade, calls for a horizontal protection for whistleblowers were the regular subject of EP Resolutions. Despite the non-binding character of the latter, those resolutions from the legislative branch of the EU, the only institution directly elected by EU citizens, carry a significant weight and demonstrate an intent to move toward a stronger, cross-sectorial protection for whistleblowers. In this context, a very interesting resolution on the protection of whistleblowers who reveal confidential information on private or public entities was adopted by the EP in October 2017. It called on the EU Commission to present an ambitious horizontal legislative proposal to establish high standards of protection for whistleblowers with a broad scope which should include the private and public sector, and should be applicable to national as well as EU institutions.[152] This EP Resolution was an initiating trigger for the EU Commission's 2018 Proposal for a Directive on the protection of persons reporting breaches of Union law,[153] analyzed in the next chapter.

References

Abazi V (2016) Leaked transparency and whistleblowers. *Verfassungsblog*

Alter C, Haynes S, Worland J (2019, 23-30 December) TIME Person of the year 2019: Greta Thunberg. *Time Magazine*

---

[150] EDPS, *Guidelines on processing personal information within a whistleblowing procedure.*

[151] EU Commission, *Impact Assessment accompanying the EU Whistleblower Directive proposal*, pp. 28-29.

[152] Recital 1 *European Parliament resolution of 24 October 2017 on legitimate measures to protect whistle-blowers acting in the public interest when disclosing the confidential information of companies and public bodies (2016/2224(INI))*, P8_TA(2017)0402.

[153] EU Commission, *Impact Assessment accompanying the EU Whistleblower Directive proposal*, p. 1.

Bieber R, Maiani F (2015) Europäisches Verkehrsrecht: Die Rechtspraxis sämtlicher Verkehrsträger. Nomos/Facultas Verlag/Helbing Lichtenhahn, Baden-Baden/Vienna/Basel

Cadwalladr C (2018, 18 March) 'I made Steve Bannon's psychological warfare tool': meet the data war whistleblower. *The Guardian*

Carvajal D, Minder R (2013, 8 August) A Whistle-Blower Who Can Name Names of Swiss Bank Account Holders. *The New York Times*

Coleman R, Jessen H (2016) EU maritime safety and pollution control: introduction. In: Jessen H, Werner MJ (eds) EU Maritime Transport Law. C.H.Beck/Hart/Nomos/Hart Publishing, Munich/Oxford/Baden Baden/Portland, pp 566–588

Datenschutzkonferenz (2018, 14 November), Orientierungshilfe der Datenschutzaufsichtsbehörden zu Whistleblowing-Hotlines: Firmeninterne Warnsysteme und Beschäftigtendatenschutz

Earth League International (2020) The World's First Whistleblower Initiative Dedicated to Wildlife Crime. https://wildleaks.org/the-first-wildleaks-report/. Accessed 13 April 2021

Fitzgerald K (2018) Whistleblowing: Not always a Losing Game. In: Sakellarious N, Milleron R (eds) Ethics, Politics, and Whistleblowing in Engineering. CRC Press, New York, pp 121–128

Gelles D (2019, 9 December) Boeing 737 Max Factory Was Plagued With Problems, Whislte-Blowers Says. *The New York Times*

International Consortium of Investigative Journalists. Luxembourg Leaks: Global Companies Secrets Exposed. https://www.icij.org/investigations/luxembourg-leaks/. Accessed 13 Apr 2021

Kausch T (2014) Studiodiskussion: Verräterische Helden? Interview with Hervé Falciani. Arte

Ma A (2019, 10 December) A Boing whistleblower says he tried to raise concerns about sloppy 737 Max production, but was ignored by the CEO, board, FAA, and NTSB. *Business Insider France*

Marsh R, Wallace G (2019, 11 December) Whistleblower testifies that Boeing ignored pleas to shut down 737 MAX Production. *CNN*

McKenzie B (2019) GDPR – German data protection authorities establish new rules for whistleblowing hotlines: Call for action – Update

Minder R (2012, 18 December) Bank Data-Theft Suspect Allowed Out of Jail. *The New York Times*

Obermayer B, Obermaier F (2016) Panama Papers: Die Geschichte einer weltweite Enthüllung. Kiepenheuer & Witschen, Cologne

Ottesen KK (2020, 3 March) Cambridge Analytica whistleblower: We should be scared about what we're going to see in this year's elections. *The Washington Post*

Perrigo B (2019, 8 October) 'The Capabilities Are Still There.' Why Cambridge Analytica Whistleblower Christopher Wylie Is Still Worried. *Time Magazine*

Pimm M (2016) Commentary on Directive 2009/16/EC of the European Parliament and of the Council of 23 April 2009 on Port State Control. In: Jessen H, Werner MJ (eds) EU Maritime Transport Law. C.H.Beck/Hart/Nomos/Hart Publishing, Munich/Oxford/Baden Baden/Portland, pp 856–901

Rettman A (2013, 5 June) Interview: EU Commissioner: Offshore Leaks transformed tax policies. *EU Observer*

Süddeutsche Zeitung. Dossier Panama Papers. https://panamapapers.sueddeutsche.de. Accessed 13 Apr 2021

Zilioli C (2016) The Independence of the European Central Bank and Its New Banking Supervisory Competences. In: Ritleng D (ed) Independence and Legitimacy in the Institutional System of the European Union. Collected Courses of the Academy of European Law. Oxford University Press, Oxford, pp 125–179

Chapter 8
A New Whistleblower Directive: Toward Stronger Protection in the EU

As demonstrated in the previous chapter, the EU has followed a sectorial approach to whistleblower protection, limiting the scope to specific areas. This approach has proven to be a weak incentive for EU Member States to adopt more comprehensive national legislations on whistleblower protection.[1] Based on the principles mapped out by the CoE Recommendation CM/Rec(2014)7 determining the effectiveness of whistleblower protection frameworks, only ten EU Member States were found to have a horizontal and comprehensive legal framework protecting whistleblowers, two having close to no protection for whistleblowers[2] and the remaining EU Member States having a protection framework limited to certain sectors, or part of the territory.[3] In the latter group, the application of existing rules was further limited through a restrictive personal scope or a narrow definition of breaches being susceptible to be reported.[4]

The patchwork of rules illustrated in Fig. 8.1 greatly compromises the effectiveness of existing provisions protecting whistleblowers.[5] In EU Member States where only a sectorial protection of whistleblowers is put in place, the fear of reporting, often linked to the uncertainty as to the exact scope of application of the law, greatly minimizes the positive impact resulting from the adoption of whistleblower

[1]EU Commission, *Commission Staff Working Document: Impact Assessment Accompanying the document Proposal for a Directive of the European Parliament and of the Council on the protection of persons reporting on breaches of Union law* [hereinafter "Impact Assessment accompanying the EU Whistleblower Directive proposal"], SWD(2018) 116 final, 23 Avril 2018, pp. 28–29.

[2]Ibid., p. 2.

[3]EU Commission, *Annexes on the Proposal for a Directive on the protection of persons reporting on breaches of Union law COM(2018) 218 final – 2018/0106(COD)* [hereinafter "Annexes on the EU Whistleblower Directive proposal"], 23 April 2018, Annex 6, p. 126.

[4]Ibid.

[5]EU Commission, *Impact Assessment accompanying the EU Whistleblower Directive proposal*, p. 12; see also Worth et al. (2018).

© The Author(s), under exclusive license to Springer Nature Switzerland AG 2021
H. C. L. Yurttagül, *Whistleblower Protection by the Council of Europe, the European Court of Human Rights and the European Union*, European Union and its Neighbours in a Globalized World 3, https://doi.org/10.1007/978-3-030-78059-3_8

No specific provision
Partial/sectorial provision
Specific provision

Member State	Horizontal law[137]	Protection of employees in the private sector[138]	Legal obligation to set up reporting channels[139]	Broad definition of wrongdoing[140]	Broad protection against retaliation[141]	Confidentiality	Specific protection in Courts (reverse burden of proof)[142]	Requirement of good faith[143]
Austria	X	X	√	√	X	√	X	√*
Belgium	X*	X	√	√	√	√	√	√
Bulgaria	X	X	X	√	X	X	X	X
Croatia	X	√	X	X*	X	√	√*	√
Cyprus	X	X	X	X	X	X	X	X
Czech Republic	X	X	√	√	X	√	√	X
Denmark	X	X	√	X*	X	√	√	X
Estonia	X	√	X	X*	X	√	√	√
Finland	X	X	√	X*	X	√	√	X
France	√	√	√	√	√	√	√	√
Germany	X	X	√	√	X	X	√	√*
Greece	X	X	X	X*	X	X	√	√
Hungary	√	√	X	√	√	√	X	√
Ireland	√	√	X	√	√	√	X	√*
Italy	√	√	√	X*	X	√	√	√
Latvia	X	X	X	X	X	X	X	X
Lithuania	X	X	√	√	X	√	X	√*
Luxembourg	X	√	X	X*	√	X	√	√
Malta	√	√	√	√	√	√	X	√
Netherlands	√	√	√	√	√	√	X	√
Poland	X	X	√	X*	√	√	X	√
Portugal	√	X	X	X*	X	X	√*	√*
Romania	X	X	X	X*	X	√	√	√
Slovakia	√	√	√	√	√	√	√	√
Slovenia	X	√	X	X*	√	√	√	√
Spain	X*	√	X	X*	√	X	√	X
Sweden	√	√	√	√	√	X	√*	√
United Kingdom	√	√	√	√	√	√	X	√*

137 Member Stes have a single, horizontal law for the protection of whistle blowers. (*) Legislation provides protection only in parts of the territory.

138 Partial protection is provided by Member States only in the financial and/or banking sector.

139 (*) Reporting channels are only prescribed by law to the certain sectors (PT, SI) or do not require the set-up of channels but refer to reporting channels such as a possibility to report to employers (HU, IE).

140 (*) Partial protection of whistleblowers only limited to cases of corruption (EE, EL, HR, LU, PT, RO, SI) or if wrongdoing that can harm the public interest (DK, ES, FI, IT, PL)

141 Partial provisions of protection since whistleblowers are only protected against some forms of retaliation such as unfair dismissal or discrimination.

142 (*) Reverse burden of proof only in some sectors (HR, PT) or not foreseen by law, but in practice (SE).

143 The requirement of good faith is very different from one Member States to another. (*) Good faith is understood as the reasonable belief that the disclosure is substantially true (IE, UK) only required by caselaw (AT, DE) or only in some sectorial laws (LT, PL).

Fig. 8.1 EU Member States' legal framework on the protection of whistleblowers (Reproduced from EU Commission, *Annexes on the Proposal for a Directive on the protection of persons reporting on breaches of Union law COM(2018) 218 final – 2018/0106(COD)*, 23 April 2018, Annex 6) regulations.[6] This can be demonstrated in the LuxLeaks case, where national judges strongly disagreed on the scope of application of the existing national whistleblower protection framework.[7] Despite a positive development in recent years, with a number of EU Member States having adopted or being in the process of adopting new domestic legislations to protect whistleblowers more effectively, some EU Member States have failed to deliver tangible results.[8]

To address this shortcoming, the European Parliament has on several occasions called on the EU Commission to consider uniform minimum standards[9] and present a legislative proposal establishing "an effective and comprehensive European whistleblower protection programme".[10] In its 2017 resolution entitled "Legitimate measures to protect whistle-blowers acting in the public interest", the EP called on the EU Commission to present a "horizontal legislative proposal establishing a comprehensive common regulatory framework which will guarantee a high level of protection across the board, in both the public and private sectors as well as in national and European institutions, including relevant national and European bodies, offices and agencies, for whistle-blowers in the EU".[11] In 2018, the EU Commission responded with a Directive proposal on the protection of persons reporting on breaches of Union law.[12] Following the ordinary legislative procedure, the finalized text was adopted in October 2019.[13] According to 288 TFEU, a Directive, in contrast to Regulations which are directly applicable in EU Member States' internal legal system after their entry into force, has to be transposed into national law, national authorities having "the choice of form and methods". In the case of the EU Whistleblower Directive, the EU Member States are given 2 years to do so.[14] This

---

[6]EU Commission, *Impact Assessment accompanying the EU Whistleblower Directive proposal*, p. 12.

[7]Ibid., pp. 12-13; see also Vandendriessche (2018), pp. 486–488.

[8]EU Commission, *Annexes on the EU Whistleblower Directive proposal*, Annex 6, p. 129.

[9]As early as 2002, MEPs asked the EU Commission about possible whistleblower protection rules, see e.g. Parliamentary question by the MEP Eija-Riitta Korhola (PPE-DE) to the Commission: *EU Standards governing whistle-blowers in the private sector*, E-0345/02, 12 February 2002.

[10]Recital 14 *European Parliament resolution of 23 October 2013 on organised crime, corruption and money laundering: recommendations on action and initiatives to be taken (final report) (2013/2107(INI))*, P7_TA(2013)0444; Recital 88 *European Parliament resolution of 12 March 2014 on the US NSA surveillance programme, surveillance bodies in various Member States and their impact on EU citizens' fundamental rights and on transatlantic cooperation in Justice and Home Affairs*; Recital 2 *European Parliament resolution of 14 February 2017 on the role of whistleblowers in the protection of EU's financial interests (2016/2055(INI))*, P8_TA(2017)0022.

[11]Recital 1 *European Parliament Resolution 2016/2224(INI)*, (emphasis added).

[12]EU Commission, *Proposal for a Directive of the European Parliament and of the Council on the protection of persons reporting on breaches of Union law* [hereinafter "Whistleblower Directive proposal"], COM(2018) 218 final – 2018/0106(COD), 23 April 2018.

[13]*Directive (EU) 2019/1937 of the European Parliament and of the Council of 23 October 2019 on the protection of persons who report breaches of Union law* [hereinafter "EU Whistleblower Directive"], OJ L 305, 26.11.2019, p. 17.

[14]Article 26(1) *EU Whistleblower Directive*.

chapter will analyze the preliminary consultations and impact assessment undertaken by the EU Commission, the development of the legislative process, and the resulting text of the Directive to better understand the objective of the initiative and the legal gaps it is aiming to fill.

8.1 The Preliminary Considerations for an EU Legislative Initiative on Whistleblowing

Prior to its proposal, the EU Commission undertook an assessment of the economic, social and environmental impact of a new legislative initiative aiming to strengthen the protection of whistleblowers across the EU (hereinafter referred to as "impact assessment"). The EU Commission systematically conducts impact assessments in order to evaluate new or amended legislative proposals, support the decision-making process[15] and determine the extent to which such proposals could tackle the specific issues identified.[16] As part of the impact assessment on an EU-wide whistleblower protection Directive, the EU Commission consulted different stakeholders and commissioned an external study to determine the quantitative and qualitative impacts and benefits of a stronger whistleblower protection framework across the EU and in national law. The impact assessment also included the recommendations of the Regulatory Scrutiny Board (RSB) following its examination of the EU Commission's draft assessment and proposal.[17] In the context of its impact assessment, the EU Commission considered the different policy options at its disposal to strengthen the protection of whistleblowers across the EU in order to determine which legislative initiative would be the most efficient to address the issues linked to a lack of whistleblower protection.

8.1.1 The Views of Stakeholders

Between March and June 2017, the EU Commission undertook consultations with different stakeholders in order to gather information about the issues arising from a lack of whistleblower protection in the EU and on national level, work out the essential elements necessary to be included in an effective whistleblower protection framework on EU level and determine which areas would most benefit from an increased whistleblower protection scheme, so as to better determine the scope of a new EU whistleblower framework: One Open Public Consultation (OPC), three

[15] Rowe (2006), pp. 460–461.

[16] Ibid., p. 454.

[17] EU Commission, *Annexes on the EU Whistleblower Directive proposal*, Annex 1, pp. 59 et seq.

targeted online consultations with professionals engaged in activities related to whistleblowing and three workshops with experts in whistleblower protection.

8.1.1.1 The Open Public Consultation

The overwhelming majority of respondents to the OPC were private individuals,[18] which demonstrates a significant public interest in the topic of whistleblower protection and the strong desire to introduce stronger protection for EU citizens. Interestingly, almost half of respondents came from Germany,[19] a country particularly resistant to introducing a national whistleblower protection despite consistent calls from German NGOs and unions for action in this area.[20] More surprisingly, about a quarter of respondents came from France,[21] where the Loi Sapin 2 was adopted in 2016,[22] establishing a comparatively high level of protection for whistleblowers in contrast with other EU Member States.[23] The adoption of the Loi Sapin 2 may have played a role in raising awareness of the French public for issues related to whistleblowing, hence a relatively high participation to the EU public consultation, but it could also reveal a level of dissatisfaction of the current legal protection afforded on the national level and the hope to increase the minimum standard of whistleblower protection through a harmonized EU legislative act.

Almost all respondents to the OPC expressed support for the protection of whistleblowers[24] in the form of legally binding minimum standards through a combination of EU and national provisions[25] in order to assist EU Member States in the fight against fraud and corruption,[26] tax evasion and tax avoidance,[27] as well as in the protection of the environment,[28] public health[29] and food safety.[30] An EU

[18]EU Commission, *Annexes on the EU Whistleblower Directive proposal*, Annex 2 p. 65: 97% of respondents took part as private individuals.

[19]Ibid.. 43% of respondents came from Germany.

[20]Köhn (2019, 15 Mai) and Strack (2008).

[21]EU Commission, *Annexes on the EU Whistleblower Directive proposal*, Annex 2 p. 65: 23% of respondents came from France.

[22]Loi No. 2016-1691 du 9 décembre 2016 relative à la transparence, à la lutte contre la corruption et à la modernisation de la vie économique (1) (Loi Sapin II).

[23]Péronne and Daoud (2017), Mignon-Colombet and Hannedouche-Leric (2017) and Hertslet and Barsan (2018).

[24]EU Commission, *Annexes on the EU Whistleblower Directive proposal*, Annex 2, p. 66: 99.4% of OPC respondents agreed that whistleblowers should be protected.

[25]EU Commission, *Annexes on the EU Whistleblower Directive proposal*, Annex 13, p. 23: 96% of individuals and 84% of organizations supported legally binding minimum standards.

[26]Ibid., p. 25: 95% of individuals, 85% of organizations.

[27]Ibid.: 93% of individuals, 78% of organizations.

[28]Ibid.: 93% of individuals, 73% of organizations.

[29]Ibid.: 92% of individuals, 73% of organizations.

[30]Ibid.: 91% of individuals, 71% of organizations.

horizontal approach to whistleblower protection was the second most popular option,[31] and found particular support among individuals when considering "protection in cases of disclosure to the public (media, web platforms, etc) where internal reporting and reporting to oversight institutions are not available, not functioning properly or cannot be expected to function properly".[32]

As part of an effective whistleblower protection framework, individuals and organizations ranked the protection against retaliation (harassment,[33] reduction of wages,[34] dismissal,[35] etc) as the most important element,[36] and the confidentiality of the whistleblower's data as the most effective way to ensure this protection.[37] The protection of whistleblowers in administrative proceedings,[38] the proper investigation of whistleblower reports or disclosure,[39] and the establishment of reporting channels to oversight institutions[40] were also considered particularly important as part of an effective whistleblower protection framework. The ranking differed between organizations and individuals in regard to the other aspects constituting an effective whistleblower mechanism. While, for example, the protection of whistleblowers in cases of disclosure to the public found particular support among individuals,[41] organizations considered internal reporting channels slightly more important.[42]

8.1.1.2 Targeted Consultations and Experts' Workshops

From the 530 invitations for consultation sent by the EU Commission, 26 public authorities responded while only one private company did.[43] Those numbers seem to indicate private companies' lack of interest in regard to whistleblower protection, which further underlines the necessity to impose binding rules which would make

[31]Ibid., p. 26.

[32]Ibid., p. 27: 39% of individuals were for EU horizontal legal provisions compared to 28% for a combination of EU and national legal provisions. (On the other hand, 33% of organizations supported horizontal legal provisions in contrast to 43% for a combination of EU and national provisions, see EU Commission, *Annexes on the EU Whistleblower Directive proposal*, Annex 13, p. 28).

[33]Ibid., p. 15: 84% of individuals, 80% of organizations.

[34]Ibid.: 84% of individuals, 78% of organizations.

[35]Ibid.: 83% of individuals, 82% of organizations.

[36]Ibid., pp. 12-13: 88% of individuals, 87% of organizations.

[37]Ibid., p. 15; 85% of individuals, 82% of organizations.

[38]Ibid., p. 13; 85% of individuals, 79% of organizations.

[39]Ibid.: 76% of individuals, 77% of organizations.

[40]Ibid.; 79% of individuals, 68% of organizations.

[41]Ibid.; 83% of individuals while only 65% of organizations supported this option.

[42]Ibid.: 68% of organizations versus 55% of individuals.

[43]EU Commission, *Annexes on the EU Whistleblower Directive proposal*, Annex 2, p. 65; 26 respondents were public authorities.

the establishment of whistleblower protection frameworks in the private sector compulsory. On the basis of information provided by certain public authorities, tax evasion and corruption were identified as the most common breaches reported by whistleblowers in the last 10 years.[44] In this respect, the consultations targeting respondents in the area of tax did not result in a clear position on the necessity to impose the tiered reporting approach, with some even advocating that the external reporting channel to tax authorities be the only reporting method protected by a whistleblower protection framework.[45] As to the general concept of the tiered model, the experts agreed that whistleblowers should indeed be encouraged to report internally first, before using external reporting channels, in order for organizations to have a chance to address the issues and protect their reputation, thus striking a fair balance between the competing interests of the parties involved.[46] However, when internal reporting channels are installed, ensuring confidentiality of the whistleblowers' identity was emphasized by the targeted stakeholders and experts as a key element to "ensure a safe alternative to silence", the latter even considering the establishment of anonymous reporting channels as an option for particularly vulnerable individuals.[47]

The views were divided on the scope and nature of an EU initiative. While some experts from the EU Member States' authorities, emphasizing the principle of subsidiarity and the necessity of an appropriate legal basis in the EU Treaties when developing a new legislative proposal, expressed a clear preference for EU soft-law,[48] other experts specialized in whistleblower protection[49] considered non-regulatory measures such as an EU Commission recommendation as insufficient, and an EU harmonization as much more favorable for companies with EU cross-border activities, given the cost benefits of having to comply with only one regulatory framework.[50] "[I]f the goal is blanket protection for workers in the public and private sector", the whistleblower specialists acknowledged that sectorial measures could be introduced as an interim period, but that a horizontal option should be pursued to remedy efficiently the current fragmentation of whistleblower protection across the EU and avoid the creation of complex legal constructs due to the diversity of sectorial Regulations which would further legal uncertainty.[51] This position was confirmed by the targeted consultations in tax matters, whose respondents predominantly favored a horizontal approach.[52]

[44] Ibid., p. 67, tax evasion represented 50% of all cases, tax avoidance 1%, and corruption 44%.

[45] Ibid., p. 69.

[46] Ibid., p. 68.

[47] Ibid., p. 67.

[48] Ibid., p. 70.

[49] Ibid., p. 66.

[50] Ibid., pp. 70–71.

[51] Ibid., p. 71.

[52] Ibid., p. 71.

Ultimately, experts and targeted shareholders agreed that, independently of the scope and nature of the EU initiative, it should be accompanied by information campaigns aiming to combat the negative image of whistleblowers and thus encourage a culture of transparency in the workplace.[53]

8.1.2 *The Policy Options Considered by the EU Commission*

Following those consultations, and on the basis of the external ICF study assessing the quantitative and qualitative impacts and benefits of horizontal or sectorial EU actions to strengthen the protection of whistleblowers[54] the EU Commission considered different policy options to promote minimum standards in whistleblower protection across the EU, drawing from the principles established by the CoE in its Recommendation CM/Rec(2014)7.[55] All policy options where based on the principles established by the CoE it in Recommendation CM/Rec(2014)7. In accordance with the key principles of EU law, those options had to be considered in the light of the principles of conferral, subsidiarity and proportionality[56] defining the exercise of EU competences under the EU Treaties. In this respect, given that no specific Treaty provision provides for an EU competence in regard to whistleblower protection, a thorough analysis of the appropriate legal ground had to be conducted. According to settled case-law, the choice of the Treaty basis for any EU initiative should rest on objective criteria, especially regarding the aim and content of the measures.[57] Furthermore, while the choice of multiple legal provisions is permissible, it is only justified when the EU measure "simultaneously pursues a number of objectives or has several components that are indissociably linked, without one being secondary and indirect in relation to the other".[58] When this is the case, it must be ensured that

[53] Ibid., p. 68.

[54] EU Commission, *Annexes on the EU Whistleblower Directive proposal*, Annexes 14 and 15 (ICF's Study on the need for horizontal or further sectorial action at EU level to strengthen the protection of whistleblowers: Final Report, Vol. I – Principal Report (Annex 14); Vol. II - Annexes 1 to 9 (Annex 15).

[55] EU Commission, *Impact Assessment accompanying the EU Whistleblower Directive proposal*, pp. 32–37.

[56] Article 5(1) TEU.

[57] CJ, Case C-300/89, *Commission of the European Communities v. Council of the European Communities (Titanium Dioxide)*, Judgment of 11 June 1991, ECLI:EU:C:1991:244, para 10; CJ, Case C-45/86, *Commission of the European Communities v. Council of the European Communities (Generalized Tariff Preferences)*, Judgment of 26 March 1987, ECLI:EU:C:1987:163, para 5; CJ, Case C-440/05, *Commission of the European Communities v. Council of the European Communities*, Judgment of 23 October 2007, ECLI:EU:C:2007:625; CJ, Case C-411/06, *Commission of the European Communities v. European Parliament and Council of the European Union*, Judgment of 8 September 2009, ECLI:EU:C:2009:518.

[58] CJ, Case C-411/06, *Commission v. Parliament and Council*, para 47; CJ, C-178/03, *Commission of the European Communities v. European Parliament and Council of the European Union*,

the different legal provisions chosen are also procedurally compatible with each other.[59]

8.1.2.1 The Excluded Options from the Outset

In view of the foregoing, the EU Commission excluded several legislative options from the start.

The Protection of Whistleblowers Under the EU Charter

The EU Commission emphasizes in its impact Assessment the essential role of whistleblowers in a democratic society, in the context of freedom of expression protected by Article 11 EU Charter of Fundamental Freedoms, and related to that, through their contribution to the work of investigative journalists.[60] Within the context of whistleblowing, a link can be drawn between Article 11 and Article 30 EU Charter,[61] the latter providing protection in the event of unjustified dismissal. Despite its vague wording and narrow application, Article 30 EU Charter is the first EU law provision which explicitly refers to this protection as a fundamental right.[62] However, while the provisions of the EU Charter have the same legal value as the EU Treaties, it does "not extend in any way the competences of the Union as defined in the Treaties".[63] Therefore, the EU Commission rightly concluded that the EU Charter cannot be used as an autonomous legal basis for the enactment of whistleblower protection rules.[64]

EU Initiatives Based on Article 50(2)(g) or Article 153(1)(a) and (b) TFEU

Article 50(2)(g) TFEU

Judgment of 10 January 2006, ECLI:EU:C:2006:4, para 43; CJ, Case C-336/00, *Republik Österreich v. Martin Huber*, Judgment of 19 September 2002, ECLI:EU:C:2002:509, para 31; CJ, Case C-281/01, *Commission of the European Communities v. Council of the European Union*, Judgment of 12 December 2002, ECLI:EU:C:2002:761, para 35.

[59] CJ, Case C-300/89, *Titanium Dioxide*, paras 17 et seq.

[60] EU Commission, *Impact Assessment accompanying the EU Whistleblower Directive proposal*, p. 1.

[61] Cobbaut (2019), p. 298.

[62] Schmitt (2019), pp. 505–506.

[63] Article 6(1) TEU; see also CJ, Case C-339/10, *Krasimir Asparuhov Estov and Others v. Ministerski savet na Republika Bulgaria*, Order of 12 November 2010, ECLI:EU:C:2010:680, para 12.

[64] EU Commission, *Impact Assessment accompanying the EU Whistleblower Directive proposal*, pp. 30–31.

The first option excluded was a Directive based on Article 50(2)(g) TFEU. According to the EU Commission, even if the provision would have allowed to introduce a minimum standard of protection in the private sector through the obligation to create internal reporting channels within private entities, it would have evidently excluded the public sector, thus limiting the scope of the EU initiative, and leaving the establishment of further means of protection such as external reporting channels or effective protection against retaliation to the discretion of EU Member States.[65]

Article 153(1)(a) and (b) TFEU

The Position of the EU Commission

In compliance with its statement that "the Treaties do not provide a legal basis for regulating the protection of whistleblowers in a horizontal way",[66] the EU Commission also abandoned a legislative initiative based on Article 153(1)(a) and (b) TFEU. According to the EU Commission, Article 153 TFEU would restrict the personal scope to workers, leaving other potential whistleblowers such as self-employed individuals or suppliers unprotected, thus going against international recommendations. In the EU Commission's opinion, the gaps left by the restrictive personal scope would not be rebalanced by a broader material scope because the protection afforded would be limited to reports concerning the health, safety and working conditions of workers, and it was doubtful whether it could be extended to an obligation to establish reporting channels and investigation procedures. The EU Commission also stated that such a focus on the health, safety and working conditions of workers might bear the risk of an increase in reports motivated by personal grievances while leaving breaches of EU law unreported. Finally, according to the EU Commission, the extensive and thus costly EU interference combined with a lack of transboundary impacts resulting from a legislative initiative based on Article 153 TFEU appeared to be inconsistent with the principle of proportionality. Therefore, the EU Commission considered the provision as inadequate for promoting a harmonized definition of whistleblowing across the EU.[67]

Opposing Views

The position of the EU Commission was contradicted by a 2017 report commissioned by the Greens/EFA Group in the EP,[68] in which Article 153 TFEU was considered an effective legal basis as it "ensures that every working relation in the

---

[65] Ibid., p. 37.

[66] Ibid., p. 53.

[67] Ibid., p. 38

[68] Abazi (2017).

EU, whether in the private or public sector, would enjoy equal minimum levels of protection in terms of disclosure and therefore ensures the highest level of unity in how reporting should be done in the EU as well as ensuring the highest level of legal certainty because it applies across the board in terms of fields and sectors".[69] Because Article 153 TFEU merely entitles the Union to "support and complement the activities of the Member States", the report acknowledges that the EU could only take measures in the form of minimum standards for a progressive implementation.[70] Accordingly, considerations should be given to the possibility of including multiple legal bases.[71] In the same vein, the Greens/EFA Group in the EP proposed a draft Directive,[72] updated in 2018 and entitled "Proposal for a Directive establishing minimum levels of protection for whistleblowers".[73] This proposal for a Directive, based on Article 4(2)(b) in conjunction with Articles 151 and 153(2)(b) TFEU,[74] chose to focus on the protection of working conditions of workers, stating that those provisions offer "the widest personal scope and highest level of protection for whistleblowers".[75] According to the authors of the Directive proposed by the Greens/EFA Group in the EP, a Directive based on those provisions complies with the principle of subsidiarity, Article 153(2)(b) TFEU being a non-exclusive competence of EU Member States, and the goal, protecting whistleblowers across the EU, being better achieved through a set of common rules laying down a harmonized definition and minimum standards so as to close the existing loopholes created by diverse national regulations.[76] Furthermore, the authors argued that the common minimum standards laid down by the Directive proposal were appropriate and necessary, thus complying with the principle of proportionality.[77]

The Horizontal Approach vs. Article 5(1) TEU

Whether or not a general protection of whistleblowers across the EU, promoted by the EP, possibly under a provision such as Article 153 TFEU, complies with the principles of conferral, subsidiarity and proportionality enshrined in Article 5 (1) TEU is highly controversial and can be traced back to the recurrent conflict regarding the division of competences between the EU and its Member States. The negative opinion of the RSB of the first impact assessment submitted by the EU Commission demonstrates the particularly contentious character of the subject. In its

---

69 Ibid., p. 10.
70 Ibid., pp. 11–12.
71 Ibid., p. 15.
72 Abazi et al. (2016).
73 Abazi et al. (2018).
74 Ibid., p. 7.
75 Ibid., p. 6.
76 Abazi et al. (2016), pp. 17–19.
77 Ibid., pp. 19–20.

examination, the RSB noted that the report transmitted by the EU Commission did not explain why "an umbrella whistleblower protection" was not considered, and then criticized the EU Commission for not having sufficiently addressed the question of subsidiarity.[78] The refusal of the Council to release the full version of an opinion prepared by its Legal Service regarding the possible legal basis for a "whistleblowers" Directive, which was made only partially accessible to the public, reinforces this observation. The letter rejecting the request for public access to this document states, *inter alia*, that "the legal advice covered by this opinion deals with issues which are particularly wide in scope and contentious. In particular, the analysis on the question of the appropriate legal bases for the proposal provided in the requested opinion goes beyond the legislative file in question and could be transposed in other similar contexts. The legal advice is therefore sensitive".[79] That said, the complete, unredacted version of the document prepared by the Council's Legal Service has since been made public.[80]

The close link between a general protection of whistleblowers and the right to freedom of expression, emphasized by the EU Commission itself,[81] represents a particular challenge to the development of a horizontal protection on the EU level, EU Member States having strongly rejected the competence of the EU in matters related to fundamental rights.[82] The opinions expressed by some EU Member States during the consultative workshops confirm this reluctance, drawing attention "to the need for any EU legislative initiative to respect the principle of subsidiarity, raising concerns about the existence of a legal competence for a horizontal approach".[83] A Directive connecting the protection of whistleblowers to the economic interests of the EU seemed therefore more probable to be accepted by EU Member States.[84] Considering the arguments put forward by the EU Commission in its analysis of a Directive based on Article 153 TFEU, the general reluctance of EU Member States and the fact that Article 153 TFEU is too scarcely used to ensure a strong regulation, a Directive ensuring a horizontal protection across sectors was considered more efficient but from the outset particularly unlikely to be accepted by EU Member States.[85] Although defying the very purpose of introducing an EU-wide legislative instrument, namely to remedy the fragmented nature of the measures devoted to

[78] EU Commission, *Annexes on the EU Whistleblower Directive proposal,* Annex 1, p. 59.

[79] Council reply to an official request by the author to access that document, 11 November 2019, *Ref. 19/2133-rh/nb*, p. 2.

[80] Legal Service of the Council, *Opinion on the Commission proposal for a Directive of the European Parliament and the Council on the protection of persons reporting on breaches of Union law ("whistleblowers" directive) – legal basis*, No. 14620/18, 14 December 2018.

[81] EU Commission, *Impact Assessment accompanying the EU Whistleblower Directive proposal*, p. 1.

[82] Racho (2016), para 8.

[83] EU Commission, *Impact Assessment accompanying the EU Whistleblower Directive proposal,* p. 52.

[84] Racho (2016), para 11.

[85] Ibid., para 15 *in fine*.

whistleblower protection across the EU, a more pragmatic approach, focusing on a more extensive yet sectorial protection of whistleblowers, appeared to be more realistic.[86]

8.1.2.2 The Integrated Multi-Sectorial Approach for a Better Implementation of EU Objectives

The Spill-over Impact of EU Law Violations

The position taken by the EU Commission in its impact assessment confirms this position. While it recognized that a strong whistleblower protection framework encouraging individuals to report on breaches of EU law is crucial for the effective implementation of EU laws and policies,[87] recalling its 2016 Communication entitled "EU Law: Better Results through Better Application",[88] the EU Commission noted that the insufficient protection of whistleblowers in domestic legislations can have a *detrimental influence on the effective implementation and enforcement of EU laws and policies* within Member States, which can in turn have a negative cross-border impact ("spill-over impacts").[89] In cases where breaches of EU law occurred in one EU Member State, the EU Commission evaluated the spillover effect to be particularly strong in areas related to the financial interest of the EU.[90] However, as seen above, there is a major discrepancy between EU Member States in regard to the level of protection afforded to whistleblowers. While some EU Member States introduced comprehensive whistleblower protection frameworks, others did not, which creates a fragmented legal landscape across the EU.[91]

Uniform Rules for Targeted Sectors

In EU Member States with no or incomplete whistleblower protection laws, individuals wanting to report on breaches of EU laws might prefer to remain silent due to a lack of protection against the negative consequences of reporting. This in turn can lead to a lack of implementation and enforcement of EU laws and policies and have negative cross-border effects. According to the EU Commission, the introduction of

---

[86]Ibid., para 16.

[87]EU Commission, *Impact Assessment accompanying the EU Whistleblower Directive proposal,* p. 29.

[88]EU Commission, *EU Law: Better Results through Better Application*, Communication from the Commission, 2017/C 18/02, 23 December 2016.

[89]EU Commission, *Impact Assessment accompanying the EU Whistleblower Directive proposal*, p. 29.

[90]Ibid.

[91]Ibid.

an EU-wide homogenous level of protection for whistleblowers, as a tool to better implement and enforce EU laws, would therefore comply with the principle of subsidiarity.[92] In consideration of the above, the EU Commission proposed different policy options to pursue the general goal of addressing "underreporting of breaches of EU law leading to serious harm to the public interest in **areas** where strong whistleblower protection can significantly contribute to expose, prevent and deter such harm",[93] in order to improve the overall enforcement of EU policies.[94] To achieve this goal, the EU initiative should focus in particular on providing legal clarity and certainty as well as raising awareness about the importance of whistleblowing.[95]

The formulation of this objective clearly underlines the EU Commission's reluctance to use the horizontal approach promoted by the EP. Instead, it focuses on a more integrated sectorial approach to address underreporting in specific areas where stronger whistleblower protection mechanisms are deemed necessary, namely the protection of the EU Budget, proper functioning of the internal market, public procurement, competition, aggressive tax planning schemes, environmental protection, nuclear safety, product safety, consumer protection, public health, food and feed safety, transport safety, protection of privacy and personal data and security, and networks.[96] However, in accordance with the "future proof" character of EU initiatives, the EU Commission acknowledged that the scope of the proposed policy could be extended if future findings demonstrated a need for strong whistleblower mechanisms in areas excluded from the current proposal.[97]

The strategy followed by the EU Commission, by linking higher standards of protection for whistleblowers across the EU to an increased implementation and enforcement of EU laws and policies, restricting thereby the material scope of the legislative initiative to certain sectors, aims to strictly comply with the principles of conferral, subsidiarity and proportionality of Article 5 TEU, and in doing so, reduce the likelihood of resistance from the EU Member States while promoting a particularly ambitious whistleblower protection framework nonetheless. The EU Commission's position is the perfect example of the proverb "choose your battles".

The Model of the Council of Europe Recommendation

According to the EU Commission, "the baseline for defining whistleblowers and for setting EU standards can be found in the 2014 Council of Europe

[92]Ibid., p. 30.
[93]Ibid., p. 32 (emphasis added).
[94]Ibid., p. 29.
[95]Ibid., p. 32.
[96]Ibid., pp. 15–18.
[97]Ibid., p. 28.

Recommendation".[98] Consequently, the minimum standards introduced by the different policy options considered by the EU Commission were primarily based on the principles laid down by the CoE Recommendation CM/Rec(2014)7,[99] whose only variable was the material scope of application.[100] The EU Commission used three criteria to determine the impact of the different policy options: The effectiveness to achieve the objective set out; the economic costs for EU Member States and employers;[101] and finally, the feasibility to implement the new initiative effectively.[102] Due to the data gap on the causal relationship between the protection of whistleblowers and a stronger enforcement of EU laws, the benefits of the respective policy options was calculated through data modelling on the basic assumption that a stronger whistleblower protection framework would increase the number of reports of breaches of EU law and thus strengthen the enforcement of EU law.[103]

In that respect, the starting point to determine the costs and benefits of the proposed policy options was the current status quo.[104] The annual operational costs[105] related to the respective EU initiatives was composed of the cost to provide internal reporting channels,[106] the cost to provide "outsourced internal reporting channels",[107] the cost to investigate and manage cases of reported wrongdoings,[108] and finally, the cost to provide annual training to raise awareness about the reporting procedure.[109] In this context, the EU Commission acknowledged that EU Member States would be affected not only through their obligation to implement and bear the administrative and transposition costs generated by a new EU legislative instrument,

[98]Ibid., p. 6

[99]Ibid., p. 33.

[100]Ibid., p. 32.

[101]Ibid., pp. 42–43.

[102]Ibid., p. 43.

[103]Ibid., p. 44; see also EU Commission, *Annexes on the EU Whistleblower Directive proposal,* Annex 3, p. 72, too few EU Member States public agencies collect data on whistleblowers to constitute a representative costs-benefits analysis.

[104]EU Commission, *Annexes on the EU Whistleblower Directive proposal,* Annex 3, p. 73.

[105]EU Commission, *Impact Assessment accompanying the EU Whistleblower Directive proposal,* p. 44.

[106]EU Commission, *Annexes on the EU Whistleblower Directive proposal,* Annex 3, p. 74; (estimated to cost 1 h of staff time per report of wrongdoing; the number of reports of wrongdoing per worker is assumed to increase as the strength of protection increases).

[107]Ibid.; (estimated to cost €1.5 per person per year, based on consultations with hotline providers and other experts).

[108]Ibid.; (estimated to take an average of 2 days of staff time per report for both internal and outsourced internal reporting channels).

[109]Ibid.; (estimated at half an hour of training per worker per year). The proportion of workers who receive training to ensure they are aware of the violations of law and reporting channels is assumed to vary by the strength of protection available in a Member State.).

but also as "employer".[110] As to private entities, while large[111] and medium[112] enterprises would be most affected by an increase in whistleblower protection, the EU Commission decided to exempt small and micro companies[113] from the new initiative, their size preventing them from causing serious harm or threat to the public interest. However, an exception was to be made to small and micro companies working in risk sectors or having an exceptionally high annual turnover.[114]

Four Policy Options

The Baseline Scenario

The Policy option 1 considered by the EU Commission, the status quo, leaves the current situation unchanged and the responsibility of introducing whistleblower protection frameworks to the EU Member States.[115] The EU Commission would merely monitor the transposition of existing sectorial regulations on whistleblower protection. This variant would evidently fail to address the issues of fragmented and therefore inefficient protection of whistleblowers and miss the objective to strengthen the enforcement of EU laws and policies.[116]

An EU Commission Recommendation

The Policy option 2 consists of an EU Commission Recommendation setting minimum standards, modeled after the CoE Recommendation CM/Rec(2014)7, which would guide EU Member States in the implementation of effective and complete whistleblower protection legislation on the national level.[117] To go beyond what the CoE recommended, the EU Commission would offer accompanying actions to help EU Member States implement those recommendations and strengthen their cooperation with the European Network of Ombudsmen.[118] However, the majority of stakeholders noted that the release of the CoE Recommendation CM/Rec(2014)7 did not lead to the increased adoption by EU Member States of stronger domestic legal frameworks to protect whistleblowers, and doubted that an EU Commission recommendation would have a different result due to the

[110]Ibid., p. 76.

[111]Ibid., p. 74; Large companies count between 250 and 44,000 employees and represent 1% of all business in the EU.

[112]Ibid., p. 75; In the EU, medium companies have between 50 and 249 employees.

[113]Ibid.; Companies with fewer than 50 employees.

[114]Ibid.

[115]EU Commission, *Impact Assessment accompanying the EU Whistleblower Directive proposal*, pp. 38–39.

[116]Ibid., p. 39.

[117]Ibid.

[118]Ibid.

unenforceability of such an instrument. This observation was confirmed by the EU Commission in its impact assessment.[119]

A Directive Based on Article 325 TFEU

The third option considers the introduction of a Directive based on Article 325 TFEU which would include all essential elements for an effective whistleblower protection regulation, including reporting channels, protection from retaliation etc., but whose material scope would be limited to areas linked to the financial interests of the EU. The Directive would be complemented by an EU Communication laying down a general EU policy framework which would include accompanying measures to help EU Member States implement the Directive and promote international best-practice.[120] In regard to the potential impact of the option on the EU Member states' justice system, the EU Commission estimated the cost of implementation to be limited given the already existing rules protecting whistleblowers in this area.[121] As for employers, the private sector would bear the highest annual operational costs linked to the establishment of internal reporting channels.[122] The stakeholders highlighted that such a Directive would leave unaddressed the issues linked to the fragmentation of whistleblower protection frameworks across the EU and create divergences between whistleblowing rules applicable to reports linked to national funds and reports related to EU funds, which would ultimately further the legal complexity and thus legal uncertainty for whistleblowers.[123] The EU Commission agreed, stating that this option "would be yet another sectorial EU legislation".[124]

A Multi-Sectorial Protection Directive Accompanied by an EU Commission Communication

The fourth and final option considered by the EU Commission consisted of a minimum harmonization Directive,[125] and a sub-option complementing the main proposition with an additional non-binding instrument.[126]

The main proposition formulated the most ambitious proposition yet and took the form of a Directive on the basis of Article 114 and Article 325 TFEU, which would

[119]Ibid., pp. 48–49.

[120]Ibid., p. 40.

[121]Ibid., p. 51; The costs on the national justice system is estimated to be around 34 million, with the strongest impact on the justice system of Spain, Latvia and Cyprus, and the least impact on France and the UK.

[122]Ibid.; EUR 916.5 million for the private sector and EUR 284.4 million for the public sector.

[123]Ibid., p. 50.

[124]Ibid.

[125]EU Commission, *EU Whistleblower Directive proposal*, Explanatory Memorandum, p. 6.

[126]EU Commission, *Impact Assessment accompanying the EU Whistleblower Directive proposal*, pp. 40–41.

have the same characteristics as the Directive described in option 3 but whose material scope would extend to the fields identified by the EU Commission[127] as particularly benefiting from stronger whistleblower regulations.[128] Under the chapter "Approximation of Laws", Article 114 TFEU gives competence to the EU to remove potential obstacles to the smooth functioning of the internal market. Article 325 TFEU is the single provision in the Chapter "Combatting fraud", and states in paragraph 1: "The Union and the Member States shall counter fraud and any other illegal activities affecting the financial interests of the Union". The sub-option 4, which would complement the Directive based on Articles 114 and 325 TFEU with the same accompanying EU Commission Communication as described in option 3,[129] was ultimately the option selected by the EU Commission.[130]

The main option offers the broadest material scope while addressing the concerns of proportionality expressed by EU Member States,[131] through an integrated multi-sectoral approach, ensuring a legal protection for whistleblowers in relevant area.[132] Despite the broader material scope, the EU Commission recognized that the number of employers targeted by this initiative would be similar to option 3, thus leading to the same expected costs on the Member States' justice system.[133] Due to the multitude of areas targeted by option 4, the annual operational costs would be proportionally higher than in option 3, with the private sector still bearing the highest economic burden.[134] The EU Commission evaluated this option to be particularly feasible and an appropriate response to the stakeholders' expectations.[135] As to the sub-option 4, the EU Commission considered the accompanying Communication to be particularly effective for raising awareness about whistleblower protection and encourage EU Member States to adopt coherent domestic regulations which would in turn ensure legal certainty.[136]

The EU Commission argued that this combination of binding and non-binding instruments would ensure consistency with the already existing sectorial whistleblower protection framework in place and fill the gaps created by the current fragmentation of the law in that field, thus playing a complementary role ensuring legal clarity and security.[137] To ensure the EU relevance, the EU Commission stated that the Directive would be applicable to areas where: (1) there was a need for

[127]Ibid., pp. 15–28.

[128]Ibid., p. 40.

[129]Ibid., p. 41.

[130]Ibid., p. 57.

[131]Ibid., p. 52.

[132]Ibid., p. 53.

[133]Ibid., p. 54; EUR 34 million, with Spain, Latvia and Cyprus bearing the highest costs.

[134]Ibid., p. 55; approx. EUR 1,000 million for the private sector, and around EUR 320 million for the public sector.

[135]Ibid.

[136]Ibid., pp. 55–56.

[137]Ibid., p. 58.

stronger enforcement; (2) the connectivity between whistleblower protection and higher reporting of Union law violations could be established and finally, (3) those violations could cause a serious harm to the public interest.[138]

8.2 The Proposal for a Whistleblower Directive

8.2.1 The Scope of Application of the Directive Proposal

8.2.1.1 The Legal Bases

On the basis of its impact assessment, the EU Commission laid down the following legal bases for its Directive proposal on the protection of persons reporting on breaches of Union law (hereinafter referred to as "Directive proposal"):

Having regard to the Treaty on the Functioning of the European Union, and in particular Articles 16, 33, 43, 50, 53(1), 62, 91, 100, 103, 109, 114, 168, 169, 192, 207 and 325(4) thereof and to the Treaty establishing the European Atomic Energy Community, and in particular Article 31 thereof

The provisions listed above refer to the areas illustrated in Table 8.1.

The provisions proposed by the EU Commission as forming a legal basis confirms the sectorial approach promoted in its impact assessment and directly reflects the sectors identified by the EU Commission which would most benefit from a harmonization of whistleblower protection rules.

With its Directive proposal, the EU Commission aimed to offer a "robust whistleblower protection" framework based on a "balanced set of measures at EU level in specific area with a clear EU dimension" in order to "enrich the EU toolkit for strengthening the correct application of EU law and respect for transparency, good governance, accountability and freedom of expression, which are values and rights on which the EU is based".[139]

8.2.1.2 The Multi-sectorial Material Scope

While the Directive proposal, as a whole, laid down all the key elements of an effective whistleblower law and put forward an ambitious whistleblower protection framework, its extent was curtailed by the material scope, exposed in Article 1 of the Directive proposal in conjunction with the Annex to the Directive proposal. Through a particularly complex system of referral, the EU Commission limited the areas of application of the Directive to a list of EU acts, all falling within the sectors identified

---

[138] Ibid., p. 58.

[139] EU Commission, *Strengthening whistleblower protection at EU level*, Communication from the Commission to the European Parliament, the Council and the European Economic and Social Committee, COM(2018)214 final, p. 12.

Table 8.1 Legal bases of the EU Commission Directive Proposal

Legal bases Directive proposal of the EU Commission 23.04.2018	
Data protection	Article 16 TFEU[a]
Strengthening customs cooperation between Member States	Article 33 TFEU[a]
Agriculture policy	Article 43 TFEU[a]
Freedom of establishment	Article 50 TFEU[a]
Mutual recognition of diploma	Article 53(1) TFEU[a]
Services	Article 62 TFEU[a]
Transport	Article 91 TFEU[a]
Include rail, road, inland waterway, sea and air transport	Article 100 TFEU[a]
Internal market	Article 103 TFEU[b]
State aids	Article 109 TFEU[b]
Approximation of laws (internal market)	Article 114 TFEU[a]
Public health	Article 168 TFEU[a] (only para. 4)
Consumer protection	Article 169 TFEU[a]
Environment	Article 192 TFEU[a]
Common commercial policy	Article 207 TFEU[a]
Prevention and fight against fraud against the financial interests of the EU	Article 325(4) TFEU[a]
	Article 31 EURATOM[b]

[a]Only ordinary legislative procedure
[b]Only Council decision, on a proposal from the EU Commission after consultation with EP

in the EU Commission's impact assessment and listed in Article 1 (1) of the Directive proposal. This intricate maneuver thus aimed to strictly respect the principles of conferral, subsidiarity and proportionality laid down in Article 5 TEU and ensure in this way a clear EU dimension to the Directive.

The Annex to the Directive proposal was divided into two parts. In this respect, when EU acts, the list of which was given in Part 2 of the Annex to the Directive proposal, already provide for reporting mechanisms, the provisions of the Directive proposal should apply, provided that the existing rules are not binding.[140] This clarification was important to preserve the specific provisions tailored to the particular reporting demands of each sector while extending the protection requirements. Indeed, while some EU acts listed in part 2 of the annex included well-developed reporting mechanisms, such as in the Regulation (EU) No 596/2014 on market abuse,[141] Directive 2013/30/EU on safety of offshore oil and gas operations,[142]

[140]Article 1(2) *Whistleblower Directive proposal.*

[141]Annex to the *Proposal for a Directive of the European Parliament and of the Council on the protection of persons reporting on breaches of Union law,* COM(2018) 218 final ANNEX 1, 23 April 2018, Part II, A (iv), p. 8.

[142]Annex to the *Whistleblower Directive proposal*, Part II, C (i), p. 9.

Regulation (EU) No 376/2014 on the reporting, analysis and follow-up of occurrences in civil aviation[143] or Directive 2013/36/EU on access to the activity of credit institutions and the prudential supervision of credit institutions and investment firms,[144] already mentioned above, others have vague formulations regarding reporting requirements, such as the Directive 2009/65/EC on the coordination of laws, regulations and administrative provisions relating to undertakings for collective investment in transferable securities (UCITS), which refers broadly to "internal control mechanisms"[145] and "disclosure and reporting requirements of the UCITS".[146]

Furthermore and in accordance with the goal to set harmonizing minimum standards[147] in the areas defined by the EU Commission in its impact assessment,[148] the proposal enumerated further sectors falling under the scope of the Directive: "(i) public procurement; (ii) financial services, prevention of money laundering and terrorist financing; (iii) product safety; (iv) transport safety; (v) protection of the environment; (vi) nuclear safety; (vii) food and feed safety, animal health and welfare; (viii) public health; (ix) consumer protection; (x) protection of privacy and personal data, and security of network and information systems".[149] However, instead of an all-encompassing sectorial approach, the scope of application of the Directive proposal regarding those sectors was limited to a list of EU acts contained in the annex to the Directive proposal, thus restricting the Directive's material scope of application to the particular spheres of those EU laws. Part 1 of the annex contained a catalogue of EU acts, categorized in sections following the order listed by Article 1(1)(a) of the Directive proposal: Section A was dedicated to all the EU public procurement laws falling under the scope of the Directive, section B listed the Directives and Regulations related to the financial services, prevention of money laundering and terrorism financing, section C enumerated the EU product safety laws to which the Directive will be applicable, etc.

In addition to those sectors listed above, the material scope of the Directive proposal also extended to breaches of rules related to the functioning of the internal market,[150] and in particular regarding corporate tax law[151] and the rules on

[143] Annex to the *Whistleblower Directive proposal*, Part II, B (i), p. 9.

[144] Annex to the *Whistleblower Directive proposal*, Part II, A(v), p. 8.

[145] Article 12 (1)(a) *Directive 2009/65/EC of the European Parliament and of the Council of 13 July 2009 on the coordination of laws, regulations and administrative provisions relating to undertakings for collective investment in transferable securities (UCITS)*, OJ L 302, 17.11.2009, p. 32.

[146] Article 19(3)(h) *Directive 2009/65/EC.*

[147] Article 1(1) *Whistleblower Directive proposal.*

[148] EU Commission, *Impact Assessment accompanying the EU Whistleblower Directive proposal,* pp. 15–28.

[149] Article 1(1)(a) *Whistleblower Directive proposal.*

[150] Article 1(1)(d) *Whistleblower Directive proposal.*

[151] Article 1(1)(d) *Whistleblower Directive proposal.*

competition,[152] breaches of State aid rules[153] and breaches affecting the financial interests of the Union.[154] Complementary to Article 1(1)(a) of the Directive proposal, those sectors further reflected the legal basis on which the Directive proposal was based.

8.2.1.3 The Personal Scope

In reference to the "whistleblower" definition provided in the CoE Recommendation CM/Rec(2014)7, the personal scope of the Directive proposal developed by the EU Commission was particularly extensive as it included individuals in the private and the public sector who become aware of breaches "in a work-related context".[155] Under the Directive proposal, "work-related" was defined as "current or past work activities in the public or private sector through which, irrespective of their nature, persons may acquire information on breaches and within which these persons may suffer retaliation if they report them".[156] A non-exhaustive list was provided to illustrate this definition: In addition to individuals with the status of workers[157] and self-employed,[158] the Directive should also apply to shareholders, managers and individuals working without remuneration, such as volunteers and unpaid trainees,[159] reflecting Principle 3 of the CoE Recommendation CM/Rec(2014)7. Furthermore, individuals working for contractors, subcontractors and suppliers,[160] and individuals "whose work-based relationship is yet to begin",[161] should also enjoy protection. The systematic of those examples demonstrated the requirement for a contractual relationship, even if only in the future. This reasoning was aligned with the CoE Recommendation CM/Rec(2014)7, which promotes an expansive approach to the personal scope of whistleblower laws based on a person's "work-based relationships" and linked the level of protection afforded to the extent of damage an individual can potentially suffer.

[152] Article 1(1)(b) *Whistleblower Directive proposal.*
[153] Article 1(1)(b) *Whistleblower Directive proposal.*
[154] Article 1(1)(c) *Whistleblower Directive proposal.*
[155] Article 2 (1) *Whistleblower Directive proposal.*
[156] Article 3 (10) *Whistleblower Directive proposal.*
[157] Article 2(1)(a) *Whistleblower Directive proposal.*
[158] Article 2(1)(b) *Whistleblower Directive proposal.*
[159] Article 2(1)(c) *Whistleblower Directive proposal.*
[160] Article 2(1)(d) *Whistleblower Directive proposal.*
[161] Article 2(2) *Whistleblower Directive proposal.*

8.2.2 A Tiered Model of Reporting

The Directive proposal modeled the structure of the principles developed by the CoE Recommendation CM/Rec(2014)7 and put an obligation on EU Member States to establish internal[162] and external reporting channels,[163] as well as protective measures against retaliation.[164] However, contrary to the CoE Recommendation, the Directive proposal established a tiered model of reporting, according to which the protection measures established by the Directive should only be applicable to individuals who had reasonable grounds to believe the information reported to be true[165] and who, when reporting through external channels, did so when internal mechanisms were inexistent,[166] ineffective,[167] not mandatory[168] or when the reporting individual was entitled to directly use external means to report breaches.[169] In cases of public disclosure, the Directive proposal only provided protection when internal and external channels proved inefficient[170] or inadequate to address the particular nature of the breach reported.[171]

8.2.2.1 Internal Reporting Channel

The Directive proposal also introduced an obligation for private and public entities to establish internal reporting channels. Indeed, with the exception of micro and small private enterprises[172] that do not provide financial services,[173] and municipalities with less than 10,000 inhabitants,[174] all private and public legal entities should establish internal reporting channels available to employees and individuals who have work-related relationships with the entities.[175] Regardless of the form through which individuals can report breaches, whether through hotlines, electronic and paper forms,[176] or physically to a designated person or department in charge of

[162]Article 4 *Whistleblower Directive proposal.*
[163]Article 6 *Whistleblower Directive proposal.*
[164]Article 14 *Whistleblower Directive proposal.*
[165]Article 13(1) *Whistleblower Directive proposal.*
[166]Article 13(2)(b) *Whistleblower Directive proposal.*
[167]Article 13(2)(a), (d) and (e) *Whistleblower Directive proposal.*
[168]Article 13(2)(c) *Whistleblower Directive proposal.*
[169]Article 13(2)(f) *Whistleblower Directive proposal.*
[170]Article 13(4)(a) *Whistleblower Directive proposal.*
[171]Article 13(4)(b) *Whistleblower Directive proposal.*
[172]Article 4(3)(a) and (b) *Whistleblower Directive proposal.*
[173]Article 4(3)(c) *Whistleblower Directive proposal.*
[174]Article 4(6)(c) *Whistleblower Directive proposal.*
[175]Article 4(2) *Whistleblower Directive proposal.*
[176]Article 5(2)(a) *Whistleblower Directive proposal.*

receiving reports,[177] the confidentiality of their identity should be ensured.[178] Diligent[179] follow-up procedures, which were defined as "any action taken by the recipient of the report . . . to assess the accuracy of the allegation made in the report and, where relevant, to address the breach reported, including actions such as internal enquiry, investigation, prosecution, action for recovery of funds and closure",[180] should also be implemented,[181] as well as an obligation to provide feedback on the ongoing process.[182] In this respect, receipt and follow-up could be undertaken by the same person or department.[183]

8.2.2.2 External Reporting Channels

According to the Directive proposal, State should also establish independent and autonomous[184] authorities, with staff members qualified[185] to receive whistleblower reports,[186] provide information[187] and feedback,[188] follow-up on reports[189] and if required, transmit relevant information to EU organs[190] while preserving the confidentiality of the reporting person's identity,[191] unless the procedure requires its disclosure.[192] In that regard, at least three kinds of mechanisms dedicated solely[193] to the receipt of reports should be put in place: The written,[194] phone call,[195] or personal[196] form. The competent authorities should also provide clear and easily accessible online information[197] on the relevant breaches susceptible to be

[177] Article 5(2)(b) *Whistleblower Directive proposal.*
[178] Article 5(1)(a) *Whistleblower Directive proposal.*
[179] Article 5(1)(c) *Whistleblower Directive proposal.*
[180] Article 3(13) *Whistleblower Directive proposal.*
[181] Article 4(1) *Whistleblower Directive proposal.*
[182] Article 5(1)(d) *Whistleblower Directive proposal.*
[183] Article 5(3) *Whistleblower Directive proposal.*
[184] Article 6(2)(a) *Whistleblower Directive proposal.*
[185] Article 8(1) *Whistleblower Directive proposal.*
[186] Article 8(2)(b) *Whistleblower Directive proposal.*
[187] Article 8(2)(a) and (c) *Whistleblower Directive proposal.*
[188] Article 6(2)(b) *Whistleblower Directive proposal.*
[189] Article 6(3) *Whistleblower Directive proposal.*
[190] Article 6(2)(c) *Whistleblower Directive proposal.*
[191] Article 6(2)(a) *Whistleblower Directive proposal.*
[192] Article 9(1)(c) in conjunction with Article 9(2) and (3) *Whistleblower Directive proposal.*
[193] Article 7(1) *Whistleblower Directive proposal.*
[194] Article 7(2)(a) *Whistleblower Directive proposal.*
[195] Article 7(2)(b) *Whistleblower Directive proposal.*
[196] Article 7(2)(c) *Whistleblower Directive proposal.*
[197] Article 10 *Whistleblower Directive proposal.*

reported,[198] the different reporting mechanisms available,[199] the reporting procedure itself[200] and the protection mechanisms afforded to reporting individuals.[201] In order to ensure reliable and effective reporting channels, which should be reviewed and, if necessary, improved upon on a regular basis,[202] the dedicated authorities should, in close consultation with the reporting individuals, keep record of the reports received through acknowledgment of receipt when appropriate[203] or the recording or accurate minutes of conversations over the phone[204] or in person.[205]

8.2.3 A Protective Framework with a Sanction Regime

Without prejudice to the EU Member States' freedom to adopt more favorable provisions,[206] individuals reporting breaches should be protected against direct or indirect retaliatory measures[207] through exemptions from liability under defamation, copyright or secrecy laws,[208] through a reversal of the burden of proof in judicial proceedings, the employer having the responsibility to demonstrate a lack of causality between the report and the negative consequences suffered by the reporting individual,[209] or through the eligibility for financial and legal assistance.[210] Preventive measures in the form of penalties should also be adopted to dissuade from retaliation.[211]

8.2.4 The Assessment of the EU Commission's Directive Proposal

The limits to the application of the Directive proposal, established through the multisectorial, EU-law focused material scope, was coherent with the EU Commission's

[198] Article 10(a) *Whistleblower Directive proposal.*
[199] Article 10(b) *Whistleblower Directive proposal.*
[200] Article 10(c) and (e) *Whistleblower Directive proposal.*
[201] Article 10(f) *Whistleblower Directive proposal.*
[202] Article 12 *Whistleblower Directive proposal.*
[203] Article 11(2) *Whistleblower Directive proposal.*
[204] Article 11(3) and (4) *Whistleblower Directive proposal.*
[205] Article 11(5) *Whistleblower Directive proposal.*
[206] Article 19 *Whistleblower Directive proposal.*
[207] Article 14 *Whistleblower Directive proposal.*
[208] Article 15(7) *Whistleblower Directive proposal.*
[209] Article 15(5) *Whistleblower Directive proposal.*
[210] Article 15(8) *Whistleblower Directive proposal.*
[211] Article 17 *Whistleblower Directive proposal.*

approach promoted in its impact assessment. However, it also represented its main deficiency as it left unaddressed the negative effects of a fragmentation of the protection hitherto offered to whistleblowers. Indeed, the sectorial coverage of the Directive proposal, though more expansive than previous EU legislative initiatives, created a complex legal web where individuals would have to determine whether the breach they wished to report had an EU-element and fell within the scope of one of the EU acts listed in the Annex to the Directive proposal. The complexity of the material scope thus minimized the effectiveness of the protection mechanism established by such a Directive, a concern confirmed by the ECA.[212] However, despite this deficiency, which had its origin in the fundamental tension at the center of the EU since the dawn of its existence, namely the question of sovereignty and transfer of competences, the significance and symbolic character of this Directive proposal should not be underestimated. The EU Commission indeed developed a groundbreaking whistleblowing framework which promoted a forward-thinking and comprehensive approach to whistleblower protection. By establishing an EU-wide whistleblower protection framework, this proposal was truly remarkable by its unprecedented scale.[213] This Directive proposal was the result of the fundamental shift in the European perception of whistleblowers which took place in the last decade and illustrated the new European consensus on the importance to establish a legally-binding, cross-border whistleblower protection framework. The fact that a supranational organization like the EU deemed it not only possible, but also realistic, to impose legal obligations upon its EU Member States in establishing a comprehensive whistleblower protection mechanism, offers an optimistic prospect of the radical changes which could be expected in regard to the future of whistleblower protection in Europe. This sets the stage for the future adoption of an international Convention on whistleblowing, as promoted by the CoE. In this sense, the proposal made by the EU Commission was truly revolutionary.

8.3 The Amendments Proposed by the European Parliament

According to the ordinary legislative procedure, Directive proposals made by the EU Commission are sent to the EP for discussion. On its part, the EP can propose amendments to a text prepared by the EU Commission. To that end, the EP Rapporteur in charge of the text leads the negotiation process between the different EP groups on the basis of the suggestions made by the different EP Committees. The Committee on Legal Affairs of the EP (JURI) and its rapporteur, Virginie Rozière,

[212] ECA, *Opinion concerning the proposal for a Directive of the European Parliament and of the Council on the protection of persons reporting on breaches of Union law*, No. 4/2018, 15 October 2018, para 12.

[213] Gerdemann (2019), p. 28.

were in charge of the Directive proposal on the protection of persons who report breaches of Union law and prepared the Committee report tabled for plenary.[214]

8.3.1 The Positions of the European Parliament Committees

8.3.1.1 Amendment Proposals Regarding the Material Scope

The Directive proposal was generally welcomed by the EP Committees,[215] despite an overwhelming agreement on the necessity to extend its scope.[216] While some committees proposed to include further provisions to the legal basis of the Directive,[217] others recommended introducing additional EU acts to the annex[218] or excluding its exhaustive character[219] in order to broaden the material scope of the Directive. Numerous committees also viewed the inclusion of the EU Charter provisions in the Directive favorably.[220]

8.3.1.2 Amendment Proposals Regarding the Personal Scope

The personal scope was also subjected to a number of proposed amendments by the EP Committees. In line with the CoE Recommendation CM/Rec(2014)7, several EP Committees proposed to extend the provision related to the status of workers within the meaning of Article 45 TFEU to former workers, whose working relationship has

[214]EP, *Report on the proposal for a directive of the European Parliament and of the Council on the protection of persons reporting on breaches of Union law (COM(2018) – C8-0159/2018 – 2018/0106(COD))* [hereinafter "EP Report on the Whistleblower directive proposal"], A8-0389/2018, 26 November 2018.

[215]Ibid.: Opinion of the Committee on Legal Affairs (JURI), p. 134; Opinion of the Committee on Economic and Monetary Affairs (ECON), p. 149; Opinion of the Committee on the Environment, Public health and Food safety (ENVI), p. 350; Opinion of the Committee on Culture and Education (CULT), p. 434; Committee on Constitutional Affairs (AFCO), p. 489.

[216]Ibid.: Opinion of JURI, p. 134 and pp. 137-147; Opinion of ECON, p. 149; Opinion of ENVI, p. 351; Opinion of AFCO, p. 489.

[217]Ibid.: Opinion JURI, p. 147; Committee on Civil Liberties, Justice and Home Affairs (LIBE), *proposed Amendment 1*, p. 188; Committee on Employment and Social Affairs (EMPL), *proposed Amendment 1*, p. 312.

[218]Ibid.: ENVI, *proposed Amendments 62 to 103*, pp. 390–430.

[219]Ibid.: CULT, *proposed Amendments 70 to 88*, pp. 480–486.

[220]Ibid.: Committee on Budgetary Control (CONT), *proposed Amendment 55*, p. 284; CULT, *proposed Amendment 44*, p. 458; AFCO, *proposed Amendment 35*, p. 508; see also EMPL, *proposed Amendment 4*, p. 313, ENVI, *proposed Amendment 2*, p.352.

since ended.[221] In accordance with the 2017 EP Resolution 2016/2224(INI), a number of EP Committees suggested to include EU Officials[222] in the personal scope of the Directive, thus imposing an obligation on EU bodies to introduce internal reporting channels.[223] Certain EP Committees introduced an even more ambitious proposal, moving away from the strictly "work-related relationship" to a broader approach, which would include individuals related to reporting persons, such as facilitators or intermediaries like journalists, into the personal scope of the Directive.[224]

8.3.1.3 An Ambitious Approach Regarding Reporting Mechanisms

Regarding the reporting procedure, the possibility to report anonymously found strong support among the different EP Committees,[225] while the tiered approach promoted by the EU Commission in its Directive proposal was overwhelmingly rejected.[226] Further protective measures, such as psychological support,[227] were also suggested to be included in the Directive. Some EP Committees proposed to establish a new EU organ to centralize the receipt of reports, such as the "Union Referral Body" brought forward by the Committee on Budgetary Control of the EP (CONT),[228] which would be an independent European authority competent to receive, investigate, follow-up and protect whistleblowers,[229] or the "European

---

[221] Ibid.: ECON, *proposed Amendment 32*, p. 166; LIBE, *proposed Amendments 65 and 70*, pp. 222–223; CONT, *proposed Amendment 58*, p. 285; EMPL, *proposed Amendment 33*, p. 328; CULT, *proposed Amendment 45*, p. 459; AFCO, *proposed Amendment 39*, p. 509.

[222] Ibid.: CONT, *proposed Amendment 59*, p. 285; LIBE, *proposed Amendment 66, 71 and 74*, pp. 222, 223 and 224; EMPL, *proposed Amendment 37*, p. 329; ENVI, *proposed Amendment 27*, p. 369; CULT, *proposed Amendment 45*, p. 460; AFCO, *proposed Amendment 40*, p. 510.

[223] Ibid.: LIBE, *proposed Amendments 88 and 90*, p. 229; CONT, *proposed Amendment 71*, p. 289; EMPL, *proposed Amendment 47*, p. 333; ENVI, *proposed Amendment 34*, p. 373; CULT, *proposed Amendment 47*, p. 464.

[224] Ibid.: ECON, *proposed Amendments 31 and 34*, pp. 165 and 166; LIBE, *proposed Amendments 68 and 72*, pp. 222 and 224; CONT, *proposed Amendment 61*, p. 286; EMPL, *proposed Amendment 40*, p. 330; ENVI, *proposed Amendment 29*, pp. 369–370; CULT, *proposed Amendment 45*, p. 460; AFCO, *proposed Amendment 44*, p. 511.

[225] Ibid.: ECON, *proposed Amendment 55, 69 and 77*, pp. 173, 177 and 182; LIBE, *proposed Amendment 94*, p. 230; CONT, *proposed Amendment 108*, p. 302; EMPL, *proposed Amendment 46*, p. 332; ENVI, *proposed Amendment 52*, p. 384; CULT, *proposed Amendment 48*, p. 464; AFCO, *proposed Amendment 57*, pp. 515–516.

[226] Ibid.: ECON, *proposed Amendment 68*, p. 177; LIBE, *proposed Amendment 127*, p. 241; CONT, *proposed Amendments 105 and 106*, pp. 300–301; EMPL, *proposed Amendment* 70, p. 340; ENVI Opinion, p. 351, *proposed Amendment 50*, p. 382; CULT Opinion p. 435 and *proposed Amendment 61*, pp. 473-475; AFCO, *proposed amendment 55*, p. 515.

[227] Ibid.: ECON, *proposed Amendment 74*, p. 180; EMPL, *proposed Amendment 90*, p. 345: AFCO, *proposed Amendment 62*, p. 517.

[228] Ibid.: CONT, *proposed Amendment 70*, p. 289.

[229] Ibid.: CONT, *proposed Amendment 87*, p. 294.

Whistleblower Protection Office (OPLA)" proposed by the Committee on the Environment, Public Health and Food Safety of the EP (ENVI), which would be an EU organ directly accessible to whistleblowers.[230]

8.3.2 The European Parliament Draft Legislative Resolution

8.3.2.1 The Scope *Ratione Materiae*

The final amendments were adopted by JURI on November 20, 2018. While keeping the sectorial approach promoted by the EU Commission, the Draft EP Directive Legislative Resolution on the proposal for a Directive on the protection of persons reporting on breaches of Union law (hereinafter referred to as "EP Draft Legislative Resolution") proposed to extend the material scope of the Directive by adding Article 153(1) (a), (b) and (e), and Article 157(3) TFEU to the legal basis of the Directive proposal,[231] discarding the exhaustive nature of the annex[232] and including further EU acts in it.[233] Article 153 TFEU, as seen above, relates to the competence of the EU in relation to social policies. While Article 153(1)(a) TFEU mentions the health and safety of workers in their workplace, Article 153(1)(b) TFEU refers to working conditions in general and Article 153(1)(e) TFEU concerns the information and consultations of workers. Finally, Article 157(3) TFEU regulates the equal opportunities and treatments of men and women in the workplace. JURI thus reinforced the social component of the Directive proposal and widened the sectorial approach by including all EU acts related to the sectors listed in Article 1(1) Directive proposal, moving away from the multi-sectorial EU acts specific systematic proposed by the EU Commission, thus promoting a broader multi-sectorial coverage.

8.3.2.2 The Scope *Ratione Personae*

Regarding the personal scope, the EP Draft Legislative Resolution included the status of workers within the meaning of national law and practice,[234] which could represent a double-edged sword if the national definition of worker is more restrictive that the EU definition. An interpretation based on the spirit and purpose of the Directive would tend to prioritize the norm with the broadest definition of worker.

---

[230]Ibid.: ENVI Opinion p. 351.

[231]Ibid.: Draft European Parliament Legislative Resolution on the proposal for a directive of the European Parliament and of the Council on the protection of persons reporting on breaches of Union law (COM(2018)0218 – C8-0159/2018 – 2018/0106(COD)) [hereinafter "EP Draft Legislative Resolution"], *proposed Amendment 1*, p. 6.

[232]Ibid.: Draft Legislative Resolution, *proposed Amendment 87*, p. 58.

[233]Ibid.: Draft Legislative Resolution, *proposed Amendments 119-154*, pp. 90–133.

[234]Ibid.: Draft Legislative Resolution, *proposed Amendment 88*, pp. 59–60.

However, without a clear regulation, this alternative option could lead to increasing confusion as to the personal scope of the Directive. Notwithstanding this risk, the EP Draft Legislative Resolution took an ambitious, yet careful stand by including facilitators into the scope of the Directive,[235] defined under the EP Draft Legislative Resolution as "a natural person who assists or aids the reporting person in the reporting process in a work-related context".[236] Based on this definition, it is doubtful that journalists could fall under the scope of the Directive, which raises a substantial issue given their essential role as "public watchdog" and intermediary between the whistleblower and the public, when all other reporting options have failed. On the other hand, the EP Draft Legislative Resolution acknowledged the gap left by the Directive proposal in regard to the work-based relationship of workers, and remedied it by including not only individuals whose work-based relationship was yet to begin but also those whose work-based relationship had ceased,[237] following the suggestions of several EP Committees and the CoE Recommendation CM/Rec(2014)7.

8.3.2.3 The Element of Good Faith

In contrast to the Directive proposal of the EU Commission, which referred to "reasonable grounds"[238] of the reporting individual when determining whether protection should be afforded, in accordance with the CoE Recommendation CM/Rec(2014)7, the EP Draft Legislative Resolution followed the ECtHR case-law on whistleblower protection under Article 10 ECHR and expressly used the concept of good faith,[239] which was defined as "the reasonable belief of a reporting person, in light of the circumstances and the information available to that person at the time of the reporting, that the information reported by that person is true and that it falls within the scope of this Directive".[240] In this context, the principle of good faith follows two main purposes: On the one hand, it protects individuals who reported false information when they could have reasonably believed in the accuracy of the information, on the other hand, it hinders abusive reports.

[235]Ibid.: Draft Legislative Resolution, *proposed Amendment 88*, p. 59. The inclusion of facilitators to the EU initiative was called for, inter alia, by the German Bar Association (2018), pp. 9–10.

[236]Ibid.: Draft Legislative Resolution, *proposed Amendment 89*, p. 61.

[237]Ibid.: Draft Legislative Resolution, *proposed Amendment 88*, p. 60.

[238]Article 13(1) *Whistleblower Directive proposal*.

[239]*EP Report on the Whistleblower directive proposal*: Draft Legislative Resolution, proposed *Amendment 88*, p. 59.

[240]Ibid.: Draft Legislative Resolution, *proposed Amendment 89*, p. 62.

8.3.2.4 A Horizontal Approach to Reporting Channels

The EP Draft Legislative Resolution abandoned the tiered model and followed an undifferentiated approach between the internal and external reporting channels.[241] In regard to the respective reporting procedures, the EP Draft Legislative Resolution reduced the timeframe from 3 to 2 months by which competent authorities should provide feedback, which could be extended to 4 months in specific circumstances, and provided for the possibility of consulting the reporting individuals during the investigation.[242] Given the often particularly vulnerable situation in which reporting individuals are, often leading to anxiety, stress, lack of sleep and depression, the shorter period of uncertainty and the consultation during the investigative process are welcome measures as they strengthen the feeling that "things are moving". For public disclosures, the EP Draft Legislative Resolution maintained the conditional approach proposed by the EU Commission.

8.3.3 *A Cause for Celebration*

The EP Draft Legislative Resolution also strengthened the protection mechanisms and introduced amendments expanding support for whistleblowers through to provision of legal advice and psychological support[243] as well as adding remedial measures in parallel to the protective measures against retaliation, such as compensation or reintegration.[244] As the Eurocadres[245] President rightly said, this draft report and the amendments adopted by JURI are first and foremost, "a cause for celebration for all Europeans who wish for a more transparent and open Europe".[246] Indeed, the additional provisions and specifications adopted by the EP further strengthened the protection framework developed by the EU Commission. While keeping the sectorial approach promoted by the Directive proposal, the EP complemented the text with additional key aspects of an effective whistleblower framework, raising the protection standards upon which negotiations between the different EU institutions could be held and increasing thereby the likelihood of a higher level of protection as a result of those negotiations.

[241]Ibid.: Draft Legislative Resolution, *proposed Amendment 98*, p. 75.

[242]Ibid.: Draft Legislative Resolution, *proposed Amendment 91*, p. 65 (internal reporting); *proposed Amendment 95*, pp. 70–71 (external reporting).

[243]Ibid.: Draft Legislative Resolution, *proposed Amendment 100*, pp. 78–79.

[244]Ibid.: Draft Legislative Resolution, *proposed Amendment 103*, pp. 82–83.

[245]Eurocadres is the Council for European Professional and Managerial Staff, the trade union for professionals and managers.

[246]Jefflen (2018, 21 November).

8.4 The Adopted EU Whistleblower Directive

On the basis of the Draft EP Legislative Resolution amending the EU Commission Directive proposal and in compliance with the ordinary legislative procedure, interinstitutional negotiations between the EP, the Council and the EU Commission were initiated,[247] also known as *Trilogue*. The *Trilogue* resulted in an agreement, which was adopted by the EP in April 2019,[248] and by the Council in October 2019.[249] The Directive (EU) 2019/1937 on the protection of persons who report breaches of Union law was published in the Official Journal in November 2019 and entered into force in December 2019.[250] With the exception of Germany and the UK, who abstained from voting, all EU Member States voted favorably for the text.[251]

8.4.1 The Scope of Application of the EU Whistleblower Directive

8.4.1.1 The Legal Bases

According to well-established case-law, the choice of the legal basis must be determined by means of objective criteria,[252] taking into account the aim and content of the measure.[253] As the Legal Service of the Council noted, the Directive "has as main or predominant aim the enhancing of the enforcement of certain areas of Union law through rules on the protection of whistleblowers".[254] To pursue the integrated

[247] Council, Better protection of whistleblowers: Council adopts its position, 25 January 2019 *Press release*.

[248] *Position of the European Parliament adopted at first reading with a view to the adoption of Directive EU (2019)... of the European Parliament and of the Council on the protection of persons who report breaches of Union law*, EP-PE_TCI-COD(2018)0106, 16 April 2019.

[249] Council, Better protection of whistle-blowers: new EU-wide rules to kick in in 2021, 7 October 2019, *Press release*.

[250] *Directive (EU) 2019/1937 of 23 October 2019 on the protection of persons who report breaches of Union law* [hereinafter "EU Whistleblower directive"], OJ L 305/17, 26.11.2019, p. 17.

[251] Council, *Voting result on the Directive of the European Parliament and of the Council on the protection of persons who report breaches of Union law*, No. 13019/19, 11 October 2019; when asked by the author on the reasons for abstaining, the Permanent Representation of the Federal Republic of Germany to the EU replied "dass Deutschland sich zu der... Enthaltung im Rat inhaltlich nicht positioniert hat", 25 February2021. The question to the United Kingdom remained unanswered.

[252] CJ, Case 45/86, *Commission v. Council*, para 11.

[253] CJ, Case C-300/89, *Titanium Dioxide*, para 10; see also CJ, Case C-376/98, *Germany v. European Parliament and Council of the European Union (Tobacco Advertising)*, Judgment of 5 October 2000, ECLI:EU:C:2000:544, para 59.

[254] Legal Service of the Council, *Opinion on the Commission proposal for a Directive ("whistleblowers" directive) – legal basis*, No. 14620/18, para 25.

multi-sectorial approach of the Directive, the use of different legal bases targeting the relevant sectors thus appears to comply with the condition laid down by the CJEU, whereby an EU measure can be based on multiple legal provisions if it "simultaneously pursues a number of objectives or has several components that are indissociably linked, without one being secondary and indirect in relation to the other" (Table 8.2).[255]

That said, the procedural compatibility between the different provisions must be ensured.[256] In this respect and with the exception of Article 31 EURATOM, which requires a qualified majority of the Council, all the provisions used as legal bases provide for the ordinary legislative procedure, also known as the co-decision procedure. In its opinion on the EU Commission Whistleblower Directive proposal, the Legal Service of the Council had in fact argued against the inclusion of Article 31 EURATOM, Articles 103 and 109 TFEU as legal bases, in accordance with its consistent position whereby "legislative and non-legislative legal bases should not be combined in one and the same Union act".[257] While the two latter provisions were subsequently abandoned in the adopted version of the Directive, it maintained Article 31 EURATOM. Articles 30-39 EURATOM refer to the protection of the health of workers and the general public against the dangers arising from ionizing radiations, Article 31 EURATOM allowing for the establishment of basic standards to that effect. The three EU institutions thus seem to have considered the role of whistleblowers so relevant in this field that they decided against the position of the Legal Service. From a procedural standpoint, while the CJEU held that the need for the Council's unanimity can jeopardize the "very purpose of the cooperation procedure, which is to increase the involvement of the European Parliament",[258] a qualified majority, as required by Article 31 EURATOM, does not undermine the essence of the co-decision procedure and is thus compatible with the other provisions used as legal bases.

8.4.1.2 The Extension of the Material Scope in National Hands

In accordance with the principles of subsidiarity and proportionality enshrined in Article 5 TEU[259] and in accordance with the EU Commission's impact assessment,

[255] CJ, Case C-411/06, *Commission v. Parliament and Council*, para 47; see also CJ, C-178/03, *Commission of the European Communities v. European Parliament and Council of the European Union*, Judgment of 10 January 2006, ECLI:EU:C:2006:4, para 43; CJ, Case C-336/00, *Republik Österreich v. Martin Huber*, Judgment of 19 September 2002, ECLI:EU:C:2002:509, para 31; CJ, Case C-281/01, *Commission of the European Communities v. Council of the European Union*, Judgment of 12 December 2002, ECLI:EU:C:2002:761, para 35.

[256] CJ, Case C-300/89, *Titanium Dioxide*, paras 17 et seq.

[257] Legal Service of the Council, *Opinion on the Commission proposal for a Directive ("whistleblowers" directive) – legal basis*, No. 14620/18, paras 41 and 43.

[258] CJ, Case C-300/89, *Titanium Dioxide*, para 20.

[259] Recital 108 *EU Whistleblower Directive*.

Table 8.2 Legal bases of the EU Whistleblower Directive

Sectors targeted in the Directive proposal	Directive proposed by the European Commission 23.04.2018	Directive adopted	Sectors targeted in the adopted Directive
Data protection	Article 16 TFEU	Article 16 TFEU	Data protection
Strengthening customs cooperation between Member States	Article 33 TFEU		
Agriculture policy	Article 43 TFEU	Article 43 (2) TFEU	Agriculture policy
Freedom of establishment	Article 50 TFEU	Article 50 TFEU	Freedom of establishment
Mutual recognition of diplomas	Article 53 (1) TFEU	Article 53 (1) TFEU	Mutual recognition of diplomas
Services	Article 62 TFEU		
Transport	Article 91 TFEU	Article 91 TFEU	Transport
Include rail, road, inland waterway, sea and air transport	Article 100 TFEU	Article 100 TFEU	Include rail, road, inland waterway, sea and air transport
Internal market	Article 103 TFEU		
State aids	Article 109 TFEU		
Approximation of laws (internal market)	Article 114 TFEU	Article 114 TFEU	Approximation of laws (internal market)
Public health	Article 168 TFEU	Article 168 (4) TFEU	Public health related to safety concerns
Consumer protection	Article 169 TFEU	Article 169 TFEU	Consumer protection
Environment	Article 192 TFEU	Article 192 (1) TFEU	Environment
Common commercial policy	Article 207 TFEU		
Prevention and fight against fraud against the financial interests of the EU	Article 325 (4) TFEU	Article 325(4)	Prevention and fight against fraud against the financial interests of the EU
	Article 31 EURATOM	Article 31 EURATOM	

the text adopted by the EP and the Council reiterates the aim of strengthening the enforcement of EU policies through the establishment of common minimum standards to protect individuals reporting on breaches of specific EU laws,[260] thus

[260]Article 1 *EU Whistleblower Directive*.

maintaining the multi-sectorial EU specific approach[261] promoted by the EU Commission in its proposal. Under the new Directive, breaches can be unlawful acts and omissions, but also abusive practices, namely acts and omissions which defeat the object or the purpose of the specific EU acts listed in the Annex.[262] Regarding the EU acts listed in Part II of the Annex to the Directive, which already include sectorial reporting mechanisms, the provision of the new Directive should apply[263] and "build as far as possible on the existing channels".[264] However, if the sectorial rules have a mandatory character, they should prevail over the rules established by the EU Whistleblower Directive.[265] Interestingly, the Directive broadens the material scope through additional EU acts in the Annex to the Directive[266] and underlines "the possibility for Member States to extend protection under national law as regards areas or acts not covered by paragraph 1".[267] While a provision allowing for more favorable treatment was already introduced in the Directive proposed by the EU Commission,[268] the additional emphasis on EU Member States' power to expand upon the material scope laid down in the Directive could be regarded as an implicit encouragement from the EU toward its EU Member States to adopt a comprehensive whistleblower protection framework on national level when transposing the Directive.

8.4.1.3 The Personal Scope of the New Directive

In general terms, the Directive applies to "reporting persons working in the private and public sector who acquired information on breaches in a work-based context".[269] Furthermore, to pursue the inherent objective to provide protection for individuals whose economic livelihood depends directly or indirectly on the entity or person they report on,[270] it also took into account the considerations expressed by the EP committees and included not only individuals whose work-based relationships have not yet started but also those which have ended.[271] In order to grant protection to the "broadest possible range of categories of persons", the EU Whistleblower Directive lays down a rather ambitious peripheral approach by

---

[261] Article 2(1) *EU Whistleblower Directive.*

[262] Article 5(1) in conjunction with Recitals 42 and 43 *EU Whistleblower Directive.*

[263] Article 3(1) *EU Whistleblower Directive*; see also Recitals 9 and 20 of the same Directive.

[264] Recital 68 *EU Whistleblower Directive.*

[265] Article 3(1) *EU Whistleblower Directive.*

[266] Annex to *EU Whistleblower Directive.*

[267] Article 2(2) *EU Whistleblower Directive.*

[268] Article 19 *EU Whistleblower directive proposal.*

[269] Article 4(1) *EU Whistleblower Directive.*

[270] Recital 36 *EU Whistleblower Directive.*

[271] Article 4(2) *EU Whistleblower Directive.*

extending the scope of application to facilitators[272] and third parties who are connected with the reporting individual,[273] emphasizing that protection should be granted irrespectively of whether the reporting individual has the EU citizenship.[274]

Article 5(8) of the Directive promotes a particularly restrictive notion of facilitator however, defining it as a "natural person who assists a reporting person in the reporting process in a work-related context, and whose assistance should be confidential". As seen above, some EP Committees had called for the definition to include intermediaries, such as journalists,[275] but the EP Draft Legislative Resolution rejected those amendment proposals and preferred the definition ultimately adopted in the Directive. With this background, it is questionable whether journalists could be understood as facilitators and enjoy protection under the adopted Directive, despite the explicit emphasis on their 'watchdog' role in democratic societies.[276] Such a restrictive formulation is particularly unfortunate considering the key role of journalists as intermediaries between the whistleblower and the public, especially considering that public disclosure is permissible under certain conditions laid down in Article 15 of the Directive. It is unfortunate especially in view of certain statements by EU Member States, such as Hungary, which emphasized that "any protection provided by the Directive for third persons other than the reporting person under its personal scope should be interpreted narrowly".[277] However, differences between Member States in this regard will be narrowed by the procedure of Article 267 TFEU, according to which the CJEU has the jurisdiction to give preliminary rulings concerning the interpretation of EU acts, a procedure aiming to ensure a uniform interpretation and application of Union law to secure the unity of the EU legal order.

8.4.1.4 National Security Matters and Classified Information

In this context, a novelty was introduced in the new Directive, excluding from the scope of application of the Directive, *inter alia*, matters related to national security[278] and classified information.[279] While being unfortunate, this exclusion is not surprising following the trilogues negotiation. Indeed, as seen above, the fields of national security and classified information are particularly contentious subjects in

---

[272] Article 4(4)(a) in conjunction with Recital 41 *EU Whistleblower Directive*.

[273] Article 4(4)(b) *EU Whistleblower Directive*.

[274] Recital 37 *EU Whistleblower Directive*.

[275] See Sect. 8.3.1.1.

[276] Recital 46 *EU Whistleblower Directive*.

[277] Council, *Statement by Hungary*, Draft Directive of the European Parliament and of the Council on the protection of persons who report breaches of Union law (first reading) – Adoption of the legislative act = Statements, 12460/19 ADD 1 REV 1, 1 October 2019, p. 2.

[278] Article 3(2) *EU Whistleblower Directive*.

[279] Article 3(3)(a) *EU Whistleblower Directive*.

respect to whistleblowing and are very often excluded from the protection coverage of whistleblower laws. National security being "the sole responsibility of each Member State",[280] it was therefore expected that EU Member States would demand the explicit exclusion of this field from the scope of application of the EU Whistleblower Directive during the negotiation process.

8.4.1.5 "Reasonable Grounds"

Furthermore and drawing upon the ECtHR case-law and the CoE Recommendation CM(2014)/7,[281] any individual reporting can only enjoy protection under the new Directive if she or he had reasonable grounds to believe that the information reported was true.[282] This condition should prevent individuals to report knowingly wrong or misleading information and thus curb malicious or abusive reporting.[283] The exclusion of the motives of the whistleblower as a qualifying factor[284] is particularly welcome and reflects the new European consensus on whistleblower protection. Another positive development is the definition of information on breaches, which encompasses "information, including reasonable suspicions, about actual or potential breaches, which occurred or are very likely to occur",[285] thus allowing for "persons who do not provide positive evidence but raise reasonable concerns or suspicions"[286] to fall under the scope of the Directive. In light of the circumstances of each case, it would be for national courts to determine the concrete elements of proof or level of suspicion necessary to affirm the reasonable grounds of the reporting individual, a national margin of discretion with the potential to raise, or, conversely, lower the level of protection offered to whistleblowers under the new Directive. That said, Article 267 TFEU will ensure that divergences between the national authorities' interpretation of "reasonable grounds" remain limited.

8.4.1.6 The Entities Targeted by the EU Whistleblower Directive

According to the EU Whistleblower Directive, private entities with 50 or more employees,[287] as well as small and micro enterprises which operate in the financial

---

[280] Article 4(2) *in fine* TEU; see also Recital 24 *EU Whistleblower Directive.*

[281] Recital 31 *EU Whistleblower Directive.*

[282] Article 6(1)(a) *EU Whistleblower Directive.*

[283] Recital 32 *EU Whistleblower Directive.*

[284] Ibid.

[285] Article 5(2) *EU Whistleblower Directive.*

[286] Recital 43 *EU Whistleblower Directive.*

[287] Article 8(3) *EU Whistleblower Directive.*

sector or in sectors where rules on whistleblowing already exist[288] and, in duly justified cases,[289] small and micro sized companies whose activities involve a certain level of risk,[290] will have to establish internal reporting channels under the new Directive.[291] In order to alleviate the financial burden of medium enterprises and mitigate the additional bureaucratic charge for private entities overall, the new Directive stipulates the possibility for private entities to outsource the management of internal reporting channels,[292] and for enterprises with 50 to 249 employees to share funds to cover the cost of receiving and investigating internal reports.[293] Public entities or entities owned or controlled by public authorities should also establish internal reporting channels, with the exception of entities with less than 50 employees or municipalities with a population under 10,000.[294] Following the same logic as for the private sector, the new Directive opens the door for shared reporting channels between municipalities, on the condition that they ensure a clear separation with external reporting channels.[295] On the EU level and in parallel to using already existing cooperation mechanisms during investigations on breaches with a cross-border character, EU Member States should examine and further develop their cooperation capacities to better perform their follow-up obligations.[296]

8.4.2 *Reporting Mechanisms*

8.4.2.1 A Middle Ground

The relationship between internal and external reporting channels was the biggest bone of contention in the discussion over the adoption of an EU Whistleblower Directive.[297] At the end, the new Directive found a middle ground between the proposed tiered model of the EU Commission and the undifferentiated approach promoted by the EP Committees. While Belgium and Bulgaria had expressed their preference for such a flexible choice between internal and external reporting channels,[298] the removal of the strict tiered approach was met with vehement opposition

[288] Article 8(4) in conjunction with Article 3(1) *EU Whistleblower Directive* and Parts I.B and II of the Annex to the *EU Whistleblower Directive*.

[289] Article 8(8) *EU Whistleblower Directive*.

[290] Article 8(7) *EU Whistleblower Directive*.

[291] Article 8(1) *EU Whistleblower Directive*.

[292] Article 8(5) *EU Whistleblower Directive*. See also Recital 54 *EU Whistleblower Directive*.

[293] Article 8(6) *EU Whistleblower Directive*.

[294] Article 8(9) *EU Whistleblower Directive*.

[295] Article 8(9) *EU Whistleblower Directive*.

[296] Recital 72 *EU Whistleblower Directive*.

[297] Reppelmund (2019), p. 307.

[298] Council, Outcome of proceedings on the Proposal for a Directive of the European Parliament and of the Council on the protection of persons reporting on breaches of Union law: Mandate for

from the side of France and Germany.[299] Notwithstanding this resistance, the tiered model, with its mandatory requirement to first use internal channels, was ultimately abandoned, the EU making a strong stand for whistleblowers. While it encourages the use of internal channels when appropriate,[300] aiming to promote "a culture of good communication and corporate social responsibility",[301] the new Directive takes into account the empirical studies which demonstrates that the preferred reporting channel is predominantly through internal mechanisms.[302] On the basis of these observations, the Directive does not formulate a strict tiered model between internal and external channels,[303] going so far as to govern anonymous reports and public disclosures under the same rules as external reporting.[304] Under the new Directive, the protection should also extend to reports made directly to EU bodies, which should be governed by the provisions related to external reporting.[305] If EU bodies already established procedures for external reporting, as it is the case of OLAF or the EU Commission, those should remain untouched.[306]

8.4.2.2 Public Disclosure Under the New Directive

Unless based on a specific national law on freedom of expression and freedom of information,[307] public disclosure is permissible under the new Directive in three sets of circumstances: When no adequate measures were taken following internal and/or external reporting,[308] when the whistleblower had reasonable grounds to believe that the breach she or he wishes to report constitutes "an imminent or manifest danger for the public interest",[309] or finally, when the whistleblower has reasonable grounds to believe that using external channels would be ineffective or could subject her or him to retaliatory measures.[310] Whether those conditions are fulfilled should be

negotiations with the European Parliament – Declarations from Member States, *Belgian Statement: Déclaration de la Belgique concernant la proposition de directive relative à la protection des personnes dénoncant les infractions au droit de l'Union* and *Bulgarian Statement: Declaration by the Republic of Bulgaria*, Interinstitutional File: 2018/0106(COD), No. 5747/19 ADD 1, 29 January 2019, pp. 3-5.

[299] Jefflen (2019, 16 December 2019).

[300] Article 7(2) *EU Whistleblower Directive*.

[301] Recital 47 *EU Whistleblower Directive*.

[302] Recital 33 *EU Whistleblower Directive*.

[303] Article 10 *EU Whistleblower Directive*.

[304] Article 6(3) *EU Whistleblower Directive*.

[305] Article 6(4) *EU Whistleblower Directive*.

[306] Recitals 69 *EU Whistleblower Directive*.

[307] Article 15(2) *EU Whistleblower Directive*.

[308] Article 15(1)(a) *EU Whistleblower Directive*.

[309] Article 15(1)(b)(i) in conjunction with Recital 80 *EU Whistleblower Directive*.

[310] Article 15(1)(b)(ii) in conjunction with Recital 81 *EU Whistleblower Directive*.

determined upon the circumstances of the case on the basis of objective criteria.[311] Public disclosure is understood under the Directive as "the making of information on breaches available in the public domain",[312] via online platforms, social media or directly to the media for example.[313]

8.4.2.3 Anonymous Reporting

Even if EU Member States have the freedom to decide whether the competent authorities should be able to receive and follow-up on anonymous reports,[314] an individual having anonymously reported on breaches through public disclosure and whose identity has subsequently revealed should enjoy protection under the Directive, provided that she or he had reasonable grounds to believe at the accuracy of the information and fulfilled the conditions laid down in the provision dedicated to public disclosures.[315]

8.4.2.4 Reporting Means

Furthermore, and irrespective of the channel used, whether internal or external, reporting individuals should have a variety of means at their disposal to report breaches, including the written form, per post, complaint box or online form, for example,[316] through telephone hotline or a special voice messaging system, or if requested by the whistleblower, through a physical conversation.[317] To allow potential whistleblowers to make an informed decision,[318] "individual, impartial and confidential advice, free of charge, should be made available",[319] and information on the modalities of internal[320] and external[321] reporting channels should be clear and easily accessible. After examination, a documentation in the form of a certification could be issued to confirm that the whistleblower is indeed protected under the law.[322]

[311] Recital 79 *EU Whistleblower Directive*.

[312] Article 5(6) *EU Whistleblower Directive*.

[313] Recital 45 *EU Whistleblower Directive*.

[314] Article 6(2) *EU Whistleblower Directive*.

[315] Article 6(3) in conjunction with Articles 6(1) and Article 15 *EU Whistleblower Directive*.

[316] Recital 53 *EU Whistleblower Directive*.

[317] Article 9(2) (internal reporting) and Article 12(2) (external reporting) *EU Whistleblower Directive*.

[318] Recital 75 *EU Whistleblower Directive*.

[319] Recital 89 *EU Whistleblower Directive*.

[320] Article 7(3) *EU Whistleblower Directive*.

[321] Article 9(1)(g) in conjunction with Article 13 *EU Whistleblower Directive*.

[322] Recital 90 *EU Whistleblower Directive*.

The new Directive also requires competent authorities to design user-friendly and secure reporting channels,[323] which preserve the confidentiality of the information received,[324] in particular regarding the identity of the reporting person as "an essential ex-ante measure to prevent retaliation",[325] unless the latter agreed to disclose her or his identity[326] or when the disclosure is required by "a necessary and proportionate obligation" under EU or national law.[327] In case the wrong department or individual has received an information transmitted through external channels, the recipient should preserve the confidentiality of the information and transfer it without delay and alteration to the competent authority.[328] Furthermore and in accordance with data protection rules, the applicable record-keeping systems should comply with the confidentiality principle and should preserve reports no longer than strictly necessary and proportionate.[329] The discretion to define the exact timeframe is left to EU Member States.

8.4.2.5 Strong Follow-up Systems

Within 7 days after the report was received, an acknowledgment of receipt should be sent back. At the request of the reporting individual, the authority receiving an external report could refrain from it, a decision it could also take if it considers that sending back such acknowledgement of receipt would compromise the principle of confidentiality.[330] However, such waiver was not provided in cases of reports made through the internal reporting process.[331] This omission could increase the vulnerability of the whistleblower and compromise the confidentiality of her or his identity. This is the reason why the internal procedural step should be aligned to the conditions set forth in the external reporting process. In case of repetitive reports devoid of new meaningful details,[332] or when the report concerns minor breaches,[333] the authorities competent to receive external reports can decide at their own discretion to discontinue the procedure.

After the receipt of a report, competent authorities have the obligation to follow-up and provide feedback, following strict deadlines. Indeed, they have 3 months if

---

[323] Recital 73 *EU Whistleblower Directive*.

[324] Article 9(1)(a) (internal channel) and Article 12(1)(a) (external channel) *EU Whistleblower Directive*.

[325] Recital 82 *EU Whistleblower Directive*.

[326] Article 16(1) *EU Whistleblower Directive*.

[327] Article 16(2) and (3) *EU Whistleblower Directive*.

[328] Article 11(6) in conjunction with Article 12(3) *EU Whistleblower Directive*.

[329] Article 18(1) *EU Whistleblower Directive*. See also Recitals 85-86 *EU Whistleblower Directive*.

[330] Article 11(2)(b) *EU Whistleblower Directive*.

[331] Article 9(1)(b) *EU Whistleblower Directive*.

[332] Article 11(4) *EU Whistleblower Directive*.

[333] Article 11(3) *EU Whistleblower Directive*.

the report was made internally,[334] 3 months with a possible extension to 6 months in duly justified cases, when the report was made through external channels,[335] to provide feedback. According to the Directive, feedback is defined as "the provision to the reporting person of information on the action envisages or taken as follow up and on the grounds for such follow-up"[336] while follow-up is understood as "any action taken by the recipient of a report ... to assess the accuracy of the allegations made in the report and, where relevant, to address the breach reported, including through actions such as an internal enquiry, an investigation, prosecution, an action for recovery of funds, or the closure of the procedure".[337] These requirements are key and aim to combat the lack of trust in the effectivity of reporting channels.[338]

8.4.2.6 Staff Training

One significant deficiency remains however. Unlike staff members competent to receive external reports,[339] individuals in charge of receiving internal reports are not required, under the new Directive, to be specifically trained to handle reports. Because the training of staff is key to ensure that reports are correctly received and handled, this omission is particularly unfortunate. It is all the more damaging when mismanaged internal reporting channels could lead to the revelation of the identity of the whistleblower, which is a significant risk, especially in cases of internal reports, violating this way one of the key element of any effective whistleblower framework and undermining the trust in the effectiveness of internal reporting systems.

8.4.3 A Retaliation Prevention Framework with Protective Measures

The EU Whistleblower Directive introduces two sets of measures: A sanction regime,[340] and a protective framework for whistleblowers against retaliation.

[334] Article 9(1)(f) *EU Whistleblower Directive.*

[335] Article 11(2)(d) *EU Whistleblower Directive.*

[336] Article 5(13) *EU Whistleblower Directive.*

[337] Article 5(12) *EU Whistleblower Directive.*

[338] Recital 63 *EU Whistleblower Directive.*

[339] Article 12(5) *EU Whistleblower Directive.*

[340] Article 23 *EU Whistleblower Directive.*

8.4.3.1 Protective Scheme

In this context, a close link is required[341] in order for a detrimental measure suffered by the whistleblower to be defined as a retaliation.[342] While the whistleblower would have to "demonstrates prima facie that he or she reported breaches or made a public disclosure in accordance with this Directive and suffered a detriment",[343] the burden of proof should lie on the author of the detrimental action to demonstrate the lack of causal link between the reporting and the detriment suffered,[344] given the resource imbalance between the whistleblower and the perpetrator, the latter being more likely to possess further documentation to explain the reasons justifying the action taken.[345] This reversal of the burden of proof is to be welcomed and reflects the CoE Recommendation CM/Rec(2014)7. To prevent a chilling effect[346] and considering the diversity of forms retaliatory measures may take, a broad definition of retaliation is necessary for an effective whistleblower protection framework.[347]

The new Directive thus took into account the considerations expressed by several EP Committees and provided for protection against retaliation in the form of psychiatric or medical referrals.[348] It also introduces an obligation to establish new supportive systems in the form of access to comprehensive information and advice,[349] as well as legal aid in judicial proceedings.[350] That aid could play an important role in ensuring an effective whistleblower framework, financial assistance being decisive for whistleblowers to effectively enforce their rights under the law.[351] To alleviate the chilling effects of ongoing retaliation during legal proceedings,[352] and reflecting the CoE Recommendation CM/Rec(2014)7,[353] the new Directive also introduces access to interim relief[354] as well as the possibility for EU Member States to provide financial and psychological support during those proceedings.[355] Furthermore, whistleblowers should be shielded from liability[356]

---

[341] Recital 44 *EU Whistleblower Directive.*

[342] Article 19 in conjunction with Article 5(11) *EU Whistleblower Directive.*

[343] Recital 93 *EU Whistleblower Directive.*

[344] Article 21(5) *EU Whistleblower Directive.*

[345] Recital 93 *EU Whistleblower Directive.*

[346] Recital 88 *EU Whistleblower Directive.*

[347] Recital 44 *EU Whistleblower Directive.*

[348] Article 19(o) *EU Whistleblower Directive.*

[349] Article 20(1)(a) *EU Whistleblower Directive.*

[350] Article 20(1)(c) *EU Whistleblower Directive.*

[351] Recital 99 *EU Whistleblower Directive.*

[352] Recital 96 *EU Whistleblower Directive.*

[353] CM, *Recommendation CM/Rec(2014)7 on the Protection of Whistleblowers*, 30 April 2014, *Appendix*, Point 26.

[354] Article 21(6) *EU Whistleblower Directive.*

[355] Article 20(2) *EU Whistleblower Directive.*

[356] Article 21(2) *EU Whistleblower Directive.*

in legal proceedings for defamation, copyright infringement, violation of trade secrets, etc., with the burden to prove that the whistleblower does not meet the requirements set by the Directive lying on the initiator of the proceeding.[357] If the access to the information reported constituted a criminal offense, national law should remain applicable however.[358]

8.4.3.2 Sanction Regime

Regarding the sanction regime, Article 23 of the Directive introduces two systems. On the one hand, it establishes penalties with the intent to dissuade employers to retaliate against whistleblowers,[359] on the other hand it imposes sanctions against individuals who "knowingly reported or publicly disclosed false information".[360] While the latter penalties should prevent abusive reporting, the Directive emphasizes that they should be proportionate in order not to have a dissuasive effect on potential whistleblowers.[361]

8.4.4 Waiver and National Transposition

Finally, the Directive underlines that while the rules established should not be used to lower the level of existing whistleblower protection standards on the national level,[362] EU Member States remain free to adopt higher standards than those established by the Directive.[363] It also stresses that the rights and remedies established cannot be waived or limited by "any agreement, policy, form or condition of employment".[364]

---

[357]Recital 97 *EU Whistleblower Directive*.

[358]Article 21(3) *EU Whistleblower Directive*.

[359]Article 23(1) *EU Whistleblower Directive*.

[360]Article 23(2) *EU Whistleblower Directive*.

[361]Recital 102 *EU Whistleblower Directive*.

[362]Article 25(2) *EU Whistleblower Directive*.

[363]Article 25(1) *EU Whistleblower Directive*.

[364]Article 24 *EU Whistleblower Directive*.

8.5 Outlook: The EU Whistleblower Directive in the EU Legal Landscape

Because the EU Whistleblower Directive provisions needs to fit in the EU legal landscape, it is particularly important to assess the future challenges the EU and EU Member States will face following the adoption of the new EU Directive on the protection of whistleblower and its transposition into national law. This final part will touch upon the main issues arising from the adoption of the EU Whistleblower Directive and shed some light on those legal conflicts.

8.5.1 Working Conditions and Equal Treatment

While the EU Commission excluded a Directive based on Article 153 TFEU in its impact assessment, it considered, in a statement on the adopted Directive, "the possibility of proposing to extend its scope of application to certain acts based on Articles 153 TFEU and 157 TFEU, after consulting the social partners, where appropriate, in accordance with Article 154 TFEU",[365] an ambitious plan encouraged by the EESC,[366] which raises however a number of questions.

8.5.1.1 Article 153 TFEU

Article 153 TFEU is the most significant legal basis for Directives regulating social policies in the EU[367] and is closely linked with Article 30 EU Charter on the protection in the event of unjustified dismissal.[368] The complex formulation of Article 153 TFEU, and the scarce examples of EU measures adopted on this legal basis makes the identification of its precise scope particularly challenging.[369] According to Article 153 TFEU, the EU is entitled to play a harmonizing role by adopting Directives laying down "minimum requirements for gradual

[365]Council, Draft Directive of the European Parliament and of the Council on the protection of persons who report breaches of Union law (first reading) – Adoption of the legislative act = Statements, *Statement by the Commission*, Interinstitutional File 2018/0106(COD), No. 12460/19 ADD 1 REV 1, 1 October 2019, p. 2. Consideration already formulated by the EU Commission in April 2019, see Annex to the EP legislative resolution of 16 April 2019 on the proposal for a directive of the European Parliament and of the Council on the protection of persons reporting on breaches of Union law (COM(2018)0218 – C8-0159/2018 – 2018/0106(COD)), *Commission statement on the Directive on the protection of persons reporting on breaches of Union law*.

[366]EESC, *Strengthening whistleblower protection at EU level*, Opinion SOC/593, 18 October 2018, para 1.4.

[367]Krebber (2016a), AEUV Art. 153, para 1.

[368]Schmitt (2019), p. 509.

[369]Krebber (2016a), AEUV Art. 153, para 1.

implementation"[370] in certain social policy fields so as "to support and complement the activities of the EU Member States".[371] The provision thus emphasizes the primary competence of EU Member States in social policy areas and reveals the reluctance of those same EU Member States to transfer legislative competence to the EU in fields related to labor law.[372] Extending the scope of the Directive on the protection of whistleblowers to EU acts based on Article 153 TFEU appears therefore particularly challenging[373] and will most certainly be met with resistance from some of the EU Member States. Even if only a few EU instruments have been adopted on the basis of this provision, the cautious formulation of the EU Commission, to extend the scope of the EU Whistleblowers Directive to merely "certain acts", demonstrates the highly controversial subject and the expectation that even such a limited extension might face strong opposition. In regard to the specific field which could be included in the EU Whistleblower Directive, Article 153(1)(b) TFEU on working conditions, seems to be the most appropriate, considering its procedural compatibility, and the general subject matter, especially if the CJEU engages in an extensive interpretation of Article 153(2)(b) TFEU[374] and has demonstrated the willingness to accept a legal basis which does not have a direct link with the subject at stake.[375]

8.5.1.2 Article 157 TFEU

In referring to Article 157 TFEU, which lays down the principle of equal opportunity and treatment between men and women in the workplace[376] and prohibits discrimination in respect of employment and occupation,[377] the EU Commission emphasizes the importance of whistleblowing to promote gender equality in the workplace and the need to consider an extension of the EU Whistleblower Directive's material scope to include reports on breaches of this principle. Equality between men and women is a core principle of EU law, enshrined in the TEU and the EU Charter.[378] While a possible extension of the material scope to certain acts based on Article 157 TFEU will face the same challenges as for Article 153 TFEU, the EU Commission's statement holds significant symbolic value and is all the more relevant in the

370 Article 153(2)(b) TFEU.

371 Article 153(1) TFEU.

372 Krebber (2016a), AEUV Art. 153, para 3.

373 Abazi (2017), p. 10.

374 Krebber (2016a), AEUV Art. 153, para 9.

375 Abazi (2017), p. 10.

376 Krebber (2016b), AEUV Art. 157, para 1; Eichenhofer (2018), AEUV Art. 157, para 2.

377 Krebber (2016b), AEUV Art. 157, para 36; Eichenhofer (2018), AEUV Art. 157, paras 13 et seq. On Gender equality in the workplace, see also CJ, Case C-14/83, *Sabine von Colson and Elisabeth Kamann v. Land Nordrhein-Westfalen*, Judgment of 10 April 1984, ECLI:EU:C:1984:153.

378 Kollonay Lehoczky (2019), pp. 401–425.

aftermath of the *#metoo* and Time's Up movements, which drew attention to the particularly precarious situation of women in the workplace, contributing to the gender pay gap and cementing the glass ceiling.

8.5.2 *Trade Secrets and the EU Whistleblower Directive*

8.5.2.1 Article 5(b) Trade Secrets Directive vs. the EU Whistleblower Directive

The points of friction between the Trade Secrets Directive and the extent of protection for whistleblowers was of particular concern for EU Member States during the interinstitutional negotiations on the EU Whistleblower Directive[379] and will most certainly be highly debated in national parliaments when transposing the EU Whistleblower Directive, when the nuances and delimitations between those concurring interests will have to be defined.[380] On the one hand, the protection of trade secrets has a substantial economic value for businesses[381] and is particularly relevant to foster competitiveness and innovation.[382] On the other hand, the public may have a legitimate interest in obtaining information which is classified as trade secrets, especially when it reveals acts of wrongdoing.[383] Individuals who may become aware of such misconduct in the course of their work-related activities should therefore be able to disclose this information without acting in breach of EU trade secrets rules. The Trade Secrets Directive stipulates in this context that "[t]he measures, procedures and remedies provided for in this Directive should not restrict whistleblowing activity",[384] laying down exceptions to the general protection of trade secrets, whereby the acquisition, use and disclosure of trade secrets are permissible, *inter alia*, "for revealing misconduct, wrongdoing or illegal activity, provided that the respondent acted for the purpose of protecting the general public interest".[385] While the constituent elements of 'general public interest' remain unclear and may potentially lead to diverging interpretations depending on the EU Member States,[386] the CJEU will contribute to a unified and consistent interpretation by means of preliminary rulings, keeping disparities within narrow limits.

[379] Council, Outcome of proceedings on the Proposal for a Directive of the European Parliament and of the Council on the protection of persons reporting on breaches of Union law: Mandate for negotiations with the European Parliament – Declarations from Member States, *Austrian Statement*, Interinstitutional File: 2018/0106(COD), No. 5747/19 ADD 1, 29 January 2019, p. 2.

[380] Racho (2016), para 21.

[381] Bauschke (2019), p. 134.

[382] Recital 2 *Trade Secrets Directive*.

[383] Nader (1972), p. 9.

[384] Recital 20 *Trade Secrets Directive*.

[385] Article 5(b) *Trade Secrets Directive*.

[386] Abazi (2016), p. 1069.

Furthermore, the formulation of Article 5(b) Trade Secrets Directive would leave the burden of proof on the whistleblower,[387] which is particularly problematic and goes against key whistleblower protection principles and the EU Whistleblower Directive itself.

On the other hand, the EU Whistleblower Directive states that "[p]ersons who disclose trade secrets acquired in a work-related context should only benefit from the protection granted by this Directive, . . . provided that they meet the conditions laid down by this Directive, including that the disclosure was necessary to reveal a breach falling within the material scope of this Directive".[388] In this context, those persons should not be made liable if they had reasonable grounds to believe that the reporting or public disclosure of trade secrets was necessary to reveal the breach,[389] the disclosure having to be considered lawful in accordance with Article 3(2) Trade Secrets Directive. However, competent authorities having received information related to trade secrets should only use or disclose them to conduct a proper follow-up.[390]

Two questions are therefore particularly relevant in the context of a disclosure of information classified as trade secrets: Can the information disclosed be defined as a trade secret under the meaning of the Trade Secrets Directive? If yes, 1) does the disclosure fall within the material scope of the EU Whistleblower directive. If it not the case, 2) can the disclosure be considered legitimate according to Article 5 (b) Trade Secrets Directive?

8.5.2.2 The Definition of "Trade Secrets"

The Trade Secrets Directive defines a trade secret as information which is not "generally known or readily accessible",[391] "has commercial value because it is secret",[392] and "has been subject to reasonable steps under the circumstances, by the person lawfully in control of the information, to keep it secret".[393] This definition gives the secret holder a certain margin of discretion in determining which information should be categorized as trade secrets.[394] While this discretion is understandable, businesses being better placed to determine which information has commercial value and should therefore remain confidential, this margin entails the risk of abuse, a risk which could be mitigated by an effective whistleblower protection framework. While the adoption of the EU Whistleblower Directive provides important

[387] Ibid., p. 1068.

[388] Recital 98 *EU Whistleblower Directive*.

[389] Article 21(7) *EU Whistleblower Directive*.

[390] Article 16(4) *EU Whistleblower Directive*.

[391] Article 2(a) *Trade Secrets Directive*.

[392] Article 2(b) *Trade Secrets Directive*.

[393] Article 2(c) *Trade Secrets Directive*.

[394] Abazi (2016), pp. 1067–1068.

specifications in regard to the circumstances in which such disclosures are legitimate and should be protected, it leaves some grey areas, as the term "general public interest" used in the Trade Secrets Directive is rather vague and seems to refer to a broader concept than the material scope of the EU Whistleblower Directive. The two Directives having to be considered complementary as "the civil redress measures, procedures and remedies provided by [the Trade Secrets Directive should continue to apply] for all trade secrets falling outside the scope of the [EU Whistleblower Directive]",[395] the interplay between both in the national legal system of EU Member States remains to be seen.

8.5.2.3 A Shaky Legal Ground

Experience shows that EU Member States tend to adopt domestic provisions faithfully to the Directives, without expanding the scope of application even if such expansion is permissible. Considering the complementarity of the two Directives, if the disclosure of a trade secret reveals a breach which is not covered by the material scope of the EU Whistleblower Directive, or if the disclosure was not made in compliance with the conditions laid down by that Directive, the reporting individual could still be exempt from prosecution if the disclosure is interpreted as being for the protection of the general public interest, in compliance with Article 5(b) Trade Secrets Directive.[396] The gap between the scope of the EU Whistleblower Directive and the conditions laid down by the Trade Secrets Directive is an issue that EU Member States will have to address. Considering that EU Member States have the freedom to expand upon the scope of the EU Whistleblower Directive,[397] the broader the material scope of the national transposition, the more coherent will it interplay with trade secrets rules.

8.5.3 GDPR vs. the EU Whistleblower Directive

8.5.3.1 A Reciprocal Influence

As seen above, the protection of personal data and the protection of whistleblowers are closely interlinked but can also come into conflict with each other. Indeed, whistleblowers have been important actors in the revelation of data protection violations by States or private entities. The digitalization of the world has opened new doors in data abuses and left individuals vulnerable to serious violations of their right to privacy. Now more than ever, whistleblowers can help strengthen data

[395] Recital 98 *EU Whistleblower Directive.*

[396] See Recital 98 *EU Whistleblower Directive.*

[397] Article 25(1) *EU Whistleblower Directive.*

protection rules and raise the alarm about violations and abuse of personal data.[398] The material scope of the EU Whistleblower Directive thus includes the protection of privacy and personal data[399] as one of the key sectors which would benefit from a stronger protection for whistleblowers across the EU.[400]

However, whistleblower reports often contain sensitive personal data, either on the whistleblowers themselves or the individuals involved. Whistleblowing procedures should therefore be carefully framed in order to ensure a strict respect of data protection principles[401] laid down by EU rules.[402] Authorities competent to receive and process whistleblower reports should comply in particular with the GDPR, Directive (EU) 2016/680 and Regulation (EU) 2018/1725 when processing personal data.[403] Under the GDPR, personal data is "any information relating to an identified or identifiable natural person ('data subject'); an identifiable natural person is one who can be identified, directly or indirectly, in particular by reference to an identifier such as a name, an identification number, location data, an online identifier or to one or more factors specific to the physical, physiological, genetic, mental, economic, cultural or social identity of that natural person".[404] This is a broad definition which needs to be further concretized in whistleblowing procedures.[405]

8.5.3.2 The EDPS Guidelines

To avoid an excessive collection of personal data, the EDPS recommends providing clear instructions about whistleblowing procedures, which should include specific details on the relevant information to be provided by whistleblowers or processed by competent authorities.[406] When irrelevant personal information is still being transmitted, such information shall not be further processed and deleted without delay.[407] Furthermore, the collection of personal information in the process of a whistleblower report and during the investigation should be stored no longer than necessary[408] and

---

[398] Recital 14 *EU Whistleblower Directive*.

[399] Article 2(1)(a)(x) *EU Whistleblower Directive* in conjunction with Annex Part 1 (J) to the *EU Whistleblower Directive*.

[400] EU Commission, *Impact Assessment accompanying the EU Whistleblower Directive proposal*, pp. 26–28.

[401] Recital 76 *EU Whistleblower Directive*.

[402] Recital 83 *EU Whistleblower Directive*. See also Annex Part 1(J)(ii) to the *EU Whistleblower Directive*.

[403] Article 13(d) in conjunction with Article 17 *EU Whistleblower Directive*.

[404] Article 4(1) *GDPR*.

[405] EDPS, *Guidelines on processing personal information within a whistleblowing procedure*, July 2016, para 15.

[406] Ibid., paras 11 and 14.

[407] Article 17 in fine *EU Whistleblower Directive*.

[408] Article 5(1)(e) *GDPR*.

a thorough information security risk assessment[409] should be undertaken in order to take appropriate measures to ensure a secure processing of personal information.[410]

Part of an effective whistleblower report mechanism compliant with data protection rules should include the provision of personal data specific information.[411] The EDPS recommends in this context a two-step procedure: A general data protection statement, and a specific data protection statement intended for the different categories of individuals involved.[412] For whistleblowers, information on the recipient (s) of the report should be made available,[413] in accordance with Article 13 GDPR. Details on the disciplinary consequences in cases of malicious reporting can also be provided in this context.[414] Individuals being the object of a whistleblower report also have a right to information on their personal data use, pursuant to Article 14 GDPR. However, the transmission of such personal data specific information to those individuals might, in certain cases, jeopardies ongoing investigation into the allegations. Thus, a possible deferral in the provision of such information should be at the discretion of competent authorities, the decision to defer having to be well argued on the basis of the circumstances of each case.[415]

As seen above in the Stuttgart case, the right of access under Article 15 GDPR can be a particularly complex challenge when the protection of whistleblowers is concerned. In this context, the "status of the requester and the current stage of the investigation"[416] should be taken into consideration to strike a fair balance between the different interests at stake, taking into account Article 23 GDPR. As a general principle, "[w]hen access is granted to the personal information of any concerned individual, the personal information of third parties such as informants, whistleblowers or witnesses should be removed from the documents except in exceptional circumstances".[417]

---

[409]EDPS, *Guidelines on processing personal information within a whistleblowing procedure*, para 33.

[410]Article 32 *GDPR*.

[411]EDPS, *Guidelines on processing personal information within a whistleblowing procedure*, paras 18-22.

[412]Ibid., para 18.

[413]Ibid., para 19.

[414]Ibid., para 19.

[415]Ibid., para 20.

[416]Ibid., para 23.

[417]Ibid., para 25.

8.5.4 The European Public Prosecutor's Office: A Future Focal Point

8.5.4.1 A New EU Organ...

In April 2017, 16 EU Member States released a proposal for a Regulation establishing an European Public Prosecutor's Office (EPPO)[418] which should "be in charge of investigating, prosecuting and bringing to justice the perpetrators of offences against the Union's financial interests",[419] a Regulation subsequently adopted in October 2017.[420] The EPPO currently has 22 participating EU Member States,[421] with Laura Codruța Kövesi as European Chief Prosecutor. The adopted EPPO Regulation acknowledges the importance of whistleblowers for the performance of the EPPO's duty and encourages EU Member States to provides "effective procedures to enable reporting of possible offences that fall within the competence of the EPPO and to ensure protection of the persons who report such offences from retaliation, and in particular from adverse or discriminatory employment actions".[422] According to the EPPO Regulation, the EPPO is competent for "investigating, prosecuting and bringing to judgment the perpetrators of, and accomplices to, criminal offences affecting the financial interests of the Union which are provided for in Directive (EU) 2017/1371 and determined by this Regulation".[423] As seen above, "breaches affecting the financial interests of the Union as referred to in Article 325 TFEU and as further specified in relevant Union measures",[424] which include Directive (EU) 2017/1371,[425] is part of the EU Whistleblower Directive's material scope and represents one of its main innovations.[426] Indeed, the protection of the financial interests of the EU "is a core area in which enforcement of Union law needs to be strengthened"[427] and where EU whistleblowing rules are proven to be

---

418Council, *Proposal for a Regulation on the establishment of the European Public Prosecutor's Office – Draft Regulation*, Interinstitutional File: 2013/0255 (APP), No. 5766/17, 31 January 2017.

419Council, European public prosecutor's office: 16 member states together to fight fraud against the EU budget, 3 April 2017, *Press release*.

420*Council Regulation (EU) 2017/1939 of 12 October 2017 implementing enhanced cooperation on the establishment of the European Public Prosecutor's Office ('the EPPO')* [hereinafter "EPPO Regulation"], OJ L 283, 31.10.2017, p. 1.

421EU Commission, The Mission of the European Public Prosecutor's Office. https://ec.europa.eu/info/law/cross-border-cases/judicial-cooperation/networks-and-bodies-supporting-judicial-cooperation/european-public-prosecutors-office_en#mission. Accessed 13 April 2021; see also OPPO official website. https://www.eppo.europa.eu/home. Accessed 13 April 2021.

422Recital 50 *EPPO Regulation*.

423Article 4 *EPPO Regulation*.

424Article 2(1)(b) *EU Whistleblower Directive*.

425Recital 15 *EU Whistleblower Directive*.

426White (2018), p. 172.

427Recital 15 *EU Whistleblower Directive*.

effective for that effect.[428] Interestingly, prior to the now adopted EU Whistleblower Directive, the EU Commission already qualified the EPPO Regulation as one of the existing EU tools on whistleblower protection.[429]

8.5.4.2 ... and Future Focal Point for Whistleblowers

For whistleblowers within EU institutions, under the EU Staff Regulations, as well as for whistleblowers in EU Member States under the newly adopted EU Whistleblower Directive, the establishment of the EPPO "will change the current landscape of law enforcement and criminal justice".[430] Indeed, the EPPO could further encourage whistleblowers to report on the one hand, and contribute to the implementation of the EU Whistleblower Directive by acting as a focal point on the other hand.[431] To that end, the adoption of its own internal rules on reporting procedures[432] would represent a welcome clarification,[433] the EPPO being able to receive information from different sources, including private parties[434] and, by extension, whistleblowers.[435] The coordination between EPPO and OLAF should also be clarified in order to ensure a coherent procedural systematic in the receipt of whistleblower reports,[436] especially in regard to internal investigations within EU institutions and bodies.[437] While a more extensive mandate could have allowed the EPPO to be a central player in receiving all whistleblower reports and in so doing, ensuring a harmonized access to information for whistleblowers across the EU,[438] the limited material competence of the EPPO[439] makes it impossible. An extension to cross-border terrorism was proposed,[440] but an inclusion of responsibilities linked to the implementation of the EU Whistleblower Directive and thus of any breach of EU acts listed thereof is highly unlikely. At most, informative and logistical competences seem to be more realistic. In regard to the territorial scope of application of

---

[428]EU Commission, *Impact Assessment accompanying the EU Whistleblower Directive proposal*, pp. 15–17.

[429]EU Commission, *Annexes on the EU Whistleblower Directive proposal,* Annex 5, p. 88.

[430]EU Commission, *2019 Review of the Guidelines on whistleblowing*, p. 4.

[431]Racho (2016), paras 24 et seq.

[432]Recital 50 in fine *EPPO Regulation.*

[433]White (2018), p. 175.

[434]Recital 49 *EPPO Regulation.*

[435]Pérez Enciso (2018), p. 270.

[436]White (2018), p. 175.

[437]Vervaele (2018), p. 16.

[438]Racho (2016), para 14.

[439]Article 22 *EPPO Regulation.*

[440]EU Commission, *A Europe that protects: an initiative to extend the competences of the European Public Prosecutor's Office to cross-border terrorist crimes,* Communication from the Commission to the European Parliament and the European Council, COM(2018) 641 final, 12 September 2018.

the EPPO Regulation, while it is limited to the jurisdiction of EU Member States,[441] the mandate of the EPPO should be interpreted "as broadly as possible so that its investigations and prosecutions may extend to offences committed outside the territory of the Member States".[442] A close cooperation between EU Member States and the EPPO would ensure an effective protection of whistleblowers across the EU, as the EPPO is able to inform about facts[443] or refer cases[444] to EU Member States competent authorities when the substance lies outside of its mandate, thus exercising a fundamental role of an EU focal point for whistleblower reports.

8.6 Intermediate Conclusion: The Way Ahead for EU Member States

EU Member States will have until the end of 2021 to transpose the EU Whistleblower Directive into their national legal systems. In doing so, EU Member States have an exceptional opportunity to go beyond the application coverage established by the Directive and use this text as a basis to develop a comprehensive and horizontal protection framework on the national level. While the EU Whistleblower Directive merely protects individuals reporting information on breaches affecting the EU interests in selected sectors, national legislators could use the transposition process so as to also include all breaches of national law, irrespective of the sector and independently of whether EU interests are concerned or not. In this context, the EU Commission explicitly encouraged EU Member States, "when transposing the Directive, to consider extending its scope of application to other areas, and more generally to ensure a comprehensive and coherent framework at national level".[445] While some EU Member States had already adopted a horizontal approach to their national whistleblower laws, this Directive could incite the other EU Member States to do the same. This way, the shortcomings resulting from the fragmented coverage offered by the EU Whistleblower Directive will be addressed to provide whistleblowers across the EU with legal clarity through a coherent and clear protection framework.[446]

---

[441] Article 23 *EPPO Regulation*.

[442] Recital 64 *EPPO Regulation*.

[443] Recital 48 *EPPO Regulation*.

[444] Recital 77 *EPPO Regulation*.

[445] EU Commission, *Strenghening whistleblower protection at EU level*, Communication COM (2018)2014 final, p. 12.

[446] Brockhaus and Kafteranis (2020); In Germany, some have argued that an extension of the material scope may be constitutionally required see Brockhaus et al. (2020b); Brockhaus et al. (2020a, 2 December).

Only time will tell if or to what extent EU Member States will make use of the possibility to expand upon the material scope of the EU Whistleblower Directive[447] and which interpretation domestic courts will provide to those provisions, unknowns which will ultimately determine the success of the EU Whistleblower Directive. Despite some shortcomings in the protection scheme and the original legal gap linked to the fragmented material scope, the newly adopted EU whistleblower Directive remains nonetheless a groundbreaking text which establishes a supranational, legally binding whistleblower protection framework, a world first. In accordance with the dynamic approach promoted by the EU Commission in its impact assessment, and the monitoring system established by the Directive, this text has all the chances to become the leading and most comprehensive supranational legal framework on whistleblower protection. This new Directive could also play a catalytic role in promoting the internationalization of whistleblower protection and contribute to the adoption of an international legally binding Convention.

References

Abazi V (2016) Trade secrets and whistleblower protection in the European Union. Eur Papers 1 (3):1065–1072

Abazi V (2017) Legal analysis on the competences of the European Union for Legislation on whistleblower protection. Report commissioned by the Greens/EFA Group in the European Parliament. http://extranet.greens-efa-service.eu/public/media/file/1/5179. Accessed 13 Apr 2021

Abazi V, Alemanno A, Bartlett Quintanilla P V, Berg J, Herman Z, Rauschenberger P, Vogel M (2016) Whistleblower protection in the public and private sector in the European Union: a draft direction. Greens/EFA Group in the European Parliament. https://www.greens-efa.eu/legacy/fileadmin/dam/Images/Transparency_campaign/WB_directive_draft_for_consultation_launch_May_2016.pdf. Accessed 13 Apr 2021

Abazi V, Bartlett Quintanilla P, Herman Z, Myers A (2018) Whistleblower protection in the public and the private sectors in the European Union: proposal for a directive establishing minimum levels of protection for whistleblowers. Greens/EFA Group in the European Parliament. https://extranet.greens-efa.eu/public/media/file/7753/5536. Accessed 13 Apr 2021

Bauschke H-J (2019) Geschäftsgeheimnisse und Bezug zum Whistleblowing – Gesetzliche Neuregelung. Zeitschrift für das öffentliche Arbeits- und Tarifrecht 7:133–136

Brockhaus R, Kafteranis D (2020) No more piecemeal tactics. *Verfassungsblog*

Brockhaus R, Gerdemann S, Thönnes C (2020a, 2 December) Ungleicher Schutz für Whistleblower - verfassungswidrig?. Zoom Event organized by Gesellschaft für Freiheitsrechte, Whistleblower-Netzwerk, Transparency International Deutschland

Brockhaus R, Gerdemann S, Thönnes C (2020b) Zu drohenden verfassungswidrigen Ungleichbehandlung durch die Umsetzung der EU-Whistleblowing-Richtlinie. *Verfassungsblog*

Cobbaut E (2019) Article 11 – freedom of expression and information. In: Dorssemont F, Lörcher K, Clauwaert S, Schmitt M (eds) The charter of fundamental rights of the European Union and the employment relation. Hart Publishing, Oxford, pp 295–313

Eichenhofer E (2018) AEUV Art. 157. In: Streinz R (ed) EUV/AEUV, 3rd edn. C.H. Beck, Munich

[447] Schmolke (2020), p. 27.

Gerdemann S (2019) Revolution des Whistleblowing-Rechts oder Pfeifen im Walde? Der Richtlinienvorschlag der Europäischen Kommission zum Schutz von Whistleblowern. Recht der Arbeit 1:16–28

German Bar Association (Anwaltverein) (2018) EU-RiL Vorschlag Whistleblowing, Stellungnahme SN51/18

Hertslet M, Barsan IM (2018) Der Schutz von Whistleblowern in Frankreich – Handlungsbedarf für Unternehmen. Zeitschrift fur internationales Wirtschaftsrecht 2:68–72

Jefflen M (2018, 21 November) Opinion: EU Parliament vote strenghens whistleblower protection. *EU Observer*

Jefflen M (2019, 16 December) Santa came early to whistleblowers. Now the work starts. Whistleblowerprotection.eu Platform initiative. https://whistleblowerprotection.eu/blog/santa-came-early-to-whistleblowers-now-the-work-starts/. Accessed 13 Apr 2021

Köhn R (2019, 15 Mai) Whistleblower haben es in Deutschland immer noch schwer. *Frankfurter Allgemeine Zeitung*

Kollonay Lehoczky C (2019) Article 23 – equality between men and women. In: Dorssemont F, Lörcher K, Clauwaert S, Schmitt M (eds) The charter of fundamental rights of the European Union and the employment relation. Hart Publishing, Oxford, pp 401–425

Krebber S (2016a) AEUV Art. 153. In: Calliess C, Ruffert M (eds) EUV/AEUV: Das Verfassungsrecht der Europäische Union mit Europäischer Grundrechtecharta, 5th edn. C.H. Beck, Munich

Krebber S (2016b) AEUV Art. 157. In: Calliess C, Ruffert M (eds) EUV/AEUV: Das Verfassungsrecht der Europäische Union mit Europäischer Grundrechtecharta, 5th edn. C.H. Beck, Munich

Mignon-Colombet A, Hannedouche-Leric S (2017) Le nouveau dispositif anti-corruption de la loi Sapin 2: quelles avancées et quelles zones d'ombre? La Semaine Juridique – Édition Générale 5:234–235

Nader R (1972) An anatomy of whistle blowing. In: Nader R, Petkas PJ, Blackwell K (eds) Whistle blowing: the report of the conference on professional responsibility. Grossman Publishers, New York, pp 3–11

Pérez Enciso P (2018) Exchange and processing of information between the European Public Prosecutor's Office and National Authorities. The case management system. In: Bachmaier Winter L (ed) The European Public Prosecutor's Office: the challenges ahead. Legal studies in International, European and comparative criminal law, vol 1. Springer, Cham, pp 253–279

Péronne G, Daoud E (2017) Loi Sapin II, loi Vigilence et RGPD. Pour une approche décloisonnée de la *compliance*. Dalloz IP/IT 11:584–590

Racho T (2016) La possibilité d'un encadrement juridique des lanceurs d'alerte par l'Union européenne. La Revue des droits de l'homme 10:1–13

Reppelmund H (2019) Whistleblowing-Richtlinie: Vorläufige Einigung zwischen Europäischem Parlament und den Mitgliedstaaten. Europäische Zeitschrift für Wirtschaftsrecht 8:307

Rowe GC (2006) Tools for the control of political and administrative agents: impact assessment and administrative Governance in the European Union. In: Hofmann HCH, Türk AH (eds) EU Administrative governance. Edward Elgar, Cheltenham, pp 448–511

Schmitt M (2019) Article 30 – protection in the event of unjustified dismissal. In: Dorssemont F, Lörcher K, Clauwaert S, Schmitt M (eds) The charter of fundamental rights of the European Union and the Employment Relation. Hart Publishing, Oxford, pp 505–534

Schmolke K U (2020) Die neue EU-Richtlinie zum Whistleblowerschutz und ihre Umsetzung in Deutschland. Zur anstehenden Regulierung on Whistleblowing in Deutschland. Working Paper 01/2020, LMU: 22-28

Strack G (2008) Whistleblowing in Germany. Whistleblower-Netzwerk

Vandendriessche A (2018) Legal developments in the protection of whistleblowers in the European Union. Eur Data Protection Law Rev 4(4):483–491

Vervaele JAE (2018) The European Public Prosecutor's Office (EPPO): introductory remarks. In: Geelhoed W, Erkelens LH, Meij AWH (eds) Shifting perspectives on the European Public Prosecutor's Office. Asser Press, The Hague, pp 11–19

White S (2018) A Matter Of Life And Death: Whistleblower Legislation in the EU. Eucrim Eur Criminal Law Associations' Forum 3:170–177

Worth M, Dreyfus S, Hanley G (2018) Gaps in the system: whistleblower laws in the EU, *Blueprint Report Series* No. 2. blueprint for Free Speech

Part V
Findings and Recommendations

Chapter 9
Conclusion

9.1 A Long Road Ahead

We Europeans have a long way ahead of us in regard to whistleblower protection. While the initiatives analyzed in this book have allowed for a fundamental shift in the discussion around the legal regulation of whistleblowing in Europe and enabled the emergence of a new European consensus, much remains to be done. Indeed, European States now bear the primary responsibility for introducing effective whistleblower protection frameworks into their national legal systems, in compliance with the recommendations made by the CoE and the Directive adopted by the EU.

While EU Member States will have to transpose the EU Whistleblower Directive until 2021, they still enjoy a particularly large margin of appreciation in regard to the material scope of their national transposition laws, which give them the possibility to develop a restrictive, sectorial and thus fragmented national protection coverage for whistleblowers, or on the contrary, use the transposition of the EU Whistleblower Directive as an opportunity to establish extensive, horizontal whistleblower laws. It remains to be seen whether EU Member States will rise to this occasion. It is also uncertain whether CoE Member States who are not members of the EU will follow the Serbian lead and adopt comprehensive whistleblower laws without an obligation to do so. Indeed, the EU example has demonstrated how certain States can be particularly reluctant to adopt whistleblower laws when not under a legal obligation.

This is the reason why the CoE and the EU should continue to play a leading role in furthering the promotion of whistleblower protection across Europe. While the adoption of dedicated national laws can contribute to an increased recognition of whistleblowers as important actors in democratic societies, changing the negative connotation associated with whistleblowing, deeply rooted in European mentalities will be a long-winded affair and demands continuous investment of those

© The Author(s), under exclusive license to Springer Nature Switzerland AG 2021
H. C. L. Yurttagül, *Whistleblower Protection by the Council of Europe, the European Court of Human Rights and the European Union*, European Union and its Neighbours in a Globalized World 3, https://doi.org/10.1007/978-3-030-78059-3_9

international and supranational institutions. More specifically and in accordance with the legal analysis conducted in this book, a set of conclusions can be drawn.

9.2 The Leading Role of the Council of Europe

The CM should remain informed about the actions taken by CoE Member States' governments with regard to Recommendation CM/Rec(2014)7, in accordance with Article 15 (b) of the Statute of the Council of Europe. Pursuant to its supervisory responsibility under Article 46 (2) ECHR, the CM should also ensure CoE Member States' compliance with ECtHR judgments in regard to whistleblower cases. On the basis of the national actions taken following the Recommendation CM/Rec(2014)7, the CoE should identify lessons learned and promote common best practices specific to the European context.

The CoE should also continue to promote stronger whistleblower protection rules dedicated to the national security sector in accordance with the Tshwane Principles. In this respect and according to PA Resolution 2060, the CoE should ensure support to whistleblowers like Edward Snowden, including political support if they are asylum seekers. In accordance with PA Resolution 2300, the CoE should continue to work on the development of a legally binding Convention on the protection of whistleblowers. Finally, the CoE should also encourage and support Europe-wide campaigns to promote awareness and understanding of the role of whistleblowers in democratic societies.

On the internal front, the CoE should reform its internal rules on whistleblowing to reflect the new European consensus and introduce the minimum standards of whistleblower protection established by Recommendation CM/Rec(2014)7. Finally, as promoted by PA Resolution 2300, the CoE should appoint a general rapporteur on whistleblowers and work on the creation of an independent European observatory, as a reliable focal point in charge of sharing best practices.

9.3 The Right to Freedom of Expression for Whistleblowers Under the ECHR

The ECtHR should adjust its jurisprudence to reflect the new European consensus on whistleblowing, and in particular, abandon the need for a "subordinated work-based relationship", abandon the criterion of the intent and motive of the whistleblower to determine the level of protection under Article 10 ECHR and specify its jurisprudence concerning the particular balancing exercise when whistleblowing in private employment relationships is at issue.

9.4 The Future of Whistleblower Protection in the EU

The EU Commission should continue to encourage EU Member States to expand the scope of application of the EU Whistleblower Directive in their national transposition measures so as to ensure a comprehensive whistleblower protection framework across the EU. The EU should also organize awareness campaigns. In this context, it should consider establishing an EU award ceremony for whistleblowers in order to promote public recognition of the contributions and sacrifices they make. Furthermore, because the costs connected to legal proceedings can be particularly high, the EU should contemplate the possibility to create an EU Fund to help whistleblowers pay their legal fees, which can be called the European Whistleblower Fund (EWF). The EU should also conduct continuous monitoring and assessments of the effectiveness of the national measures adopted in transposing the EU Whistleblower Directive so as to adapt the rules where appropriate, in accordance with the "future proof" character of EU initiatives. To lead by example, the EU should reform its Staff Regulations and the corresponding implementing provisions to reflect the new European consensus on whistleblower protection. In this respect, the CJEU should align its jurisprudence to the emerging European consensus on whistleblower protection, especially in regard to the burden of proof, so as to consolidate its jurisprudence and offer EU whistleblowers the highest level of protection.

9.5 Final Thoughts

As demonstrated throughout this book, the European whistleblowing principles established over the last decades now reflect many of the international best practices in regard to whistleblower protection.[1] To fully align with international standards however, certain grey areas will need to be clarified on the national level. First, the personal scope promoted by the CoE, the ECtHR and the EU remains primarily work-based, with the risk to exclude third parties like intermediaries, natural like legal persons, who can face similarly harsh sanctions for having helped whistleblowers outside of any work-related context. Also, the exclusion of national security matters from the scope of application of the EU Whistleblower Directive emphasizes the perpetual point of friction between national security and whistleblowing. It is hoped that the Recommendation CM/Rec(2014)7 and the ECtHR's case-law will alleviate this shortcoming and encourage European States to adopt strong reporting and protection schemes for whistleblowers working in the national security, defense and intelligence sector. Similarly, while current European measures have primarily promoted a framework intended to provide better protection for whistleblowers, it is expected that the new generation of whistleblower recommendations will increase the focus on potential incentives, mirroring the

[1] See also Feinstein et al. (2021), pp. 13–34 and Appendix 2.

leading whistleblowing model implemented in the U.S. The Market Abuse Regulation and certain EU tools analyzed in this book have already hinted at this future evolution. The data collected by European States in monitoring the impact of their whistleblower laws will be essential information to assess the pertinence of existing measures and enable tailored adjustments of whistleblower rules in accordance with new findings.

Finally, the global crisis sparked by the COVID-19 pandemic, bringing to light the worldwide impact of national cover-ups, may well become a decisive driver for the adoption of an international convention on the protection of whistleblowers. Such an initiative, though sector specific, gained momentum in late 2020 with the European Council President Charles Michel's proposal to adopt an international Treaty on pandemics.[2] Supported by the UK Prime Minister Boris Johnson,[3] it reflects an international recognition that stronger report systems are needed on the world stage to prevent global threats to the public interest. Indeed, according to the European Council press release, such treaty should not only ensure risk monitoring, it would also include "a more efficient system of alerts and information sharing". While Mr. Michel held that such a pandemic treaty would be within the framework of the WHO, he also emphasized that "the objective is to do better ... in all areas where we recognise it is in our interest to strengthen cooperation", a particularly positive declaration which may open the door for a more comprehensive approach to international reporting.

Indeed, the greatest challenges facing the world today can only be addressed through greater international cooperation, the need to establish transnational reporting channels thus appears essential to counterbalance a lack of effective reporting means on the national level. From internet-based crimes to viruses, threats to the public interest are no longer constrained by national borders. Whistleblower laws, however, remain mainly country-specific. In regard to the GDPR for example, Edward Snowden held that it "is undoubtedly a major legal advance, but even its transnationalism is too parochial: the Internet is global".[4] The same applies to the EU Whistleblower Directive, the CoE Recommendation CM/Rec(2014)7 and the ECtHR's case-law. While those regional efforts are undoubtedly a very significant step forward, the international impact of cover-ups can only be addressed through a global approach to whistleblowing.

In 2000, the Organization of American States (OAS) commissioned Thomas Devine, Robert Vaughn and Keith Henderson with the drafting of a model whistleblower law[5] intended to reflect the highest international standards in the

[2]European Council, Press release by President Charles Michel on an international Treaty on Pandemics, 3 December 2020, *Press release.*

[3]Reuters Staff (2021, 15 February).

[4]Snowden (2019), p. 331.

[5]Vaughn et al. (2003), pp. 858–859.

subject matter.[6] The first draft presented in 2000, with the aim to guide States in the adoption of their national anticorruption laws within the framework of the Inter-American Convention Against Corruption, included, inter alia, a right to asylum under international law.[7] While the final draft adopted in 2013 excluded such possibility,[8] it has become increasingly clear today that individuals who use their right to free speech to report on matters of international public interest should be afforded international protection. Similarly to the call by the Independent High Level Panel of Legal Experts on Media Freedom to provide safe refuge to journalists at risk,[9] the same is true for whistleblowers at risk. An international legal instrument on whistleblower protection could provide such mechanism. From a global reporting system to an international protection framework, a legally binding instrument could establish an international whistleblowing system under the UN framework, allowing for early-warning on global threats, and put signatory States under an obligation to afford protection to whistleblowers at risk, by granting asylum, providing visas or consular support.

Similarly to the draft model law developed by Mr. Devine and his colleagues, which provided for a right to asylum under international law, an international protection framework should be put in place. Such protection should be afforded based on whistleblowers' right to freedom of expression. Indeed, as emphasized by the former Special Rapporteur David Kaye, whistleblower protection "rest upon a core right to freedom of expression", a right enshrined both in the Universal Declaration of Human Rights and the ICCPR.[10] A legally binding instrument based on this right, in the form of an international treaty on whistleblowing or an additional protocol to the ICCPR, would allow for the extension of the scope of application to all individuals who disclose or help disclose information on threats to the public interest, the right to the truth thereby becoming enforceable under international law. When asked about the pertinence of such an international treaty, the former Special Rapporteur David Kaye responded that while ideal in the long term, short-term solutions should be provided considering the lengthy process of an international undertaking.[11] National and regional initiatives to protect whistleblowers, such as the transposition of the EU Whistleblower Directive or the promotion of the CoE Recommendation CM/Rec(2014)7 and the OAS Model Law on whistleblowing, thus appear to be the primary priorities in the short- to mid-term.

---

[6]OAS, *Model Laws and Legislative Guidelines*. https://www.oas.org/en/sla/dlc/mesicic/leyes.html. Accessed 13 April 2021.

[7]Devine et al. (2000), Article 17.

[8]OAS, *Model Law to facilitate and encourage the reporting of acts of corruption and to protect whistleblowers and witnesses*, OEA/Ser.L, SG/MESICIC/doc.345/12 rev. 2, 22 March 2013.

[9]Yeginsu (2020).

[10]UN, *Report of the Special Rapporteur on the promotion and protection of the right to freedom of opinion and expression David Kaye*, A/70/361, 8 September 2015, para 5.

[11]Response to the question asked by the author on the possible adoption of an international convention on whistleblower protection, at European Forum Alpbach Conference (2020, 2 September).

That said, with only a quarter of the world having dedicated whistleblowing statutes,[12] the current COVID-19 crisis may well have an accelerator effect on the adoption of an international treaty, States having a particularly strong interest in establishing an international reporting and protection scheme to promote whistleblowing on global threats to the public interest.

References

Devine T, Vaughn RG, Henderson K (2000) Model law protecting freedom of expression against corruption. Organization of American States, Washington, DC

European Forum Alpbach Conference (2020, 2 September) Effective anti-corruption whistleblower protection. Panel discussion, moderator: Myers A, Speakers: Hershman M, Kaye D, Vella C

Feinstein S, Devine T, Pender K, Allen C, Nawa R, Shepard M (2021) Are whistleblowing laws working? A global study of whistleblower protection litigation. International Bar Association/Government Accountability Project

Moyo S (2021) Letter from the President of the IBA. In: Feinstein S, Devine T, Pender K, Allen C, Nawa R, Shepard M (eds) (2021) Are whistleblowing laws working? A global study of whistleblower protection litigation. International Bar Association/Government Accountability Project

Reuters Staff (2021, 15 February) European Council President welcomes support of UK PM to work on pandemic treaty. *Reuters*

Snowden E (2019) Permanent record. Macmillan, London

Vaughn RG, Devine T, Henderson K (2003) The whistleblower statute prepared for the Organization of American States and the global legal revolution protecting whistleblowers. George Washington Int Law Rev 35:857–902

Yeginsu C (2020) Report on providing safe refuge to journalists at risk. High level panel of legal experts on media freedom

[12]Moyo (2021), p. 5.